SOCIAL MEDIA MARKETING WORKBOOK

2023

Jason McDonald, Ph.D.
© 2023, JM Internet Group

https://www.jm-seo.org/
Tel. 800-298-4065

"The perfect is the enemy of the good." – Voltaire

TABLE OF CONTENTS

0
INTRODUCTION

Welcome to the *Social Media Marketing Workbook 2023!*

My name is Jason McDonald, and I will be your "virtual guide" through the jungle of social media platforms – from Facebook to Twitter, YouTube to TikTok, Instagram to Pinterest, LinkedIn to Blogging, and beyond. Along the way, I will give you a **framework** to understand social media marketing – that it's a **party**, and you are the **party organizer**. I'll give you **structural tips** to set up your brand on each platform. I'll return again and again to the theme of "**content marketing**" – your own content, curated content, UGC or User Generated Content, and interactive content. I'll give you **tips**. I'll show you free **tools**. I'll point to when and how to use **advertising** as a complement to **organic** efforts. I'll guide you **step-by-step** on the basics of setup and posting on each individual platform.

New for 2023, I'll emphasize the twin concepts of a) a "**classic**" social media platform like Facebook or LinkedIn, in which you generally see content posted by "friends," "connections," or "brands" you follow, and b) a "**recommendation engine**" such as TikTok, in which you heavily see content that matches your "content interests" whether or not you are connected to that person or brand. You'll find that nowadays, we are all "content marketers" as well as "social media marketers." I'll also emphasize that you increasingly need to **advertise** to make social media work for you. The days of free, "organic" reach are swiftly coming to an end, not just on Facebook or Instagram, but on all platforms. That said, there remain exciting free/organic opportunities if you know how to find and manipulate them in your favor.

By the end of this Workbook, you'll understand social media from the perspective of a *marketer* (not just a *consumer*). You'll understand the basic structure of each platform. You'll have keen insights into how to use each platform for marketing as well as knowledge of helpful free tools. You'll know what content works and what content is a waste of time. You'll know the basics of advertising and know where to look to learn more. And, if you put in the effort to complete the free companion worksheets, you'll have a macro "social media marketing plan" as well as several "micro plans" for each platform.

In short, you'll know what to do and how to do it.

Why Market via Social Media?

If you own a business or work as a marketing manager at a business, you're probably intrigued by **social media** as a **marketing platform**. Hardly a day goes by that the "traditional" news media doesn't talk about Twitter, Instagram, TikTok, Facebook, or YouTube, often in the context of some new way to reach customers and build buzz. Between TV shows like *Dr. Who* or podcasts like *This American Life* encouraging you to "like" them on Facebook, or your next-door neighbor or perhaps a business competitor bragging about their latest tweet or "Reels" upload to Instagram, it seems like everyone is promoting their Facebook Page, their YouTube channel, their reviews on Yelp, or encouraging you to check them out on TikTok. What do they understand that you don't get? Or, even if you get a lot, what are secret tips and tricks that can improve your marketing even further? Social media is everywhere, and yet it can seem very confusing to the uninitiated. What is this *magical marketing*, and how does it work?

Let's Talk about You

Let's talk about you for a moment. Perhaps you own a small business, perhaps you're the marketing manager at a mid-sized company producing ball bearings, or perhaps you are an ad agency guru charged with setting up a Facebook plan for a local non-profit. It's easy to be overwhelmed and natural to feel like you're not sure how to market on social media. Perhaps you're just starting out with a **Facebook Page** for your **business**, or perhaps you've seen your teenager spend hours on **Instagram**, **TikTok**, or **Snapchat**, or you realize that the female shopping demographic is "on" **Pinterest**. Perhaps the hip coworker dressed in black or one of his friends has looked down on you condescendingly when you don't understand the difference between a *hashtag* and a *retweet*. Or you've painfully learned that **Facebook** business reviews can make (or break) your business only after an unhappy customer trashes you online. Social media, after all, is all around us in today's 24/7 desktop, tablet, and mobile phone environment, and it does not seem to be simple!

Maybe you have already attempted a Facebook Page, a YouTube Channel, or a Pinterest board, but it hasn't really worked out. Maybe you've downloaded TikTok and tried to understand not just what the buzz is all about but how brands use TikTok for their digital marketing. "How does social media really work?" you wonder. "What's all the fuss about, and can it really bring in customers and make sales?"

Don't worry. Enter the Social Media Marketing Workbook to the rescue!

This book will explain the "how" – a step-by-step, systematic method for effective social media marketing. But before we dive into the "how," let's step back for a minute and ask the "why":

Why market on social media?

Here are some reasons why **social media marketing** is valuable:

- **Your customers are on social media.** Nearly everyone uses Facebook – from teenagers to grandmas, business executives to flight attendants. Every day nearly five billion videos are watched on YouTube, and nearly everyone is on one of the social platforms, whether that is Facebook or Instagram, TikTok or YouTube, LinkedIn or Twitter. By marketing via social media, you can "fish where the fish are."

- **Social media is big.** Facebook, the largest social media platform, has over two billion users worldwide and climbing; LinkedIn sports over 800 million members as "the" network for B2B marketers. Indeed, new platforms continue to rise – not just TikTok but the rebirth of Reddit, the rise of Nextdoor, and one never knows if Tumblr might make a comeback. Every day, over 250 million hours of video are watched on YouTube, and so on and so forth.

- **Social media is free**. Facebook, YouTube, TikTok, Instagram, Pinterest... are, of course, free to use. Users love them because, "for free," they get access to their friends and family, plus content from brands they love. And in terms of marketing, there is a lot you can do, for free, to build your brand, spread eWOM (electronic word of mouth), help you stay top-of-mind with your customers, and even "get shares" or "go viral." (*"Free," as we will learn, does not mean easy or no hard work involved – more on that later!*)

- **Social Media builds your brand.** Quick name a car company! Was it Toyota? Tesla? BMW? Car companies spend millions on paid ads (and on social media) so that when I say car, you say "Toyota" (or "Tesla" or whatever). They've built their brand recognition and brand identity so that consumers are primed to have warm, fuzzy feelings before they step on a car lot or visit a car website. Social media is a key part of staying top of mind: engaging content on Facebook, Instagram, TikTok, etc., can "build your brand" so that you will "sell more stuff."

- **Social Media can reach not only existing but also new customers.** Between organic ("free") and paid reach on sites like Instagram, Facebook, YouTube, or Twitter, you can not only stay in touch with your existing customers, but you can also be discovered by new customers. Unlike on search engines like Google (where customers must proactively look for you), on social media, you can be discovered as customer No. 1 shares information with customer No 2. You can also be discovered not when a customer is proactively searching for you but when he just happens to be checking his Facebook news feed or browsing photos on Instagram.

- **"Recommendation Engines" Create Content Marketing Opportunities.** Today's most exciting trend is the "recommendation engine" concept. Led by TikTok, platforms as diverse as YouTube and Instagram are increasingly smart and increasingly suggesting content to users. *Dog lovers see more dog videos. Cat lovers see more cat videos.* This occurs even if they do not "like" or "follow" the publishers of this content.. And this creates a huge opportunity for you to reach "new" customers: just create fun, viral, shareable, snackable content (especially video) that matches their interests. Easier said than done, but the trend toward content marketing creates exciting opportunities for free, organic reach (just as you thought it was all about advertising).

- **You can advertise on Social Media.** While consumers may react negatively to advertising in the abstract, most will nonetheless react positively to ads that specifically target their interests and needs. Facebook, Instagram, Twitter, YouTube, LinkedIn, Pinterest, TikTok – indeed, every major social media platform offers targeted advertising that - when done right - can be an effective way to build your brand and sell more stuff. The reality today is that more and more platforms are becoming "pay-to-play." Accordingly, smart marketers have set a 2023 New Year's Resolution to become savvy social media *advertisers* as much as *marketers.*

Social Media (Seems) Complicated

Social media, however, is also **complicated**. First of all, *using* social media is one thing, and *marketing* on social media is another. That snappy teenager might understand how to *use* TikTok, but this doesn't mean she knows how to *market* on it. Even many experienced marketers are befuddled, as their knowledge of traditional marketing channels does not translate easily to social media networks like Instagram or Twitter. Indeed, many businesses simply fail at social media marketing, either doing nothing or spinning their wheels with endless busy work. They don't understand how social media functions, and they fail to see the incredible marketing opportunities beneath the surface of this huge but messy, brave new world of marketing. Quite simply, you have to invest some time to learn "how" to market on social media.

Or, in today's new environment, many marketers complain about the demise of organic ("free") reach on Facebook, Instagram, and YouTube and avoid learning about and deploying the incredible advertising opportunities on each network. "If you can't beat 'em, join 'em," goes the old saying, but many marketers refuse to work with the gurus at Facebook, YouTube, or Pinterest, who spend their days brainstorming how to make ads engaging and effective on their platforms. YouTube, Facebook, Pinterest, and the gang – after all – aren't charities. They're *for-profit businesses* based on *advertising*. So how do you advertise? How can you advertise to build your brand and sell more stuff?

Fortunately, the *Social Media Marketing Workbook* will provide you with food for thought, tips and tricks, and practical action items to make your social media marketing more effective.

Who is This Workbook For?

This workbook is aimed primarily at **small business owners** and **marketing managers**. **Non-profits** will also find it useful. If you want to build buzz around your company or brand, increase your sales or sales leads, or expand your reach from your most loyal customers to their friends and family and to the friends and family of those friends and family, this workbook is for you.

If you are a person whose job involves advertising, marketing, and/or branding, this workbook is for you. If you are a small business that sees a marketing opportunity in social media of any type, this workbook is for you. And if your job is to market a business or organization online in today's Internet economy, this book is for you. Anyone who wants to look behind the curtain and understand the mechanics of how to market on social media (from Facebook to LinkedIn, Twitter to Yelp, Pinterest to YouTube to TikTok, and beyond) will benefit from this book.

Anyone who sees – however dimly – that social media could help market their business will benefit from this hands-on workbook. And even if you are a skilled practitioner, this book will add value by helping you to think strategically about how to market via social media and, as we go platform by platform, reviewing tips, tricks, and secrets that you might not know about.

Oh, and if you're a student or perhaps an *un-* or *under-*employed marketer, and you're building job skills, this Workbook will help you join the digital revolution by "going social." Marketing today has "gone digital," meaning that Search Engine Optimization (SEO), advertising, review marketing, and social media marketing are the skills you need to be a high-payed, high-powered marketer in 2023. This Workbook teaches you the cornerstone skill of how to market on social media, but check out my other digital marketing books at **http://jmlinks.com/books** to educate yourself on SEO, Google Ads, or digital marketing more generally.

How Does This Workbook Work?

This workbook starts with an overview of **social media *marketing***. Beyond the positive "can do" attitude that I assume you already have, the next most important asset is a "mental model" of what social media is, what social media marketing is, and the roles in this narrative between you as a content producer and your customers as content consumers.

It's simple. If social media is a **party**, then **using social media** is akin to just *showing up at a party*. **Marketing** on social media, in contrast, isn't about showing up. It's about ***throwing*** the party!

Understanding this distinction between "attending" the social media party and "throwing" the social media party is the subject of **Chapter One**.

SOCIAL MEDIA MARKETING = THROWING GREAT "VIRTUAL PARTIES"

Chapter Two is the next most important concept: **content marketing**. You need wonderful food and entertainment to keep your party going, and content is the "food and entertainment" of social media marketing. Accordingly, Chapter Two will explain to you how to set up and maintain a content production machine to feed all your social channels. New for 2023 is the concept of a "**recommendation engine**" and how your content marketing must cater not just to friends, family, and social connections but to the "AI" or "Artificial Intelligence" that increasingly gives users more of what they like.

Chapters Three through **Twelve** are deep dives into social media marketing, one platform at a time. We'll start, for example, with **Facebook**. First, we'll provide an overview of how Facebook works, explaining everything from profiles to pages, likes to comments to shares, algorithmic pleasure to posting rhythm. Marketing on Facebook will become much clearer as we work through Facebook in plain English, written for "mere mortals." Along the way, I'll provide **videos** and **worksheets** that will act as "Jason as therapist," so you can fill them out and begin to outline your own unique Facebook marketing plan. Chapter **quizzes** help you test your knowledge and generate a nifty certificate suitable for framing and/or to place on your refrigerator. My goal is for you to not only *understand* Facebook marketing but actually to begin to *do* marketing on Facebook. Ditto for LinkedIn, Twitter, Instagram, TikTok, YouTube, and the rest of the gang.

Table of Contents

⟫ Meet the Author

My name is Jason McDonald, and I have been active on the Internet since 1994. I have taught SEO, Google Ads, and Social Media since 2009 – online, at Stanford University Continuing Studies, at both AcademyX and the Bay Area Video Coalition in San Francisco, at workshops, and in corporate trainings across these United States. I love figuring out how things work, and I love teaching others! Social media marketing is an endeavor that I understand, and I want to empower you to understand it as well.

Learn more about me on Twitter or LinkedIn at *@jasoneg3*, on the Web at either **https://www.jasonmcdonald.org/** or at **https://www.jm-seo.org/**. Send me an email at **jason.mcdonald@jm-seo.net**. Or just call 800-298-4065, say something flattering, and my secretary will put you through. *(Like I have a secretary! Just call if you have something to ask or say)*. Visit the websites above to follow me on Twitter, connect with me on LinkedIn, or follow me on Facebook. *Sorry, my Snapchat, Instagram, and TikTok are so crazy; they're for friends and family only.*

Take My Classes

I teach SEO and Social Media Marketing online for Stanford Continuing Studies. If you'd like to learn more or get an email alert when registration is open, visit **http://jmlinks.com/classes**. The classes build on the books and focus on practical, hands-on knowledge of SEO and Social Media Marketing successes.

⟫ SPREAD THE WORD: TAKE A SURVEY & GET $5!

If you like this workbook, please take a moment to take a short **survey**. The survey helps me find errors in the book, learn from student questions, and get feedback to improve future editions. Plus, by taking the survey, I'll be able to reach out to you, and we can even become friends. Or, if not friends, at least friends on the Internet or Facebook, which isn't quite the same thing, but still, it's pretty good.

Here's how –

- Visit **http://jmlinks.com/survey**.
- Take a short **survey** about the book.
- I will rebate you $5.00 via Amazon gift eCard.

How's that for an offer you can't refuse?

This offer is limited to the first 100 participants and only for participants who have purchased a paid copy of the 2023 edition of this book. You may be required to show proof of purchase and the birth certificate of your firstborn child, cat, or goldfish. If you don't have a child, cat, or goldfish, you may be required to prove telepathically that you bought the book.

» QUESTIONS AND MORE INFORMATION

I **encourage** my students to ask questions! If you have questions, submit them via **http://jmlinks.com/contact**. There are two sorts of questions: ones that I know instantly, for which I'll zip you an email answer right away, and ones I do not know instantly, in which case I will investigate, and we'll figure out the answer together.

As a teacher, I learn the most from my students. So please don't be shy!

» REGISTER YOUR BOOK

Finally, this workbook is meant to leverage the power of the Internet. Register your Workbook to access a cornucopia of **free** resources:

- Go to **http://jmlinks.com/2023smm**
- Reenter this password: **2023smm** at the welcome screen.
- Follow the instructions to enter your email.

You can also register the book at the JM Internet Group Website (**https://www.jm-seo.org**); just click on "register a book" on the left menu.

Once you register, you get access to –

- **A PDF copy of this book.** Read it on your PC or tablet, and the links referenced in the book become clickable. This is a great way to extend the book into myriad resources such as example websites or social media pages, FAQ's, support or help from the major vendors, and videos.

- **My social media marketing dashboard** – an easy-to-use, clickable list of the best tools for social media marketing by category (e.g., Facebook tools, Twitter tools, etc.).

- *The Marketing Almanac* – a collection of up-to-date social media tools in detail. While the *Dashboard* identifies my favorites, the *Almanac* compiles the universe of free social media tools as well as free tools for SEO and Google Ads.

- **Quizzes** – an easy way to test your knowledge and reinforce what you're learning. The devil is in the details, and the quizzes test your devilish knowledge medium-by-medium.

- **A Free Pony** – OK, sorry, you won't actually get a free pony. But you will get a wealth of free information so that you'll not only know the basics of social media, you'll know how to "keep up" with ever-changing landscape.

Jump Codes

Throughout the book, I reference the website **http://jmlinks.com/** plus various "jump codes." If you're reading in PDF format, the links are clickable. If you're reading in hard copy or on the Kindle, I advise you to fire up your Web browser, bookmark **http://jmlinks.com/,** and then enter the codes. Note that the website is "http" and not "https" (secure) as the site is nothing more but a means to jump to the real resources referenced in this book.

Here's a screenshot:

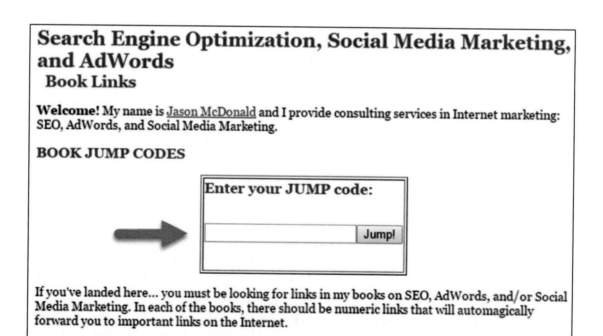

For example, **http://jmlinks.com/16s** would mean first go to **http://jmlinks.com/** and enter "16s" in the jump code box. Your browser will then "jump" you to the referenced resource.

VIDEO. Watch a video tutorial on how to use "jump" codes at **http://jmlinks.com/jump**.

OK, now that we know what this workbook is about, who it is for, and our plan of action...

Let's get started!

▶▶ COPYRIGHT AND DISCLAIMER

I knew you just couldn't wait for the legal stuff. *Calm yourself down, and get ready for some truly fun reading.*

That's a *good thing*. This workbook is **independent**. My aim is to "tell it as I see it," giving you no-nonsense information on how to succeed at social media marketing.

In addition, please note the following:

- All trademarks are the property of their respective owners. I have no relationship with nor endorsement from the mark holders. Any use of their marks is so I can provide information to you. Don't confuse them with me or me with them. I'm just a poor intellectual, and they are big, rich, powerful corporations with teams of money-grubbing lawyers.

- Any reference to or citation of third-party products or services, whether for Facebook, LinkedIn, Twitter, Yelp, Google, TikTok, Yahoo, Bing, Pinterest,

YouTube, Instagram, Snapchat, or other businesses, search engines, or social media platforms, should not be construed as an endorsement of those products or services tools, nor as a warranty as to their effectiveness or compliance with the terms of service with any search engine or social media platform.

The information used in this workbook was derived at the time of publication. However, social media marketing changes rapidly, so please be aware that scenarios, facts, and conclusions are subject to change without notice.

Additional Disclaimer. Internet marketing is an art and not a science. Any changes to your Internet marketing strategy, including SEO, Social Media Marketing, and online advertising, are at your own risk. Neither Jason McDonald, Excerpti Communications, Inc., nor the JM Internet Group assumes any responsibility for the effect of any changes you may, or may not, make to your website or social media marketing based on the information in this workbook.

Additional Additional Disclaimer. Please keep your arms and legs in the vehicle at all times, be kind to one another, and do not cut other people off while driving. Please remember that everything you say and do online becomes part of your digital footprint, and when aliens download the digital records of earth in the year 2027, you'll either be remembered as a kind person or a jerk. Choose to be kind.

▶▶ ACKNOWLEDGEMENTS

No man is an island. I would like to thank my beloved wife, Noelle Decambra, for helping me hand-in-hand, managing our busy household and raising two wonderful girls, and as my personal cheerleader in the book industry. Gloria McNabb has done her usual tireless job as first assistant, including updating this edition as well *The Marketing Almanac*. I'd like to thank my two daughters, Hannah and Ava; especially Ava, who, as a teenager in the trenches of today's "social media generation," has found the patience to explain TikTok to me at least three times while constantly reminding me, "Dad, Facebook is not cool." Last but not least, I would also like to thank my black Labrador retriever, Buddy, and our rescue dog, Zero, for countless walks and games of fetch, quizzical looks when I talked out loud to these beloved animals about the vagaries of Pinterest or TikTok, as well as I refined my ideas about marketing and about life. Those of you who own a dog will understand; those of you who don't, well, get a dog. "Dog" is "God" spelled backward for a reason.

And, again, a huge thank you to my students – online, in San Francisco, and at Stanford Continuing Studies. You challenge me, you inspire me, and you motivate me!

1
PARTY ON - SOCIAL MEDIA MARKETING

You know the 1979 song "Girls Just Want to Have Fun" by Cyndi Lauper? Or the 1991 movie, "Thelma and Louise?" Well, the YouTube video of the former now has over 1 billion views, and the ending scene of the latter has over 1.9 million. Here's the upshot: people (not just girls) want to have fun. Sometimes it works out really well as in the Cyndi Lauper song, and sometimes, not so much, as in the "Thelma and Louise" movie – but in all cases, people are pursuing their self-interest in a good time.

They go to Facebook to see posts by friends and family, they go to Instagram to see pictures and videos, they go to Pinterest to find cool stuff to buy or make, and they (increasingly) go to YouTube shorts, Instagram Reels, and TikTok to just "be entertained." And you can even make the claim that they go to Twitter to "have a good argument" because there is nothing more fun than being on the "We're Totally Right, and the Other Side is Idiots" team on Twitter, relishing in one's own virtue, knowledge, and just general goodness vs. the evil, horrible, nasty people on the other side. **People want to have FUN on social media**. That even includes LinkedIn, which is the most serious and most career-oriented of platforms, as what is more "fun" than being knowledgeable in your job (and getting a big, fat raise) or finding that dream job for your career advancement?

Social media is all about "fun." It's a party and you – my friend – are the party-thrower. I want you to learn to throw fantastic parties on Facebook, elegant career mixers on LinkedIn, and over-the-top jams on TikTok and YouTube. I want you to be Cyndi Lauper, with thousands of adoring fans, and not Thelma and Louise careening over a canyon to their doom (oops, spoiler alert).

This book is really a book about how to throw parties. As such, it focuses on the middle, productive ground – part **theory** and part **practice**. It gives you a framework for how to "think" about social media marketing as well as concrete advice on how to "do" social media marketing on each particular network.

This first Chapter is about *how to think about social media marketing*. What is social media marketing? Why are you doing it? What should you do, step-by-step, to succeed?

Let's get started!

To-Do List:

» Understand that Social Media Marketing is Like Throwing a Party

» Recognize the Social Media Marketing Illusion

» Identify Relevant Discovery Paths

» Establish Goals and KPIs

»» Checklist: Social Media Marketing Action Items

»» Deliverable: a "Big Picture" Social Media Marketing Plan

» UNDERSTAND THAT SOCIAL MEDIA MARKETING IS LIKE THROWING A PARTY

Have you ever **attended** a party? You know, received an invitation, showed up, said hello, and spouted out various meets and greets to other guests, ate the *yummy* food, drank the liquor (or the diet soda), hobnobbed with other guests, ate some more food, danced the night away, thanked the hosts, and left?

Attending a party is all about showing up, enjoying the entertainment and food, and leaving.

Have you ever **used** Twitter? Facebook? Instagram? LinkedIn? TikTok? You know, logged in, checked out some funny accounts, read some posts, posted back and forth with friends and family, checked your updates, and then logged out?

That's *attending* a party. That's *using* social media.

Using social media is all about logging in, enjoying what's new and exciting, and logging out.

Throwing a party, however, is something entirely different from **attending** a party. Similarly, **marketing** via social media is something entirely different from **using** social media.

This Chapter explores the basics of social media *marketing*: **throwing** the "social media party" vs. just **showing up**. That word *marketing* is very important: we're exploring how to use social media to build our brand, promote the visibility of our company, product, or service, and even (gasp!) use social media to sell more stuff. Ours, my friend, is a "party with a purpose" – to build our brand and (ultimately) sell more stuff.

BECOME A GREAT SOCIAL MEDIA PARTY ORGANIZER

Social media **marketing** is the art and science of **throwing** "great parties" on Twitter, Facebook, LinkedIn, Pinterest, and the like in such a way that people not only show up to enjoy the party but also are primed to buy your product or service.

Let's explore this analogy further: how is social media *marketing* like *throwing a party*?

Here are three ways:

Invitations = Promotion. A great party needs great guests, and the first step to getting guests is to identify an attendee list and send out invitations. Who will be invited? How will we invite them – will it be face-to-face, by phone call, email, postal mail, etc.? For your social media marketing, you'll need to identify your target audience(s) and brainstorm how to get them to "show up" on your social media page via tactics like sending out emails, cross-posting your Facebook to your Twitter, or your LinkedIn to your blog, advertising, or even using "real world" face-to-face invitations like "Hey, follow us on Twitter to get coupons and insider deals."

Social media marketing requires having a promotion strategy.

Food and Entertainment = Content. Will your party have a band, a magician, a comedian, or just music? What is your entertainment strategy? What kind of food will you serve - Mexican, Chinese, Tapas, or something else? Similarly, for your social media marketing: why will people "hang out" on your Facebook page or YouTube channel? Will it be to learn something? Will it be because it's fun or funny?

Social media marketing requires having a content marketing strategy, a way to systematically produce yummy content (blog posts, infographics, images, videos) that people will enjoy enough to "hang out" on your social media page or channel.

Hosting = Ongoing Management. As the host of your party, you'll "hang out" at the party, but while the guests are busy enjoying themselves, you'll be busy meeting and greeting, making sure everything is running smoothly, and doing other behind-the-scenes tasks. Similarly, in your social media marketing, you'll be busy coordinating content, interacting with guests, and even policing the party to "kick out" rude or obnoxious attendees.

Social media marketing requires ongoing behind-the-scenes management, often on a day-to-day basis, to ensure that everything is running smoothly up to and including dealing with "rude" guests.

SOCIAL MEDIA MARKETING IS THROWING A 24/7 PARTY ONLINE

In addition, you want to think like a "party detective." Let's assume you're going to throw your spouse an amazing 40th birthday party. Before that party, you'll probably start attending other gatherings with a critical eye – noting what you like and what you don't like, what you want to imitate, and even reaching out to the magicians, bands, and bartenders to find out what they cost and possibly hire them for your own party.

Inventory Other Parties

You'll "inventory" other parties and make a list of likes and dislikes, ideas, and do-not-dos, and use that information to plan your own party systematically.

As a social media marketer, therefore, you should "attend" the parties of other brands online. Identify brands you like (some of my favorites - REI, Whole Foods, Rustic Cuff, Chipotle, Author / Actor Matthew McConaughey, Bishop Robert Barron, CEO Jeff Bezos, fitness guru Shaun T, nerd brand Thermo Fisher Scientific), "follow" or "like" them, and keep a critical eye on what they're doing. **Inventory** your likes and dislikes, and **reverse engineer** what other marketers are up to. And in your industry, do the same. Follow companies in your own industry, again with the goal of "reverse engineering" their social media marketing strategy, successes, and failures.

For your first **TO-DO**, identify some brands or public figures you admire and "follow" them on Twitter, LinkedIn, Facebook, TikTok, etc. Start making a list of what you like, or dislike based on reverse engineering their online marketing strategy. Become a good user of social media, but with an eye to the marketing strategy "behind the scenes." Here are the steps:

1. **Log in** to one of your **social media accounts** (e.g., Twitter or Facebook).

2. Using the search function, **search for keywords** that are relevant to your business. If you are a wedding planner, for example, search for keywords such as 'wedding planning' or 'weddings' or 'party planners.'

    a. You can use a special Google search of *site:network* as in *site:facebook.com* "accounting firms" to use Google to find interesting items on any social media site rapidly. Note: there is NO SPACE between the ":" and the network. Visit **http://jmlinks.com/12v** to see this search query in action. You can also watch a **video** on this at **http://jmlinks.com/16g**.

    b. Use the *Social Media Marketing dashboard > keyword tools* to research keyword "themes" around which your customers search and talk. Imagine a water cooler conversation by your customers on theme X or theme Y – identify which topics are relevant on social. Visit **http://jmlinks.com/smmdash** > keyword tools to begin.

3. Write down or **bookmark accounts that you find**. If you search for "hamburgers," and you find the Facebook page of the Palo Alto restaurant, "The Counter," then "like" that Page on Facebook and/or bookmark it. You'll need a list of five to ten companies that are like yours and/or that you can see are doing a good job on the platform. Do the same for their LinkedIn, TikTok, Instagram, Pinterest, etc., accounts.

4. Begin to **inventory** what you **like** and **dislike** about how they are running their social media effort. For Facebook, for example, do you like their cover photo (that is, the long rectangular photo or video at the top of a brand's Facebook Page)? Why or why not? Do you like their profile picture (that is, the square smaller image that appears in posts by the Page)? What about the items that they post – text, photos, videos – and/or the "themes" of their content? Imagine you are attending their party not "to have fun" but to "reverse engineer" how they are putting it on. What works? What doesn't? Write this down on a spreadsheet or document.

We'll return to this process for each platform, but whether you're an experienced social media participant or not, start to look at social media as "parties" and start to step back and ponder what's going on on Twitter, Facebook, YouTube, etc., as the work of "party throwers" in interaction with "party attendees."

A Party with a Purpose

Another fact to notice is that brands like Whole Foods or REI, or public personas like Khloe Kardashian or Shaun T – in contrast with the average John Doe or Sally Jones - are on social media for an "ulterior motive," usually to "build their brand" and "sell more stuff." Social media marketing, in short, is like throwing a *party with a purpose*. While the birthday party you're throwing for your spouse on her 40th birthday is hopefully just a labor of love, corporate parties are not so benevolent. For example, the real-world corporate parties I've gone to in Silicon Valley have a business objective. You may show up at the Synopsys party at the *Design Automation Conference* or the Analog Devices' event at the *Consumer Electronics Show*, eat their food, drink their liquor, and enjoy their entertainment, but they want something in return. They want you – as the partygoer – to listen to a spiel by their CEO or product marketing manager on their latest product, they want you to get a "warm and fuzzy feeling" about their brand, and they want you to think of them the next time you're ready to purchase something.

The same is true for corporate "parties" on social media marketing. These are parties with a purpose, which you can generally break down into two interrelated subgoals:

- Build **brand equity** among target customers, giving them a warm and fuzzy feeling that they "like" the brand so much they'll be favorably inclined to buy its product and/or service; and/or -

- **Get a sale** by selling the product or service right then and there.

  o Or, a few steps before the sale, a goal might be to get a sign up to an email newsletter, or a **sales lead / registration** from a free eBook or software download offer, etc. The "goal" of social media marketing can be to "acquire sales leads" in the form of names, company names, email addresses, phone numbers, etc., in exchange for "something free" like a software download, free eBook, or free consultation.

Whether they're subtle about it (*just get that warm and fuzzy feeling*), or they're aggressive about it (*act now, and get a special discount for following us on Twitter*), social media "parties with a purpose" aren't exactly the same as a family party or gathering. Brands want something from their attendees: better **brand equity** (that "warm and fuzzy feeling") and, ultimately, more **sales**.

BUILD YOUR BRAND TO "SELL MORE STUFF."

As you begin to pay attention to competitors and brands that seem to "get" social media, I want you to be just a bit cynical and look for the goals behind their "parties with a purpose" on Twitter, Facebook, LinkedIn, TikTok, and the like. What's in it for them, and how do they blend this purpose into their "oh so fun" parties on social media? What's in it for their customers? And what's the *quid pro quo* of why users show up at the party while the party producer goes to the trouble and expense of throwing the party? What's REI's goal for its Facebook page vs. what are the reasons why users show up at REI's Facebook "party?" Why do users watch Martha Stewart on YouTube, and why does Martha Stewart go to the trouble of creating a robust YouTube channel?

And as for you –

Question: What do you want to get out of your "social media marketing party?"

A Brand Example: Rustic Cuff

For example, I love the brand, Rustic Cuff, which is a Tulsa-based business that produces artisan-style bracelets. Rustic Cuff is very active on social media and does a really good job at it. Take a look at their website at **https://www.rusticcuff.com/**, scroll down to the bottom, and click over to their social icons. You'll see that they're active on Facebook, Instagram, Pinterest, and YouTube.

Here's a screenshot of their Instagram account (**https://www.instagram.com/rusticcuff/**):

Notice that they post often, that they have 105,000 followers, and that their posts are visually "fun." Next, step back, scroll down their account, pay attention to what they're posting, and be a bit cynical. Ask why? Rustic Cuff isn't a charity, after all. This is a business, a business that wants to build its brand and sell more stuff. As you pay attention to Rustic Cuff's posts on Facebook, Pinterest, and Instagram, you'll notice two types:

> **Buy Our Stuff Posts.** These are posts that, rather shamelessly, connect the social media experience with an "act now!" feature to encourage a user to skedaddle on over to RusticCuff.com and buy something. These are probably less than 20% of their posts. **Purpose**: get people to buy their stuff.
>
> **Fun Posts.** These are posts either by Rustic Cuff or by users that seemingly share their passion for beautiful jewelry and stylish stuff. These are probably more than 80% of their posts. **Purpose**: build positive brand equity.

For example, here's a "buy our stuff" post to Instagram showcasing two beautiful gold and silver cuffs:

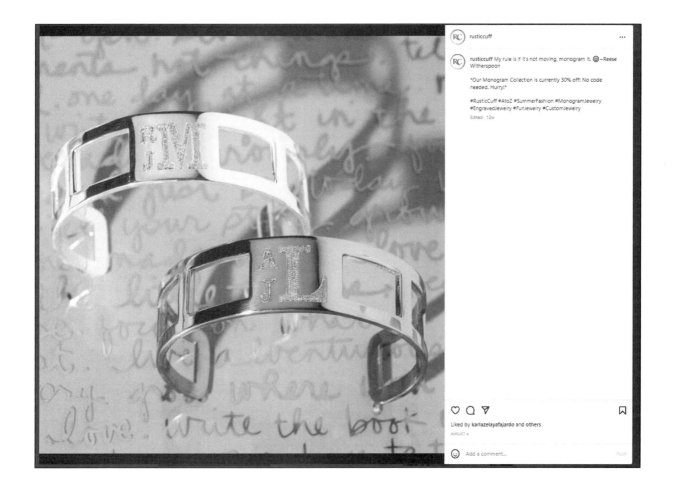

Don't get me wrong. There's nothing unethical about this post; it's just a straightforward "buy our stuff post." But compared with many of their other posts (which focus on building up positive brand equity), this post is just a bit more *shameless* and direct towards a transactional plea. It literally says, "Our Monogram Collection is currently 30% Off!" It's a shameless "buy out stuff" type of post.

Indeed, here's a screenshot of their Instagram account on the mobile app (where most people use Instagram). Notice the prominent link to "shop," that is – **yes, please** – you can purchase their products via Instagram:

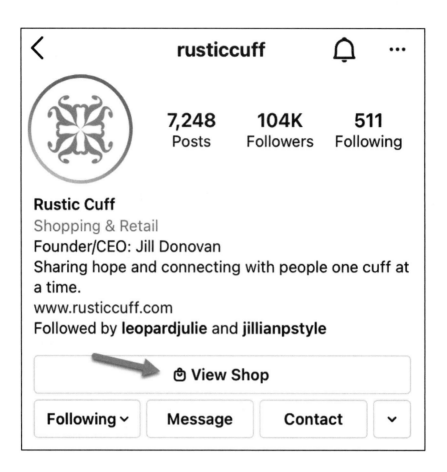

Now, not all posts are of the "buy our stuff type." In fact, many, many more are meant to "build the brand" by sharing motivational messages.

For instance, check out this post from Rustic Cuff posted on September 15, 2022:

This post is inspirational. It's motivational. It challenges us all to try, even if we are going to fail. It's good advice for anyone trying to master social media marketing! You gotta start somewhere, and you gotta ALWAYS be learning. Notice how it has 299 likes and multiple comments. Users love this kind of content on Instagram! And notice how it doesn't say "Buy our stuff" but rather "builds the brand" by positioning Rustic Cuff as an aspirational, motivational company. To be cynical, the reason these sorts of posts are made is to make you feel good about "buying their stuff."

"Reverse Engineer" Brands on Social Media

By looking at the posts of brands like Rustic Cuff (or Chipotle, or Wendy's, or REI, etc.) that do social media well, you'll realize that there's a mix of "buy our stuff" posts with other less transactional, more "feel good" posts such as the company's charismatic CEO sharing her words of wisdom, their customers having fun with their "cuffs," and even inspirational messages.

Rustic Cuff is throwing a "party with a purpose" but doing so in such a wonderfully fun, engaging way that it's not in-your-face or obnoxious. The jewelry and photography of the bracelets are beautiful. The engagement with style is engaging. But it is there. They want you to buy more Rustic Cuff products, either *indirectly* because you "like" their brand and have positive feelings about them or *directly* because you've seen a pin to Pinterest, a Facebook post, or something on Instagram that pulls you directly into their eCommerce store.

In summary, Rustic Cuff isn't on Facebook, Instagram, and Pinterest "just for fun." They have a marketing purpose: build their brand and (ultimately) get people to buy their stuff. Once you understand this strategy, I assure you that you'll see it everywhere by every brand that does social media well. It's called **content marketing,** and it's a key element to "parties with a purpose."

Find and Reverse Engineer Companies to Emulate

How do you throw great parties? By attending them in "stealth mode." So it goes with Social Media Marketing. How do you do it well? Your first task is to go on Twitter, Facebook, Instagram, LinkedIn, TikTok, and other networks to identify companies that intrigue you. "Like" or "follow" them and start to think about their social media marketing "as if" you were attending their "party." Look for the "purpose" behind their parties and how they blend this "purpose" into their content marketing strategy.

There are two sorts of companies that you want to identify:

1. **Companies-to-emulate**. Identify big brands that may not be in your industry but do social media well. Many big consumer brands such as Wendy's, Chipotle, Target, REI, Martha Stewart, or even Shaun T are crushing it on social media. These are companies that, while not necessarily like your own, are the *superstars of social media.*

2. **Competitors**. Search by keyword or relevant content themes for your company on Facebook, Twitter, LinkedIn, etc., to identify competitors that are similar to you. Take your "real world" competition, visit their website, and track down their social accounts. These competitors are companies *similar to your own.*

You don't want to do social media in a vacuum. You don't want to face a blank canvas or blank screen. It's "social" media – which means you need to pay attention to companies-to-emulate, competitors, your own customers, industry, etc. Imitate what's working well. "Steal" and "reverse engineer" the strategies of companies-to-emulate and competitors. Often, you can't just follow the competition in your industry; if your industry is behind the times, you can't mine the pathetic, sad, Luddite competitors that you face for ideas of how to market on social media. Instead, look to the Shaun T's, the REI's, the Chipotle's, etc., of the social world for ideas and inspiration.

At the end of this exercise, you should have a list of five to fifteen companies that you are going to follow on social media. Welcome to *Spy-vs.-Spy* social media edition.

>> RECOGNIZE THE SOCIAL MEDIA MARKETING ILLUSION

As you begin to identify and monitor brands that you like on a given social media platform, you may be tempted to conclude that it's either really easy or they are just geniuses. Successful social media is based on **illusion**, however, just like successful parties are based on illusion.

How so?

Let's think for a second about an amazing party. Think back to a holiday party you attended, a great birthday or graduation party, or even a corporate event. Was it fun? Did it seem magical? It probably did.

Now, if you've ever had the (mis)fortune of planning such an event — what was that like? Was it fun? Was it magical? Yes and no, but it was also probably a lot of work, "in the background," to make sure that the party ran smoothly.

I went to a wedding once, and the "rent-a-priest" literally started reading a Jewish wedding script, stopped herself, and said, "Oh Jesus, this is a Christian wedding." She ran out to her car, came back with a different script, and started again. Needless to say, the "illusion" of the perfect wedding was shattered, and the couple ultimately got divorced. The point is that a really good party — such as a wedding, a Bar Mitzvah, or a 40th Birthday — has an illusion that it's all "spontaneous," all "perfect," all "magical." But it's not.

The Party Illusion

Great parties have an element of **illusion** to them: they *seem* effortless, while *in reality* (behind the scenes), an incredible amount of strategy, planning, and hard work goes on. Similarly, great social media marketing efforts (*think Katy Perry or Lady Gaga on YouTube, think Whole Foods on Facebook or blogging, Airbnb or Aeromexico on Instagram, Chipotle or Wendy's on TikTok, or REI, Zappos, Burt's Bees, or even Nutella on Twitter*), create an illusion. They (only) "seem" spontaneous; they (only) "seem" effortless. But in the background, a ton of work is going on to promote, manage, and grow these "social media parties."

ILLUSION IS COMMON TO GREAT PARTIES AND GREAT SOCIAL MEDIA MARKETING

With respect to social media marketing, this **illusion phenomenon** often creates a weird problem for you vis-a-vis management. Your boss might mistakenly believe that "social media is easy" and/or "social media is free." You, as the marketer, might have to educate him or her that it only "looks" easy or "seems" free. Social media marketing requires a ton of strategy, hard work, and (gasp!) even money or sweat equity to make it happen. Among your early tasks in social media marketing may be to explain the "social media marketing" illusion to your boss.

It only seems easy. It only seems free.

For your second **TO-DO**, organize a meeting with your boss and/or marketing team. Discuss all the things that have to get done to be successful at social media marketing, ranging from conducting an **inventory** of companies-to-emulate and competitor efforts to **setting up basic accounts** on Twitter, Facebook, Instagram, LinkedIn, etc., to **creating content** to share on social media (images, photos, blog posts, infographics, videos), to **monitoring** social media channels on an on-going basis, and finally to **measuring** your successes. Educate the team that although it might not take a lot of money, social media marketing does take a significant amount of work!

We're planning an awesome party here, people. It's going to take a ton of work, it's going to be a ton of fun, and it's going to be incredibly successful!

Now, *please don't get discouraged or overwhelmed.* It seems hard, and it seems like a ton of work, but once you know what to do and you become systematic at doing it, you can do amazing social media marketing in just a few hours each week. Like preparing to get in shape, you'll need to commit to regular activities. But, like getting in the best shape of your life, thousands of people do it and do it well. It takes discipline, but YOU CAN DO IT!

Imagine me greased up and sweating like Shaun T with my shirt off, jumping rope in front of you, yelling, ARE YOU READY? Pop music is blaring; one of my groupies is saying, "It takes real work. It takes real effort, and guess what — that's just the warm-up!" Electrifying pop music is blaring over the loudspeakers. My ab muscles are jingling in front of your desk, and I'm leading you and your team (plus your boss) in a chant: WE CAN DO THIS! WE CAN DO THIS!

Now, stop imagining me as Shaun T. It's getting weird.

And here's a screenshot of the amazing, incredible, motivational Shaun T fitness guru Facebook Page (at 1.8 million followers) at **http://jmlinks.com/52v**.

I'm not even a real Shaun T fan (I have 12-pack abs, meaning 2X the desired six-pack, after all). But I admire anyone with 1.8 million followers on Facebook, 1.1 million followers on Instagram, 277K followers on Facebook, and 180 K on YouTube. Not to mention an influencer like Shaun T, who is already "all in" on TikTok with 722K followers on this new network. The man projects an amazing can-do spirit, one that combines motivation with the technical knowledge of how to get in shape. Now, let's get back to our computers, potato chips, and iPhone cameras and make an incredible social media marketing strategy for your business! We can do this! Sitting down! Burning no calories! Munching on potato chips!

Know the Question and Find the Answer

Once you start to view social media marketing as a systematic process, a great thing will happen: you'll formulate concrete, *specific* questions. You'll formulate concrete, *specific* tasks, such as "how do I create an infographic?" or "what are the dimensions of a Facebook cover photo?" and "how do I schedule my posting to Twitter?"

I am going to share with you one of my best-kept secret websites. It's an amazing, powerful website that can literally answer almost any question. It's called **Google**, and you can find it at **https://www.google.com/**. Bookmark this site. It's very useful.

Here's a screenshot:

OK, let me be serious. Once you formulate a specific question, such as "What is the character limit of a tweet?" or "What is a branded hashtag?," you can Google it, to find the answer.

IF YOU KNOW THE QUESTION, YOU CAN GOOGLE THE ANSWER

Once you realize, for example, that Facebook allows cover photos and that smart Facebook marketers swap theirs out from time to time, you can create the "questions" of "How do you create a cover photo for Facebook?," "What are the dimensions of a Facebook cover photo,?" etc. Now that Facebook allows videos as cover photos, you can Google, "How do you set up a video as your Facebook cover?" You can type specific questions into Google to find the answers; Google will point you to the official Facebook help files as well as other helpful blog posts or answer sites on the Web. Indeed, people often make amazing "how to" videos on YouTube, and once you know a question, you'll almost always find someone who has made a YouTube of the answer. (YouTube is my second favorite top-secret site to find answers; check it out at **https://www.youtube.com/**).

Yes, I know I'm being tongue in cheek, but you'd be amazed at how few people actually realize that they can Google their marketing questions about social media or look up YouTube videos that show you how to do such-and-such step-by-step.

In addition, all of the social media platforms have official help files, such as at **https://help.twitter.com** or **https://www.facebook.com/help**. You can Google your questions as well as go directly into the official help files. Ironically, the technical aspects of social media marketing, such as "how to share a YouTube video?" or "what are the character limits to a Tweet?" are actually easy to solve. Once you know the question, you can Google or YouTube the answer.

▶ IDENTIFY RELEVANT DISCOVERY PATHS

In my opinion, the more challenging problems are not usually the technical ones. The more challenging problems originate either in a) a vague marketing vision for your company and/or b) a poorly thought-out content marketing strategy. Before we plunge into Facebook, LinkedIn, Twitter, and social media platforms on a step-by-step basis, therefore, let's turn first to some of the bigger questions in marketing, such as:

> *What do you sell?*
>
> *Who wants it and why?*
>
> *How do customers find you?*
>
> *How (and why) do customers become excited about your brand?*
>
> *What prompts them to buy your product or service?*
>
> *What changes a one-time customer into a super fan, a super sharer, an evangelist on social media who will like, comment, and share your brand to social media success?*

Let's focus on the important question of "how customers find you." A great social marketer will have a very specific understanding of the paths by which customers find their product, service, or company. This understanding then guides –

> *How much should you focus on SEO (Search Engine Optimization)? How much should you focus on Google Ads? How much on Facebook? On LinkedIn? On Yelp? Or Twitter? Should you buy ads on television or (gasp!) send out unsolicited email (spam)? Is Pinterest worth the effort? What about ads on social media; should you advertise or focus solely on organic?*

It makes sense if you think like a fisherman and think of your customers like fish. If your "fish" tend to be on Facebook, then you need to prioritize Facebook in your marketing strategy; if your "fish" tend to be using LinkedIn, then you need to prioritize

LinkedIn; if your "fish" tend to read reviews on Yelp, you need to prioritize Yelp. And if your fish are 13 years old and endlessly share their day-to-day hopes, dreams, and fantasies on TikTok, well, you better get tiktok'in.

The Five Discovery Paths

How do customers **"discover"** you? This is perhaps *the* most important question in marketing. Why? Because if a customer can't find you, if a customer doesn't learn about you, if a customer isn't jazzed about your brand, they can't buy your product or service. And if you don't have a firm grasp on how customers discover you, you don't know where to put your marketing efforts. You can't *fish for the fish* when you don't know *where the fish are*. You'll be advertising on billboards when they use Google. Or advertising on Google when they use Facebook. Or focusing on organic posts on Instagram when they use reviews on Yelp. Or doing the Internet when they're all in the real world. Or sending postcards through the US mail, or using the print Yellow Pages when you've been living in a cave for the last two decades and failed to realize that nearly everything (but not absolutely everything) is online.

In short, many businesses fail to understand *how customers discover them (Question #1)* and *how they, as marketers, can influence how customers find them (Question #2)*. How might customers find you? Let us count the ways.

SEARCH. The **search** path occurs when the customer is "searching" for a company, product, or service. For example, a customer is hungry. He types "pizza" into Google or Yelp. He browses available restaurants, chooses one, and shows up to get pizza. He *searched* for pizza. He *found* pizza. He *bought* pizza. The search path is the province of **SEO** (Search Engine Optimization), largely on Google, but also on sites such as Yelp or Amazon that work via "keywords" to help customers find stuff that they want. **Google Ads** advertising is also helpful on this path.

The search path exists in the "real world" as well, as for example, when a customer goes to a mall and looks at the kiosk map to find out which stores sell gifts, or when a customer uses a directory of business accountants, or perhaps even when a customer asks friends or family if they "know any good painters." The key concept in search is that the customer knows what he wants, and he proactively goes searching for it.

REVIEW / RECOMMEND / TRUST. The review / recommend / trust path is based on "trust indicators." In it, the customer already has created a list of vendors he might use, but he is researching "whom to trust." In this path, he might use the "reviews" and/or "stars" on Facebook, Yelp, Airbnb, TripAdvisor, or Google as "trust indicators" to predict which pizza restaurant is good (or bad). **Reviews** and **stars** are the most common trust indicators in social media marketing, but having a robust

Facebook page with many followers and interesting posts can also be a "trust indicator." Having an expert-looking profile on LinkedIn can be a "trust indicator" for a CPA or an architect. A recommendation from a friend or colleague also plays into reviews and trust. The review / recommend / trust path is all about a customer "asking for help" from friends, family, business colleagues, or online review sites like Yelp, Amazon, TripAdvisor, etc. The key concept in review / recommend / trust is the reliance on *external validations* such as recommendations from friends or stars on Yelp.

EWOM / SHARE / INFLUENCERS. Wow! That pizza was great! Let me take a selfie of myself chowing down on the pizza and post it to Instagram. Or, wow, here is a cat video of cats at the pizza restaurant puzzled by the self-serve soda fountain. It's "gone viral" on TikTok and has sixteen million views! Or, oh my goodness, Oprah has just recommended we read the novel, *An American Marriage* by Tayari Jones, so let's buy it on Amazon and get started.

The **share path** occurs when a customer loves the product, service, or experience with enough passion to "share" it on social media – be that via electronic word of mouth (eWOM), a share on his or her Facebook page, a "selfie" on Instagram, or a viral video on YouTube or TikTok. Others find out via shares from their friends or influencers, and suddenly yours is the most popular pizza joint in town. Indeed, **influencer marketing** is a type of marketing that straddles both the review / recommend / trust marketing and the share path; an "influencer" like Kim Kardashian recommends new jewelry, and then everyone goes out to buy it. The *influencer* is just a "trust indicator" *par excellence* with the push of *share* behind him or her.

In a sense, therefore, the "share" path is the flip side of the review path. The key concept in share is when a customer or influencer pro-actively "pushes" her love of your product or service to friends, family, or business colleagues. The "share" path is more proactive, and the review / recommend / trust path is more passive, but they are closely related.

INTERRUPT. The interrupt path is the bad boy of marketing, both online and off. Interrupt marketing occurs when you want to watch a YouTube video, but before you can watch it, you are forced to view an annoying ad. Or it's the ads on TV that we "must" watch (at least had to watch before DVRs came along) before we see the live sports event we want to enjoy. Or, it's when you get a "cold call" or "spam email" from a recruiter who's viewed your Profile on LinkedIn and forced their unsolicited message into your LinkedIn alerts. Interrupt is largely **advertising** and largely advertising to "push" products that people aren't proactively looking for. But just because people hate it doesn't mean it isn't useful. Spam works, and so do TV ads.

BROWSE. The browse path is all about getting your message *adjacent* to what a person is reading or viewing. In it, you're looking for something, reading something, or watching something, and alongside comes something else. For example, you go to

YouTube to look up "how to tie a tie," and in the suggested videos at the end might be a video for Dollar Shave Club. Or you might see Dollar Shave Club videos suggested at the right of the screen. You're not proactively looking for Dollar Shave Club, but you see their information as you "browse" for related content on sites like YouTube, Facebook, or blogs. Or, you go to the mall "to shop" and happen to wander into a boutique, only to buy the newest dog toy - something that you really hadn't been considering buying in the first place. Or you read a blog or perhaps the *New York Times* online or go to an industry trade show and just "happen" to notice a new product or service. The **browse path** is about getting your product or service *adjacent* to something the customer is looking at.

These are the five **discovery paths**, and as you look to your marketing, you'll see that everything in promotion can fit into one of these paths. There are both digital and non-digital examples of them. A door-to-door salesman, for example, is engaging in interrupt just as an unsolicited spam email or telemarketing call is, too. An ad on a billboard is "browse," just as an ad on the *New York Times* online is browse, too. Every promotional choice fits into one of the five discovery paths.

You'll also quickly realize that most marketing in the "real world" isn't pure. It has elements of more than one path. When you get an influencer to recommend your product, for example, you're using both the *share* path and the *review / recommend / trust* path. Or, when you use SEO to propel a blog post to the top of Google, you're using both the *search* path and the *browse* path to get your product or service in front of potential customers. They find an interesting blog post through a Google search, they read it, and then they discover your product or service "adjacent" to the post. The marketing or promotional mix will often seek to engage customers across a range of paths, but it's useful to see them as distinct discovery methodologies.

All of these paths can come into play in an effective social media marketing strategy. Your job is to identify your customers, figure out where they hang out on social media, and position your message in front of their "eyeballs" to use the industry slang for getting *what you sell* in front of *how they see*.

Outline Your Marketing "Big Picture"

For your third **To-do**, download the **Big Picture Marketing worksheet**. For the worksheet, go to **http://jmlinks.com/2023smm** (then enter the code '**2023smm**' to register your workbook), and click on the link to the "Big Picture Marketing."

In this worksheet, you'll write a "business value proposition," explaining what you sell and who are the target customers. You'll also identify the most relevant "discovery paths" by which potential customers find your products. You will begin to realize that there is a "method" to the "madness" as you identify where your customers are and how best to reach them.

» ESTABLISH GOALS AND KPIS (KEY PERFORMANCE INDICATORS)

Marketing is about measurement. Are we helping our brand image? Are we getting sales or sales leads? How do we know where we are succeeding and where there is more work to be done? Why are we spending all this blood, sweat, and tears on social media marketing anyway? Is it paying off?

In today's overhyped social media environment, many marketers feel like they "must" be on Twitter, they had better get on TikTok, or they "must" have a presence on Pinterest, etc. All of the social media companies – Facebook, Twitter, Pinterest, TikTok, Yelp – have a vested interest in overhyping the importance of their platform and using fear to compel marketers to "not miss out" by massively jumping on the latest and greatest social platform. **Social media guilt**, however, is to be avoided: if you define a clear business value proposition, know where your customers are, and establish clear goals and KPIs (Key Performance Indicators), you'll be able to focus on those social platforms that really help you and ignore the ones that are just hype.

AVOID SOCIAL MEDIA GUILT: YOU CAN'T (AND SHOULDN'T) USE EVERY NETWORK

Let's identify some common **goals** for effective social media marketing. The boss might have an ultimate "hard" goal of getting sales leads or selling stuff online. Those are definitely important, but as marketers, we might look to intermediate or "soft goals" such as nurturing a positive brand image online or growing our online reviews.

Generally speaking, social media excels at the "soft goals" of growing brand awareness, nurturing customer conversations, encouraging reviews, and the like, and is not so good at immediate, direct goals like lead captures or sales. Here are common goals for social media marketing:

> **eWOM (electronic Word of Mouth).** Every brand wants people to talk about it in a positive way, and today a lot of that conversation occurs on social media. If you are a local pizza restaurant, you want people "talking" about you and your pizza on Yelp, on Facebook, on Twitter as a great place to get pizza, eat Italian food, cater a wedding, or host a birthday party for little Jimmy. As marketers, a

common goal for social media is to grow and nurture positive eWOM, which might be positive conversations on Facebook, positive reviews on Yelp or Google My Business, relationships between customers and us and among customers, and the sharing of our brand across media.

Customer Continuum. *A prospect becomes a customer, a customer becomes a fan, and a fan becomes an evangelist.* For example, I'm hungry. I search for "great pizza" in Palo Alto, California, and I find your pizza restaurant. I try your pizza, thereby becoming a customer. It's good, and I'm a fan: if someone asks me, I'll recommend *Jason's Palo Alto Pizza.* And finally, I love your pizza so much, I wrote a positive review on Yelp, I created a YouTube video of me eating your pizza, I took a selfie for Instagram, and I have a new blog on Tumblr about your pizza. As marketers, we want to encourage customers to move to the right on the customer continuum: *from prospect to customer, customer to fan, fan to superfan, and superfan to evangelist.*

Superfans vs. Influencers. A major goal of your social media marketing, therefore, is to encourage "superfans." Superfans are folks who love your brand so passionately they not only follow you on Facebook, connect with you on LinkedIn, or subscribe to your YouTube channel. They like, comment, and (most importantly) share your content with others. *If you're Jesus, these folks are your disciples.* They spread your message (often for free). They can be compared with "influencers," who are people who have their own followers and "sell" their influence to the highest bidder. Think "free word-of-mouth" (Superfans) vs. "paid endorsements" (Influencers). Both are useful, but a major goal of social media is to nurture a community of "superfans" around your brand.

Customer from Hell. You also need to be aware of (and seek to mitigate) the "customer from hell" who can hate a brand so much that she writes a negative review on Yelp, posts negative comments on Facebook, or creates a viral YouTube video about your terrible pizza. (**Reputation management** is the industry term for being aware of both positive and negative social media discussions about your brand). Social media marketing is also about reputation management and especially mitigating "customers from Hell."

Social Trust. Customers want pizza. Customers read reviews. Customers use reviews to decide which pizza restaurant is probably good. Similarly, when customers want to go to a theme park, they might check out the Facebook page. They like theme parks that have lively Facebook pages over those that have boring Facebook pages. **Social trust indicators** are all about mental "shortcuts" that customers make to identify possible vendors, services, or products. A common goal of social media marketing, therefore, is to nurture positive trust indicators about our brand online: reviews, especially but not only.

Stay Top of Mind. You visit the pizza restaurant, one time. That encounter is an incredible marketing opportunity! As a marketer, I want to convert that "one touch" to "many," that single encounter to staying "top of mind" so I can remind you about my business, products, and/or services and entice you to come back. I want you to follow us on Twitter, so I can Tweet special deals, promotions, what's cooking, and stay "top of mind," so that when you're hungry again, you think, *Jason's Palo Alto Pizza*. I want you addicted to my fun Instagram feed, my clever TikTok, and even to connect with us on LinkedIn for your business catering needs. Using social media to convert *one touch to many* and *stay top of mind* is an excellent goal.

Promotion, promotion, promotion. Social sharing – getting customers to market your brand to their friends, family, and colleagues – is probably the most common social media goal. You want your customers to Instagram their happy kids having a great pizza party at your pizza restaurant! You want your customers to share tweets about their amazing corporate catering event with their Facebook friends. And you want your customers to share your informative industry blog post on cybersecurity with their contacts on LinkedIn. *Encouraging social promotion is a key goal for SMM.*

Your **TO-DO** here begins by simply taking out a piece of paper, opening up a Word document, and jotting down "soft" and "hard" goals for your social media marketing efforts. For extra credit, start to hypothesize which goals might be best accomplished on which social media network.

The Virtuous Circle

When you add up all of the goals listed above, and probably a few you may have identified that I've missed, you get to the **virtuous circle** of social media marketing. When your social media marketing efforts are working well, you can create a positive feedback loop.

The more positive reviews you have on Facebook, the more customers you get, the more customers you get, the more positive reviews. The more followers on Twitter you get, the more chances you have to get them to share your discounts, the more discounts they share, the more followers you get. The more people who like / share / comment on your Facebook page, the better your score in the Facebook algorithm (a measurement of how engaging one's content is), the better your reach, the more people see your content, the more people see your content, the more shares you get on Facebook, the better your reach. The more people who watch your TikToks, the better the algorithm pushes you out to new prospects which causes more people to see your TikToks…

Nurture a Virtuous Circle

Nurturing a virtuous circle should be a major goal of your social media marketing efforts. You want all of these "soft goals" to turn into "hard goals": a positive brand image to lead to more sales and a stronger bottom line. All of this can be measured.

For your next **To-do**, download the **Marketing Goals Worksheet**. For the worksheet, go to **http://jmlinks.com/2023smm** (then enter the code '**2023smm**' to register your workbook), and click on the link to the "Marketing Goals Marketing."

In this worksheet, you'll identify your "hard" goals, whether you have something "free" to offer, and your "soft" goals on social media. Ultimately, these big-picture goals will be translated into much more specific goals, germane to a social medium such as YouTube, Twitter, or Facebook. Don't forget to conceptualize what a *virtuous marketing circle* would look like for your company. Visualize social media marketing success; you'll get there step-by-step.

» Remember the Big Picture

At this point, you've begun your social media marketing journey. You've understood that social media marketing is about "throwing" the party more than "attending the party." You've realized you need to start "paying attention" with regard to what other marketers are doing on social media, with an eye to "reverse engineering" their marketing strategy so that you have ideas of what you like and do not like in terms of social media. You've started to brainstorm "discovery paths" and "goals" for your SMM efforts.

And you've realized that once you've identified your goals, identified relevant social media, set up your social accounts, the really hard work will be a) promoting your social media channels and b) creating the kind of content that makes them want to "like you," keep coming back for more, and share your message with their friends, family, and/or business colleagues.

You've understood that **promotion** and **content creation** are the big ongoing tasks of successful social media marketing.

⚏ CHECKLIST: SOCIAL MEDIA MARKETING ACTION ITEMS

Test your knowledge of the "Big Picture" of Social Media Marketing! Take the *Social media marketing quiz* at **http://jmlinks.com/qzsm**. Next, here are your "Big Picture" **Action Items**:

❑ **Research** whether your customers (and competitors) are on social media. If so, which networks? What are they doing? What interests them, and why?

> ❑ Identify *competitors* to reverse engineer as well as **companies / brands / influencers to emulate**. "Like" their Facebook pages, "follow" them on Instagram, etc.

>> ❑ Begin to "reverse engineer" what they are doing on social media. How are their accounts set up? What **technical features** are they using on each platform? What type of content are they posting – their own, other people's content, UGC (User Generated Content), or interactive?

>> ❑ What **content** is getting the most engagement as measured by likes, comments, and shares? Why might this be so?

>> ❑ **Imitation** is the highest form of flattery. What structural or technical aspects do you see in use by competitors or companies-to-emulate that you can use? What content strategies do you see being deployed that you, too, can utilize?

❑ **Identify** your **discovery** paths. Which paths (*search, review (recommend, trust), eWom (share, viral), interrupt, browse*) are the most relevant to your business and customers?

❑ **Identify** the platforms (Facebook, LinkedIn, TikTok, Twitter, etc.) that seem to be "where your customers hang out." What are they doing there? What content is engaging them and why? What are competitors doing? We will return to this issue as we go over each platform, but you have to start somewhere. So start looking at platforms through the prism of your customers.

❑ **Formulate** (and write down) your **KPIs** (*key performance indicators*) or social media marketing **goals** such as eWOM, movement along the customer continuum, prevent "customers from hell," grow trust indicators, stay top of mind, or leverage social media promotion not to mention "hard goals" such as eCommerce sales or sales inquiries.

»» DELIVERABLE: OUTLINE A SOCIAL MEDIA MARKETING PLAN

Now that we've come to the end of Chapter 1, your first **DELIVERABLE** has arrived. For the worksheet, go to **http://jmlinks.com/2023smm** (then enter the code **'2023smm'** to register your workbook), and click on the link to the "Social Media Marketing Plan Big Picture Worksheet." By filling out this plan, you and your team will establish a vision of what you want to achieve via social media marketing.

2
CONTENT MARKETING

If social media *marketing* is throwing amazing Facebook fiestas, incredible Pinterest parties, and unbelievable YouTube soirees that not only attract and engage your potential customers but also lead them towards a better perception of your brand and even result in real sales or sales leads ... well, "content," in short, is the "food and entertainment" of social media marketing. It's simple if you think about it. *No food, no party. No great food or entertainment, no great party.* You gotta have **content** just like you gotta have food and/or entertainment to get your party started (and keep it going).

Whether it's Instagram or Pinterest, Facebook or LinkedIn, YouTube or Twitter, you need to create and maintain a **content marketing machine** – a nearly endless series of blog posts, infographics, memes, photos, tweets, and/or videos that will feed the hunger for content of all your social channels.

In this Chapter, I'll overview the elements of your **content marketing machine** and give you tips and tools to enable high-speed and efficient production of content for social media.

Let's get started!

TO-DO LIST:
- » Understand the Basic Structure of Social Media
- » New for 2023: "Recommendation Engines"
- » Identify Content You Can Easily Produce
- » Identify Content Formats
- » Identify Buyer Personas and Content Themes
- » Produce Your Own Content on Schedule
- » Blog, Blog, Blog: You Gotta Blog, Vlog, Phlog, and Post
- » Curate Other People's Content
- » Encourage User-Generated Content
- » Interact with Interactive Content
- » Carrot and Outreach Marketing

>> UNDERSTAND THE BASIC STRUCTURE OF SOCIAL MEDIA

Social media has a structure. Your content is like *water* that is *poured* into the *structure* of social media. Structure influences content. Thus, the first key to success with content is to understand the basic structure of social media:

1. **Users and brands produce content**. Users and brands upload content (videos, photos, images, text posts, etc.) to their accounts or channels.

2. **Users are connected to other users and brands**. Other users "follow" brands or "like" other users.

3. **Users see and consume content when connections post it**. As friends and brands post content, users who are connected to them see or consume this content.

4. **Platforms reward engagement**. In addition to monitoring who is connected to whom, the "algorithm" of each platform monitors content that gets **engagement** as measured by likes, comments, and shares. It then pushes that content out further: thus, "content that gets engagement" gets even more "engagement" via the algorithm.

As content producers, we thus face a **structural reality**. We must get users to "follow" our brands on social media! And we must get users to like, comment, and share our content piece-by-piece!

There's no point in having fantastic content on Facebook, for example, if no one follows your business Facebook page. It doesn't matter if you have a YouTube channel with incredible content if no one subscribes to your channel, and so forth and so on. The structural reality is that you must get users to "follow" your brand on each platform, and you must get users to "like," "comment," or "share" your content.

>> NEW FOR 2023: "RECOMMENDATION ENGINES"

Engagement has always been an important part of the algorithms of each platform. But with the rise of TikTok, **engagement** is beginning to replace **social connections** as the primary metric of success or failure. TikTok is the first platform that is truly a "recommendation engine" first and a "social platform" second. Previously, platforms like Facebook, LinkedIn, and Twitter put the primary weight on who a user followed.

Social connections among users and brands were the key aspect in the content algorithm.

TikTok, in contrast, stands this on its head. Yes, users can and do follow other users and brands, but TikTok heavily emphasizes **engagement**. The algorithm snoops at users in the background and monitors not only whether they like, comment, or share a video but their **hover time** and **watch time**. If a user hovers on a video and/or if a he or she watches the video to completion, the algorithm figures out what the video is about and pushes similar content to that user **regardless of whether he or she is connected to other users or not**.

Dog lovers see more dog videos. Cat lovers see more cat videos, and iguana lovers see more iguana videos. **And they see these videos not just from connected friends and brands but also from non-connected brands.**

TikTok pushes content from **"strangers"** to viewers as much, or more than, from "friends" to "friends."

On TikTok, it doesn't really matter who you follow. **It matters what type of content keeps you engaged.**

TikTok, I would argue, is thus the first "recommendation engine." The other platforms, especially YouTube and Instagram, are following suit. They are beginning to prioritize engagement and beginning to "suggest" content from users that a person does not yet follow, i.e., "strangers."

This has enormous implications for your content strategy. First and foremost, **you must create engaging content.** Content that gets likes, comments, and shares – yes, but also content that spurs users to dwell on it, to consume it completely. But second, you must create content that spurs "hover time" and "watch time." And third, this means you are marketing as much to "strangers" as to followers of your brand.

This means:

#1 – Grow your follows, likes, comments, and shares. Yes, you still want customers to follow your brand on social and "smash that like button" on Facebook, Instagram, YouTube, etc.

#2 – Think about strangers. How does your content appear to a person who has never seen your brand? How can you convert this stranger into a prospect, customer, superfan, or even brand evangelist?

#3 – Grab their attention. "Dog bites man" is not news. "Man bites dog," however, is news. Shocking! Outrageous! Over-the-top! That kind of headline, thumbnail, and first few seconds of content is what snags users' attention (both followers and strangers). We increasingly live in a "clickbait" world.

#4 – Foster engagement. Increasingly, however, you must create content that spurs engagement as measured not just by likes, comments, or shares but also by hover time and watchtime (on video). Once you have their attention, follow up with fun, helpful, "sticky" content that encourages them to stick around and subscribe.

In summary, there is now both a social aspect and a "recommendation engine" aspect to success at social media.

» IDENTIFY CONTENT YOU CAN EASILY PRODUCE

With that in mind, let's turn to content. We're all good at something. Some of us can cook, and some of us can't. Some of us can take photos, and some of us can't. Some of us can write, and some of us can't. This is true for individuals, and it's true for companies as well. This is also true for companies as they work on their social media marketing.

Let's look at REI (**https://www.rei.com/**), for example. As a company that lives in the outdoor industry, REI is a company that is "good" at –

- **Taking photos and videos**. REI staffers take brilliant photos of the outdoors, photos that feature its products. Check out REI's Instagram at **https://www.instagram.com/rei/** to see for yourself.

- **Writing**. REI staffers write with passion about the environment and about how much fun it is to "get outdoors." Check out REI's blog at **https://www.rei.com/blog**.

- **Motivating customers to create content**. REI constantly encourages UGC or *user-generated content*, as its customers upload videos and stories about the outdoors and interact on the company's social media channels. Check out the REI hashtag *#optoutside* on Twitter and Instagram. You can view it on Twitter at **http://jmlinks.com/52w** and on Instagram at **http://jmlinks.com/52x**.

To see more of REI's content in action (posts, blog posts, videos, images), simply browse the company's Facebook Page at **https://www.facebook.com/REI/** and admire the remarkable content marketing machine of this online retailer.

You, Too, Can Create Content

REI's content marketing machine may seem formidable, and it is. REI is a huge corporation in a very fun, very photogenic industry with many passionate outdoor men and women acting like fans. REI has tremendous advantages. But guess what? You, too, can create great content for your own social media marketing machine.

Before you feel daunted and give up, remember you probably aren't competing against the likes of REI, Disney, or Airbnb. You're competing against other companies in your own sad, pathetic industry, and they aren't any smarter or better than you. (*Ok, your industry isn't sad and pathetic, but you know what I mean. It's not inhabited by titans of industry or geniuses like Einstein.*). **You don't have to run faster than the bear, just faster than your buddy**. So, with a little luck, some strategy, and some hard work, you can (and must) create a content marketing system to produce content to feed your social media needs.

Take Rustic Cuff, for example, which started as a small, woman-owned business in Tulsa and grew into a powerhouse of fashion at **https://www.rusticcuff.com/**. Check out their Instagram, Facebook, Pinterest, and YouTube. Each social channel is amazing! Or check out Numi Organic Tea at **https://numitea.com/** and their social channels like Instagram or Facebook. Or, if you think social media is only for B2C (Business-to-Consumer) businesses, check out B2B (Business-to-Business) ThermoFisher Scientific at **https://www.thermofisher.com/**.

With active channels on YouTube, Twitter, Facebook, and LinkedIn, each company shows you that businesses - small and large, consumer and B2B - have all plunged into social media and can (and are) succeeding. It takes effort, and the organic tea niche is different from the custom bracelet niche, and the B2B niche of selling high-tech gadgets is different from the niche involved with what your business does and sells. Identify, research, and dominate your niche even as you look to best-in-class companies like

Rustic Cuff, REI, Thermo Fisher, Numi Organic Tea, or others that are great to *emulate* but should not *intimidate* you for your future success as a social media marketing maven.

Remember: you (and your company) are experts in something (hopefully, your products or services or at least something that relates to your products or services). You (and your company) are passionate about something (hopefully how your products or services are used). All you really have to do is use your iPhone to take pictures of this, your laptop to write about it, your Android phone to take videos, and some nifty online tools to create cheesy quotes about it, tweet about it, create infographics, about it, etc., etc.

> **Share your knowledge and your passion. Become a "helpful expert" to your customers!**

That's what content marketing is really all about.

Your first **TO-DO** is to inventory your own and your company's skill set. What type of content is going to be relatively easy for you, your company, and even your own customers to produce? If you're a pizza restaurant, for example, it's going to be pretty easy to whip out an iPhone and snap a photo of happy customers enjoying a birthday celebration, if you're a wedding planner, it's going to be pretty easy to take a quick video with the bride and groom on their special day, and if you're a CPA, it's going to be relatively easy to write a short blog post about upcoming changes to the federal tax code and how they impact married couples. Can you take photos? Can you shoot a video? Can you write?

Or perhaps you love quotes. It's not going to be hard to go to a website such as Pablo (**http://jmlinks.com/29b**) and input a few motivational quotes that relate to your industry, pick an image, and generate a "quotable photo" for Facebook or Instagram. Perhaps you love data, and you can generate infographics using free tools such as Easely (**http://jmlinks.com/29c**), where you can input data and images and create eye-appealing infographics. And, finally, perhaps you're up for a more beefy type of writing, and you can conceptualize and write a free eBook. You can download templates from Hubspot (**http://jmlinks.com/29d**), or even go whole hog and write an eBook for Amazon using their free KDP services (**http://jmlinks.com/29e**).

Another point is whether you like **interaction**. Some people live on their phones; others live on Twitter or LinkedIn or Facebook, etc. They love interacting with others on social media. Appoint these folks to your social media content team, and have them find interesting content from others and like, comment on, and share it. Have them monitor your own brand content and, again, like, comment on, and share the comments of others. Interactive content is yet another type of content that needs to be part of your plan, just as "working the room" would be one of your tasks as a party host. Shake hands, say hello, ask about the wife or husband and kids, share the news of the day.

WORK THE PARTY

The point of this exercise is to get you thinking about what type of written or visual content you can easily and systematically feed your social media channels. What are you good at, and what will come easily? Where are there easy opportunities to generate content, whether that be a photograph or a blog post?

» IDENTIFY CONTENT FORMATS

What kind of content do people generally want? What kind of content gets shared? Among the most popular and commonly shared items on social media are the following:

Photos. Photographs and images are the bread-and-butter of Facebook, Instagram, and even Twitter.

Memes. From *grumpy cat* to *success kid*, memes make the funny and memorable, sticky and shareable on social media. I love memes; just go to Google, type in "social media memes" and click on "images" to get a quick laugh.

Infographics and Instructographics. From how to tie a tie to sixteen ways you can help stop global warming, people love to read and share pictures that tell a story, hopefully with facts.

Blog Posts. An oldie but goodie: an informative, witty, funny, informational, or fact-filled post about a topic that matters to your customers.

Short Text Posts or Tweets. Funny, important, moving, informative quotations. Cute and clever quips on industry events. Even within the 280 character limit of Twitter, you can share ideas that are short, sweet, and powerful.

Slideshows. From Slideshare to just posting your PowerPoints online, slideshows are a hybrid visual and textual cornucopia of social sharing fun.

Videos. If a picture tells a thousand words, a video can tell ten thousand. YouTube is a social medium in its own right, but the videos themselves are content that can be enjoyed and shared on networks like Instagram, TikTok, and Facebook.

These are just the *formats* of content, the *genres* of information as it were. They're just empty shells. Your job is to identify which formats will be the easiest for you and your company to produce and to then start your content production machine. We'll return to them in a moment, but for now: a) understand that content "lives" in various formats such as text, photos, or video, b) start to think about which formats are going to be easiest for you to produce, and c) which formats are most likely to spur engagement from your target customers.

» IDENTIFY BUYER PERSONAS AND CONTENT THEMES

Your second **TO-DO** is to brainstorm the **buyer personas** and **keyword themes** that customers care about and the type of content that they'll be interested in and will find engaging. These are interrelated, just as the foods that guests want and the types of guests are interrelated. Kids like French fries and Coca-Cola; adults like fine French wines and camembert cheese.

Build a Keyword or Content Theme Worksheet

While **keywords** do not play as tight a role in social media marketing as they do in search engine optimization (SEO) or Google Ads, you still want to identify customer social media themes, whether these be "pain points" or "points of interest." What are people talking about on social media, what are they searching for on Google, and where does a topic that interests customers intersect with what you have to offer? You must get inside your customers' heads and brainstorm not only the types of content (images, blog posts, infographics) that interest them but also the content itself (i.e., What does it explain? What does it describe with passion? What does it convey as a photo?)

A good way to conceptualize this is to have a meeting with your marketing team and conceptualize **buyer personas** – stereotypical mockups of typical customers.

A Palo Alto pizza restaurant, for example, might brainstorm **buyer personas** like:

> **The Hungry Worker Bee.** This is a man, aged 27-35, who works in downtown Palo Alto, and is looking for a quick bite to eat. He likes pizza and is value-conscious plus time-sensitive.
>
> **The Office Manager.** She works in a nearby office and is charged with ordering catering for office meetings. She's interested in fun, lively food that's easy to get and fits within her catering budget.

The Busy Mom or Dad. This person has a few young kids and lives close to Palo Alto. They're looking for either quick pizza delivery for a Thursday night or perhaps a venue for their kid's birthday party.

Next, take each persona and brainstorm the types of content/themes that they'd be interested in. The *Worker Bee*, for example, would be interested in learning about coupons, discounts, and special offers of the "pizza of the day." So you'd need to generate either coupon codes or perhaps short tweets about a "pizza of the day" that features *kale* and *pesto* and is on sale with a secret coupon code known only to your followers on Twitter.

The *Office Manager*, in contrast, might be interested in blog posts about how to throw better office parties or catering ideas that are fun for yet another weekly sales meeting.

And the *Busy Mom or Dad* might want to view (and share) photos of their kids (or the kids of their friends) having a blast on Birthday Night at the local pizza restaurant. Each buyer persona, in short, has certain content interests. Hubspot produces a nifty buyer persona tool at **http://jmlinks.com/29s**. Answer a few questions, and the tool will literally create a buyer persona profile complete with a photo.

Tools to Research Keyword Themes

Once you've brainstormed a few buyer personas, role play "as if" you were that buyer persona and write down the keyword themes that might interest that person. To use a different example, let's say you're a wedding planner; you'd realize that the *bride-to-be* is an obvious buyer persona, and she'd be interested in topics such as "how to plan a wedding on a budget" or "tips on selecting the best wedding venue," or "how to deal with divorced parents and their new spouses at a wedding reception," etc.

Or imagine your company sells insurance; you'd identify a buyer persona of the *busy thirty-year-old dad* with two kids, who wonders, "what's the best way to set up a living trust," or "what's the difference between term life insurance and whole life insurance," and you'd write a nifty blog post or perhaps create an eBook. By role-playing, you get "inside the head" of each buyer persona and identify the topics that would interest them as a photo, as a blog post, as a tweet, as a video, etc.

Here are some fun tools that can help you brainstorm keyword themes for your social media content:

SeedKeywords (**http://jmlinks.com/29f**). Simply type in a scenario, and this tool generates a URL you can email out to your team members. Then, each can input the keyword themes that they think that "buyer persona" might be interested in.

RiteTag (https://ritetag.com/). Again, input a "starter" word or hashtag, and this tool will show you related hashtags and metrics on popularity (shown visually by keyword size). It's based on Twitter but is really useful for any theme.

Answer the Public (http://jmlinks.com/51e). Ignore the creepy man. Enter some "seed keywords" that you think your target customers might talk about on social media. Browse suggestions. This is a really awesome tool to brainstorm keywords (after you get past the creepy man).

Google AdWords Keyword Planner. If you have a Google Ads account, and especially if you're spending a couple of hundred dollars per month, you can use this Google tool to research keywords, related keywords, volumes, and value. The reality is that what people search for on Google is also often what they talk about on social. To access it, visit Google Ads at **https://ads.google.com/**, log in, then click on the "tools" icon at the top right, and then click on "Keyword Planner."

If you have a budget, I also highly recommend that you use Buzzsumo (**http://jmlinks.com/29j**). For $99 a month, this tool allows you to input a keyword and see the most shared content on Facebook, Twitter, Pinterest, Reddit, and Links. Here's a screenshot of the most shared content for the keyword *wedding tips*:

So your steps are:

1. Log in to Buzzsumo.com.

2. Enter a keyword such as "organic food" or "tax refund" and select a time horizon such as "past month" or "past year."

3. Sort by network, such as Facebook, Twitter, or Pinterest.

4. Click to view the most shared content.

   a. Reverse engineer what it's about.

   b. Hypothesize why it received so many shares.

5. Click back and click on "View sharers" to see which influencers on Twitter shared the content.

The tool also allows you to enter the domain of a competitor or popular blog in your industry and see the most shared content as well. For example, enter rei.com to see the most shared content from that domain. Here's a screenshot:

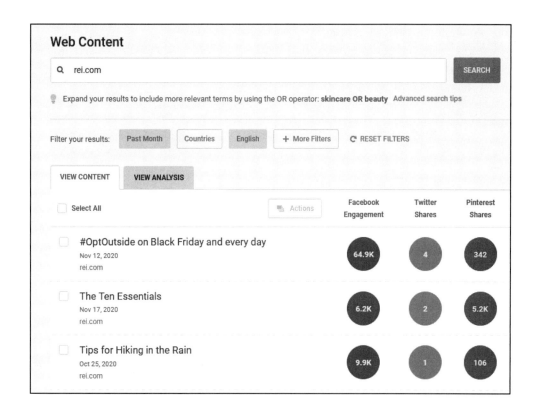

You can also sort by network to see the most shared content on Facebook, Twitter, Pinterest, and blog links.

As you research keywords, look for themes that connect "what your customers want" with "what you offer." These are your primary themes; that is, themes that directly or very closely touch on what you offer. An example would be a Palo Alto pizza restaurant that would have themes like "pizza" or "Italian food."

Don't miss **adjacent keyword themes**. A Palo Alto Pizza Restaurant, for example, should realize that its customers will also be talking about and interested in content themes such as "places to eat in Palo Alto," "where to take a client to lunch," "things to do in Palo Alto, etc." Even themes like "birthdays" or "Memorial Day" would be relevant themes. You always want to "fish where the fish are," so look not only for keyword themes that are spot on to what your company offers but also for *adjacent* keyword themes. Aeromexico, to use a different example, is an airline that flies to Mexico, but its social media keyword themes aren't just "airlines" or "cheap air tickets" but also keywords such as *travel, best tourist destinations in Mexico, Latin America, things to do in Mexico City*, etc.

For your third **To-do**, download the **Keyword Worksheet** and the **Content Marketing worksheet**. For the worksheet, go to **http://jmlinks.com/2023smm** (then enter the code '**2023smm**' to register your workbook), and click on the link to the "Content Marketing." On the **keyword worksheet**, fill out the tab marked "Social Media Themes." On the **Content Marketing Worksheet**, fill out the sections on buyer personas and keyword themes.

» PRODUCE YOUR OWN CONTENT ON SCHEDULE

Now that you have your buyer personas and keyword themes in hand, you can return to your list of content formats that are easy for you to produce and then look for opportunities. You're looking to marry "content that's easy to produce" with "content that your customers want." Here are some content ideas using the idea of a Palo Alto pizza restaurant:

- **Birthday Customers.** Identify customers who are coming to the restaurant to celebrate a birthday. For example, have each waiter or waitress ask customers, "Is anyone celebrating a birthday today?" If so, ask if you can take a picture of their birthday party and share it to the company Facebook page. Get their emails and email them an alert that their party has been "shared" (*because they will likely then reshare it with their friends and photos*).

- **Incentives**. Many restaurants already give the birthday customer a free dessert such as an ice cream sundae or brownie. Make sure that your restaurant has some incentive for customers who are celebrating a birthday to identify themselves. For example, "Check in on Facebook" and be entered to win a free pizza on your birthday! Coupons, special deals, discounts – these are all types of content that you can and should produce for social media.

- **Photo or Quick Video**. Take a photo or shoot a quick video. When the waiter or waitress brings out the birthday dessert, make sure that they have a mobile phone handy and ask the customers for consent to take a celebratory photo. Be on the lookout for other customer photo opportunities such as anniversaries, holidays like Valentine's Day or Cinco De Mayo, gatherings of friends, or even that group of business customers on a quick lunch.

- **Contests and Challenges**. For Cinco de Mayo, have a **contest** for the person who can eat the most chips and guacamole. Or have a **contest** for the best recipe for guacamole. **Challenge** your customer to see who can flip the lid of a burrito bowl without spilling. Chipotle, for example, is a brand that crushes it in terms of contests and challenges. Check out their "Chipotle Lid Flip" challenge at http://jmlinks.com/57a or via the hashtag *#Chipotlelidflip* on Instagram and TikTok.

- **Reminders**. Get the email address, if possible, of one or all of the customers, or leave a card with the check that says "Check our Facebook Page and Instagram Page" for our birthday photos and birthday photo contest. Your email newsletter is a form of content marketing; don't neglect it.

- **Promotions**. Paid advertising is a type of content. Smart social media marketers increasingly don't ignore advertising but rather get their ads to work with their organic content (and vice-versa). In fact, where advertising ends and organic begins is a fuzzy line nowadays.

In this way, you have an easy-to-understand content production system for your wait staff. Every time there's a birthday, they're going to ask for permission to take a photo and enter that photo in your Instagram / Facebook photo contest.

Next, let's look at **blog content**. You'll realize that one of your buyer personas is the busy office manager in Palo Alto who's looking for ideas for inexpensive, fun catering for the weekly sales meeting. You want your pizza restaurant to be discovered by her and get in the rotation for caterers. She's probably looking for blog articles on human resources, catering, and employee morale, as well as caterers in Palo Alto. So, in this case, you'd identify fun article topics for your blog on "how to boost employee morale with better office parties," or "tips on catering for employees who have diverse dietary needs," etc. In this case, you'd identify someone at the pizza restaurant who is a decent writer and assign the writing task of creating at least one blog post per month on the topic of "Palo Alto Catering" and related keywords.

Or, take your buyer persona of the Hungry Worker Bee. These people often go to Twitter or Instagram, searching for daily lunch specials, special deals, and information on "what's cooking." In this case, your content would be as simple as a daily tweet/photo with a discount code or hashtag, such as *#PaloAltoPizza25* that they simply need to say upon ordering to get the discount. Or, perhaps you realize that *#tacotuesday* is a trending hashtag on Twitter every Tuesday, so your content production task is to piggyback on the buzz about *#tacotuesday* by having a taco-style pizza ready every Tuesday. You then tweet out a short tweet with a picture on Twitter and Instagram and use the relevant hashtags.

In each case, you're identifying a format of content (*photo, blog post, video,* or *tweet*) that fits into the keyword themes that your target customers care about. You then figure out what content needs to be produced, who needs to produce it, and when it needs to be produced. Your **TO-DO**, here is to return to the **Content Marketing Worksheet** and populate the section on a Content Schedule. It should answer the following questions:

- What **content format** can be (easily) produced, such as photos, videos, blog posts, tweets, etc.?

- What **keywords** or **content themes** does this content touch upon that matter to your target customers?

    o Don't miss **direct** themes (such as pizza or Italian food) vs. **indirect** themes (such as Irish-American holidays like St. Patrick's Day, what to do in Palo Alto, or even themes like how to cater for a great office party).

- **Who** is going to produce this content?

- **When** are they going to produce it? (Not just Tuesdays, but at what "event" or "moment," such as "Every time we have a birthday customer, we will offer to take a fun photo," or "Every Mother's Day, we will have a customer contest asking customers for their favorite memory of their Moms.")

- **Where** will this content be **posted** on social media? Will it go to Facebook, Instagram, your blog, Twitter, YouTube, etc.?

Successful content marketing is about being **systematic**. It's about being **smart**. And it's about being **lazy**. Look for easy, ongoing content opportunities.

≫ BLOG, BLOG, BLOG, YOU GOTTA BLOG, VLOG, PHLOG, AND POST

Any business that's serious about social media marketing must have a blog if for no other reason than a blog gives you an easy place to put your articles, infographics, photos, and videos that you can then reference on Twitter, Facebook, Pinterest, etc.

You gotta blog!

If you don't have a blog on your website, ask your web designer to set one up immediately, preferably at your domain.com/blog. The easiest platform to use is WordPress. If you can't use WordPress or set one up on your own domain, I recommend Google's Blogger platform at **https://www.blogger.com/**. Tumblr (**https://www.tumblr.com/**) is another good one with the added benefit that it is a social media network in its own right.

Blogs are so important for social media content that I want to spend some time on blogging. I'm assuming you have set up a company blog, so structurally, you're ready to write your first post. (If you've already written a few posts, you can also revisit and re-optimize them as indicated below).

Your blog and the blog posts on it can serve any or all of three purposes.

1. as a **trust indicator** to substantiate your company as a "helpful expert."

2. as an **SEO asset**, that is - as a way to get to the top of relevant Google, Yahoo, and Bing searches via basic SEO) (*This is covered in-depth in my SEO Workbook, so we will not cover it here*).

3. as **content** for posting and **sharing** to your social media networks.

4. as a **place to put** other content such as videos or photos.

Each of these, conceptually, are different things, but one blog post can be oriented towards one, or all, of them. For example, a blog post on "Seven Tax Tips for Expatriates Living in the USA," can be a *trust indicator* substantiating your CPA firm as experts in international tax issues, it can be an *SEO asset* helping get your company to the top of relevant Google searches, and it can be *content* that you can share on social media networks like LinkedIn to stay top of mind among potential customers and encourage social sharing.

Identifying Content Themes for Your Blog

What should you blog about? What type of content should you create? The answer is to identify **content themes** that touch on what your target customers want to know about. Clients seeking international tax advice, for example, would be interested in reading blog posts on ways to minimize double taxation or what types of behavior are most likely to provoke an IRS audit. Persons planning a wedding might be interested in comparing the merits of a "destination wedding" in Mexico with an "at home" wedding in Los Angeles. And persons interested in cybersecurity for their corporations might be interested in a blog post with an infographic on the twelve most common security holes in a typical corporate network.

A Strong Blog Touches on Content Themes that People Care About

Emotion, Emotion, Emotion (and Some Utility)

In general, successful social media content is content that hits **emotional** themes such as usefulness, being counterintuitive or counterfactual, being shocking, provoking fear or outrage, or being funny. It's really all about utility or emotion; outside of LinkedIn (which is the most serious network), emotional triggers are by far the most common content!

Accordingly, if there is an "emotional" angle to your blog post, be sure to touch on it and be sure to include it in your headline.

> *Once you have the keyword target, the next step is to write a catchy headline and write a catchy blog post that hits on either emotion or usefulness.*

Let's take the example of a Los Angeles CPA firm that has expertise in international taxation issues. Our keyword research has identified the FBAR (Report of Foreign Bank and Financial Accounts) requirements, which require reporting of overseas assets as a "hot button" issue among our buyer personas. We might then take the topic of "FBAR compliance" and spin out blog headlines such as:

> *Why FBAR Matters to Your Clients (Even If They Don't Know It Yet) ("utility").*
>
> *Why What You as a CPA Don't Know About FBAR Is Going to Cost You ("fear").*
>
> *The FBAR: An Outrageous Intervention of the Government in our Lives ("shocking")*
>
> *An FBAR Tragedy: A Small Businessperson Forced into Bankruptcy ("Outrage or sentimentality")*

Fun tools that will help you "spin" blog topics and titles for social media are the Portent Idea Generator (**http://jmlinks.com/17g**) and Hubspot's topic generator (**http://jmlinks.com/9w**).

Vlog, Phlog, and Post: Other Forms of Blogging

Blogging, of course, refers to the written word. A good blog post has a strong concept, a catchy headline, and somewhere between two and five paragraphs. Pretty much every business needs to have a blog unless your business is just so visual that you can get by with just photos or videos. You should expand your definition of blogging, however, to include other forms of rapid-fire content. Let's discuss each type:

Vlog or video blogging. You can blog with the printed word, but you can also "video" blog" or Vlog on YouTube but also on native content on Facebook, Instagram, TikTok, and even LinkedIn. Indeed, with the rise of "stories" on Instagram and Snapchat, this is yet another type of "day in the life" video blogging. So think about short video content you can share across channels, and like blogging, this content can be very "spur of the moment."

Phlog or photo blogging. Photos are the bread and butter of Instagram and Facebook, so think of being systematic as you produce photos of products, services, customers, events, etc.

Posting. You can post straight text on Facebook, Twitter, or LinkedIn. These short posts (< 280 characters on Twitter) are like micro blog posts. Again, be systematic about the content that you'll share in text format. It can be as simple as posting "TGIF" on Friday, "I love Taco Tuesday!" or "The only thing we have to fear is fear itself," with some additional commentary about your industry or trends within it.

As with a more robust blog post, each type of "micro" blogging, "photo" blogging, or "video" blogging follows the same rules. Know what your audience wants and create content that touches on your keyword themes. Think interactively – what will your target customers like, comment on, or share? Give priority to emotions and counterintuitive content. Emotions work better than facts, and anything that's counterintuitive works better than things that are not. Brainstorm content that is "man bites dog," not "dog bites man."

Think systematically. What can you produce easily and on schedule? It's easier if you think of content that's authentic and spontaneous vs. thinking that each piece of content needs to be a masterpiece that will stand for centuries.

Share Systematically on Schedule with Hootsuite

Finally, now that you have a well-written blog post (photo, video, etc.) that touches on trending industry themes of interest to key customer segments, it's time to share it. Post it to your blog, and then use a URL shortener like **http://bitly.com/** or

http://tinyurl.com/ to shorten your long blog URL. Rebrandly (**https://www.rebrandly.com/**) is a service that allows you to use a custom URL.

Once you have a piece of content and a URL, shorten it and then paste it into Hootsuite (**http://jmlinks.com/29k**). Summarize the topic, and post it strategically to your Twitter, Facebook, LinkedIn, and wherever else appropriate. (If you don't like Hootsuite, Buffer or Later are competitor applications).

Here's a screenshot of a post to LinkedIn, Facebook, and Twitter via Hootsuite that is "just text:"

You can schedule your posts across time and platforms, thus making it very easy to "plan ahead" and populate your social channels for any given week or month.

To sum up, once you know a keyword theme, the process of creating a blog post (or another type of blog-like content) is as follows:

1. **Identify the blog concept and relevant content themes**. These define what the blog post is about and which keywords people are likely to search for. Use a tool like Buzzsumo (**http://jmlinks.com/29j**) to see what's already being shared on social media sites.

2. **Outline the content and write a rough draft**. Just as in all writing, it's good to write out a rough draft. A good blog post should have about four to five paragraphs of text. "Less is more" when it comes to social media, so make the blog post pithy and informative.

3. **Identify a provocative image**. Whether it's on Instagram, Facebook, or LinkedIn, people respond to images. Use a royalty-free image site such as Pixabay (**https://pixabay.com/**) or Unsplash (**https://unsplash.com/**) and find an image that conveys the essence of your blog post.

4. **Write a catchy, keyword-heavy headline**. It's no accident that popular sites like *Buzzfeed* and *Huffington Post* use shocking or provocative headlines! *Dog bites man!, Explore the latest scandal! Lose weight without exercise!, etc.* People react to and share content that hits an emotional nerve, and the headline is the first step toward a strong emotional reaction.

5. **Finalize the content**. Review your content and make sure it is easy to read, preferably with lists and bullets.

6. **Share the content**. Identify the appropriate social media platform, such as LinkedIn, Twitter, Facebook, Instagram, etc., and share your post. Use a tool like Hootsuite to organize and schedule your shares.

VIDEO. Watch a video tutorial on how to write social media-friendly blog posts at **http://jmlinks.com/16p**.

Your Blogging Objectives

In terms of social media marketing, your blog objectives are a) to stay "top of mind" among customers and their contacts, b) to substantiate your organization's brand image as a "helpful expert," and c) to encourage "social sharing" so that friends of friends, and colleagues of colleagues, can become aware of your company and its products or services. A strong blog post can be great as a trust indicator, great for SEO, or attractive for social media sharing, or all three! So, start blogging as well as vlogging, phlogging, and sharing short posts!

» CURATE OTHER PEOPLE'S CONTENT

Effective content for social media comes in four main types: your own content, other people's content, user-generated content, and interactive content. We've already discussed your own content, such as text, blog posts, photos, or videos that you will conceptualize and create on a regular basis. But because you'll need a lot of content to feed your social media channels, you will generally never be able to generate enough on your own. For this reason, let's turn to the second type of content – **other people's content**, often called "**curated content**."

Curate is just a fancy word that means identifying useful content in your industry, summarizing it via a short headline or summary paragraph as in a tweet, and sharing this content on your social networks like Twitter, Facebook, LinkedIn, etc. I, for one, do a lot of content curation on Twitter and LinkedIn. You can check me out on Twitter at **http://jmlinks.com/37m**. Here's a screenshot of my sharing of a link to a New York Times article on social media:

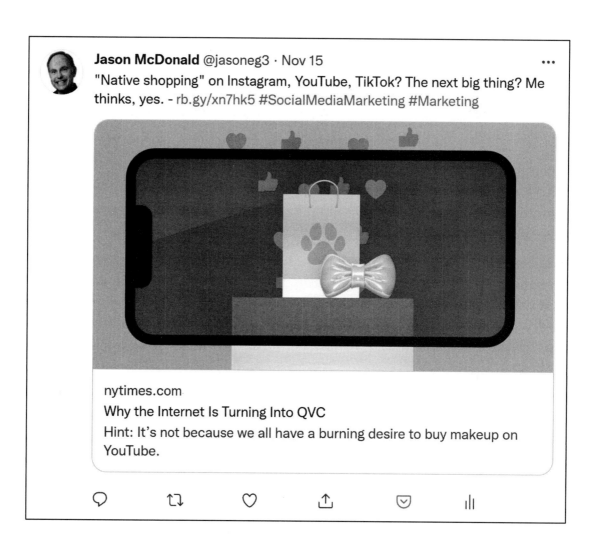

Jason McDonald @jasoneg3 · Nov 15

"Native shopping" on Instagram, YouTube, TikTok? The next big thing? Me thinks, yes. - rb.gy/xn7hk5 #SocialMediaMarketing #Marketing

nytimes.com
Why the Internet Is Turning Into QVC
Hint: It's not because we all have a burning desire to buy makeup on YouTube.

By diligently paying attention to blogs, publications, and trade shows on SEO, Social Media Marketing, and AdWords (via tools like *Feedly.com, Buzzsumo.com, Drumup.io*), I systematically identify, read, and "curate" the best content for my followers. I thus have other people's content to share on my own social media channels (Twitter, LinkedIn, Instagram, Facebook, etc.) and thereby work to stay top of mind with my target customers and position myself as a "helpful expert."

Be a Helpful Expert

This idea of a "helpful expert" is a good way to wrap your head around content curation. You'll position your lead employees and/or your company as a whole as a "helpful expert" by looking through all the junk and noise in your industry, identifying the best / most useful content from industry blogs, gurus, and publications, and then sharing this content to your own social media channels. If producing your own content is all about being a good *photographer*, *writer*, or *videographer*, content *curation* is all about being a good *editor*.

The steps to content curation are:

1. Identify your **content themes** (which you have hopefully already identified above), including broader industry themes for which you might not want to produce your own content, but you might want to monitor for relevant content.

2. Systematically **research and identify content**. Browse industry blogs, portals, websites, social media feeds, etc.. Separate the wheat from the chaff, meaning throw away the low-quality content and identify the truly interesting content that will interest your target customers.

3. **Summarize** this content in short format, ideally less than the 280 characters of Twitter, including a short URL to the full content using a URL shortener like bitly.com or tinyurl.com.

4. **Share** this content to your social media channels on a regular basis, using scheduling software like Hootsuite (**http://jmlinks.com/29k**) or Buffer (**http://jmlinks.com/29m**).

Advantages and Disadvantages

You might be tempted to ask why you should curate the content of others vs. using your own content. While it's certainly true that producing your own content is better (because you can control the message and directly promote your own company or product), few of us have the budget or resources to produce sufficient content on our own to fill our content pipeline. To stay top of mind with customers, you need a lot more content than you'll be able to produce yourself.

There are thus advantages and disadvantages to your own content vs. other people's content. The advantage of other people's content is that it is easy to get, while the advantage of your own content is that it's yours; you can customize it to your desired message. The disadvantage of other people's content is that you do not control the message (and it thereby promotes them to some extent), while the disadvantage of your own content is that it takes time and effort to produce. It's a lot like the food at our party analogy. The advantage of other people's tacos is that they take less effort on your own part, but (if they're good) they promote the actual producer of those tacos. The advantage of your own tacos is that they taste better (hopefully), and they promote you as the guru of tacos, but the disadvantage is that they are more work.

Going back to review the "types" of content you may want for your social media marketing content machine; you'll see that you have –

Your own blog post vs. the blog post of an industry guru

Your own photograph vs. the photograph of a great photographer

Your own quote vs. a famous quote by somebody else

Your own webinar vs. the webinar being put on by industry luminaries.

Go back and review some companies that are doing social media well (e.g., Whole Foods, REI, HP, Bishop Robert Barron, Seth Godin), and you'll see that many of them mix and match "their own content" and "other people's content" plus sometimes they commentate on the content of others (a "hybrid" model).

Let's drill down into other people's content.

Finding Other People's Content to Share on Social Media

You want to start systematically identifying great content in your industry and queuing this up to be shared on your social networks. Your goal is to be a "helpful expert," the person who tells others, "Hey! Did you know that so-and-so is having an amazing free webinar on Thursday?" or "Hey! Did you see that our industry journal just published an in-depth study on such-and-such topic?" Other People's Content or OPC is easy to find, easy to share, and helps to position you as the person or company that really has its ear to the industry pulse.

How do you find quality content produced by other people? How do you do this in an easy and systematic way?

Fortunately, there are tools to help you systematically identify and share other people's content. (All are listed in *The Marketing Almanac, content marketing section* and on my *Social Media Marketing Dashboard*). Here are some of my favorites:

Bookmark / Read Industry Blogs. Identify the top industry blogs in your industry, bookmark them (and/or input them to Feedly), plus follow them on social media as on Facebook, LinkedIn, Twitter. You can share their content with your followers, plus commentate on content that they're producing. To find blogs in the first place, go to Google and type in a keyword that is relevant to your company's industry and the word "blog." For example, visit **http://jmlinks.com/12w**, which is a sample search for blogs on *proteomics*

Google Searches. Enter your keyword themes into Google. Click on the *Tools Menu > Past Month.* Alternatively, click on the *News* tab. This is a good way to find timely blog posts and articles on your keyword themes for sharing. See it in action for "organic food" at **http://jmlinks.com/37n**. You can input these "saved searches" to your Start.me page as well.

Google News. Google News is one of the best free tools to aggregate information. Log in to your Google / Gmail account, and visit **https://news.google.com/**. Once you do so, you'll get an email alert when Google finds new news, and this content will appear in Google News on the left under "saved searches." You can also manage your feed by clicking on "For you" on the left and adding keywords or topics. Watch a video on how to use Google News for social media marketing at **http://jmlinks.com/46y**.

DrumUp (https://drumpup.io). DrumUp integrates easily with most social media platforms and helps you curate and share content that is useful to your followers.

Feedly (http://feedly.com) - Feedly is a newsreader integrated with Google or Facebook login. It's useful for social media because you can follow important blogs or other content and share it with your followers. It can also spur great blog ideas.

Easely (http://easel.ly) - Use thousands of templates and design objects to easily create infographics for your blog. A competitor is Piktochart (**http://piktochart.com**).

Buzzsumo (http://buzzsumo.com) - Buzzsumo is a 'buzz' monitoring tool for social media. Input a keyword, select a date range like "last week," and this tool will show you what is being most shared across Facebook, Twitter, LinkedIn, etc. You can also input a domain such as *nytimes.com* or one of your industry blogs and also see what is being most shared from that domain.

Google Alerts (https://www.google.com/alerts) - Google alerts allow you to input keywords and then receive daily or weekly alerts of new items that the Google search engine finds on those keywords. It's useful, but I like Google news better.

A final nifty tool is Start.me (**https://start.me/**). Sign up for this free service, and you can build a personalized dashboard with links to all your favorite industry blogs, key tools like Feedly or Buzzsumo, canned searches on Google, etc. You can even share these dashboards with your team. Imagine having a Monday afternoon assignment of launching your Start.me personalized dashboard, browsing Feedly and key industry blogs, checking your Google alerts, and then quickly identifying interesting content, summarizing it, and sharing it to your social media networks by scheduling it to Hootsuite. *We're talking about the systematic production of content marketing here, factory edition.*

By being systematic, you can fill your social media content pipeline in just a couple of hours a week.

"I want to be a machine." ~ the artist, Andy Warhol

Keep Your Secrets Secret

And, as part of the social media illusion, you don't have to share the amazing tools above with your customers. They'll just think you are gung-ho awesome. The "illusion" of effective social media marketing will work in your favor; you will be perceived as the industry guru that somehow never sleeps and is aware of every important industry trend, "how to" video on YouTube and key article that's up for debate in the industry blogosphere.

» ENCOURAGE USER GENERATED CONTENT (UGC)

Never forget the *social* element of social media. Don't think of this like a project you'll do by yourself; you need employees in your company to help, and you need the participation of your customers and fans. You'll want to enlist the support of other employees in your company, especially the frontline, customer-facing staff, to look for content opportunities. If at all possible, you also want to encourage user-generated content or UGC. UGC is both cheap (your users will be doing the heavy lifting) and engaging, as users love to share and see their own content.

Here are some ways to encourage UGC:

> **Ask**. Simply ask for feedback. Don't just post a photo to Instagram or Facebook. Post a photo with a query. Post a picture of your latest "Taco Pizza" concoction and ask users if they think they'll like it. Don't post a photo that says "Happy Mother's Day" to Facebook, but rather post a photo of a mom and child and ask users to share their favorite memory of their own mom.

> **Have Contests.** Within reason, contests are a great way to solicit UGC. Don't just post a picture of a cute kid at his birthday party eating pizza in your restaurant. Post the photo of the kid, and ask them to enroll in your "cutest kid of the month" contest as measured by Facebook and Instagram likes. Want to see what contests are up and out on Instagram? Check out the hashtag *#contest* at **http://jmlinks.com/52y**.

> **Sponsor Challenges.** Especially on youth-oriented platforms like Instagram, YouTube, and TikTok, brands can create silly challenges that motivate customers

and superfans to chime in. For example, check out the "#challenge" hashtag on TikTok or Instagram. It's full of brand-sponsored "challenges" that encourage UGC.

Conduct Surveys. Use your blog, Twitter, or Facebook to engage in customer surveys. Twitter, for example, has made the app easy to use; simply select the "Add Poll" icon on a Tweet. For Facebook, merely Google "Facebook Poll App," and you'll find an assortment of free and paid apps for Facebook. SurveyMonkey and Google also offer free / paid versions of survey software.

Use Hashtags. Especially on Instagram, but also on Twitter, you can set up a branded hashtag just for your customers to share posts about your products or services. Airbnb does this on Instagram with *#airbnb* (**http://jmlinks.com/29p**), as do vendors like REI with *#optoutside* (**http://jmlinks.com/29q**). If you're in a fun industry where people like to "show off," you may not even have to incentivize people with a contest to get them to generate photos, tweets, or other content that promotes your brand!

You can also commission content, for example, by sending bloggers free product samples and asking them to blog or video blog about your products or services. (If you do so, you'll need to have them identify per FTC regulations that they were given free stuff). Search YouTube for *unboxing* (**http://jmlinks.com/29r**), for example, and you'll discover there's a whole genre of unboxing or haul videos in which people showcase and talk about products.

Influencer marketing is yet another buzzword for UGC. It has come to mean paid or at least promoted content. So for influencer marketing, you:

1. Identify influencers who reach the types of customers you want to reach.

2. Reach out to them via email, their agents, or emerging marketplaces such as Octoly (**https://www.octoly.com/**). Most influencers require at least free product, if not a paid promotion fee.

3. The influencer then shares to his or her social following some type of content about your product or service. It could be a product review, a coupon or special deal, a contest, etc.

UGC is all about encouraging customers, fans, superfans, and even (paid) influencers to talk about and "spontaneously" share content to their social channels that casts your product or service in a positive light. Your **TO-DO** here is to brainstorm which users are most likely to spontaneously create positive content about your company, product, or service. How do you identify them? How do you motivate them? How can you nurture them?

» INTERACT WITH INTERACTIVE CONTENT

Finally, as you are working on your own content, curated content, and UGC, don't forget that social media is really all about interactivity. The fourth type of content is "**interactive content**," a fancy word describing the back-and-forth between a brand and its customers or among the customers themselves. All of the algorithms favor content that engages people as measured by likes, comments, and shares. A YouTube video that "goes viral" usually does so because people like it, comment on it, and share it. Ditto for a Facebook post that gets a lot of traction or a tweet that shows up prominently in Twitter moments. As you create content, curate content, or catalyze UGC, always think:

1. **What's in it for them?** Why would a user even want to passively read or consume this piece of content in the first place?

2. **Why would they like it?** What will cause them to hit the "like" button, and why?

3. **Why would they comment on it?** What prompt can you devise that will engage them in a conversation around this piece of content?

4. **Why will they share it?** Content that gets shared extends your reach, and saying that something "went viral" really means that people engaged with it so fervently that they massively liked it, commented on it, and shared it. But why?

Next, flip this around and realize that you, as a content producer and brand, need to interact with the content of others. If someone comments on your YouTube video, respond back in the comments. Do the same if someone comments on your Facebook or LinkedIn post, tweet, etc. If someone reviews you on Yelp, respond to the review and say thanks. If they engage with you, engage back with them. Have conversations with your fans and superfans across all channels.

Be Interactive. Set a goal of a daily or weekly log-in to each and every one of your social channels. Scan for user comments, and comment back. Thank people for reviews on Facebook, Google, or Yelp. "Tag" people in photos on Instagram or Facebook. Follow the followers of your competitors. Reach out to influencers, superfans, and prominent people on Twitter and talk "to" them about your keyword themes. Be interactive both with people who have commented on your content; be proactively interactive with new people, especially on platforms like Twitter or LinkedIn, where it's considered OK for people to strike up online conversations with strangers.

Look for Content and Engage with It

Moreover, look for content by your users, potential users, and by influencers. Find their content and engage with it by liking, commenting on, and sharing it. Here's just one example based on LinkedIn.

1. Sign in to your LinkedIn account.

2. In the search bar, type in a keyword theme that matters to your company and/or customers.

3. Click the button marked content.

4. Scroll through content posted by others to LinkedIn and like, comment on, and share content that's relevant to you and your brand.

Here's a screenshot:

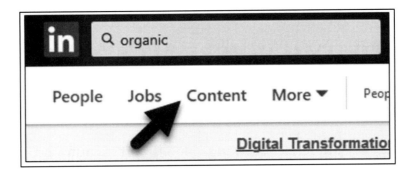

Do the same with hashtags across Facebook, LinkedIn, Twitter, and Instagram. Identify key hashtags and engage with the content being shared across them. Here's a screenshot for the hashtag *#organic* on Instagram at 47 million posts:

In this way, across all the networks, you can quickly identify content put up by others on themes that matter to your business. You can then like, comment on, and share that content. Indeed, people respond to the "flattery" that you took the time to read, like, comment on, and even share their content.

It's not just LinkedIn or Instagram, of course. You can do the same process on all of the networks. Find posts on Facebook that matter to your brand and comment on them, find tweets on Twitter that matter to your brand and like or comment on them, find videos on YouTube that matter to your brand, and thumb up / thumb down, comment on, and share them. Interactive content means making this process of searching for and engaging with others a key part of your content marketing strategy.

INTERACTIVITY IS WHERE "IT'S AT" ON SOCIAL MEDIA

Interactivity can be as simple as following, liking, commenting on, and sharing the content of other brands or individuals in your industry. Or it can be as complicated as identifying "influencers" more powerful than you and systematically drawing them into a conversation or interaction. By engaging with this content, you'll draw the attention of others and become part of the conversation. No one likes people who just talk. Any good conversation is about talking and listening, listening and reacting, sharing and bringing others into it. Social media, in summary, is a *conversational* platform, not a *broadcast* medium.

New for 2023 is the trend towards "duets" and "commentary" on both TikTok and YouTube. On TikTok, a "duet" is when one user comments on the video of another user. "Duets" can even go viral on Twitter. You can check out "duets" on TikTok at http://jmlinks.com/57c. TikTok also has quite a bit of commentary videos. This is similar to YouTube, where content is often tagged "commentary," and usually means one user clips a video from another user and then comments on it in video format. You can see sample YouTube commentary videos at **http://jmlinks.com/57d**. In both cases, these are "interactive" content strategies.

» CARROT & OUTREACH MARKETING

At this point, you've begun your social media marketing journey. You've understood that social media marketing is about "throwing" the party more than "attending the party." And you've realized that the really hard work will be creating the kind of **content** that makes potential customers want to "like you," keep coming back for more, and share your message with their friends, family, and/or business colleagues.

> **Content creation** and **promotion** are the most important ongoing tasks of successful social media marketing!

With that in mind, I would like to draw your attention to a high-value type of content marketing. It's what I call "**carrot and outreach**." In this strategy, you identify something "free," such as a Webinar, an e-Book, a free online consultation, or some other type of content that is not only free to the user but so enticing that they will give you their name, company name, email, and telephone. *Your* "free carrot" is given in exchange for *their* contact info so that you or your sales team can follow up.

Here's an example:

1. You are a B2B company selling something professional, such as anti-virus, anti-phishing software to companies concerned about online security.

2. You create a free Webinar that is short, informative, and fun, entitled "The Unseen Dangers of Managing Your Business Online." This webinar highlights the issues around viruses, phishing, and other scams that plague corporate users on the Internet.

3. You promote your free webinar via teasers, paid ads, short clips, etc., using both paid and free tactics on key social networks such as Twitter, Facebook, and LinkedIn.

4. Interested persons register for your webinar.

5. You produce the webinar as a "Facebook / LinkedIn / Twitter live event" and record it so you can repurpose that content later.

6. You capture the names, company names, email addresses, and phone numbers of the attendees.

7. Your sales staff follows up with these prospects and makes sales.

"Carrot and outreach" marketing is used most frequently in B2B and professional services. But it can also be used in B2C marketing. For example, a dog groomer might offer a free online consultation on dog beauty issues. Or a tax preparation service might offer a free financial analysis. An e-commerce company might offer a heavily discounted or free sample in exchange for registration. The sky is the limit: just identify some type of "free" content, a promotion or outreach strategy to promote it, and your follow-up strategy.

Email marketing (discussed in Chapter 10) is ideal for "carrot and outreach." For example, you can brainstorm an exciting, fun, "must-read" email newsletter. The newsletter in and of itself can be your "carrot." Or you might identify an eBook. Alternatively, think of using a DRIP campaign, which is a series of automated email responses that go out before or after your "anchor" "carrot" content. You can see an example of this strategy at **https://www.jm-seo.org/free** , which promotes my free "Marketing Almanac" ebook and uses DRIP marketing to follow up with folks who download it. A few days after the first download, the user gets a teaser message offering more information on my books. DRIP, like the drip, drip, drip of a leaky faucet, means sending out message after message in an automatic fashion. Learn more about DRIP campaigns at **http://jmlinks.com/57g**.

»» CHECKLIST: CONTENT MARKETING ACTION ITEMS

Test your knowledge of Content Marketing! Take the *Content marketing quiz* at **http://jmlinks.com/qzcm**. Next, here are your Content Marketing **Action Items**:

❑ Identify **buyer personas** and **keywords** or **content themes**. Create a *Keyword Worksheet* identifying your keywords on a continuum from "adjacent" or "educational" to late-stage or "transactional" keywords.

❑ **Research** content by **competitors and companies-to-emulate** using a tool like Buzzsumo to identify the *most shared content* and reverse engineer why. Brainstorm how you, too, can create highly interactive or shareable content.

❑ Identify the **four types of content**: your own content, other people's content, UGC (User Generated Content), and interactive content. What will be your easiest and most effective mix of content?

    ❑ Create a **content map** for your own content to be produced. These might be simple text, photos, videos, memes, infographics, etc. Pay attention to **content format** and identify which format is easiest for you to produce.

    ❑ Set up **tools** like Google News, Feedly, DrumUp or Buzzsumo to pre-identify the content of others. Sort through the noise and identify content that positions your brand as a "helpful expert."

    ❑ Brainstorm **UGC content opportunities** and, if possible, set up the "systems" to begin encouraging UGC. Consider creating contests or challenges that spur your customers to "spontaneously" share content.

    ❑ Set aside a specific time each day or week to identify and interact with **interactive content**, whether as posted by customers or fans to your own brand channels or by customers or fans across hashtags and relevant content themes.

❑ Create a **content calendar** identifying the type of content you will produce, when it will be produced, and who will produce it.

❑ **Share your content** in a systematic way using a scheduling tool such as Hootsuite or Buffer.

❑ Brainstorm a free "**carrot**" such as an eBook, Webinar, or free consultation, and then use "carrot" and "outreach" marketing to connect social media to your sales funnel. Consider using a **DRIP** campaign via email.

Check out the **free tools**! Go to my *Social Media Marketing Dashboard > Content Marketing* for my favorite free tools on content marketing. Just visit **http://jmlinks.com/smmdash**.

»» DELIVERABLE: A CONTENT MARKETING PLAN

Now that we've come to the end of Chapter 2, your **DELIVERABLE** has arrived. For the worksheet, go to **http://jmlinks.com/2023smm** (then enter the code '**2023smm**' to register your workbook), and click on the link to the "Content Marketing Worksheet." By filling out this plan, you and your team will create a plan for all the yummy content, both yours and that of other people, that you'll need to fill your social media pipeline.

3
FACEBOOK (ORGANIC)

Facebook is a great place to begin your Social Media Marketing journey! Here are five good reasons.

First, Facebook is – by far – the **largest social media platform**, with over two billion active users and countless individual profiles, business pages, and groups. Survey after survey ranks Facebook as the most used social media platform.

Second, once you **understand the dynamics of Facebook** – *Profiles and Pages, Timelines and Posts, Likes, Comments, and Shares*... you'll more easily **understand the dynamics of other social media** like LinkedIn, Twitter, or Instagram.

Third, the Facebook **algorithm** rewards posts that foster engagement – that is, likes, comments, and shares. This aspect of "rewarding engagement" is common not just to the Facebook algorithm but to all platforms – Twitter, LinkedIn, YouTube, Pinterest, TikTok, etc. If you master the art of *engagement* on Facebook, that will help you master *content marketing* on all platforms.

Fourth, because of its extensive **reach** and its nuanced **targeting** options, Facebook is an incredible **advertising** platform. Throw in the fact that Facebook owns Instagram, and Facebook advertising options are second to none in social media!

Fifth and finally, Facebook is **fun**! Social media marketing should not be thought of as a chore but as a way to get closer to your customers and build a community of evangelists around your company, product, or service.

The question is not whether your customers are on Facebook but rather what they are doing and how you can brainstorm a social media strategy to reach them.

Let's get started!

TO-DO LIST:

» Come to Terms with Mark Zuckerberg
» Explore how Facebook Works

» Understand the Facebook Algorithm

» Inventory Companies on Facebook

» Set up and Optimize Your Facebook Page

» Tools to Manage Your Facebook Business Page

» Brainstorm and Execute a Posting Strategy

» Promote Your Facebook Page and Posts for Free

» Work with "Superfans" on Facebook

» Odds & Ends: Groups, Events, Facebook Live, etc.

»» Checklist: Facebook (Organic) Action Items

»» Deliverable: a Facebook (Organic) Marketing Plan

» COME TO TERMS WITH MARK ZUCKERBERG

Before we dive into Facebook for marketing, we need to discuss its wunderkind founder, Mark Zuckerberg. Just 38 years old, Zuckerberg is an "accidental billionaire," meaning he lacks deep experience in corporate strategy and management. He owns the largest social platform ("Meta," that is - Facebook, Instagram, WhatApp, etc.), and he (and his advisors) have manipulated the stock structure in such a way that, for all intents and purposes, Zuckerberg is 100% in charge of the company, responsible to no one. When you buy Meta stock, when you use Facebook, or when you do marketing on Facebook (whether free or paid), you are playing in Zuckerberg's sandbox. Zuck's in charge, one hundred percent.

Recently, the accidental billionaire has gone whole hog into the "Metaverse." The "Metaverse" is a geeky, nerdspace in which we are all supposed to don virtual reality "headsets" and "interact" with each other in this new computer-simulated reality. Allegedly, we'll all love this. We'll all buy NFTs (non-fungible tokens) and conduct meetings, and be thrilled at the "Metaverse" to the abandonment of real interaction in the real world and probably to the neglect of our Facebook posts and Instagram shares. Why would we need to share anything about our "real lives," after all, when we'll live in the "Metaverse?" (To visit Meta's information site on business in the Metaverse, visit **http://jmlinks.com/58v** or visit the Meta homepage at **https://www.meta.com/**).

Zuckerberg's vision of the "Metaverse," in short, is a sort of benign "Matrix" (the 1999 dystopian movie starring Keanu Reeves). Our eyes, ears, and brains, will plug into the "Metaverse," and we will transcend the boring human existence of friends, family, food, spouses, children, grandkids, gardening, hiking, politics, exercise, and probably even sex. Zuckerberg envisions this as a paradise, a paradise in which he and his fellow wunderkind nerds will be in charge, making money and ruling over us mere mortals.

As you have probably guessed, I am not a fan. I think the "Metaverse" is stupid, and count me out, 100% out. I like my dogs. I love my wife. I enjoy sex. I adore my kids, and I actually cherish "reality." A "VR" headset makes me seasick, or rather "Brave New World" sick. Be that as it may, however, Zuckerberg is captain of the Facebook Titanic, and he's taking us all on a journey into the "Metaverse" whether we want to go or not. Since the time of the "Meta" announcement, Facebook stock has fallen from around $325 a share to around $98 at the time of this writing, Zuckerberg has lost about ½ of his wealth, and as of November 2022, the company has announced its first massive layoffs of about 10,000 employees. Stocks and employment aren't our concern here. But the transition to "Meta" is impacting us marketers:

- **Facebook has lost its sense of direction**. The company's core product – Facebook - is almost an orphan, neglected by its owner, and consequently, it's lost its cool factor with the young and is universally perceived in a negative fashion by the marketing community. What is Facebook today? What is Zuckerberg's vision not of the "Metaverse" but of his core business, Facebook, and its companion, Instagram? This is entirely unclear, and – without a captain – the twin ships of Facebook and Instagram are adrift in a very competitive market.

- **The management interface of business Pages (as we shall see) is increasingly chaotic.** Terms and features appear and disappear without a rhyme or reason, and things are named and renamed in a chaotic and confusing fashion. Managing a business on Facebook seems slightly more complicated than managing a nuclear reactor or curing cancer at this point. It's a mess, both at the organic and advertising levels.

- **Faceobook has little to no technical help.** Now that the company is transitioning to the "Metaverse," so many products have been reconfigured and renamed that both the written Facebook help files and the pathetic technical help available via chat or phone are inaccurate and confusing. It's not only that things have changed at Facebook. It's that you often can't find the answer even if you want to, and even if you have "help" from the demoralized "Meta" employees chained into the "Metaverse."

In summary, Facebook 2023 is the Titanic. The Captain seems to have gone insane, the ship is sinking, and we (as marketers) are on board. But it's still the Titanic. It's huge – it's the largest social platform, and it remains heavily used! Facebook and Instagram aren't going away, and they do represent significant marketing opportunities! The Titanic didn't sink in a minute, and Facebook / Instagram / Meta won't go down in a minute either. It's not dead yet, and there's still time for a rebirth. New management, anyone?

As we explore Facebook marketing, just try to have a good attitude and recognize that what might have previously been a simple task may have become a "Hunt for Red October" as the company is destabilized by the transition to the "Metaverse" and by its zillionaire baby boss, Mark Zuckerberg. Try to maintain your "good attitude" and focus on what you're trying to accomplish: using Facebook to reach prospects, customers, and superfans in such a way as to "build your brand" and "sell more stuff."

» EXPLORE HOW FACEBOOK WORKS

To understand Facebook as a marketer is to understand the "F's": friends, family, fun, photos, and "fake." Before you set up (or optimize) a Facebook Page for your business before you start posting, before you start advertising, and before you start measuring your successes and failures, take some time to step back and ponder what real people are doing on Facebook. What you'll find is folks sharing posts, photos, and videos about their "wonderful" lives. For now, log on to Facebook and observe the "party" and what people are doing at it. This is an important point for all social platforms:

> Before you attempt to use a platform as a *marketer*, experience it as a *user*. What are "real people" doing on this platform? What content types and content themes are creating engagement? Don't bully your way into a platform, and just start shouting. Listen first. Then participate.

I'm assuming you have a personal Facebook profile; *if you do not,* simply go to **https://www.facebook.com/,** or download the mobile app for your phone, and sign up. Check out Facebook help at **https://www.facebook.com/help/** - just click on "get started on Facebook." Once you sign up – as an individual – you'll have a **profile**.

If you're new to Facebook, make a list of your friends and family, including, if possible, their email addresses. Log on to Facebook and search for them by name. Send out "friend requests" and monitor "friend requests" that are coming to you as well. Grow your network of friends on Facebook if you haven't already. Note that Facebook, like LinkedIn but unlike Instagram, Twitter, TikTok, YouTube, or Pinterest, requires that users "be friends" in order for the interactive magic to occur. If you have an established Facebook account, you probably know this already.

Next, start posting photos of your family, your dog, your trip to Las Vegas, or whatever, to your "timeline." When you log in to Facebook on your desktop or your phone, look at your "news feed." Your *news feed* will show you the posts of the friends and family with whom you are connected; when they post to their *timeline*, it will show in your *news feed* (with some caveats about the *Facebook algorithm*; more about this later). Similarly, when you post to your timeline, those posts will show on the news feed of your friends when / if they log into Facebook, whether on their computers or their phones.

The timeline and news feed are interrelated symbiotically. For example:

My daughter Hannah and I are **friends** on Facebook. One of us has proactively accepted the other's "friend request."

Hannah **posts** a picture of something she finds interesting to her Facebook **timeline**.

I see that picture when I log in to my Facebook **news feed**.

Here's a screenshot of my timeline, where I can share a status update with text and/or photos or videos with my friends:

If I post something to my *timeline*, it has a very strong chance of appearing on Hannah's *news feed*. I post, and she sees it because we are "friends," i.e., connected on Facebook.

The reverse is true as well. Here's a post by Hannah about her new puppy, Levi, that appeared in my news feed:

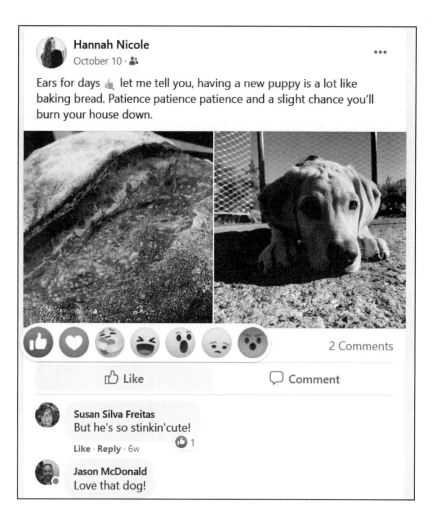

Notice how I have commented on the post, "Love that dog," as has our mutual friend, Susan. Thus:

Posts to *my timeline* show up in Hannah's *news feed*.

Posts by Hannah to her *timeline* show up in my *news feed*.

The core idea to all of the social platforms is this **relationship**: what you post to your "timeline" has the ability to show up in the "news feed" of people who are connected to you (and vice-versa). Now, the algorithm intervenes, of course, but this is the basic idea of all social networks.

Note as well the role of Susan. Posting doesn't happen only between two people but "among" people. I am connected to Hannah. She is connected to me. We are both connected to Susan. Hannah posts, I posts, Susan comments, Susan posts, Hannah comments, I "like it," and so on and so forth. Even more important, this can occur not just among people but among people and brands. Hannah posts, I posts, and Whole Foods posts. We can all "see" each other's content and like, comment, or share it.

When I post to my timeline, therefore, a post has the chance to be shown in the news feed of *everyone* with whom I am friends on Facebook; when *anyone* with whom I am a friend on Facebook posts to his or her timeline, that post has an opportunity to appear on my news feed. And vice-versa, all day long 24/7 until the end of time.

Here are the important takeaways:

1. **The News Feed is Dominant.** Few people, if any, go from the news feed and click over to the Pages of businesses or even the Profiles of friends. It's all about posts to the timeline and the readership that lives on the news feed. The news feed is "where it's at."

2. **Content**. You need a lot of content to succeed at marketing on Facebook! The news feed is like a swift river of content, so you – as a marketer – must frequently post to have a chance of being noticed. You'll need text, images, and video to succeed at content marketing on Facebook.

3. **Your Facebook Business Page isn't That Important.** While it is important to optimize your business Page on Facebook, few customers will proactively visit your Page directly. Most will only see your posts in their news feed. So spend most of your time and effort on where the action is: getting posts to appear on the news feed of customers and target customers. Once you've done the basics to set up your Facebook Page, focus on content, content, and then more content rather than tweaking the look and feel of a Page few people will see!

4. **Create Content that is Truly Engaging.** Because of how competitive the news feed is, you MUST create fun, informative, **engaging**, and interactive content. Boring, "buy my stuff" content won't work on Facebook. Interactive and engaging content – content that is counterintuitive, fun, engaging, and over-the-top, "you gotta see this" – is king, queen, and jack on Facebook.

The Five F's: Friends, Family, Fun, Photos, and Fake

As you begin to examine Facebook from the perspective of a marketer, pay attention to what people are sharing and engaging with. You will see it falls into the themes of friends, family, fun, photos, and fake:

- **Friends, Fun, Family.** Whether shared in **photo** format, as an **image**, as a **video** or just as plain **text**, Facebook is a place where people share stuff about their friends and family. Notice how many likes, comments, and shares fun photos of friends and family garner on Facebook. Facebook is a giant, collective social scrapbook.

- **What I'm Doing Today.** Alongside photos and texts of friends, family, and fun, people share text, photos, and even videos of what they're doing today. Posts of the peach cobbler they just made, their beautiful garden tomatoes, or perhaps their dog doing a weird trick – these "here's my life" type of fun photos are a huge theme in Facebook content as well.

- **Photos.** Photos dominate Facebook! Photos of friends at the beach, at Disneyland, High School graduations, Bar Mitzvahs, new babies. People are constantly posting photos with short commentaries, generally about friends, family, and fun.

- **Video content**, while less common, is even more engaging. *Facebook Live* allows people to stream content in real-time. *Facebook stories* also emphasize photo and video content.

- **Fake.** As we will discuss in a moment in more detail, Facebook is often "fake." People share the happy and successful moments of their lives but not so much the sad and unsuccessful events. Facebook is how we project our lives as we wish them to be, not 100% as they truly are.

- **Politics and Outrage.** Yes, sadly, there are the political folks on Facebook, and they have their place. Political conversation and outrage have their place on Facebook, though many people don't like politics on the platform and respond negatively, if at all. But some folks live and breathe it.

And –

- **Games, Social Contests, Challenges, Groups.** For some people, Facebook is a place for social games. There are also groups on Facebook which allow people to collaborate and communicate, as for example, a "group" of people taking a High School class in US History or a "group" of people who share a passion for black Labrador retrievers. Contests and often silly "challenges" are put out by brands and can "go viral" as person after person enters a contest or challenge.

- **News & Commentary.** Increasingly, Facebook is becoming a major source of news. Thus, people log in and see news posts (often by the media, often shared by friends), and "like," "comment," or "share" these news items. Note that news appears primarily on the app, not on the desktop version.

Notice as well a theme that we'll come back to on other social platforms like Instagram: **narcissism**. We live in the age of the selfie, and people love to share content that positions themselves as AWESOME.

> *Look at our happy family at Disneyland! Look at me and my date at the Cheesecake Factory! Wow, look at these cool photos of me when I went skydiving in Peru over Machu Pichu with my girlfriend and pet cat and took a selfie to memorialize it so you can (enviously) see how incredible my life is.*

Facebook, you see, is full of **fake**, of how life ought to be or at least of how life might be if everyone was really as "into" everyone else's narcissistic lifestyle as it might seem. To listen to an informative podcast on how the "fake" of Facebook can impact your own psychology, check out **http://jmlinks.com/29v**. (On a side note, once you realize that your own life will never live up to the fake happiness you see on Facebook, you'll be better adjusted, happier, and more realistic about finding true meaning in this maze called life).

Facebook Through the Eyes of a Marketer

Be that as it may, the marketing goal is to understand the *vibe* or *culture* of Facebook so that your company's marketing message can blend in and build on this culture to nurture your brand image, grow your customer connections, and ultimately sell more stuff. The content you post on Facebook must mesh with the culture on Facebook, which is friends, family, fun, photos, and fake.

As you research Facebook, ask yourself these questions:

1. Are your **customers** on Facebook?

2. If so, what are they posting and interacting with? What's really **engaging** to them? What **content themes** are directly or indirectly related to your brand?

3. How can you **tailor your marketing message** so that it seems "natural" given Facebook's focus on friends, family, and fun? Either –

   a. **Directly**, showcasing your company's fun product or service; or

   b. **Indirectly**, showcasing an activity adjacent to your company's product or service (more about this in a moment).

Searching Facebook for Posts

Return to your content marketing plan and get out your content themes. Research whether people are posting and talking about your themes on Facebook. If so, fantastic. If not your primary themes, perhaps there are adjacent themes next to what your company sells or does? You're looking for content and conversations that either directly or indirectly relate to your brand.

To search Facebook, log in to Facebook, and look for the search bar at the top. You'll see *Search Facebook* in gray text. (Note: for purposes of simplicity, we'll use the desktop version of Facebook, though most users use the mobile version). Enter a keyword such as "organic food." Here's a screenshot:

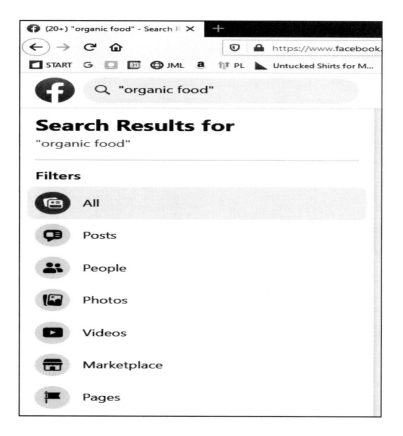

Next, scroll down the column that pops up. You can search Facebook by keyword for:

Posts – these are posts by people about the keyword you just entered.

People – these are people who have this keyword in their bio and/or posts.

Photos – these are photos posted to Facebook on the keyword.

Videos – these are videos posted to Facebook on the keyword.

Marketplace – these are things being bought and sold via Facebook.

Pages – these are business pages that have the keyword in their bio and/or posts.

Places – these are local businesses and hangouts in the "real world."

Groups – these are groups on Facebook that touch on the keyword.

Events – these are events being talked about on Facebook on this keyword.

Let's focus on Posts, which gets to what people are posting and interacting with on this keyword theme. Click on *Posts* from among the tabs across the top. Scroll down, change

"Posts From" to "Public Posts," and you'll see posts by users on these keywords. Here's a screenshot for "organic food":

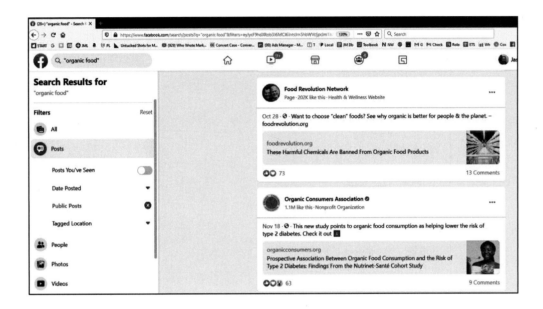

Play around with different keywords, and search posts for content that has been posted on them. Note as well that when you enter a keyword, Facebook gives you "search suggestions," which is a good way to discover content themes relating to your brand. Here's a screenshot for organic:

As you enter keywords and search, you can click on any Page or Profile that has posted on that topic and see the publicly available information. You can also filter for dates, posts from you, your friends, groups, pages, as well as all public posts. In this way, you can zero in on posts on Facebook on topics related to your business.

Remember that there are two possibilities: content themes that are *directly* relevant to your business vs. themes *adjacent* to your business. You're looking for both types of content themes – *direct* or *indirect/adjacent*. Why? Because there's no point in posting content that people aren't already interested in and engaging with on Facebook.

> Your goal here is to use **content themes** to figure out whether customers are engaging with topics of interest to your brand on Facebook, and if so, how. You're also looking to identify company Pages and groups that are relevant to your business.

To understand the difference between *direct* and *adjacent* themes, consider airlines on Facebook. Air travel is anything but fun. Passengers are stuck in cramped quarters with total strangers, fed peanuts and soft drinks, suffer through terrible WiFi, and are subject to TSA searches and endless flight delays. I don't know of many people, even those who fly first class, who truly love air travel itself. But the *destinations* are another story. Who doesn't want to go to Cancun or Paris? Who isn't interested in visiting the Pyramids or Beijing? So in terms of keyword themes possible on Facebook, we have:

direct themes:

air travel

airlines

airfares

SouthWest Airlines ("brands")

vs.

adjacent themes:

Cancun

Beijing

The Pyramids

You can see right away that the *direct* keyword themes don't really fit Facebook's culture of friends, family, and fun, but the *adjacent* or *secondary* keyword themes do. A little research will confirm this; try entering a few of the keywords listed above into the Facebook search bar. Which topics are getting more posts, and which topics are getting more interaction as measured in likes, comments, and shares?

This insight means that if you're an airline, therefore, you can't really share content that *directly* relates to your product or service because it's not very fun or pleasant. But you can share content that's *adjacent* to your product or service, such as the destinations to which you fly or perhaps the great people who are your employees and customers.

For example, check out this post by Aeromexico on its Facebook Page:

The post emphasizes the adjacent theme of the "Dia de Muertos" (Day of the Dead), the incredible culture of Mexico, and the fun of a destination journey during this holiday. It doesn't emphasize a crowded flight, airport delays, lousy food, and obnoxious fellow travelers. It's the *adjacent,* not the *direct* content theme that fits the culture of Facebook.

IDENTIFY DIRECT AND ADJACENT CONTENT THEMES

Returning to your own business, research your keyword themes that are *directly* related to your business vs. those that are *adjacent* to your business. Start asking yourself, "What is this conversation about?" and "How could your company participate in this conversation in a meaningful way that also showcases your brand?" You'll see a lot of posts by businesses on Facebook, but pay attention to the likes, comments, and shares of individual posts to gauge whether real customers are actually engaged in this conversation. So your questions are:

1. Are customers posting on keyword themes that matter to your business, either *directly* or *indirectly (adjacently)*?

2. Are these themes getting a lot of interaction as measured by likes, comments, and shares?

3. How can you (as the marketer) create content that will interact with customer-based content yet be authentic and non-salesy?

4. Will your content focus on directly relevant themes, adjacent themes, or perhaps both?

Are You a Fun Company or Not Fun Company?

At an abstract level, look deep into your company's soul, and ask yourself which Facebook strategy makes the most conceptual sense:

Are you a **fun company** in a **fun** and **photogenic industry**? If so, post fun photos or photos of your product or service directly. (Example: REI at **https://www.facebook.com/REI/**).

Or, are you a **not-fun company** *adjacent* to a fun and photogenic industry? If so, post photos of "fun" things adjacent to your product or service. (Example:

AeroMexico airlines at **https://www.facebook.com/AeromexicoNA/** – in which the service itself (*air travel*) isn't nearly as much fun as the adjacent activity (*tourism*).

Or, are you a **not-fun company** in a **not-fun industry**? If so, you'll have to think out of the box on content creation for Facebook. (Example: Progressive Insurance at **https://www.facebook.com/progressive/,** which posts lots and lots of content that has little to do with insurance, directly).

Not all products or services will work on Facebook; that's OK, too, as your mission is to identify which social media networks work most easily for your company and focus on those. Perhaps LinkedIn or Twitter will work better for your brand; if so, the point of your research on Facebook is to eliminate it as a content marketing target. That's OK. Zuckerberg can take it, really.

As you build out your Facebook content and posting strategy, dig into what brands are doing as opposed to individuals:

- What are your competitors doing that seems to be working as measured by likes, comments, and shares? (*Be careful with competitors – if they are posting a lot but getting little engagement, that's a sign that their strategy is NOT working, and you shouldn't copy it*).

- What are companies-to-emulate doing, and what is working for them? Why or why not?

At this point, don't worry about the technical details. Just spend some research time focusing on customers and on brands. Figure out the basic Zeitgeist for Facebook as it may relate to your own marketing goals.

» INVENTORY COMPANIES ON FACEBOOK

Make a list of companies (both competitors and companies-to-emulate) that you admire on Facebook. You want to monitor them and reverse engineer what they're doing that's working.

Imitation is the highest form of flattery, and identifying successful brands to reverse engineer is the easiest way to master marketing on Facebook.

So, now we are going to shift gears from **profiles** (individuals) to **Pages** (companies). You'll want to identify companies that are on Facebook and reverse engineer their marketing strategy.

Ways to Search Facebook

First, return to the **content themes** that matter to you and your potential customers. For example, if you are a maker of organic baby food, you would use the key phrases "organic food" and "baby food" to identify companies that are already on Facebook. If you are a company that organizes bird-watching tours, then you'll be searching Facebook for keywords like "birding," "birding tourism," or perhaps "ecotourism." As you find companies that seem to be doing a good job with Facebook marketing, you'll be making an inventory of what you like/dislike about their Facebook marketing in terms of their cover photo, profile picture, tabs, and posting strategy above all else.

Your **TO-DOS** here are to identify companies that seem to "get" Facebook and to inventory what you like or dislike about how they have set up their Facebook Page and how they are posting content to Facebook.

Returning to the first step, here are the two best ways to find commercial Pages to inventory for your Facebook marketing plan.

Method #1 - Search Facebook Directly. Simply type into the search box your keyword as in "organic food." Next, at the top tab, click on "Pages." Here is a screenshot:

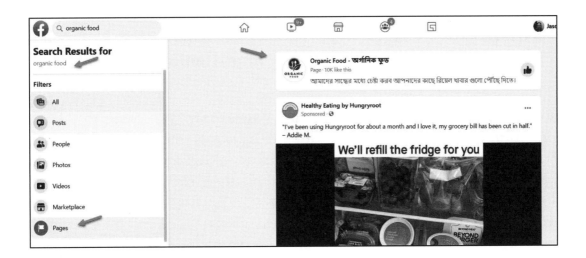

And then, after you click "Pages," you'll be able to browse business Pages that relate to your keyword search. Next, click into Pages, looking to identify companies that seem to "get" Facebook, like them in your personal profile (so you can keep an eye on them), and begin to inventory your likes/dislikes in terms of their Facebook strategy.

Method #2 - Identify Facebook Pages via Google Search. Go to Google. Type into the Google search box *site:facebook.com* "organic food." (Note: use quotation marks around multi-word phrases for best results). Google will then return you a list of commercial Pages on Facebook with that term in it. To see this in action, go to **http://jmlinks.com/2i**. Here's a screenshot:

It's very important that there be no space between *site* and *the colon*. It's *site:facebook.com* not *site: facebook.com*. You can use this tactic on Google for any social media; as for example, *site:yelp.com massage therapists Boston*, or *site:twitter.com industrial fans*. Once you know your keyword themes, using Google in this fashion is a great way to browse a social media platform to find relevant companies to reverse engineer.

VIDEO. Watch a video tutorial on how to use the site: command to search Facebook for social media marketing at **http://jmlinks.com/16g**.

Method #3 - Identify Facebook Pages via Buzzsumo. Buzzsumo (**http://jmlinks.com/29j**) tracks shares across social media platforms, including Facebook. For $99 / month, you can use this tool to drill into what content is getting engagement vis-à-vis your keyword themes and then click "up" to the Pages and Profiles that are sharing this content. Simply sign up for an account and click into *Content > Web* and then search by keyword. Next, click on the "Facebook Engagement" link and sort by the most engaging content by keyword and time period.

Here's a screenshot for "organic food:"

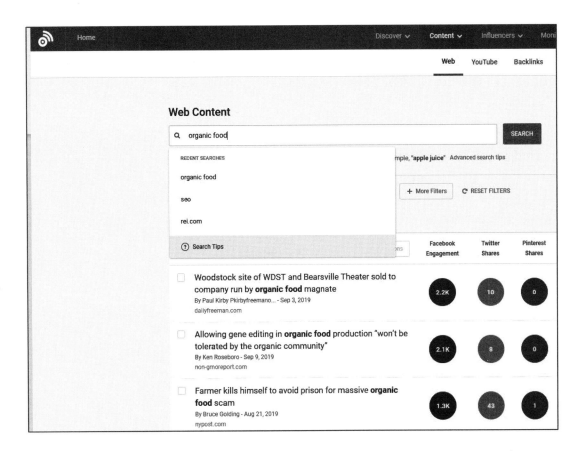

In this way, you go from *keyword > most popular content > pages and profiles that have shared that content > ideas for your own content strategy on Facebook.*

IDENTIFY COMPANIES WHO DO FACEBOOK WELL AND INVENTORY THEM

Don't be afraid to "like" companies on Facebook (even your competitors) in your individual account. In fact, I strongly encourage it. By "liking" companies you actually "like," you'll experience how they market to you, and you can then reverse engineer this for your own company.

Identify a shortlist of between three and ten companies to monitor on Facebook. Remember to focus on the two different types of companies:

Competitors. Companies that are very much like your own company, that is direct competitors and companies that are closely like your own.

Companies to Emulate. These can be companies like REI, Geico, or Navy Federal Credit Union that really seem to understand social media marketing and do a good job on Facebook.

At this point, you should have a vibrant personal profile on Facebook (connected to many friends and family members), some business pages to watch (both competitors and companies-to-emulate), and a list of content themes both direct and adjacent to monitor for your company. You are in "stealth mode," researching what is going on on Facebook that is truly relevant to your brand.

Analyze Posts by Competitors and Other Companies

Returning to the regular Facebook interface, once you "like" a company, its posts have the opportunity to show up in your news feed. We'll dive into why, or why not, in a moment. But for now, let me share with you a trick so that you can easily find the posts by Pages that you've decided to monitor.

Log in to your Facebook personal account, then scan down the left column and look for a link to Pages. Here's a screenshot:

Click on that, and then click on "Liked Pages." That will give you a quick list of pages that you like or follow. You can also bookmark this URL (**https://www.facebook.com/pages/?category=liked**) to your Start.me screen, so that you can quickly get into Pages you are following on Facebook.

For your second TO-DO, download the **Facebook Research Worksheet**. For the worksheet, go to **http://jmlinks.com/2023smm** (then enter the code '**2023smm**' to register your workbook), and click on the link to the "Facebook Research Worksheet." You'll answer questions as to whether your potential customers are on Facebook, identify brands to follow, and inventory what you like and dislike about their Facebook setup and marketing strategy.

» UNDERSTAND THE FACEBOOK ALGORITHM

To market successfully on Facebook, you need a detailed understanding of its **structure** and how it works. Most importantly, you need to understand the difference between a profile and a Page and what "like" means vis-a-vis a Page and/or a post, as well as *comment* and *share*. You also need to understand how Facebook's **structure** interacts with its **algorithm** via **content engagement**.

Let's review this:

- **People have "profiles."** This is *Jason McDonald*, a real person, for example. I have a *profile* (not a *Page*) on Facebook.

- **When two people "friend" each other by exchanging a "friend request," Facebook puts them in a like relationship.** If I "friend" my friend, Tom Jones, and he accepts this request, then he and I are connected via Facebook.

- **When two profiles are connected, if person A posts to his timeline, person B will see that post on his news feed** (with the *Facebook algorithm* caveat that the news feed can be very busy, and Facebook prioritizes the posts of friends with whom you interact over those whom you ignore).

  o **People interact with a post** by "liking" the post, "commenting" on the post, and/or "sharing" the post, thereby essentially re-posting it to their own timeline so that their own friends can see/interact with the post. In the background, The Facebook **algorithm** keeps track of which profiles, Pages, and posts are the most interactive and favors them in the news feed across the social network.

- **Companies have Pages not Profiles.** A *profile* (person) creates a *Page* (company) and then manages it as an Admin.

- **When a person ("profile") "likes" a business "Page," this creates a Facebook relationship between the "profile" and the "Page."** When I like

Safeway (**https://www.facebook.com/Safeway**), that means that when Safeway posts to its timeline, it might show on my news feed. By "liking" Safeway, I have given it permission to talk to me via Facebook.

- o **People interact with a post** by a Page by "liking" the post, "commenting" on the post, and/or "sharing" the post, thereby essentially re-posting it to their own timeline so that their own friends can see/interact with the post. In the background, the Facebook **algorithm** keeps track of which posts are the most interactive and favors them in the news feed across the social network.

To read the Facebook help files on setting up a business Page, go to **http://jmlinks.com/1c**. Note that you can technically create not just "Pages" for local businesses or places, companies, organizations, institutions, brands, or products. You can also create "public figure Pages" for artists, bands, or public figures (think CEO of your company, a la Martha Stewart), or even Pages for causes or communities. For most companies, you'll choose either the local business option, the company option, or the brand/product option.

It Gets Complicated

Here's where it gets complicated. The engineers at Facebook want **engagement**: they want people to be "hooked" on Facebook, staying on the platform as much as possible. It's a bit like drugs and drug dealers, to be honest. Thus they "reward" content that keeps people on the platform, content that is engaging or even "addictive." The algorithm thus "scores" profiles, pages, and even individual pieces of content. The more "engaging" it is, the higher its Facebook algorithm score and the more Facebook shows it to people. And the reverse is true. If you post boring content, few people see it, and over time you get a "reputation" as a boring entity on the platform.

In essence, the *more* entertaining you are, the *more* people see your content. The *less* engaging, the *less* so. (This is true not just on Facebook but on ALL platforms – TikTok, YouTube, LinkedIn, Twitter, etc.).

ENGAGEMENT = LIKES, COMMENTS, & SHARES

Let's return to the basics. When a Page posts to its timeline, that post will show up on the news feed of "profiles" (people) who have liked it based on several factors:

- The individual (a.k.a., "the profile") must have liked the Page in advance.

- If the individual previously liked the Page and generally liked posts by the Page and/or commented on them and/or shared them, then the *Facebook algorithm score* of that Page is improved. The higher the *Facebook algorithm score* (based on more interaction between that Page and the individual), the more likely it is that the post by the Page will show in the particular individual's news feed.

- A real-time analysis of the post: the faster and wider a post gets interactivity (likes, comments, and shares), the more powerful is the *Facebook algorithm score,* and it, therefore, gets even more publicity.

In essence, Facebook monitors whether users interact with the posts of a Page: the more users who interact with the posts of a Page, the higher the assessment of that Page and its posts, and the more likely users are to continue to see posts by the Page in their news feed.

If you post a piece of content to your business Page on Facebook, how likely is it that a fan of your Page, is going to see it in his or her news feed? The probability is a function of the **algorithm**, essentially:

- Content that generates a lot of likes…

- Content that generates a lot of comments…

- Content that generates a lot of shares…

    o Etc., etc., etc.…

Factor in your "reputation" as a content producer as well. Are you generally exciting? Or boring? The long and short of the Facebook algorithm as a marketer is the *more engaging* a post (profile, page, photo, video, meme, text…) is, *the more* it will show in the news feeds of your fans. Therefore:

Encouraging engagement is the #1 goal of your Facebook marketing!

To use an example, let's look at the Mayo Clinic and me on Facebook.

1. I like the Mayo Clinic business Page on Facebook (**https://www.facebook.com/MayoClinic**), giving it permission to talk to me via Facebook.

2. The Mayo Clinic posts images, photos, blog post summaries, etc., to its Facebook Page timeline, such as tips on how to live healthy, information on diseases, and even information on how to keep your pets healthy.

3. I like these posts, I "comment" on these posts (*"Oh, yes, I am going to eat more kale!"*), and even better, I "share" these posts on my own timeline by clicking the share button.

Here's a screenshot of a recent post by the Mayo Clinic:

If you look closely, you can see that this post has 174 likes, 15 comments, and 26 shares. The post has done very well on engagement! If I like, comment, and/or share it, I am also telling the algorithm that this is an interesting post. I am helping to push it along, perhaps even making it "go viral."

Behind the scenes, therefore, Facebook is more likely to push this post in front of Mayo Clinic fans because the more engagement a post gets, the more predictive that is that it will get even more engagement. Facebook lives off of this "virtuous circle," and again and again across all social networks, you'll see that driving engagement is the Holy Grail of success at social media marketing.

Engagement, however, is relative, and every brand on Facebook is engaged in a competitive struggle to keep their fans engaged with content. Compare this post to a post by REI, which features a cute cat in a tent:

This post has 1,800 likes, 671 comments, and 224 shares. It's in a different league, entirely, from the Mayo Clinic post. Notice that it is a highly **emotional** appeal based on a cute photo of a cat and our attachment to our pets. Notice as well that it mimics what real people post on Facebook: pictures of themselves, their pets, and their "fun" social outings.

In both cases, **social resonance** encourages likes, comments, and shares. And notice how in both cases, the posts have interesting text, provocative photographs, and links to a blog post or video. By *design,* the posts are meant to engage the audience.

Returning to my relationship with the Mayo Clinic post by "liking," "commenting," or "sharing" this post, I, too, am telling Facebook I am engaged with the Mayo Clinic Page.

The more I do this, the more I will see its posts in my news feed.

Now, flip this around as marketers, your goals become:

- To increase your *Facebook algorithm score* (and the probability that people will see your posts in their news feed), you MUST get more likes, comments, and shares of your posts!

- To get more **engagement**, you must post content that is fun, content that mimics posts about friends, family, fun, photos, and fake, content that is emotional, content that is "awwwwww," content that is outrageous, content that is counter-intuitive. You get the picture: don't be boring!

Encouraging **engagement** is the name of the game when it comes to Facebook marketing. Indeed, a "share" is the best of all, followed by a "comment" and then by a "like," in terms of how the Facebook algorithm assesses your engagement.

ENGAGEMENT IS GOAL #1 FOR CONTENT ON FACEBOOK

Let's dig deeper here.

Posting strategy is all about what you post and using those posts to drive up engagement and improve your Facebook algorithm score. So, first, you've used content marketing to identify the types of content that interest your target customers; second, you've created photos, videos, and written blog posts that connect "what you have" with "what they're interested in." Now you want to think about packaging that content in such a way that it spurs them to like, comment, and/or share that content on Facebook.

What drives people to engage? The answer is, first and foremost, **emotion**. Anything that sparks an emotional reaction of "how shocking," or "Oh my gosh, I didn't know that," or "I heartily agree with that idea," or "*Aw, shucks, I love puppies and babies and* *mommies and I want to support our troops too, and I hate pollution and bad people and criminals and scams…"* Anything that provokes an emotional reaction, especially one that inclines a person to click "YES! I agree," is what you're after. Oh, and **utility** is good, too, like "the secret to poaching eggs" (*Don't use vinegar despite what you see on YouTube, seriously*)… or something **counterintuitive** (like, *check out the trend for flaming hot Cheetos turkey for Thanksgiving*)… is also likely to work.

Here's a post about "free tacos," a promotion from Taco Bell relating to stolen bases during the World Series with 3,600 likes, 279 comments, and 787 shares:

What's better than tacos? Free tacos! Better than free tacos? Free tacos when your team has stolen a base! It's fun. It's emotional. It's free. It's photogenic, and – not surprisingly – people "engage with it." People love tacos. People really love free tacos. And the Facebook algorithm really loves engagement!

The point, as a marketer, is to realize that our posts – not just on Facebook but on all social media marketing – need to be emotional, useful, and/or counterintuitive. People interact with and share "man bites dog," not "dog bites man."

MAN BITES DOG = ENGAGEMENT

Here are example categories of posts that are likely to spur customer interactions:

- **Sentimental Posts**. Posts of kittens and puppies, posts of kids, posts of moms and dads, posts of moms and dads holding kittens and puppies. Posts about the 4th of July, posts about how much you love a cause... Brands on Facebook often post "sentimentality bait," i.e., posts that people click the "like button" to indicate that they "agree" with the cause. So every Mother's Day, you can see brands posting pictures of mothers and their kids, and people clicking the "like button" on these posts because they like their mothers... which is increasing the Facebook algorithm score of these posts and of these Pages.

- **Utility**. Posts that explain "how to do" stuff, especially things that are counterintuitive or funny. Such as "Ten Ways Not to Ask a Girl Out," or "Five New Ways to Lose Weight While on a Vacation."

- **Counterintuitive**. Posts that take things you "think" you know, and explain that they don't really work like you think they do. Especially common are things that people "think" are safe, but in fact are dangerous such as rawhide dog chews (*who knew that they were dangerous?*).

- **Funny**. Humor is big on Facebook. Posting jokes, funny quotes, videos, images (memes), etc. Things that make people laugh, get them to click like, comment, or share. Queue the funny babies, babies with dogs, and of course, cat videos.

- **Surveys, Polls, Contests, and Challenges**. Asking your audience a question and getting them to use the comments as a way to interact with that. *Take this quiz and learn which Star Trek character best describes your love life.* Contests and challenges are big not just on Facebook but across platforms, especially Instagram and TikTok. What kind of contest or challenge might your brand create?

- **Quotes**. Sentimental, humorous, make-you-think quotes, especially when hoisted on top of picturesque and contemplative scenery like mountains or fuzzified people. *Do or do not. There is no try – Yoda from Star Wars.*

- **Outrage**. Things that make people angry, so angry that they comment, "like" the posts in the sense of opposing the thing that outrages them, and even share the post to their friends. Outrage is very big on Facebook, and brands (rather cynically) leverage this outrage to increase their Edgerank. *Click "like" if you think dolphins shouldn't die in Tuna nets, animals shouldn't be abused, etc., for example.*

- **Controversy**. Controversy, but in a good way, can be very good for your posts to Facebook. For example, avoid posting touchy subjects like abortion or gun control, but do post on "fun" controversies such as *"Is a bikini or a one-piece a better bathing suit?" "Is it OK not to serve turkey on Thanksgiving?," or "Which is better a cat or a dog?"*

In all cases, a good-looking photo or video is a must. Look back at the brands you have "followed" or "liked," and begin to notice how they are using strategies like emotion, fun, outrage, humor, or other ways to spur interactivity.

FACEBOOK REWARDS YOU FOR ENGAGING POSTS!

Here are some brands that I admire in terms of their Facebook marketing, all of which build their engagement by sharing interactive content on a regular basis:

Bishop Robert Barron (https://www.facebook.com/BishopRobertBarron) – known as the Catholic social media superstar, Bishop Barron shares history and theological insights, and shows how something as ancient as Catholicism can leverage new media to grow its reach and build its brand.

Navy Federal Credit Union (https://www.facebook.com/NavyFederal) – if you monitor its Page, you'll see a steady dose of sentimentality, especially pictures of military men with babies (a double whammy: *yes, I support our troops, and, yes, I like babies!*).

The Super Dentists (https://www.facebook.com/TheSuperDentists) – this San Diego kids dentists takes something not-so-fun (dentistry) and effectively builds eWom, one-touch-to-many, and even social sharing via pictures, contests, sentimentality posts and the like.

REI (https://www.facebook.com/REI). REI is an outdoor sports retailer and uses Facebook to share "how to" information about hiking, campaign, and other outdoor sports, promote its products, and build a community around people who like the outdoors (and love its products).

Taco Bell (https://www.facebook.com/tacobell) – the edgy youth brand is a master at building awareness, creating the "fourth meal" (just what obese America needed), and making factory food fun.

Metamucil (https://www.facebook.com/Metamucil/) – there, I admit it. I use Metamucil! Any brand that can take something so private, and grow a Facebook page to 233,000 fans, has got to be doing something right. "Reverse engineer" how a product you probably didn't think of as friends, family, and fun uses social media on a regular basis (pun intended).

Now the point of all this, as marketers, isn't that we really love babies and military personnel (although we probably do). It's to:

- Improve our *Facebook algorithm score* to increase the probability that our Facebook fans will see our posts.

- Use our built-up *Facebook algorithm score* to propel posts that market our products or services into the news feeds of our fans, for free.

This gets to **posting rhythm**. Smart marketers will post ten or twenty "fun, fun, fun" posts to drive UP their *Facebook algorithm score*, and then one "buy my stuff" post that has a good chance of showing in the news feed. So your posting rhythm should be something like 80% fun stuff and 20% or less "buy my stuff" posts:

Fun, Fun, Fun, Fun, Fun, Fun, Fun, Fun, Fun, Buy My Stuff, Buy My Stuff Fun, Fun, Fun, Fun, Fun, Fun, Fun, Fun, Fun,

In other words, smart marketers build up their *Facebook algorithm score* by posting lots of fun, interactive content, and then "spend" their *Facebook algorithm score* with a "buy my stuff" post. Rinse and repeat as needed.

Get Your Fans to Share

Even better, business Pages on Facebook will post items that their fans are likely to share with their own friends. If you post something to your Facebook Page (e.g., a contest to win a free week's supply of your product or a silly "challenge" that relates to your content themes), and your Facebook fans share it with their friends and family, well, you've hit a home run. Why? Because Facebook (and people) pay a heck of a lot more attention to posts by people than to posts by Pages. So, by all means, post stuff to your business Page that excites your fans so much that they do the sharing! (We'll return to the importance of fans and superfans at the end of this Chapter).

If it Works, Keep Doing it

I've already pointed out that Taco Bell gives away free tacos after a "stolen base." But here's another thought. They don't just do this once. They do this again and again; if you find something that works, copy it over and over. Taco Bell has been doing this for years. **Taco Bell uses Facebook to spur engagement with its most devoted fans.** For example, here's a post about a "referendum" to bring back (or not) the Double Decker Taco or Enchirito. Note that it has 1,800 comments and 365 shares:

Now, that's a lot of engagement! The point is that this promotion was used to create tons of "spontaneous" shares by fans of Taco Bell, thereby leveraging the "superfans" of Taco Bell to create viral buzz on Facebook. Remember – a share means that the friends of a friend see the post, thus the "superfan" of Taco shares to her friends, and they see her enthusiasm for this critical referendum. So ask yourself, what is your "Taco promotion" that your fans will take over the finish line (to mix sports metaphors)? And once you find content that works, keep doing it.

Contests and Challenges

Another content theme that you see on Facebook is "contests" and "challenges." The former usually means that the brand requires fans to do something to get something free. The latter usually is just a shout-out to do something that is kind of hard to do and then share this on Facebook. The former means you get something free; the latter means that you're just cool and talented. The former appeals to users' interest in free stuff; the latter appeals to their desire to "show off."

Search Facebook for "contests" and "challenges" to see current examples. Even better, look for the hashtags *#contest* and *#challenge* as in:

> **https://www.facebook.com/hashtag/contest**
>
> **https://www.facebook.com/hashtag/challenge**

"Reverse engineer" contests and challenges in your industry, and then brainstorm your own. "Engagement" can be nurtured. It's not necessarily spontaneous.

Facebook Rewards Posts by People over Posts by Pages

The reason for this tactic is that the *Facebook algorithm score* of people is much, much higher than the *Facebook algorithm score* of company Pages. So, to the extent that you can create a post that will be shared on Facebook, you can get your fans to market your company's products. Don't think in terms of only the *Facebook algorithm score* of your Page but also in that of your customer evangelists or superfans (those people who not only like your Page but interact heavily with your posts by liking them, commenting on them, and even sharing them to their own friends and family).

Let me repeat that:

> The *Facebook algorithm score* of people is much higher than that of company Pages. **So getting your customers, fans, and superfans to share your posts is a fundamental component of an effective Facebook marketing strategy.**

For example, here's a post showcasing a "fitness challenge" with 26,000 likes, 1,100 comments, and 1,900 shares:

Note that it is also in video format. It's fun. It's intriguing. It asks for comments. It's "designed" to foster engagement, and the Facebook algorithm clearly loves it.

Compare that with this "buy our stuff" post by Navy Federal Credit:

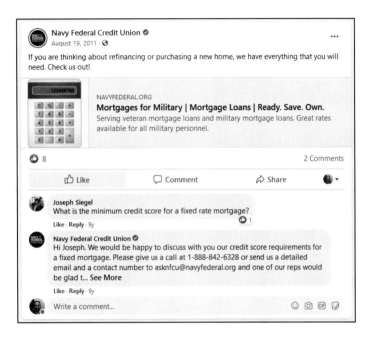

This post has only 8 likes, 2 comments, and zero shares.

But you can't just do engagement posts. You also need "buy my stuff" posts. Why? Because you have two (interrelated) goals on Facebook: 1) build up engagement, and 2) "spend" this engagement on posts that lead to a goal, such as a purchase or sales lead. You can't just post for engagement, and you can't just post to sell your stuff.

You need to do both.

If you reverse engineer the content strategy of Navy Federal Credit Union on Facebook, you'll see that the brand is posting items to drive up interactivity (fun stuff), and then occasionally posting items that are aimed to sell its products or services (serious stuff). So its posting rhythm is:

> *fun, fun, fun, fun, fun, fun, fun, fun, fun,* **buy our stuff***, fun, fun, fun, fun, fun, fun, fun,* **buy our stuff***, fun, fun, fun, etc*

.

There are two factors at work here:

> ***Engagement***: improving the *engagement* of posts by a Page improves the *visibility* of all its posts to some degree. (Note: this is also a reason to pay attention to the

time of day because *engagement* is determined "on the fly," and if a post does well "out of the gate," it will tend to do better over time).

Social Sharing: getting the fans of a Page to share the posts with their own friends and family.

Generally speaking, posts that are highly interactive get boosts on both measures. As you reverse engineer the posting strategy of competitors and/or brands that you admire on Facebook, notice how they try to spur either one or both of the above.

VIDEO. Watch a video tutorial on how to identify and inventory competitors and companies to emulate on Facebook at **http://jmlinks.com/16q**.

» SET UP AND OPTIMIZE YOUR FACEBOOK PAGE

Now that you've got the basics of Facebook down, it's time to set up or optimize your own company Page. A good way to do this is to compare/contrast Pages that you like and use your inventory list to identify to-dos. Let's go down item by item to see things you need to do in terms of Facebook Page Setup. (Note: this content refers to the "New" page experience (**http://jmlinks.com/58t**; if you're still running the "Classic" experience, I recommend you upgrade.)

After you've set up a Page, you need to toggle between your "Personal Profile" and your "Business Page." To do so, log in to your Facebook account, then find "Pages" on the left, then "Pages you manage" and then click "Switch Now." Here's a screenshot:

Alternatively, on the top right menu, click on your profile and then "See all profiles." Find your Business Page and switch into it.

Now, you're inside your Business Page. We're not going to click into more advanced features such as "Professional Dashboard" yet. We're just going to do the basics.

First, let's set up and optimize our basic Page features:

- **Cover Photo**. Click "Edit Cover Photo" and you can upload and change your Business Page's cover photo.

- **Edit Page**. Click "Edit" and this will get you into "Edit Page." Here you can edit your "Profile Picture," "Cover Photo," "Bio," and "Intro."

- **About Info**. Click into "Edit your About Info," and edit your business category, physical address, website, and other information about your business.

- **Rating / Reviews**. This is an important feature. Click into *Edit > Edit Page > About Info > Rating*. Here you can turn "on" or "off" the ability for customers to review your business.

- **Sections**. You can also manage your Page Layout under the *"More" tab > Manage Sections*. Here you can check / uncheck key features such as Questions, Likes, Reviews Given, etc.

- **Three Dots**. On the far right, look for the "three dots." Click here, and you can edit your "Action Button," which is your CTA (Call to Action) that appears on your page as well as other minor functions.

At this point, you've accomplished the basics. You've set up a Facebook Page for your business and optimized its structure.

Start Posting

The workhorse of your Facebook strategy is to post content. To do this, just click on the "What's on your mind" box that appears at the far right. Here's a screenshot:

You can simply start typing, post some text, and upload a photo or video. The buttons underneath – Live Video, Photo/ video, or Reel – refer to types of posts. A "Reel" is a short video in the TikTok format.

Finally, you can "feature" or "pin" a post (or a series of posts) by clicking into *Featured* > *Manage* or on a post clicking on the three dots to the right. Here's a screenshot:

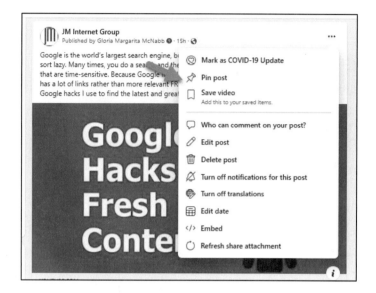

Note that when you "Pin" a post it shows up in your "Featured" section, which is the first set of items a user sees when he or she clicks into your business Page.

For your third **TO-DO**, download the **Facebook Setup Worksheet**. For the worksheet, go to **http://jmlinks.com/2023smm** (then enter the code '**2023smm**' to register your workbook), and click on the link to the "Facebook Setup Worksheet." You'll answer and outline the basic setup issues for your Facebook Page.

» TOOLS TO MANAGE YOUR FACEBOOK BUSINESS PAGE

Beyond the basics of your Facebook Page, there are some key tools to manage things at a more sophisticated level. Let's review those now.

> **Professional Dashboard.** Logged in as your Facebook Page, click on "Professional Dashboard" on the left menu. This provides insights into the engagement of your posts, giving you key data points for you to learn what posts people like and which ones they do not. Click "See more insights" on the top right. Here, you can find additional data on your Facebook Page and its Posts, as well as interactions with fans. Then, on the left menu, you can click into "tools" —

Events. Create or manage "events" here. "Events" are either online or real world events to which you can invite customers and others.

Jobs. You can post job announcements to your Facebook Page.

Page Access. Here, you can control which employees can manage or access your Facebook Page. I highly recommend you have at least two managers, and be sure to de-invite any employee if you let them go as any Page manager can delete the Page, permanently.

Moderation Assist. This feature allows you to use Facebook AI to manage comments by users. For example, you can ban posts by people who have no friends (i.e., bots), posts that have profanity, or even upload a list of "stop" words to automatically prevent posts on "hot" topics.

Fan Engagement Tools. You can give "badges" to your superfans or do other incentive programs to help them get excited about your Page.

Business Apps. You can browse paid apps in the Facebook app store. Many of these assist with e-commerce applications.

Meta Business Suite / Business Manager. These are two interrelated terms and products on Facebook. "Business Manager" is being discontinued in favor of "Business Suite." The primary purpose of Business Suite is to allow one Profile to manage more than one Business Page. Thus, this is most useful if you are an agency or ad consultant. To access Business Suite, go to your Page and then click on "Professional Dashboard." Then on the left menu, look for "Meta Business Suite." You can also download it as an app on Google Play or the Apple App store (Look for "Meta Business Suite.") It's a pretty good way to manage both your Facebook and Instagram activity if you're more of a phone than a desktop person.

Here are some of its key features –

Manage More than One Business. If you have more than one Business Page, you can access them all through Meta Business Suite. Just use the pull-down menu at the top left.

Post to Both Facebook and Instagram. If you've unified your Facebook Page and Business Instagram account, you can post to both here.

Post Content. On the center right, you can create a post, Reel, or Story.

Planner. This allows you to see and schedule posts into the future.

Content. You can gain insights into posts, Reels, and stories, and their engagement.

Insights. You can see even more data on engagement across posts, Reels, and stories.

Inbox. You can manage your Facebook messages from customers, here. Also, at the top right under "Automations" you can set up Chatbots and other messenger automations for your Business Page. You can also see and manage comments to your posts, here.

All Tools. You can see even more tools here, as well as see your billing information.

Creator Studio. Creator Studio is my favorite way to manage a Business Page on Facebook. However, it's hard to get to Creator Studio. One way is to log in to your Business Page, then click on "Professional Dashboard." Next, scroll to the bottom of the left column and click on "Stars." This will get you into Creator Studio, then click on "home" on the top left. Alternatively, use this URL: **https://business.facebook.com/creatorstudio/**. Once inside Creator Studio —

Post. You can post instantly or schedule posts, Reels, or Stories by clicking on the "Post something" box in the middle of the page. When you're ready to post, you can post it instantly or click on the down arrow and schedule a post into the future. You can also manage the distribution settings and set an end date for a post.

Insights. You can drill into "insights" for your Page as a whole, posts, videos, or other creative elements.

Pre-published. Use this feature to see "scheduled" posts. I have no idea why they use the strange term, "pre-published," but what they mean is scheduled posts.

Create New. At the top left, click "Create New," and you can easily "go live" as well as create a post, Reel, or story. This is an easy way to "go live" on Facebook from the desktop.

Published. You can see posts you've published, as well as stats on their performance.

Inbox. Manage your inbox in Creator Studio, responding to fans.

Settings. Easily toggle into the "settings" for your Page. Here, you can manage who has administrative access and add or remove people as necessary.

Finally, let's talk about **Page settings**. These are not easy to access with the tools above, although there is a link in Creator Studio. To access Page settings, log in as your Page and be at your Page. Next, click on your Page Profile Icon (Top Right). Select "Settings and Privacy," "Settings," and then "Privacy." Here you can manage the visibility of your posts as in "who can see your posts," whether you want your Page to be visible to Google, and if you want to be able to receive messages as your Page. Here's a screenshot:

Privacy Settings and Tools			
Privacy shortcuts	Manage Your Page Go here to update your contact information and more.		
Your Activity	Who can see your future posts?	Public	Edit
	Review all your posts and things you're tagged in		Use Activity Log
	Who can see the people, Pages and lists you follow?	Public	Edit
How people find and contact you	Do you want search engines outside of Facebook to link to your Page?	Yes	Edit
	Recommended Similar Page	On	Edit
Messaging	Allow people to message your Page?	On	Edit

You can also "block" nefarious individuals from interacting with your Page here. Just select "blocking" on the left menu. You can also manage how individuals can post to your Page (as in blocking profanity), under *Privacy > Public Posts* and then in the middle of the Page, "Content moderation."

Importantly, "Page Access," as in who is an Admin of your Page is not here. That is managed under *Your Page > Professional Dashboard > Page Access*. Throughout this process, remind yourself that Zuckerberg is off playing in the "Metaverse." Thus, the "teams" at Facebook are essentially left without a coherent leader. There is no single coherent vision at Facebook as to how all of this should work together.

» BRAINSTORM AND EXECUTE A POSTING STRATEGY

Don't fall into the trap of over-focusing on your Page and Page setup! That's not where the action is on Facebook. The action (for users) is on the **feed**. Most of what shows up on the feed is:

Posts. Posts by other people, ads, and posts by Pages (that is text, photos / images, and video).

Reels. Reels show on the phone app and on the desktop as short videos.

Stories. Stories are short, once-a-day photos or videos as to "what's happening."

Do not overfocus on your Page setup options to the detriment of your **content marketing** and **posting strategy**. You must systematically produce and share a ton of content on your Facebook Page! A good goal is at least one post per day to your Facebook Page, if not two or even three. Post text, photos, and videos. Post Reels. Post to your Story. Post stuff that your Superfans will see and love and that THEY will SHARE to THEIR friends and family. Post, post, post, post, and then post some more – quantity, yes, but even more, quality – engaging, fun posts.

Choose a Post Type

When you first log in to your Page, you'll see a blank box that says, "Create a post." Here's a screenshot:

The most common post type is to write some text, click Photo/Video, and then post. This is the vast majority of posts you will see. The second most common would be a video post.

There are, however, more complex options. Click on the three on the bottom right, for instance. Here's a screenshot:

You can thus beef up your posts or create variants such as an "Ask me" or a "Covid-19 Update" post. If you're curious as to what one is, just click on it (such as "Watch Party") or search Facebook help for that term (e.g., "watch party").

Turn to the content marketing section of the *Marketing Almanac* for a list of tools that will help you find other people's content and create your own. I recommend Hootsuite (**http://jmlinks.com/29k**) to manage all your social postings across platforms, but I also recommend that you vary your posting strategy so that you have some posts that go live instantly, some that are "natively" scheduled inside of Facebook and still others that are posted by a third-party app like Hootsuite or Buffer. This is so as to cover all your bases vis-à-vis the Facebook algorithm.

Four Types of Content for Facebook

Remember the four types of content and flesh out what type(s) will make the most sense for you on Facebook:

> **Your Own Content**. This is creating blog posts, photos, videos, infographics, and other fun and engaging content yourself. Note that the format that gets the highest engagement is generally native video (videos that are uploaded directly to Facebook), and the content with the highest engagement is always built on emotion.

Other People's Content or Content Curation. This is using tools like Feedly or Buzzsumo to identify fun and engaging content by others and share this on your Facebook Page as a "helpful expert."

UGC / User-Generated Content. This is creating opportunities like Facebook contests or hashtags that encourage users spontaneously to create content and share it either to your Page or about your brand on Facebook.

Interactive Content. This is logging in as your Page and commenting on the posts (and/or comments) made to your Page and its posts, plus identifying and interacting with the contents of fans and superfans.

Throughout, remember that ALL content you post on Facebook needs to be focused on friends, family, and fun with a good dose of emotions and counterintuitiveness to encourage social sharing. The only exception is the 10-20% of your posts that will be "buy my stuff" type, but even for those, try to tilt your message towards friends, family, and fun.

For your fourth **TO-DO**, download the **Facebook Posting Worksheet**. For the worksheet, go to **http://jmlinks.com/2023smm** (then enter the code '**2023smm**' to register your workbook), and click on the link to the "Facebook Posting Worksheet." You'll systematically build out a posting strategy based on the four types of content.

Once you get this done, it's time to post. Remember that Facebook marketing requires a commitment of time and resources. You can even create an editorial calendar and assign **TO-DOS** to team members so that you and your team members are posting to Facebook on a regular basis.

How frequently should you post?

Because the Facebook news feed is very crowded, you can safely post quite frequently, even several times a day. But this differs with your audience, so pay attention using the Insights tab as to what posts get the best response and whether the time of day matters. Pay attention as well to your Page likes and unlikes to see if your posts are delighting or annoying your followers.

Experiment and measure, and you'll figure out a posting rhythm that works for you.

POST 80% OR MORE ABOUT "FUN," AND 20% OR LESS ABOUT "BUY MY STUFF"

Don't forget that most of your posts (80% or more) should be about friends, family, and fun, and only a few (20% or less) should be direct pitches to buy your stuff. If you oversell your stuff, your fans will ignore your posts, unlike your Page, and your *algorithm score* will suffer.

» PROMOTE YOUR FACEBOOK PAGE AND POSTS FOR FREE

Once you've set up your Page and started to post content to it on a regular basis, you've essentially "set up" your "party." You've created a good-looking Facebook Page for your business, and you're posting so frequently that when someone lands on the Page, they'll see there's a lot of fresh, fun, and engaging content. These "trust indicators" will encourage them to like your Page, thereby allowing you to post to your timeline and (hopefully) reach them when they check their news feed.

Now it's time to send out the "invitations," that is, to promote your Facebook Page to users. In and of itself, a Facebook Page will not be self-promoting!

Remember: social media is a party. You must have yummy food and entertainment for people to show up and stick around — that is, great and engaging content. So as you promote your Facebook Page, always keep front and center "what's in it for them?" — what will they get by "liking" your Facebook Page and checking it out on a regular basis? What content will they find on your Page that will excite and engage them?

Let's focus first on free ways to promote your Page and its posts. Here are some strategies:

- **Real World to Facebook.** Ask customers face-to-face to like your Facebook Page. If you are a museum store, for example, be sure that the cashiers recommend to customers that they like your Facebook Page? *Why? Because they'll get insider tips, fun do-it-yourself posts, announcements on upcoming museum and museum store events, etc.* If you are a dentist's office, ask them to like your Facebook Page perhaps to be entered in a contest for a discount or gift certificate. Have all customer-facing employees ask customers to like your Facebook Page, and train them with a ready answer as to why "liking" your Facebook Page is worth it.

- **Hashtags and Trending Topic.** While not as important on Facebook as on Instagram, Twitter, and LinkedIn, hashtags do exist on Facebook. Create a "custom hashtag" for your brand and/or research hashtags on Facebook and include them in your posts. See **http://jmlinks.com/43e** for an example, and see **http://jmlinks.com/43g** for more information.

- **Cross-Promotion**. Link your website to your Facebook Page, your blog posts to your Facebook Page, your Twitter to your Facebook Page, etc. Notice how big brands like REI do this: one digital property promotes another digital property.

- **Facebook Messenger for Business.** Facebook Messenger is a text message app owned and operated by Facebook. It is highly popular, especially outside of the USA. To enable messenger on your Facebook Page, click "Settings" at the top of the Page, then click "Messaging." Next, then check the box to allow people to contact your Page. Learn more at **http://jmlinks.com/43p**. Commercial products are also available called "chatbots," which use Artificial Intelligence (AI) to automate this process; simply Google "Facebook Chatbot" to find an array of vendors who offer these services.

- **Email**. Email your customer list and ask them to like your Page. Again, you must have a reason why they'll like it: what's in it for them? Have a contest, give away something for free, or otherwise motivate them to click from the email to your Page, and then like the Page. You can even upload a customer email list, and Facebook will use it to "suggest" your Page to matches. See **http://jmlinks.com/37r**. You can also let Facebook "invite" your (personal) friends on Facebook to like your Page. Just click on the three dots on your Page and then "Invite Friends."

- **Interact with Other Pages**. Interact with other Pages, share their content, comment on timely topics using #hashtags, and reach out to complementary Pages to work with you on co-promotion. Use the Facebook search feature to find other Pages that are interested in your keyword themes and comment upon them while logged in as your Page. To learn how to do this, visit **http://jmlinks.com/43h**.

- **Use Facebook Plugins**. Facebook has numerous plugins that allow you to "embed" your Facebook Page on your website and thereby nurture cross-promotion. To learn more about plugins, visit **http://jmlinks.com/31a**. Another good plugin is the Facebook button for WordPress at **http://jmlinks.com/44b**. In this way, your blog can promote your Facebook Page, and your Facebook Page can promote your blog. Similarly, your YouTube videos can promote your Facebook Page, and your Facebook Page can promote your YouTube Videos.

- **Leverage your Fans and Superfans**. People who like your Page are your best promoters. When they first like your Page, when they comment on a post, when they "check in" to your local business on Facebook, and especially when they share your posts, their friends see this. Remember, it's *social* (!) media, and encouraging your customers to share your content is the name of the game. Create content that your users will proactively want to share, such as funny memes, contests with giveaways, scholarship opportunities, coupons, useful "how to" articles, etc.

- **Interact with Your Fans and Others**. Your Facebook Page shouldn't just be one-way. When a fan likes, comments, or shares your post, respond to them in the comments section. Empower your employees as individuals and your brand as a Facebook Page to talk with customers on Facebook. Respond to reviews posted by customers to your Facebook Page as well.

- **Identify Influencers**. Find people on Facebook who have a lot of personal followers and who are willing to work with your brand. Some may want to charge money; some may be free. But regardless, identify and reach out to high-profile individuals who can share your Page content to their followers. Always remember to explain to any influencer what's in it for them: it may be a direct payment, it may be a free product sample, it may be co-op promotion, but there has to be something "in it" for them (or they won't do it).

Local Businesses: Reviews and Check-ins

Local businesses have two promotional tactics that are very important. First, there are customer **recommendations** on Facebook (formally called "Recommendations and Reviews"). A "local business" that enters a physical address into Facebook enables the "review this business" feature. Once the feature is enabled, you can then ask customers to review you on Facebook (by email, face-to-face, etc.); and then, when they write a review, Facebook may alert their friends and family, thereby leveraging one happy customer to reach new customers. To learn more about reviews on Facebook, visit the help file at **http://jmlinks.com/43f**.

Here's a screenshot of the "Review Tab" for "Tacos for Life," a popular Taco Chain with a location here in Tulsa:

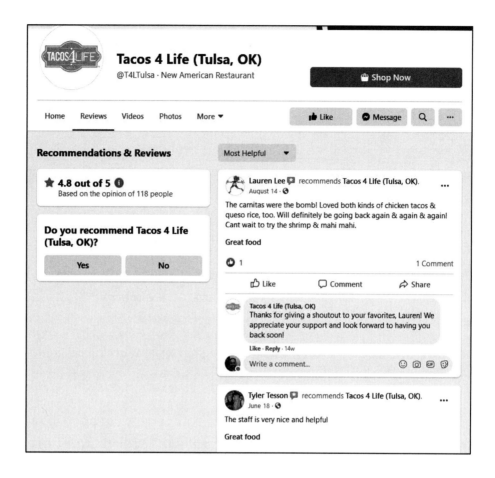

You can see that it has 118 reviews and a 4.8 out of 5 star rating. Lauren Lee thinks that the "Carnitas are the bomb," while Tyler Tesson thinks that "The staff is very nice and helpful." Reviews encourage "social spread," since when a customer writes a review, the Facebook algorithm can highlight this to friends and family. Study after study shows that people are most likely to believe friends and family when making a purchase decision. If you drill further into reviews on Facebook, however, you'll notice that they are not always positive; **brands can't control which reviews are posted**, so be ready for good or bad reviews if you enable this feature!

I discuss review marketing (such as reviews on Google, Yelp, and other local platforms) in much greater detail in my *SEO Workbook*. Suffice it to say in terms of Facebook, however, that if you enable reviews, you want to encourage happy customers to write reviews and be ready to deal with unhappy customers, attempting to assuage their concerns to the greatest extent possible.

Something as simple as ASKING happy customers, "please review us on Facebook" can make a world of difference in increasing your review count on Facebook. Simply motivate your employees when they encounter a happy customer to ask, "Hey. Could you do us a favor? Write us a review on your Facebook page." You can even generate text messages and email links to make it super easy for your most devoted customers to "share the love" via Facebook reviews.

Check-ins on Facebook

The second benefit of being a local business on Facebook is "Check-ins." "Check-ins" allow customers who are at a physical brick-and-mortar store to "check in" via Facebook on their phones. This means that their friends and family can see that they've checked in, thus giving social credence and social spread to your business. Any local business should make sure that they are correctly set up as a local business on Facebook and have enabled the check-in feature. Then, encourage customers face-to-face to check in to the business. Perhaps, for example, have a weekly contest among customers who check in to win something like a $50 gift certificate. You can even use "check in" at a trade show or real-world event by temporarily making your business address the same as the convention center and have people "check in" at your trade show booth. To learn more about Facebook check-ins, visit **http://jmlinks.com/37q**.

» ODDS & ENDS: GROUPS, EVENTS, FACEBOOK LIVE, ETC.

While posts by Facebook Pages constitute the lion's share of marketing on Facebook, there are other opportunities. Let's run through those now.

Facebook Groups. One of the best ways to work with fans and superfans is to create a group for your brand. A group means that anyone can post, however, so you do not have the kind of control that you do with a Facebook Page. But Facebook Groups are definitely worth checking out if you have a core of devoted fans and superfans. You can use a group to discuss upcoming new products or services, discuss industry events, comment about ideas that surround your brand, etc. Think of a group as you would think of an informal customer meeting at your brick-and-mortar store.

Search Groups. You can search groups in your industry by using the search bar in Facebook and typing in a keyword such as "organic" or "weddings." Then click "Groups" to browse groups. You can also type in the name of a competitor or company to emulate to see if a competitor or company to emulate has created a group. Groups are a good way to nurture interaction among your super fans, those fans who care about your business so passionately that they want to know everything about you, stay up-to-date, and even share tips, secrets, and admiration among themselves. The industry lingo for this is "brand groups." For instance, check out the "brand group" of passionate Instant Pot fans at **http://jmlinks.com/54w**.

Group Marketing (Direct). If you decide a "branded group," focused on your company, products, or services is for you, here are some things to think about. First and foremost, what's the point of the group? Why will customers want to join it? After all, a group is, by definition, interactive. Anyone can post, and anyone can chime in. So your best group is one that is customer-focused and almost "runs by itself." You, as the group manager, should really take a back seat and let the customers lead the way. Second, you can take the lead in some instances by sharing inside stories, tips, secrets, tricks, etc., about your company or product/service. The best groups are really for "superfans." Third, you can make a group private or public and adjust the settings to give you control over who gets in and how. You can also moderate the comments (or choose not to). Learn more about the technical issues of Facebook Groups at **http://jmlinks.com/43j**.

Group Marketing (Indirect). Another way to market via Facebook groups is to join them as an individual and promote your own company by being a "helpful expert." A photographer, for example, might join groups focused on weddings and then share her expertise on how to take great photos. A company that sells crafting and quilting products might have its CEO join and contribute to Facebook groups the focus on arts and crafts. Or a company that sells birding tours might join groups on birding and contribute useful content, photos, and posts to enthusiasts for birds. The point here is to be useful, relevant, and an expert and let the publicity flow back to your brand in a low-key way.

Facebook Events. If your company can host real-world events or even live or virtual events on Facebook, you can set up an event. Just as in the real world, an event lives on a calendar and is an opportunity for people to learn more, purchase tickets., etc. Think of an event like a book reading, poetry slam, or perhaps a fashion show at your store just in digital format. Learn more at **http://jmlinks.com/43k**.

Facebook Live. Persons and Pages can now stream live video on Facebook. Learn more about Facebook Live at **http://jmlinks.com/43m**. The trick here is to figure out what type of video content your fans would like to see (and participate in) live. It's great for product demos, lectures, book readings, and other types of content that might exist "in the real world" but translate easily into video. To see examples of what's being streamed right now live on Facebook, visit **http://jmlinks.com/43n**.

Facebook Appointments. You can use Appointments on Facebook to let customers book services with your business from your Facebook Page. Click into your Facebook Page and then the blue CTA (Call to Action) button on the right underneath your cover photo. Select the "Book with you" option and follow the instructions.

Facebook Stories. Brands can create "stories," which are short video vignettes of a "day in the life" of your business. Originally started on Snapchat and Instagram, these are yet another way to stay in touch with your superfans. Learn more at **http://jmlinks.com/53a**. For story ideas from brand pages that you follow, you can go to *facebook.com/stories* or visit **http://jmlinks.com/53b**. The best stories share fun, interactive, and "insider" information about a "day in the life" of your brand.

Each of the above is a special use of Facebook. They're not for every business. The main questions to ask yourself are:

1. Will your customers be interested in using this feature? Why or why not?

2. What will your share / talk about / post to the feature? If it's an event, for instance, what kind of event will it be? What will happen at the event? If it's a group, what will be the reason for the group, and what will you (and others) share on the group that will be interesting? If it's live, what will happen during the live broadcast?

3. How much time will it take for you as a business to engage via the platform?

4. How will you promote it? A Facebook group, Facebook live, or Facebook event will not promote itself. You have to promote it, just as you'd promote the real-world equivalent.

»» Checklist: Facebook (Organic) Action Items

Test your knowledge of Facebook! Take the *Facebook marketing quiz* at **http://jmlinks.com/qzfb**. Next, here are your Facebook **Action Items**:

❏ **Research** Facebook to find out whether your customers are on it and what they are doing. Identify **content themes** that are either directly relevant to your brand or adjacent to it.

> ❏ **Identify** both **competitors** and **companies to emulate**; "reverse engineer" their Page setup and posting strategies.

> ❏ **Investigate** which types of **posts** are getting the most **interaction** from fans and why. Pay attention to whether these are in keyword themes directly related to your products or services or just adjacent to them (or both).

❏ **Set up and Optimize your Facebook Page**. Identify profile and cover photo art. Select the appropriate sections, including whether to enable the "review" tab or not and whether to allow posts to the Page by fans.

❏ **Optimize Your Page Settings**. Identify Page administrators. Turn off or on key settings such as message filters, blocked users, check-ins. Pin posts to the featured slot. Go through each and every setting for your Page and make sure it is what you desire.

❏ **Manage Your Facebook Page with Tools**. Access and optimize your Facebook Page directly, and/or use "Professional Dashboard," "Meta Business Suite" or "Creator Studio" to upload and schedule posts. Create posts, Reels, and/or Stories.

❏ **Brainstorm a Content Strategy.** Begin to systematically create blog posts, photos, videos, etc., that match your marketing strategy to the interests of your target fans. Seek to encourage likes, comments, and shares. Consider doing Facebook live broadcasts or setting up a company-specific branded hashtag or Facebook group.

❏ **Promote your Facebook page** via the real world, cross-promotion among Internet properties, and other free promotional tactics. Grow your Page likes.

❏ **Measure your Facebook results** using KPIs such as the growth of Page likes, the volume of interactivity of individual posts (e.g., likes, comments, and shares), and whether Facebook is generating traffic to your website up to and including sales or sales leads.

Check out the **free tools**! Go to my *Social Media Marketing Dashboard > Facebook* for my favorite free tools on Facebook. Just visit **http://jmlinks.com/smmdash**.

»» DELIVERABLE: A FACEBOOK (ORGANIC) MARKETING PLAN

We've come to the end of our chapter on Facebook, and your **DELIVERABLE** has arrived. For the worksheet, go to **http://jmlinks.com/2023smm** (then enter the code '**2023smm**' to register your workbook), and click on the link to the "Facebook (Organic) Marketing Plan." By filling out this plan, you and your team will establish a vision of what you want to achieve via Facebook.

4
FACEBOOK (ADs)

Facebook (along with Instagram) is the largest social media *advertising* platform. Facebook / Instagram knows a lot about your customers: their age, their sex, their geographic location, and (most importantly) their interests. Are they dog people or cat people? Are they getting married or ready to retire? Do they vote Blue or vote Red? Do they like movies, and if so, which genres? Eat vegan or love BBQ? The beauty of Facebook advertising is its nuanced **targeting**: you can "slice and dice" your customer targets and reach those people most likely to get jazzed about your brand and buy your stuff. You can reach not only your existing customers but new customers. You can even attempt to "poach" the customers of your competitors! In this Chapter, we'll review paid advertising opportunities on Facebook / Instagram.

Let's get started!

TO-DO LIST:

» Advertise on Facebook: Basics

» Use Facebook Ads Manager

» Target Your Ads on Facebook: Audiences

» The Facebook Pixel, Conversion API, & Customer List

» Advertise on Facebook: the Superfan Strategy

» Measure Your Results

»» Checklist: Facebook (Ads) Action Items

»» Deliverable: a Facebook Advertising Plan

» ADVERTISE ON FACEBOOK: BASICS

The "organic" or "free" reach of business Pages on Facebook is in steep decline. The news feed is more crowded than ever. People are more interested in the posts of their friends and families than in posts by brands. Add to this the shellacking that Zuckerberg and Facebook have taken from the US Congress for "fake news," plus the massive decline in stock price due to the "Metaverse" debacle, and it's no surprise that Facebook has severely tilted its algorithm to *suppress* posts by organizations and brands and *promote* posts by friends and family. The result is that nine times out of ten, you have to **advertise** on Facebook in order to succeed.

Let me emphasize this:

> *For all intents and purposes, you MUST advertise as a brand to succeed at Facebook. The days of a truly "free" organic strategy on Facebook are over.*

Your Facebook Page won't promote itself. You have to have a promotion strategy that combines free efforts, paid efforts, and hybrid pay-to-free efforts to get the word out. You can browse Facebook's official information on advertising at **http://jmlinks.com/58u**, but let me walk you through the basic opportunities here.

Basic Ad Opportunities

First, log in to your business Page. On the left menu, look for "Ad Center" and click on that. "Ad Center" is your hub for creating and managing ads for your page. Here you can see existing ads and their performance, set up or modify your billing, and add media to your ad inventory. Click the blue "Create Ads" to see the most basic opportunities. Next, you'll see four options:

Get started with Automated Ads. This option means let Facebook AI think for you. You answer some questions and let Facebook build out the best ads to meet those objectives. If you have a lot of budget, are pressed for time, and just generally want to use Facebook / Instagram for branding, this is a good (albeit inefficient) option. A lot of your spend will be wasted, however.

Create New Ad. This will guide you step by step into the ad formats and options. We'll explore setup and targeting options below.

Boost a Post. This is the easiest and most straightforward option to use Facebook ads to help an organic post. We'll explore setup and targeting options below. You can also select "Boost existing content" on the left menu to see existing posts and easily boost them.

Boost an Instagram Post. This is the same idea, but on Instagram. We'll explore setup and targeting options below.

Returning to your Facebook page, you can also click on "Create ads," "Create Automated Ads," "Boost Post," and/or "Boost Instagram Post" to retrieve these options.

The Most Common Strategy: Boost a Post

For now, let's assume you want to do the simplest thing, which is to boost a post of yours on Facebook to people who already like your Page. Boosting a post means paying Facebook to put your post to the top of the news feed; it's paying Facebook to prioritize your post in its algorithm so that customers and potential customers are likely to see it. Your goal is to get them to see your post, engage with your post, and hopefully "like" your business Facebook Page.

You can start the boost process in two ways:

1. Log in to your Facebook Page. Then click the "Boost Post" on the left. Next, find the post you want to boost and select the blue "Boost Post" button.

2. Alternatively, just log in to your Facebook Page. Scroll down until you find the post you want to promote, and then click the blue "Boost Post" button on the far lower right corner. You can also do this as you create the post itself. This is the easiest way to boost a post.

Once you've clicked on the blue "Boost Post" button, you should see something like this:

We'll discuss targeting in detail below. For now, let's keep it simple. Your objective is to "boost" a post to reach people who already follow your Facebook Page. You are basically paying Facebook a fee so that your posts reach your existing customer base. Why? Because "organic" reach is so minimal that a little advertising / boosting of a post will go a long way toward making Facebook work for your business.

Here are some options:

Goal. Click into "goal," and you can de-select "automatic" (i.e., Facebook thinks for you). You can select from "get more messages" to "get more calls." If you're using a post focused largely on your Facebook marketing, select "get more engagement" to push it to people who are likely to "like" your Page and its content.

Ad Optimization. This option lets Facebook manipulate your creative based on the platform.

Button. Here, you can select from options such as "sign up" to "learn more." You can also create an intake form for a webinar, lead gen, or service request.

Audience. This controls the targeting options. For the simplest option, select "People who like your Page" or "People who like your page and people similar to them." Once you choose an option, here, you can set the geo target as in "People who like my Page" and are 25 miles from San Jose, California.

Duration. Set a duration for your ad.

Total Budget. Set a budget.

Placements. Here, you can select from Facebook, Instagram, and/or Messenger.

In our simple scenario, you are paying Facebook for "organic" reach. Thus, boost a post to either people who already follow your Page and/or people who are likely to do so. For a couple of hundred dollars per month, you can essentially retrieve much of the "organic" reach of your Page that has been lost due to changes at Facebook.

Summary: Boosting a Post and Targeting It

In summary, here are the steps to the most basic way to promote your Facebook content through advertising:

1. **Create a post** that has a brief headline or summary, a compelling image or video, and – if desired – a link to your website, blog, YouTube channel, e-commerce store, etc.

    a. Be sure that this post fits into the culture of friends, family, photos, and fun.

    b. If possible, make the post something that people are likely to engage with and even like, comment, or share with their own friends and family!

2. **Boost this post** on Facebook to any combination of:

    a. People who like your Page;

    b. People who like your Page and people similar to them.

    c. People who live within 25 miles of a city or zip code or another geographic target

I recommend a minimum budget of $300 / month for your average small business, and for a larger business, the sky's the limit. **Note**: we will revisit targeting options in a moment, as they are VERY important. So far, we are just boosting a post to our existing customer base.

» USE FACEBOOK ADS MANAGER

Facebook Ads Manager is a dashboard to manage all your ads in one place. It's a more robust interface than *Ad Center*. I recommend you use *Ads Manager* if you are doing a lot of advertising and if you want to do more than just "boost" a post.

To access it, log in to your Facebook Business Page, then click "Ad Center," then scroll to the bottom and click on "Ads Manager." You can also bookmark this URL: **https://business.facebook.com/adsmanager/**. Be careful, however, if you have more than one business Page or account. At the top pull-down menu, make sure you are in the *correct* business account. In addition, be very careful when it comes to the credit card and billing. The platform has a nasty habit of defaulting back to your personal credit card. If you don't see "Campaigns," "Ad Sets," and "Ads," click on the left into the "Campaigns" icon to get to the right place.

Let's explain what this structure means:

Account. This is at the top under the pull-down menu. This is the "owner" of the Ads Manager and is the "responsible party" who will pay the bill.

Campaign. This is an umbrella bucket that contains ad sets and ads.

Ad Sets. This is an umbrella bucket that contains the network (Facebook, Instagram, and/or Messenger), budget, and targeting settings.

Ads. This is the ad creative such as text, photos, and/or videos.

Thus, one Account can have multiple Campaigns, one Campaign can have multiple Ad Sets, and one Ad Set can have multiple ads. When you click "into" a Campaign, you'll immediately see the Ad Sets that live in that Campaign. When you click "into" and Ad Set, you'll see the ads that live in that Ad Set.

Ads Manager puts all your advertising in one dashboard, allowing you to see everything at once. It also allows you to create new ads, whether these are boosting existing posts, or totally new ad content. An advantage here is if you want to run an ad, but do not want your existing followers to see it; you can set up an ad in Ads Manager (as compared with boosting a post, where by definition, everyone sees it).

Inside Ads Manager, click on the "hamburger menu" at the top left. This opens up access to issues like billing, business settings, page posts, etc.

» TARGET YOUR ADS ON FACEBOOK: AUDIENCES

Targeting is the "secret sauce" of advertising on Facebook or Instagram. If you sell wedding dresses, you can target brides-to-be. If you sell dog toys, you can target dog lovers. And if you sell vacation cruises, you can target people who are thinking about vacations. Targeting is where it's "at" on Facebook!

Targeting settings can be accessed in multiple ways:

Boosting a Post. When boosting a post, click into *Audience* and then click edit.

Ad Center. Inside of Ad Center, click on *Tools > Audiences* on the far right.

Meta Business Suite. Click on the "hamburger" menu on the left for "All Tools" and then "Audiences."

Ads Manager. Click on the "hamburger menu" on the top left, and then "Audiences."

Before we get into audiences, however, note that there are three options ONLY visible from "Boost Post:"

People who like your Page

People who like your Page and people similar to them

People in your local area

These three "audiences" can be accessed if, and only if, you boost a post. These are the very valuable ways to pay a little money to Facebook to reach folks who already like your Page, people similar to them, and/or people in your local business area. These options are NOT available in the "Audience" function.

With that in mind, let's return to "Audiences" from "Ads Manager." Hover over "Create Audience," and you'll see three options:

Custom Audience. This is an audience of people who have interacted with your business, as in visited your website or given you their email address.

Looklike Audience. This is letting Facebook AI create an audience that "looks like" another audience, such as people who already like your Facebook Page or people who visited your website.

Saved Audience. This is using Facebook targeting, as for example, "Women in San Jose who are considering marriage."

Let's start with the last one, first, **"Saved Audience**." Click "Saved Audience," and you'll see options like this:

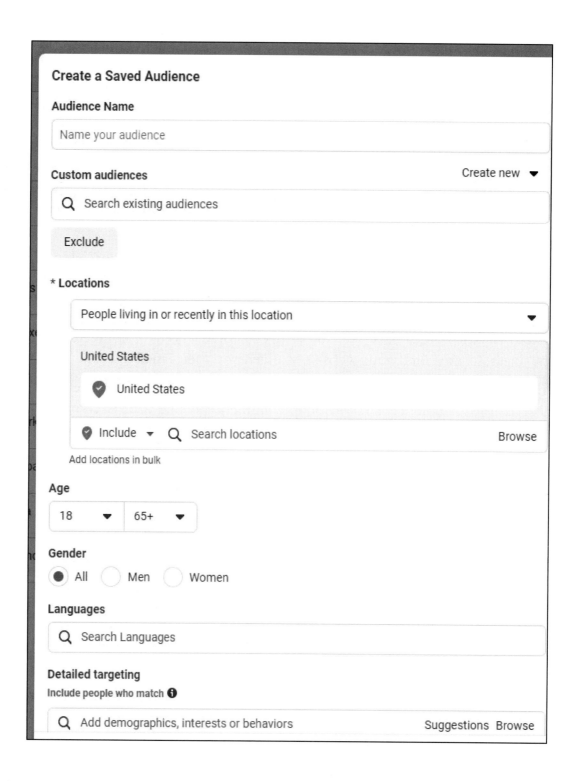

Create a Saved Audience

Audience Name

Name your audience

Custom audiences   Create new ▼

🔍 Search existing audiences

Exclude

* Locations

People living in or recently in this location   ▼

United States

📍 United States ✓

📍 Include ▼   🔍 Search locations   Browse

Add locations in bulk

Age

18 ▼   65+ ▼

Gender

⦿ All   ◯ Men   ◯ Women

Languages

🔍 Search Languages

Detailed targeting
Include people who match ❶

🔍 Add demographics, interests or behaviors   Suggestions Browse

Let's review these options. "Locations," of course, means selecting people who live in a country, state, city or zip code. "Age" means their age. "Gender" means men or women. "Languages" means English, Spanish, German, etc.

"Detailed Targeting" is the really interesting aspect. Here, you can start typing a keyword like "wedding" or "golf" and Facebook will return interests that match. Here's a screenshot for "golf":

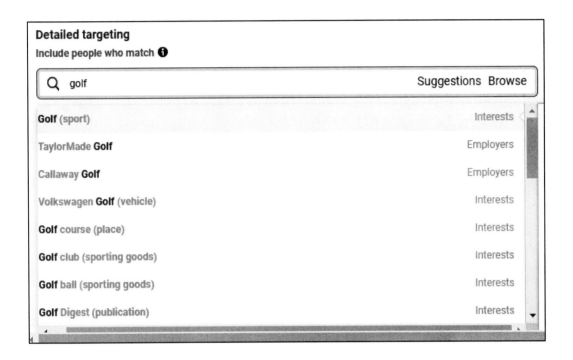

"Interests" means that they are interested in this keyword or topic. "Employers" means that they work for the entity on the left. As you select them, they are "expansive," meaning if you select "Golf" and then enter "Weddings," you'll get people who are interested in "golf" OR in "Weddings." Thus the best practice is to be very narrow here and create a unique targeting group for each specific target. Thus, you can create a "Saved Audiences" of:

> *San Jose > 25-45 age > Men > Golf*
>
> *United States > 45-65 age > Men or Women > Fishing*
>
> *California > 45-55 > Women > Rodeo*

The sky's the limit here. Once you create an audience, you can "attach" it to a Boost or to an ad in Ads Manager. So your to-do is to brainstorm your most important audiences and create them.

You can also "narrow" your audience with exclusions. So you can have an audience of:

Texas > 25-45 > Men > Books > but not Rodeo

To do this, click on "Narrow Audience" at the bottom. You can also do Boolean "Ands" by clicking "Must also match" as in women who are "getting married" and "like rodeo." And finaly you can browse categories by clicking "Browse."

"Browse" gets you demographics, interests, and behaviors, which are broad buckets. For example, you can select *Demographics > Education Level > College Grad.* And, again, you can mix and match these with other characteristics to get *Texas college grads between the ages of 25-45 who are men who like books but not rodeo.* Just be aware that if your targeting is too narrow, Facebook will complain and not run your ads.

Once you create and save an audience, it will be visible as an audience when you "Boost a post" or create an Ad Set in Ads Manager.

Audience Insights: How Big is an Audience?

Here's a pro tip. You can dig deeper into Audiences via the "Audience Insights" tool on Facebook at **http://jmlinks.com/54x**. It's hard to find in the interface, but it's inside of Ads Manager. Click the nine-dot menu at the top left, then scroll down to "Analyze and Report" and then "Audience insights." If necessary, select your business (again). Next, click on the blue "filter" at the top, and you can filter by location, age, gender, and (most importantly) interests.

For example, enter "United States" as your location and "organic food" as the interest. You can then see how big this audience is and the breakdowns by gender and age. Here's a screenshot for *United States > fishing*, showing an audience size of 68 million people:

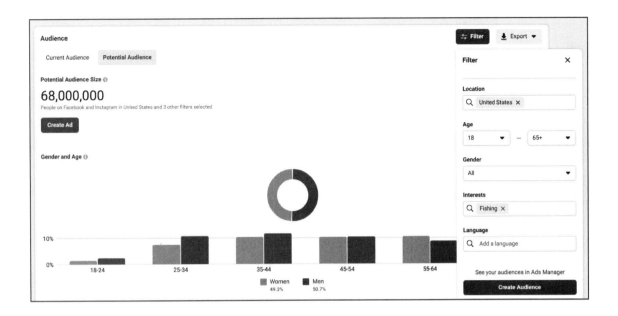

This gives you a way to see how large an audience is based on your criteria.

» THE FACEBOOK PIXEL, CONVERSION API, AND CUSTOMER LIST

The next concept in Facebook Advertising is what is called "Custom Audiences." "Custom Audiences" refer to people who have interacted with your business in some way, whether on Facebook directly, on your website, and/or by giving you their email address. Facebook allows you to "snoop" on your customers and then use this data to target / retarget / remarket to them on Facebook, plus share data on if they "convert" once they leave Facebook and visit your website. "Remarketing" means showing your ads to people who have ALREADY interacted with your business; as for example, a person who has visited your website can then be shown Facebook ads when she is on Facebook.

"Customer List," in short, is a type of "remarketing": showing ads to people who have already interacted with your business in some way. This can be very nuanced – as in showing one ad to people who have made a purchase, another ad to people who have visited your website (but not made a purchase), and still another ad to people in Cleveland, who visited your website, and purchased red sneakers but not a blue dress.

Let's review the technical aspects.

The Facebook Pixel (Rebranded to the "Meta" Pixel)

The **Facebook Pixel** is a tracking system deployed by Facebook across the Internet. Basically, you – as a website owner – add the "Facebook Pixel" to your web server.

Note: the "Facebook Pixel" has been rebranded to the "Meta Pixel" as part of Facebook's transition to the "Meta" concept, but I will use the old name as most of the help files online still refer to it as the "Facebook Pixel."

The Pixel allows Facebook to combine the data it already knows about a person via Facebook with the data it collects on your website via the Pixel. You, as the marketer, can thus participate in this massive invasion of consumer privacy (*oops, I mean this wonderful method of targeting ads to your customers*) by adding the Facebook Pixel to your website and cooperating with Facebook's snoop technology. (See **http://jmlinks.com/43c** for full information on the Facebook (Meta) Pixel). If you're running WordPress on your website, you can download and install the "Pixel Cat" plugin, which makes it relatively easy to install the Facebook Pixel on your website. Just search for "Pixel Cat" as a plugin when logged in to your WordPress website or visit **http://jmlinks.com/43s**. If you're running Google Tag Manager, it can also be done via Google Tag Manager (**http://jmlinks.com/58x**).

Once installed, the Facebook Pixel can be used to create a **custom audience**. Broadly, you can create an audience of everyone who hit your website; more narrowly, you can create sub audiences, such as an audience of persons who hit your website but did not convert or persons who hit specific pages or sections (such as men's clothes, women's clothes, or teenagers' clothes if you were an e-commerce clothing vendor, for instance). You can then use these audiences and sub audiences to target your ads on Facebook. An e-commerce site that sold jet skis, for example, could target all website visitors with ads on Facebook or, more cleverly, target only those visitors who did not convert and buy a jet ski. A clothing store could target ads to men, women, and teenagers separately, and so on and so forth. You can also assume that folks who hit your website are good prospects to like your Facebook Page, so you can use the Facebook Pixel to grow likes to your Facebook Page, and then boost posts and set up other types of Facebook ads so that your website grows your Facebook Page, and your Facebook Page grows your website and desired actions such as selling stuff on an e-commerce store or driving web feedback forms.

The Pixel, in short, unifies your website with your Facebook Page. It's awesome!

Installing and setting up the Facebook Pixel, however, is not easy. It's sort of something designed by computer geeks, for computer geeks. You may need to reach out to a technical webmaster for help with the installation and conversion issues. You can also go to Fiverr.com and just search "Facebook Pixel" (or "Meta Pixel") to find experts who can install the Pixel technology for you.

Once the Facebook Pixel is installed, it may take about 14 days to collect enough data. If you have a big website with lots of traffic, it can be faster. If your website doesn't have a lot of traffic, however, the Pixel might not work at all. You need about 20,000 visits a month to your website for it to function. We'll assume you've installed the Pixel and have enough website visitors for it to work.

It's going to get complicated at this point. Bear with me and be patient. Facebook's advertising platform is very complicated, the support files are sparse, and there is no phone support. But it's worth slogging through the pixel installation and then creating custom audiences to take advantage of this incredible way to target customers.

Here's how to create a Custom Audience using the Facebook Pixel:

1. Log in to your Facebook business Page by first logging into your personal Facebook account and then clicking on Pages on the left. It can also be found at **http://jmlinks.com/43y**.

2. Get to "Ads Manager" by clicking on the downward chevron marked "Manage Ads" at the top right of Facebook. You can also just go to **http://jmlinks.com/43z**. Be sure to click on the correct company's Ads Manager (if, for some reason, you have more than one account). This step may not be necessary in all cases.

3. On the top left, where it has the nine dots and the "Ads Manager" text, click the Menu and then "Audiences." Here's a screenshot:

4. Click the blue "Create Audience" and select "Custom Audience."

5. Click "Website."

6. Follow the steps there, as you should see your website visitors and options such as visits to a specific page or conversions. Here's a screenshot:

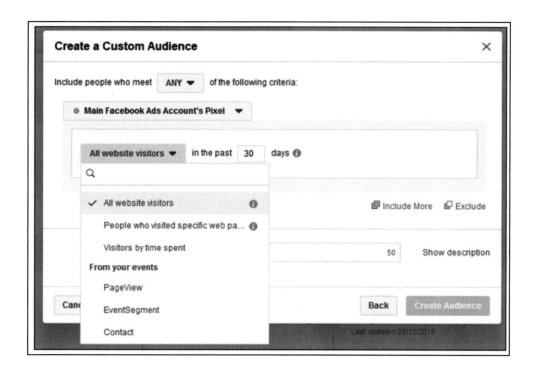

And once you've installed and set up the Facebook Pixel, you can further drill down to create sub-audiences. Here's a screenshot:

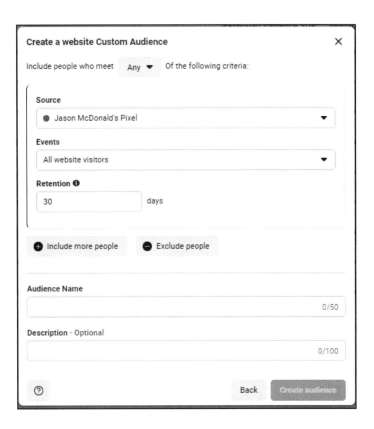

Once you've done this, you should start to see your Pixel audience available when you boost a post, advertise your page, or promote your website via Facebook advertising. Note, also, underneath your pixel you will see "Include more people" and "Exclude people" – these are the ways that you can do "Boolean" searches as for example:

People who hit my website but did not make a purchase.

People who hit my website who live in Cleveland, Ohio

People who hit my website, did not make a purchase, but like cats

Etc.

In summary, your steps are:

1. Install the Facebook / Meta Pixel on your website.

2. If desired, modify the Pixel so that you can track visits to key web pages and/or conversions on an e-commerce or lead generation site.

3. Log in to Facebook and get to the "Audiences" section in Facebook Ads Manager.

4. Define a "custom audience" based on your Facebook Pixel (all website visitors) or a sub audiences (non-converters, visitors to key pages, etc.).

Once defined, you can then use and reuse your Facebook Pixel as a "custom audience" to boost a post, advertise your page, or advertise a link to your website. You can also "slice and dice" your Facebook Pixel (the total audience) into many subaudiences. You may have to click on "Custom Audiences" to see it. Here's a screenshot:

I know it can be frustrating to set up the Pixel, but it is well worth it. Facebook does a terrible, rotten, no good, crazy job of making the Pixel easy to install and manage. Facebook's user interface sucks. Their tech support sucks. But, once you've installed the Pixel, you can laser-target people who hit your website with Facebook or Instagram ads. People who have visited your website are the most likely people to be or become your superfans, make a purchase, request more information, etc.

Installing the Facebook pixel is a fight worth winning!

Even better, once the pixel is installed, you can use "events" in Facebook to differentiate among groups. For example, you could have one custom audience of people who shopped for "women's clothes" vs. people who shopped for "men's clothes." Or a group of people who bought things ("customers") vs. people who did not ("prospects). Or a group of people who put things in their cart but abandoned it, that is, did not purchase anything. "Events" is a special way of programming your use of the pixel and targeting your ads. Check with your resident computer nerd to set up audiences and sub audiences via the pixel. Learn more about using events and the pixel at **http://jmlinks.com/57h**.

The Pixel is Dying (at Least on Apple iPhones)

New since 2020 are big changes to how the Facebook Pixel can track behavior on Apple devices, especially those running iOS 14 and higher. In a nutshell, Apple is not cooperating with Facebook Pixel tracking technology, and users now must "opt-in" to being tracked. Even worse, "cookies" are being slowly discontinued across the Internet. This is called the "Post Cookie World" or "Cookieless Future." These are funny terms to mean that it is getting harder and harder to track users across the Internet. The "Pixel" is already dead on Apple iPhones, it looks to be dead on Android phones soon, and even on the desktop, talk of the "death of cookies" means the "death of the Pixel."

These two looming changes are already having a huge negative impact on Facebook Pixel tracking. You can read more at **http://jmlinks.com/57e**.

Facebook Conversions API

As the Pixel fades into oblivion, Facebook has struck back against Apple's privacy initiative with CAPI: the Facebook Conversion API. CAPI is pretty technical, so I recommend you find a "computer geek" who works with your website to enable this feature. CAPI basically sends data from your website directly to Facebook, and Facebook rematches this to its data on users. Take that, Apple!

The good news is that many major e-commerce platforms like Shopify now support CAPI integration.

Here are the steps:

1. **Install the Conversion API on your website**. This can be done through "partner" e-commerce platforms such as Shopify, Woocommerce, or Wix OR

through direct installation on your website OR through third parties such as Google Tag Manager.

2. **Verify the insallation**. Make sure that data is flowing to/from your website to/from Facebook/Instagram. You can see this data in Facebook under "Audiences."

3. **Define "events" to slice and dice your audience**. For example, separate people who "made a purchase" from people "who did not." This may require a computer geek to set up.

4. Use this data to **set up "custom audiences"** in Facebook.

Facebook strongly recommends that you install BOTH the Pixel AND the CAPI as both are combined to track user behavior. You can read more about CAPI at **http://jmlinks.com/57f**. If you're on Shopify, check out their help file at **http://jmlinks.com/58w** or Google your platform plus "Facebook Conversion API" ("CAPI") as in "Woocommerce Facebook Conversion API" to find the latest help files.

Customer List and Other Options

A third advanced targeting technique is to called "Customer List." Here, you upload a list of customer email addresses and Facebook matches its own massive list of user emails against your list to create a custom audience based on your email list. Here's how.

1. Log in to your *Facebook Page > Ads Manager > Audiences*.

   a. Be sure to click over to *Assets > Audiences*, which should get you to **http://jmlinks.com/44a**.

2. Click the blue "Create Audience" and select "Custom Audience." (You may be prompted to upgrade to Facebook Business Manager).

3. Select "Customer List."

4. Then either Add customers by uploading a customer email list directly or if you are using MailChimp, follow the instructions there.

You can view the help file at **http://jmlinks.com/58y**. There are other less important ways to create custom audiences; here's a screenshot from Meta Ads Manager:

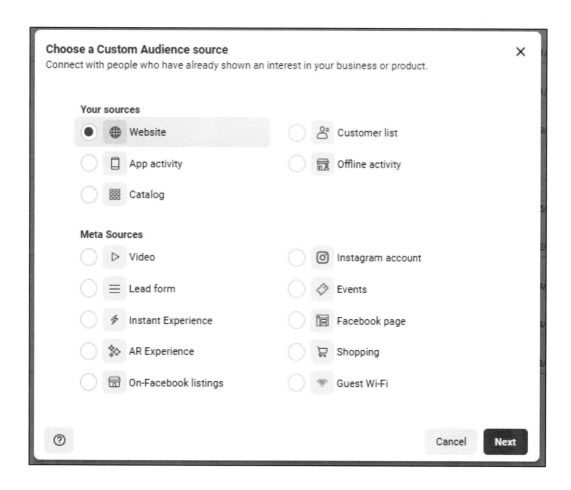

Ultimately all of them live under the "Audience Tab" in Facebook Ad manager at **http://jmlinks.com/44a** whether these are "saved" or "custom" audiences. Just be aware that Facebook refers to them as *audiences*, *saved audiences*, and *custom audiences*.

"Lookalike" Audiences: Facebook AI at Work

Finally, you can create a "Lookalike Audience," which means Facebook will look at your Facebook Page, Facebook Pixel and/or CAPI data, or other data sets, and attempt, through the miracle of artificial intelligence (AI), to create an audience of similarly minded people. To create a "Lookalike Audience," get to Audience Manager as described above. Then,

1. Click the blue "Create Audience" button and then "Lookalike Audience."

2. In the pull-down under Source, select either your Facebook Page or your Facebook Pixel audience.

3. Select a location such as Texas or Oklahoma. It needs to be pretty big, as this won't generally work for a city or a zip code. But you can experiment.

Once created, your Lookalike audience will appear named as "Lookalike – People who…" when you target an ad. A "Lookalike audience" is essentially using Facebook to mimic the characteristics of those people who either visit your website or have already liked your Facebook Page.

» ADVERTISE ON FACEBOOK THE SUPERFAN STRATEGY

The organic reach of your Facebook Page isn't very strong as compared with the reach of fans and superfans. One solution is raw advertising as discussed above. But there's another way, a hybrid between organic reach and raw advertising.

I call this the "Superfan strategy."

You can "use" your fans, superfans, and influencers to broaden your reach on Facebook. Fans, of course, are people who have liked your Page, and superfans are those who have liked your Page and are highly engaged with your brand. Influencers are those who have a really broad and engaged audience themselves.

Think of targeting fans, superfans, and even influencers with your content via advertising, and then make this content so engaging that **they want to share it** with their audience. The Superfan Strategy means getting advertising to reach fans, superfans, and influencers and "content marketing" to create content that is likely to be shared.

Here's how to do this:

1. Create a piece of **compelling content**, such as a post that is highly emotional, has a great image, and a message that fits your brand, such as a contest, giveaway, sentimental or shocking message, something counterintuitive, etc.

2. **Boost** this **post**.

3. Select the option "**People who like your Page**."

Because people who already like your Page are – by definition – fans and superfans, you can use advertising to reach them, and then because you've created compelling and shareable content, get them to share this content with their friends and family. Alternatively, you can create a "saved audience" of influencers such as people who work at the New York Times, Huffington Post, and Newsweek – that is, influencers like journalists and bloggers.

This is how content gets started in the sharing process on Facebook, and indeed, how a lot of content "goes viral." It's boosted through advertising to fans, superfans, and influencers at the get-go.

For example, here's a post by REI entitled, "OptOutside," building on their phenomenally successful campaign to close their doors on "Black Friday" and encourage people to "opt out" of the mass consumerism that hits our country on the day after Thanksgiving:

Notice how this has 2400 likes, 118 comments, and 138 shares. Most likely behind the scenes, there was an initial advertising push to get this post out in front of REI's fans and superfans. Notice as well that the content fits their brand identity as a somewhat anti-consumerist brand that encourages nature, is a bit of a "humble brag," and leverages their superfans' sense of superiority over the dumb shoppers who flock into the mega stores on Black Friday. If you're cynical, you could even say that many people will "virtue signal" their support of *#optoutside* by liking, commenting, and even sharing this type of content.

REI is using great content that supports its brand and is highly shareable in combination with advertising to create a post that "goes viral." REI is leveraging fans and superfans (plus their motivation to "support" a cause) to promote its message through Facebook.

So it's not advertising OR organic reach on Facebook; it's advertising AND organic reach by using the latter to ignite the former.

> **VIDEO.** Watch a video on Facebook advertising and superfans at **http://jmlinks.com/43t.**

» MEASURE YOUR RESULTS

Facebook offers good measurements for your organic and advertising efforts. Log in to your Facebook Page, and then click on the "Insights" tab on the left menu. This gets you into the *Professional Dashboard > Insights* data. Here you'll find an overview of your Facebook activity and a post-by-post breakdown of the reach of a post and the engagement. A graph will tell you when your fans are most engaged. You can select "Pages to watch" and keep an eye on your competitors – even down to which posts of theirs were the most interactive.

For any of your posts, click on the post and then "See insights and ads," and a popup window will give you drill-down information. Here's a screenshot of a post to the JM Internet Group Facebook Page:

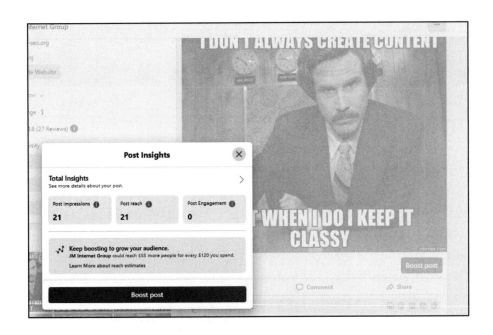

The data shows you how many people engaged with the post and how (likes, comments, and shares).

And here's a screenshot of a post of content that was boosted:

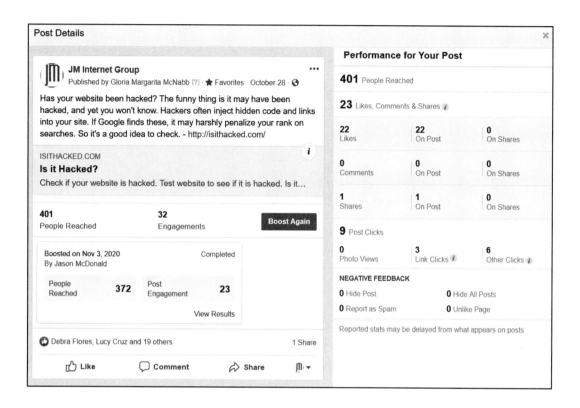

Pay attention to the *reach*, *likes*, *comments*, *shares*, and *clicks* of all your posts (both organic and advertised). All of this influences the *Facebook algorithm score* of your Page. The *more interactive* your Page and posts are, the *higher* your reach, and the *higher* your reach, the *more* people will see your posts and Page.

You'll also very clearly see that posts that are "boosted," that is supported by advertising, have a much bigger reach and, therefore, a bigger opportunity for likes, comments, and shares vs. posts that rely on free, organic reach.

You can also hover with your mouse over the comments and shares to see who did what, and even "invite them" to like your Facebook Page.

Returning to your "Professional Dashboard," you can click down into Your Page, Posts, and/or Audience to see more detailed data on engagements. Here, again, under Posts you can see pretty detailed information on the engagement of an individual post. Here's a screenshot:

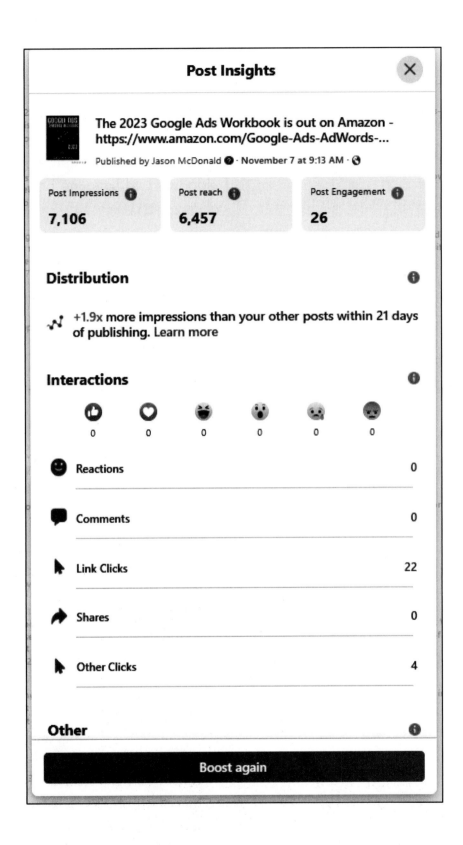

Obviously, "boosted" or "advertised" posts will get more engagement.

All in all, Facebook provides excellent insights into who is interacting with your posts and Page. Use this information to make your Page better and better as measured in posts that garner more likes, comments, and shares.

»» CHECKLIST: FACEBOOK ACTION ITEMS

Test your knowledge of Facebook! Take the *Facebook marketing quiz* at **http://jmlinks.com/qzfb**. (Before or after you do, check out the free, official Facebook learning site called "Blueprint" at **http://jmlinks.com/53e**.) Next, here are your Facebook (Ads) **Action Items**:

❑ **Master "Boosting" A Post**. Identify posts that are likely to have high engagement and "boost" them to people who already like your Facebook Page. This is the easiest and most basic Facebook ads strategy.

❑ **Brainstorm a Content Strategy.** Ads that do well on Facebook are images and video and have "high engagement" type of content. Thus, brainstorm the types of ad format, content, and offers that are most likely to spur engagement as measured by likes, comments, and (most importantly) shares.

❑ **Understand Facebook Saved Audiences.** Make sure you understand the differences between a "saved" audience, a "custom" audience, and a "lookalike" audience. Start with "Saved" audiences as the easiest way to "slice and dice" potential customers on Facebook.

❑ **Set up Facebook (Custom) Audiences.** Set up and save custom audiences to Facebook, such as the Facebook Pixel audiences, CAPI audiences, and audiences from email lists. Verify that your installation is correct and consider further audience segregation as in "customers" vs. "non-customers."

❑ **Master Targeting on Facebook Ads.** Use your existing Page followers, "Saved" audiences, "Custom Audiences," and "Looklike Audiences" to target the right ad to the right person at the right time.

❑ **Measure your Facebook results** using KPIs such as the growth of Page likes, the volume of interactivity of individual posts (e.g., likes, comments, and shares), and whether Facebook is generating traffic to your website up to and including sales or sales leads.

Check out the **free tools**! Go to my *Social Media Marketing Dashboard > Facebook* for my favorite free tools on Facebook. Just visit **http://jmlinks.com/smmdash**.

»» DELIVERABLE: A FACEBOOK ADS PLAN

We've come to the end of our chapter on Facebook, and your **DELIVERABLE** has arrived. For the worksheet, go to **http://jmlinks.com/2023smm** (then enter the code **'2023smm'** to register your workbook), and click on the link to the "Facebook Ads Plan." By filling out this plan, you and your team will establish a vision of what you want to achieve via Facebook.

5
LINKEDIN

If **Facebook** is all about *friends, family*, and *fun* – a kind of 24/7 *company picnic*, **LinkedIn** is all about *business networking* – a kind of 24/7 online *corporate party*. For example, compare what happens on LinkedIn with real-world events such as big trade shows like the annual *Consumer Electronics Show* in Las Vegas. These industry conference "parties" feature free food and entertainment, a speech or two by major CEOs, plus lots of *business networking* between vendors and potential customers. Breakout sessions help people learn new skills and keep up with industry trends. Folks are dressed in "business casual," "ready to learn," and "ready to network" for their companies and their careers. LinkedIn simply takes these activities and moves the "professional party" online.

Besides **business networking**, LinkedIn is also used heavily for recruiting and job search. But due to our focus on marketing, we will ignore that important activity. Instead, this Chapter focuses on **how to market a business on LinkedIn**, specifically the three big opportunities: 1) helping employees to optimize their **profiles**, 2) using LinkedIn to **network** with customers and prospects, and 3) leveraging a **company page** for your business. We'll also discuss the basics of **advertising** on LinkedIn.

Let's get started!

To-do List:

» Explore How LinkedIn Works

» Optimize Your LinkedIn Profile (and Your Employees', Too)

» Schmooze on LinkedIn: Your Social Rolodex

» Be Active on LinkedIn: Posts, Articles, and Video

» Be Active on LinkedIn: Connections, Comments, and Groups

» Use LinkedIn Company Pages

» Promote Your LinkedIn Profile, Posts, and Pages

» Advertise on LinkedIn

» Measure Your Results

»» Checklist: LinkedIn Action Items

» EXPLORE HOW LINKEDIN WORKS

Let's review the basic structure of LinkedIn:

- **Individuals have LinkedIn profiles**, which function as online resumes listing skills, education, and interests. Profiles allow one individual to "connect" with another individual; once connected, any post by individual No. 1 will show in the news feed of individual No. 2. In this sense, LinkedIn profiles function in the same way as Facebook profiles: you send *connection requests* (the same as *friend requests* on Facebook), and once accepted and connected, you and the other individual can directly check each other out, communicate via LinkedIn messaging, and see posts to each other's news feed.

- **Individuals can join groups.** Groups on LinkedIn are a big marketing opportunity! As at a major trade show, LinkedIn has "break out" groups by topic (from petroleum engineering to marketing to advertising to WordPress web design and beyond) that bring like-minded people together in a professional way. Note, however, that it is *people* (and not business *Pages*) that participate in groups.

- **Companies can have LinkedIn Pages.** Companies create business Pages on LinkedIn. The good news is that the "organic reach" of Pages on LinkedIn is much, much better than that on Facebook. Individuals can follow companies and by doing so, give permission for that company to communicate with them. Posts by the company have a chance to show in the news feed of individuals who have "followed" a particular company. Company Pages can also advertise on LinkedIn.

- **Posts and the News Feed.** When an individual shares a post or article to his or her LinkedIn profile, or a company shares a post on its LinkedIn Page, those posts show up in the news feed of connected individuals. Like Facebook, LinkedIn has a posting rhythm in which individuals and businesses compete for eyeballs and attention.

Structurally, therefore, LinkedIn is very similar to Facebook. *Profiles and connection requests, Pages and following, posts and news feeds.* It is also similar in content: people posts just text, text with a photo or image, text with a link to a blog or website, and/or native video.

A More Business-Oriented Culture

The **culture** of LinkedIn, however, is far more serious and business-oriented than Facebook. On LinkedIn, people are in "learning" and "business mode," sharing information and posts about business trends and topics, not the latest photo of their baby, cat video, or SNL skit that has gone viral. Common LinkedIn posts are about industry news, a job promotion, a corporate webinar, or perhaps commentary on business and national news. LinkedIn's content is far more serious and business-oriented than that shared on Facebook. Content marketing for your business on LinkedIn thus needs to fit the business- and career-oriented themes of the network.

In addition, the **structural** similarities between LinkedIn and Facebook hide a very different **pattern of interaction**. Whereas on Facebook, the center of marketing is the business *Page*, on LinkedIn, the center of gravity lies with the personal *profiles* of employees. Whereas on Facebook, you primarily interact with business Pages in terms of marketing, on LinkedIn, you primarily interact with the *employees* of various businesses. Ironically, marketing on LinkedIn centers on *persons* (i.e., your employees), while marketing on Facebook centers on *brands* (i.e., your company page).

LinkedIn's Center of Gravity is the Personal Profile

LinkedIn's center of gravity, in summary, is *person-to-person interaction*. This makes sense if you compare a company picnic (Facebook) with a business networking event (LinkedIn). Whereas at the former, you interact with the company (who brings the food and entertainment and pays for the party), at the latter, you interact with the employees of the company, talking about industry events and schmoozing about shared interests. In a business environment, you don't network with *companies*, after all. You network with the *individual employees* of a given company. Ironically, marketing on LinkedIn is thus focused on person-to-person activities vs. on Facebook, where it is more brand-to-person in nature.

Don't Talk to Strangers?

Another difference concerns stranger marketing. Whereas on Facebook, most of us are suspicious of friend requests from people we don't know or only barely know, on LinkedIn, it is much more common to send a connection request "out of the blue" or to a person you just met. Ironically, talking to strangers is more difficult on Facebook than it is on LinkedIn! And, whereas on Facebook, it's impolite to ask what one "does for a living" or to "pitch business ideas" on LinkedIn, this is so important as to be a core function. With even the most tangential of connections on LinkedIn, you can easily reach out and ask for a relationship. For example, here's a screenshot of me reaching out to *New York Times* journalist Nellie Bowles, with whom I am a second-level connection:

By clicking the three dots and then "connect," I can ask to be her "LinkedIn connection," as it were. People on LinkedIn, in short, are in **business networking mode,** and it's OK to connect to strangers and talk about and talk up your business, up to and including sales pitches (within polite reason). This makes it a fantastic social medium for business-to-business marketing!

LINKEDIN IS THE 24/7 BUSINESS NETWORKING EVENT

In addition, LinkedIn **groups** are quite vibrant, especially in more technical subjects. For a technical sector such as oil and gas, for example, people increasingly use LinkedIn groups as a way to keep informed about their industry. LinkedIn's robust technical groups are thus one example of LinkedIn's focus on "lifelong learning." Another is **"LinkedIn Learning" (https://www.linkedin.com/learning/)**. LinkedIn Learning showcases LinkedIn's goal to be about more than job search or even business networking. LinkedIn wants to become the place for professional "lifelong learning," and it's off to a great start. Finally, although business Pages do exist on LinkedIn and are increasingly important for business-to-business companies, their utility is much weaker than on Facebook for business-to-consumer companies. On the other hand, the organic reach of business Pages on LinkedIn is much better as compared to Facebook.

LinkedIn is a Team Sport

Perhaps the most important distinction is to think of Facebook as a *company-first* marketing platform and LinkedIn as an *employee-first* marketing platform. Whereas on Facebook, you can manage your marketing "top-down," using your company Page as your primary customer interaction vehicle, on LinkedIn, you must rely heavily on your employees. Every customer-facing employee needs to be "on board" with your LinkedIn marketing. He or she needs a robust LinkedIn profile and a passionate commitment to schmooze with other LinkedIn members through outreach, posting, and group participation. To succeed at LinkedIn as a business, each and every customer-facing employee must actively participate as an individual, and your company should manage its own LinkedIn business page in tandem. LinkedIn, in sum, is an **employee team sport**.

> *Employee participation* + *an active* **LinkedIn business page** = *LinkedIn marketing* **success**.

In fact, LinkedIn even has a paid service called the "My Company Tab," which enables employee co-promotion with your business at **http://jmlinks.com/31f**.

You = You and Your Employees on LinkedIn

Throughout this Chapter, I will often refer to an individual "you" as participating in LinkedIn, but remember when I say "you," I mean "you" as an individual as well as "you" as a team of like-minded, enthusiastic employees. Whether your company consists of just one employee, five employees, or five hundred employees, the real key to LinkedIn success is to get everyone "on board" and participating! Go team!

Search LinkedIn

You'll need to research LinkedIn to estimate its value to your business marketing efforts. For your first **TO-DO**, log on to LinkedIn, and search by keywords that are relevant to your company or industry. Identify persons, groups, and companies that are active on these topics.

Simply type a keyword of interest into the search bar at the top of the LinkedIn page (e.g., "organic food" if your company is involved in the organic industry, or "oil and gas" if your company works in the petroleum industry). Then, in the scroll window, select, "See all results." Here's a screenshot for the keyword "petroleum" as a search:

Across the bottom you can see clickable buttons into subcategories such as "Jobs, Companies, Posts, Groups, Events, People, etc." These are your drill-down options.

To search for people on LinkedIn who have "petroleum" in their bio, for example, click "people." This will get you people whose profiles and/or activity contain the target word. Here's a screenshot for the keyword "petroleum" and then "people:"

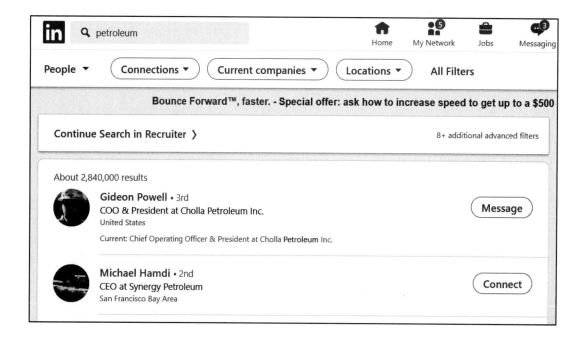

You can then click on any person and see his or her activity. By selecting "Connections," you can narrow this down to 1st, 2nd, or 3rd level connections, and you see more information for 1st level connections, of course. (1st level connections are people who have already accepted your connection request or vice-versa, whereas 2nd level connections are connections of connections, and 3rd level are connections of connections of connections). You can also select "companies" to see companies who have the keyword on their LinkedIn Page. You can then "follow" these companies just as you would on Facebook, and you can drill into their employees as well.

Next, you can search for posts that contain the keyword by clicking "Posts." Here's a screenshot for "petroleum" posts by my 1st level connections:

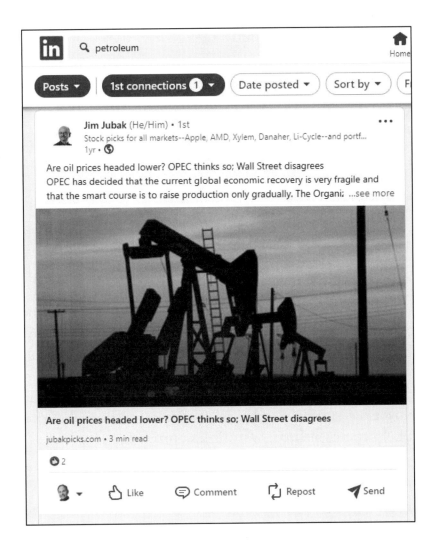

You can scroll down to browse content on these keywords, and you can click on any person who posted a piece of content. You can also like, comment, and share posts that interest you or serve your marketing goals. In this way, you can quickly scan who's posting what about a keyword such as "oil and gas."

You can also select "Groups" to see what groups exist and, again, see how active people are on a content theme. Here's a screenshot for "oil and gas" groups:

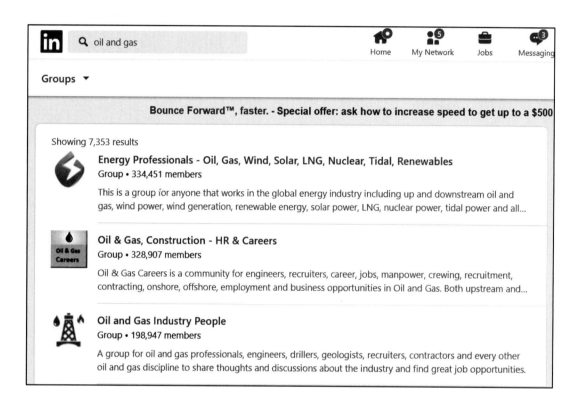

In this way, LinkedIn takes the industry trade show online. Take a content theme that matters to your company and quickly see what's going on vs. people, posts, groups, and pages. But remember as you do so that the center of gravity is personal profiles, posts, and groups, not so much company Pages. LinkedIn's own marketing propaganda will try to convince you it's all about your company Page, but in my opinion, LinkedIn is much more employee- or profile-centric. As you research how LinkedIn works, don't miss their robust help center at **http://jmlinks.com/45y**.

For your next **TO-DO**, download the **LinkedIn Research Worksheet**. For the worksheet, go to **http://jmlinks.com/2023smm** (then enter the code '**2023smm**' to register your workbook), and click on the link to the "LinkedIn Research Worksheet." You'll answer questions as to whether your potential customers are on LinkedIn, identify individuals and companies to follow, and inventory what you like and dislike about their LinkedIn setup and marketing strategy.

» OPTIMIZE YOUR LINKEDIN PROFILE (AND YOUR EMPLOYEES', TOO)

The **personal profile** is the foundation of LinkedIn. Just as on Facebook, an individual needs to set up a LinkedIn profile and populate it with information about him or herself. Unlike on Facebook, however, this personal profile has a strategic role in business marketing. As a business owner or marketer, therefore, you'll want your own well-optimized profile, but you'll also want to motivate your CEO, other key executives, and any employees that are customer-facing to set up and optimize their LinkedIn profiles. Make sure that each and every "customer-facing" employee has an optimized LinkedIn profile.

The **TO-DOS** here are:

1. **Sign up** for LinkedIn as a personal profile (and encourage everyone else in the company to sign up as well!) Have everyone make LinkedIn a part of their daily keeping-up-with-our-industry routine.

2. Identify the **content themes** that represent your business value to other people, that is, keywords that "describe you" as a businessperson and/or a company or non-profit, such as "WordPress web designer," "CPA," or "Business Coach for startups," or "Apple iPhone App development firm."

3. **Optimize** each employee personal profile so that it –

   a. Clearly and quickly represents your **personal business value proposition** as well as that of your **company**.

   b. Is **findable** via LinkedIn search by **keywords**.

   c. Establishes **trust** in you and your company as an authority and someone who is worthy of a business partnership.

First and foremost, think of **search** and **trust**. By search, we mean that people will go to Google and/or LinkedIn after they have met you or a key employee. They'll *search* you on the Internet with an eye to deciding whether you have any skeletons in your closet, whether you seem knowledgeable about your subject, and whether you seem like a good person to do business with. This trust will *flow up* to the company as well. Nowadays, people go to networking events such as trade shows and return with business cards and email addresses. They then *vet* these people and their companies by searching for them on Google and on LinkedIn. Indeed, you can optimize your LinkedIn profile to show high on Google or Bing searches for your own name plus keywords.

Think of your LinkedIn **profile** as your **public resume**. Think of your employees' profiles' as their **business cards** to exchange at an industry trade show.

To see my LinkedIn profile via Google search, for example, just search for "Jason McDonald Social Media" on Google and look for the link to LinkedIn; or simply visit my "public" LinkedIn URL at **https://www.linkedin.com/in/jasoneg3/**. Note that my LinkedIn profile appears in about position four on a Google search for *Jason McDonald Social Media*. Here's a screenshot of how my LinkedIn profile surfaces on the Google search for "Jason McDonald Social Media":

> www.linkedin.com › jasoneg3 ▾
>
> **Jason McDonald - Senior SEO / Social Media Director - JM ...**
>
> I am a teacher, corporate trainer, and **SEO** / AdWords / Social Media Consultant. I love to figure out how things work, and explain that to others in a fun and ...

The concept here is when someone meets me (*or meets you, or meets a key employee*), they'll often go back to their office and "Google" you or look you up on LinkedIn before they reach out for a business relationship. As a marketer, you want to use LinkedIn to show prominently in a search for your name plus keywords, plus you want your LinkedIn profile to show off your expertise and talents. Just like a real (paper) resume, your LinkedIn resume (profile) should be optimized to be found and to put your best foot forward. It should also be publicly viewable without the necessity of being logged into LinkedIn.

Think your name plus keywords. There are 34,900,000 results on Google for *Jason McDonald*. So people would search not just for *Jason McDonald* but for *Jason McDonald* plus keywords to check me out. *Jason McDonald SEO, Jason McDonald Social Media,* or *Jason McDonald Google Ads*. Do likewise for yourself and key employees. What keywords best describe your utility to customers? Are you *Aileen Smith, the Accountant, Jake Harris, the Javascript Programmer*, or *Jeevan Lakshmi, the Environmental Architect?*

Optimize Everyone's LinkedIn Profiles

Now it's time to call a "group meeting" of your employee team. Have them each optimize their LinkedIn profiles vis-à-vis your target keywords and target customers. It is essential that **all** key, customer-facing employees optimize their LinkedIn profiles.

> **Remember**: *LinkedIn is a team sport: you need every employee "on board" with full and eager participation! If they're ho-hum about this, explain that this new, optimized profile will be very useful to them after they get fired for lack of enthusiasm and they're out looking for a job! (Just kidding — now smile for your LinkedIn profile picture).*

As you work with key employees, let's turn to the steps to **optimize** a LinkedIn profile for search and trust.

> **A "Helpful Expert" via Keywords.** What value do you provide for others in a business relationship? Remember: you are NOT looking for a job. Generally, you are positioning yourself as a "helpful expert" in a defined area. Are you a WordPress expert? An expert CPA for small businesses? An architect with a focus on eco-friendly design? Brainstorm and define the logical keywords that someone would append to your name. There are, for example, many "Jason McDonalds" in this world. But I want to rank and be trusted as the Jason McDonald that can help you with **SEO**, **Social Media**, and **Google Ads**. Thus, I embed those keywords in my profile and write it well enough to convey my value as a helpful expert in those endeavors.

> **Once you have identified your keywords, weave them strategically into your LinkedIn profile, starting with the LinkedIn professional headline.**

To access these features, click on *LinkedIn > Me > View Profile* while logged in to LinkedIn. Then click on *View Profile*. Here's a screenshot:

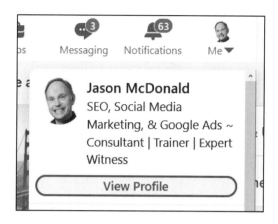

Next, hover over an area, and click on the pencil icon to edit. Here's a screenshot:

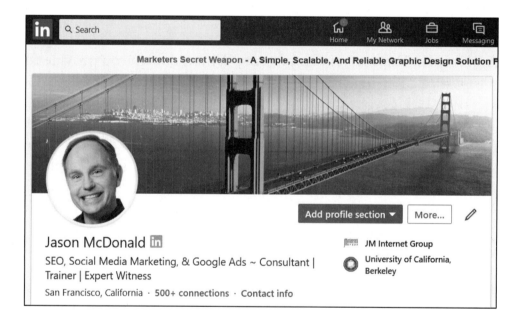

At this point, you should be in the "edit profile" section of LinkedIn. Let's go through the optimization step-by-step. (Note: some of these features may appear in a different order in your Profile than as listed below).

> **Headline**. This is the most important text on your LinkedIn profile for discoverability via search and as a quick statement of your value as a "helpful expert." It should answer the question, "What can you do for me?" Here's a screenshot of mine:

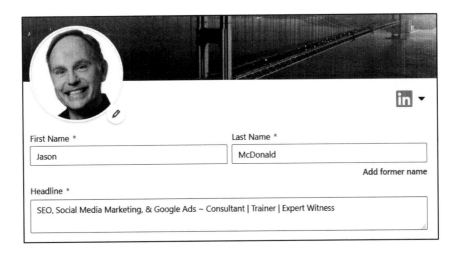

Current (Position). This is your current job, so state it well.

Country, Zip Code, Locations within this area, and Industry. Fill out as appropriate.

Website. You can now add a direct link to your personal website or your "about" page on your company's website.

Audio Recording. You can pronounce your name, plus add in a little pitch about how you are a "helpful expert."

About. Like a real resume, this describes your skills and experience. *Do NOT write this like you are looking for a job if you are NOT looking for a job!* Instead, use ALL CAPS and other ways to break up the content. Populate it with relevant keywords that people might search on LinkedIn, and make it easy to read. It should state your business value proposition succinctly. Write this "as if" you were explaining to someone at a business networking event what you do and how this is relevant to what they might need.

Media. Add links to external documents, including SlideShares or YouTube videos.

(Note: You may have to click out of "edit intro" and back into the more general "edit profile" section to access the next items).

Experience. Here's where you input your current and past employment. If your company is on LinkedIn with a company page (and, of course, it should be), a logo will be available. Again, write succinct summaries of current and past employment that contain logical keywords (do not overdo this), and explain how you can help an interested party to accomplish something of business value.

Licenses & Certifications. List any professional certifications here. I am officially certified in Google Ads, for example, so I list that in this section.

Education. Don't be shy. Populate your education section with your educational achievements, not only degrees but any awards or extra-curricular activities.

Accomplishments. Input any languages you speak as well as certifications. I speak Klingon fluently, so I put that here. (Humor is part of my brand, get it?)

Interests. LinkedIn will populate this with companies and groups you follow. So find some, and follow them.

Audio & Video. New for 2023: via the "mobile app" you can add a "how to pronounce your name" audio clip as well as an introductory video. Use these to quickly state your "value proposition" for customers.

Add New Profile Section. If you like, you can beef up your profile even further by adding publications, skills, honors, patents, etc. This is located on the top right in blue.

VIDEO. Watch a video tutorial on how to optimize your LinkedIn Profile (as well as that of key employees) at **http://jmlinks.com/16r**.

A Word about Interests

At this point, we are optimizing your LinkedIn profile for **search** and **trust**. In terms of interest and groups (which you can see at the very bottom of your LinkedIn profile), therefore, you might consider joining groups not because you plan to participate in them actively but because they convey your interests and skills. For example, I am a member of both the Harvard and UC Berkeley alumni associations really, just to convey that I am smart and attended these prestigious institutions. Similarly, I am a member of Ad Age and WordPress experts groups to convey my interest and expertise in those topics. (I don't actually participate in these groups in any serious way – I'm too busy!) Think of groups like you would think of college extracurricular activities on your resume: to convey interests and skills.

Here's a screenshot of my LinkedIn "Interests," which is people I follow and groups I belong to:

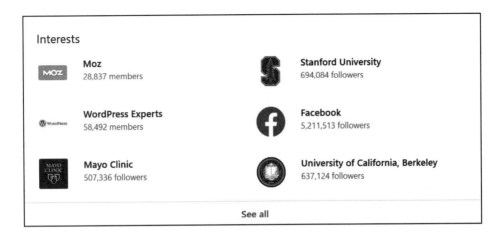

Don't I look impressive? That's the point of my personal profile – to wow potential customers that I'm smart, I'm skilled in technical things like SEO, social media marketing, and Google Ads, that I went to prestigious schools, teach for Stanford, and participate in lively groups on my areas of core competency. Is this a bit hyped up? Yes, that's the point. Explain to every employee in your company that if they don't toot their own horn, no one else will.

Contact and Personal Info

You want to make it easy for people to contact you via LinkedIn. At this point, stay logged in to "edit profile" and click up to the very top of the page. Find the "Contact info" link and click on that. Here's a screenshot:

Once you click the "Contact info" link, you can then edit how to contact you. This is important as it allows connections to contact you. Click the pencil icon and edit these sections.

Here's a screenshot:

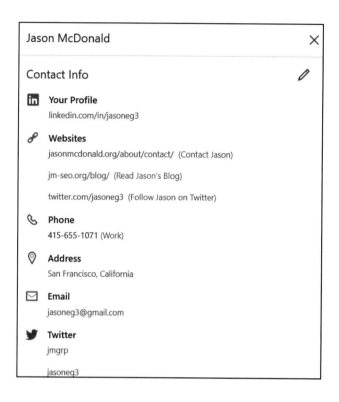

A tip here is if you select "Other" under websites, then you can write a custom caption. You can see that I've selected "Other" and then written "Contact Jason," which is a direct link to my blog's contact page. This then appears to potential contacts like this:

In this way, I make it easy for anyone to contact me via LinkedIn, even if they are not yet a connection. Note: I would not put my physical address on LinkedIn; there's really no purpose, and there are too many crazies on the Internet. You can (and should) enter your city if you're interested in local connections. But other than that, I recommend you fill out each section.

Next, optimize your public profile and URL. To do this, click out of "edit contact info" and back up. Then on the right side, find "Edit public profile and URL." Click on that. Then click on Edit URL to edit your public URL (visible to Google). Choose something short, sweet, and stable. You do not want to change this after you select a public URL.

Next, edit your visibility settings. Generally speaking, you want to be 100% public on LinkedIn, but people often configure their visibility settings incorrectly. Click *Me > View Profile,* and then on the far right, click "Edit public profile & URL" and scroll way to the very bottom until you see "Edit Visibility."

Here's a screenshot:

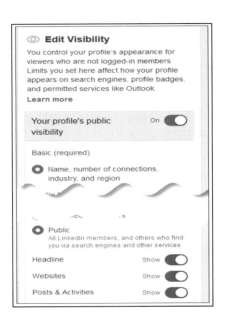

Mine is set to **Public**, meaning outsiders can see my information. I also have selected "show" for all the features. Generally, most of us want to be highly visible on LinkedIn, so I recommend setting ALL these elements to "show." An exception might be a very prestigious CEO or venture capitalist who only wants to be visible to their LinkedIn connections. But most customer-facing employees should be visible to everyone. Note, however, that only 1st degree connections can see your contact information, such as your email address or phone number, which is why under "contact info," I recommend you include links to your public blog, website, or contact page as well as your Twitter handle, as these are visible to all people on LinkedIn, regardless of their connection level.

Finally, if you scroll to the very bottom and click on "Public Profile Badge," LinkedIn will give you the HTML code so that you can put a direct link on your personal blog, company website, etc., to your LinkedIn profile. This is great for cross-fertilization and to establish yourself as a "helpful expert" on other venues. Here's a screenshot:

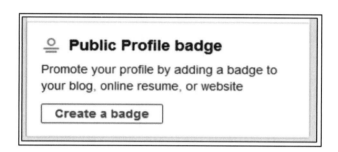

A word about privacy. For most of us, we want to be highly **visible** *(non-private)* on LinkedIn. We want potential customers, friends, and business associates to find us easily. Therefore, set your public profile as "visible to everyone" and check all of the boxes below. *If, for some reason, you do NOT want to be publicly visible on LinkedIn, then set the visibility and checkboxes accordingly.*

One of the more common mistakes people make is to think of their LinkedIn profile like their Facebook profile. Whereas on Facebook, you often want to be *invisible/private* to strangers; on LinkedIn you often want to be *visible/public* to strangers. Accordingly, setting your LinkedIn to *private* defeats the purposes of search and trust as part of your LinkedIn marketing.

For most people, therefore, I recommend that they set LinkedIn to fully *visible/public*.

GENERALLY, LINKEDIN IS *PUBLIC* PROFILE & *PUBLIC* COMPANY, WHILE FACEBOOK IS *PRIVATE* PROFILE & *PUBLIC* COMPANY

At that point, you're done with populating and optimizing your LinkedIn profile for **search** and **trust**. Congratulate yourself and your employee team: you've optimized your LinkedIn public resumes!

For your next **TO-DO**, download the **LinkedIn Profile Worksheet**. For the worksheet, go to **http://jmlinks.com/2023smm** (then enter the code '**2023smm**' to register your workbook), and click on the link to the "LinkedIn Profile Worksheet." You'll answer questions to help you set up and optimize your LinkedIn Profile.

Skills and Recommendations

While building out your profile, you'll notice that some people have many **skills** and **recommendations** on LinkedIn. Like references for a resume, these are generally all positive. Here's a screenshot of my skills:

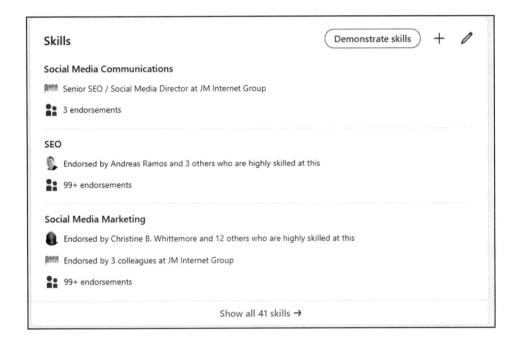

If you want to be endorsed for a new skill, click the "Plus" sign and add it. LinkedIn will prompt your connections to endorse you for this and all your skills, so over time, you'll build up a bunch of endorsements. To go one step further, check out the "Demonstrate skills" option. In certain technical areas, you can take a test, pass it, and then show a badge on your profile.

Next, take a look at **recommendations**. Here's a screenshot:

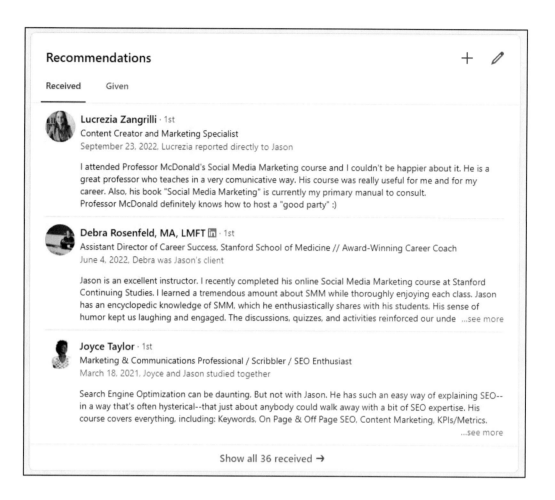

Note: you control whether recommendations show on your public profile; you can suppress any you do not like. In both cases, your LinkedIn connections are endorsing or recommending you, thus giving you social clout that you're an expert in a given area.

Solicit Recommendations and Endorsements

Your **TO-DO** here is to ask for recommendations and endorsements from friends, coworkers, and business colleagues. One of the best ways to get them is to do them for other people proactively. After completing a project with an outside vendor, for example, connect to that person on LinkedIn and write him or her a glowing recommendation and endorsement. Often, they will reciprocate. *(This is called "preemptive" recommendations in LinkedIn lingo.)* You can also click on the "Ask for a recommendation" and follow the prompts to ask a LinkedIn connection for a recommendation. And if you click the "pencil" icon, you can reorganize how your recommendations appear.

Regardless of how you solicit them, getting many positive recommendations and endorsements will make your LinkedIn profile shine.

» SCHMOOZING ON LINKEDIN: YOUR SOCIAL ROLODEX

Nearly everyone needs an optimized personal profile on LinkedIn, if for no other purpose than a job search. For those whose job is "client or customer-facing," meaning identifying, interacting, and schmoozing with potential clients, the primary purpose of LinkedIn is to *schmooze*. (Schmoozing, of course, is a wonderful Yiddish word for business networking: expanding your circle of business contacts, nurturing their respect for you, and keeping top of mind so that when they have a business opportunity, they think of you).

By nurturing your 1st level contacts and being active on LinkedIn, you can use LinkedIn as your online social rolodex, extending beyond just people you actually know to people you'd like to know for your business needs. Let's investigate schmoozing on LinkedIn, namely:

1st level contacts: these are people who have accepted your connection requests.

2nd level contacts: these are 1st level contacts of your 1st level contacts (*friends of friends*, as it were).

3rd level contacts: these are contacts of contacts of contacts.

LinkedIn Connections: What's Your Bacon Number?

Your "Bacon number" is a term coined to humorously point out that nearly everyone on the planet is connected to actor Kevin Bacon. Cher, for example, has a Bacon number of two because she and Jack Nicholson appeared in *The Witches of Eastwick*, and Jack Nicholson and Kevin Bacon appeared in *A Few Good Men*.

So Cher is a 1st level connection with Jack Nicholson and a 2nd level connection with Kevin Bacon. (*Which means that my Bacon Number is a four because my Mom knows Cher, Cher knows Jack Nicholson, and Jack Nicholson knows Kevin Bacon*).

How does the Bacon number concept relate to LinkedIn? LinkedIn uses the same system universally: you can *direct message* or *see the email* of your 1st level connections, and you can see through your 1st level connections to your 2nd level, for example:

Cher can message via LinkedIn or email Jack Nicholson directly. (1st level).

Cher can "see" that Jack Nicholson is connected to Kevin Bacon, and ask Jack to "introduce" her to Kevin, or at least mention that she "knows" Jack Nicholson (2nd level).

Unlike on Facebook, you can easily see your 2nd or 3rd level connections on LinkedIn. To see your 1st or 2nd level connections, just hit the search bar with a "blank search." Then select "People" and then 1st or 2nd to see your connections by level. In this way, I can see that I have 5,100 first level connections, and 1.6 million (!) 2nd level connections (connections of connections). To browse 3rd level connections, the easiest thing to do is to type a keyword into the search bar such as "accounting" or "WordPress," click search, then *People > 3rd+*. You can communicate with each level in different ways.

1st Level Connections

1st level connections are the best. You can directly message/find the email of anyone who is your 1st level connection. To do so, simply search on LinkedIn for the name of someone with whom you are already connected. Then:

> Click on the **blue** "Message" box. This sends them a message via LinkedIn, and in most cases, will also send them an email alert that they have a message waiting on LinkedIn.
>
> or –
>
> Click into an individual person and then click on the "**Contact info**" tab, and you can view their email address, phone number, and address.

Or, let's assume you're trying to find a connection that has a particular interest or skill. Rather than typing a person's name into the search box, type a keyword/keyphrase such as "WordPress," or "Joomla," or "Accountant for small business," and hit search. Across the top, click on "People." Next, filter by 1st, 2nd, or 3rd level connection plus additional keywords. Filter for 2nd level connections, for example.

Here's a screenshot:

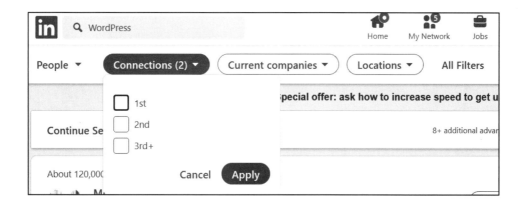

Check the box marked "1ˢᵗ," and then you can search your 1ˢᵗ level LinkedIn connections by keywords, as in this example for those 1ˢᵗ level connections I have who indicate "WordPress" in their profiles. LinkedIn also has more advanced filters, which you can get to by clicking the "All filters" button at the top right.

Essentially, you are able to use LinkedIn as a searchable rolodex of 1ˢᵗ level business contacts: define what type of person you want to contact (or prospect), search for them, and reach out directly. In this way, LinkedIn is like a huge virtual rolodex to organize and manage your business contacts.

HAVE A REASON OR "CARROT" TO CONNECT

Just as you would in the real world, remember that you need a reason to be contacting them, some type of "carrot" or "bait" to start a conversation. Perhaps your business has a new webinar or eBook, perhaps you're going to be at a real-world trade show and want to invite them to a wine and cheese event, perhaps you're going to be in their city and want to stop by and say hello. You need a reason why you're reaching out, and that reason shouldn't be a shameless just "buy your stuff" type of reason.

Working with 2ⁿᵈ Level Connections

While you can direct message (send emails or see the email addresses of) 1ˢᵗ level connections, this is not true of 2ⁿᵈ level connections (who are the 1ˢᵗ level connections of your 1ˢᵗ level connections). You can find 2ⁿᵈ level connections by the same process of search (either by name or by keyword). You can then view their profile and click the "connect" button to ask for a connection. For example, here's a screenshot of a 2ⁿᵈ level connection for me, Lynette Davis, who shows up via a search for "WordPress":

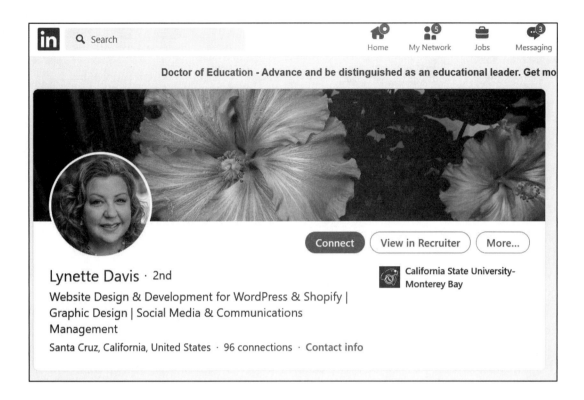

I can also see just below this my 1ˢᵗ level connections that know Lynette. So, if – for point of argument – I know John Doe, who knows Lynette, then I could reach out to John, first, and ask him if he is OK with me mentioning his name, and then I can message Lynette and mention I know John. To do that, I click on the blue "Connect" button and then the "Add a note" feature to send a custom message:

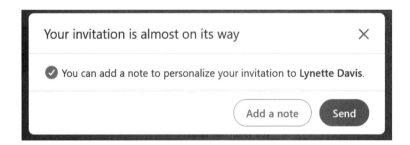

In this way, Lynette is more likely to accept my request to connect. Alternatively, of course, I could just mention that I met Lynette at a trade conference or have some other reason why we should connect. She'll also be able to see that we're connected through 1ˢᵗ level connections, so she's pretty likely to accept. Indeed, most people are on LinkedIn to network, so they're likely to accept connection requests if they seem professional and relevant. Just don't spam out connection requests, or you'll get banned from the platform.

Another technique to grow your connections is to:

1. Search LinkedIn by keyword, such as "marketing managers" or "WordPress designers" or "small business owners."

2. Identify 2nd level connections, and request connections based on some type of relevancy.

3. Be sure to have a "reason" or "carrot" for the connection, such as a shared interest, or perhaps a content "carrot," such as an upcoming webinar, new book, participation at a trade show, etc.

Note if you use this process, you'll be able to see 1st level connections in their entirety. For 2nd or 3rd level connections, you need to find the "Connect" button and have a "reason" that they should connect to you. Usually, it's a shared interest, a real-world relationship, or perhaps a "carrot" that makes connecting with you worthwhile such as a free webinar your company is having, a free eBook, a free consultation on something actually useful. Don't be too spammy, but you don't need to be too shy, either. Most people are eager to connect with relevant business connections on LinkedIn.

In some cases, you'll be required to know the email of the person with whom you want to connect; thus, always be on the lookout for the emails of potential clients. Many people list their email addresses on their business cards, so business cards retain a lot of usefulness.

Sometimes you will NOT see the "connect" option, so you have to try some non-LinkedIn method to get to this person. In this scenario, then, you can:

1. Upgrade your LinkedIn account to a paid account and use InMail to reach out to this person.

2. Click on their "contact info," and if they have a Twitter account, you can reach out via Twitter.

3. Take their name and some pertinent information, Google them, and reach out via their blog or website.

For example, here's a screenshot of a 3rd level person who has inputted his contact info:

In this way, I can start the relationship "off" of LinkedIn, and then once we know each other in some fashion, send a connection request which is more likely to be accepted. Most people are pretty open, however, and in my experience, generally, accept connection requests even if they are "out of the blue."

You can mix and match job titles and keywords. I often search for "professor" (a job title) and then "social media marketing" (a keyword phrase) to identify professors who may be teaching marketing courses and are interested in assigning my book. Then, I look for 1st, 2nd, and 3rd level connections. If we're not connected, then I send a custom message such as this:

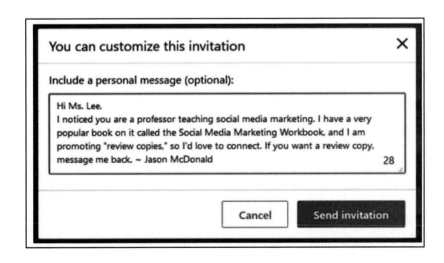

In your case, then you have these steps:

1. Identify by searching by keyword and/or job title, potential LinkedIn connections.

2. Click the "connect" button (if available).

3. Have a reason or "carrot" as to why they should connect to you for your personalized note.

Carrot and Outreach Marketing

As you build up your connections, you want to identify reasons why they would like to connect to you. "What's in it for them" is always the question to ask when reaching out on social media. I teach my students that this is "carrot and outreach marketing," essentially:

1. Brainstorm a "**carrot**" that will be enticing to your prospects. This might be a "free webinar" or a "real-world wine and cheese event." It might be an eBook. It might be a really substantive free consultation on a timely topic.

2. Have this carrot ready, as in have it ready to send in a response email or a feedback form on your website.

3. Research relevant prospects on LinkedIn via keywords.

4. Connect with them and include your "carrot" in your message.

5. When they respond with interest, send them your carrot, and begin a fruitful relationship with them.

Here's a typical LinkedIn scenario for 1st and 2nd level connections.

Let's suppose you are the sales manager for a company in the Proteomics industry. (*Proteomics is the large-scale study of proteins and is used heavily in industry to analyze organic materials*). You're going to "Proteomics World" in Boston, and you'll be introducing your new "Proteomics 2023 widget" product to the industry. You are planning on having one of those fun-filled wine and cheese parties, where your company will roll out the red carpet with free food and wine, and in exchange, attendees will be updated on your new "Proteomics 2023 widget." It's a business meeting with a little fun, a little free food and drink, and some salesy information about your new widget.

Your job is to get people to attend. You go to LinkedIn and search for:

Proteomics

Check: People

Check: 1st level

(You also select Locations > Greater Boston area, as the show is in Boston).

You then direct message all of these 1st level people and invite them to the wine and cheese event. Remember: social media is a *party*, not a *prison*, and in terms of content, you have something *fun* and *interesting*: your *wine and cheese event*.

Next, do your search by keyword, filter for 2nd level connections. Find a connection that interests you, and click on his or her name. When LinkedIn asks you for a custom note, explain that you'll be at Proteomics world in Boston, and you'd like to invite them to your wine and cheese event. They'll be likely to accept because it's relevant and sounds fun. You can do this as well for 3rd level connections.

Once your 2nd or 3rd levels accept your connection request, then they become 1st level connections, and you can directly message them via LinkedIn. Thus, the "circle of schmoozing" continues…

Alternatively, you can send what LinkedIn calls paid "InMail Messages" (see **http://jmlinks.com/3m**), but it's probably more effective to reach out for connections directly. After all, people trust people they know more than a "cold" call or a "cold" InMail / email.

> *It's not what you know (in business). It's who you know.*

The bottom line, therefore, is to use your 1st level connections to get to your 2nd levels, and the **TO-DO** for LinkedIn is to be expanding your 1st level network constantly, but how?

VIDEO. Watch a video tutorial on how to work with 1st and 2nd level connections on LinkedIn at **http://jmlinks.com/16s**.

Seek to Grow Your LinkedIn Connections

If having many connections is the name of the game on LinkedIn, how do you grow your connections? Here are some strategies:

Ask. Continually ask every business person you meet for their email, and then look them up on LinkedIn. Next, click the Connect button and then fill out the information as indicated (you'll need their email and then write a note as to how you met them). I recommend customizing your personal notes, such as "*Hi Sallie! You and I met at Proteomics world last week, and I'd like to connect with you on LinkedIn.*" If she accepts, she becomes a 1st level connection.

> **No Spamming**. Be respectful of LinkedIn's professional culture. Don't spam out contact requests willy-nilly. In fact, if you are overly aggressive, LinkedIn can ban your account for life due to spammy outreach.
>
> **Have a Reason or Carrot**. Have a reason why you're seeking a connection, especially something beneficial to the target. Don't have the attitude of "please connect with me because I want to sell you something." Rather have the attitude of "please connect with me because it's in YOUR interest Mr. Prospect, and here's why."
>
> **Lifetime Limit**. Be aware of the lifetime limit of 30,000 total connections and a weekly throttle of about 100 requests per week, designed to prevent connection spamming.

Reach out to People Who Viewed Your Profile. Over time, people will "check you out" on LinkedIn. LinkedIn monitors who viewed your profile. Even at the free account level, and even more with a premium account, you can see who looked at your profile and then reach out to them with a connection request, explaining, "Hey, I see you looked at my profile. Let's connect!" To see who viewed your profile, look to the far left under your picture and click on "Who viewed your profile." If you don't see it there, just visit **http://jmlinks.com/46d**.

Identify People and Ask for Connections. A few years ago, LinkedIn frowned on this strategy. But now, it's not difficult to reach out to total strangers. If you limit your outreach requests to ten or fifteen a day, and they are relevant, you shouldn't have any problems. First, identify a keyword search that identifies your customers (e.g., "small business"). Then reach out to 2nd or 3rd level connections. Add in an introductory note as for example, "I see we are both interested in small business, and I thought we should connect." Services such as LinkedIn Helper (**https://www.linkedhelper.com/**) can automate this process, but be careful as any automated or spammy outreach strategy is against LinkedIn's Terms of Service. Use at your own risk!

Get People to Ask You. Even better than asking people to connect to you is to get them to ask you. Ideas for this would be:

- **Real World to LinkedIn**. If you give a presentation at a trade show, ask attendees to connect with you on LinkedIn. Include LinkedIn on your business cards, and literally mention LinkedIn when you meet business associates in real life.

- **Your Website or Blog**. Place the LinkedIn icon on your website or blog, and encourage visitors to connect. (To generate a personalized LinkedIn badge, click on *Me > View Profile > Edit public profile & URL* and scroll to the very bottom).

- **Other Social Media**. Connect your LinkedIn to your Twitter, Facebook, blog, etc., and encourage people who already follow you on Twitter, for example, to connect with you on LinkedIn. If you have an email list, ask people to connect with you by emailing them.

Uploading Your Contacts. LinkedIn is happy to scour your email connections directly. To do this, click on *My Network*, and then on the left, find the icon that says, "Add personal contacts." If you also have the email address of potential connections, you can allow LinkedIn to look at your email contacts and then match you with potential connections.

To do this:

1. Click on "My Network."

2. On the left, click under "Add personal contacts" under "your connections."

3. It will then prompt you with icons for Gmail, Yahoo, Outlook etc., or you can upload an email address file (such as a customer list).

    i. You'll then get a visual prompt of potential connections, and you can check or uncheck the persons you want to send connections requests to. Again, be careful not to be spammy with this.

Be careful with this! In my experience, it can be very spammy and annoying as LinkedIn doesn't really give you many customization options. You can read the help file on importing email addresses into LinkedIn at **http://jmlinks.com/53h**.

The bottom line for you and your team is to do everything you can to encourage business contacts to connect with you on LinkedIn, because the more you grow your 1st level contacts, the more you can directly connect to them, and the more you can use them as introductions to their 1st level contacts, i.e., your 2nd level contacts. *Schmooze, schmooze, schmooze* to grow your LinkedIn network!

With Whom Should You Connect?

There are different strategies in terms of reaching out, or accepting, the connection requests of others on LinkedIn. There is no right answer. For someone who is customer-facing (e.g., sales), he or she should probably accept *every* inbound request. For someone who is a venture capitalist, he or she might accept requests only from people they really know. Another strategy is only to accept requests from people for whom you'd actually do a favor in real life. I generally accept everyone who wants to connect with me, and then if they start spamming me with messages, I disconnect from them. Typical connection strategies are thus:

- Connect with everyone who sends you a connection request, regardless of whether you know them or not. Then disconnect, if they spam you.

- Connect only with people you actually have met in real life or some capacity, as for example, people you've met at a trade show or know via a LinkedIn group.

- Connect only with people you actually know in real life, like coworkers, people at customer companies you've done projects with, etc.

- Connect very selectively, like only with people who are very close business connections. (A venture capitalist or CEO might use this strategy).

- Connect only with people who would help you move or connect only with people who will help you move bodies. I'm just kidding, of course, but you can be very selective if you "have the money" or "have the influence" and are more the recipient of requests than the sender. A famous venture capitalist with a bag of money, for example, can be very choosy. A newly hired sales guy at a tech firm, not so much.

There's no right or wrong answer.

Are Paid LinkedIn Accounts Worth It?

Unless you are an active recruiter, an active job seeker, or an outbound salesperson actively "cold calling" or prospecting, I do not generally recommend paid LinkedIn accounts. The main advantages of a paid LinkedIn account (of which there are several types) are:

- Enhanced cosmetics for your profile, such as a larger photo and the prestige of a "premium" account;

- Ability to turn on "LinkedIn Open Profile," which allows ANYONE to message you via LinkedIn regardless of whether they are 1st, 2nd, or 3rd level connections. To learn more, visit **http://jmlinks.com/53f**.

- Better positioning when applying for a job;

- Access to everyone who's viewed your profile in the last 90 days;

- Ability to see 3rd degree profiles;

- Additional search filters and the ability to filter and save search results (great for sales prospectors);

- Learning Resources via LinkedIn learning.

- Up to 15-30 InMails per month to directly contact anyone on LinkedIn, even if you are not connected; and/or (depending on the package you get)

- More detailed analytics.

To learn more about LinkedIn Premium, visit **https://premium.linkedin.com/**.

Your **To-do** here is to brainstorm a logical connection philosophy. If your purpose on LinkedIn is to use it for customer outreach and heavy schmoozing, then connecting with anyone or everyone makes sense. If your purpose is more passive or more secretive, perhaps just using LinkedIn as a public resume and/or keeping up-to-date on industry trends, then connecting only with real-world connections makes sense. Remember: once you accept a connection request, you become a 1st level connection, meaning that person can directly contact you via LinkedIn and email, as well as see your contact information. Similarly, he or she can see your 2nd level connections (unless you block that in settings). So, if you need to be more secretive, then be more judicious about with whom you connect. If not, not. There is no right or wrong connection strategy: just pre-think a strategy that makes sense for your marketing objectives.

And, remember, it's not just about "you," it's about "you" and "your team." LinkedIn is a team networking sport at the corporate or business level!

Brainstorming a Schmoozing Strategy

For your next **TO-DO**, download the **LinkedIn Schmoozing Worksheet**. For the worksheet, go to **http://jmlinks.com/2023smm** (then enter the code '**2023smm**' to register your workbook), and click on the link to the "LinkedIn Schmoozing Worksheet." You'll brainstorm your strategy for growing your LinkedIn connections. (Remember to do this with each and every customer-facing employee).

» BE ACTIVE ON LINKEDIN: POSTS, ARTICLES, AND VIDEO

In the real world of business, it's a truism of marketing that you need to "look active." People respect people who are involved and engaged and look down on people who seem to be doing nothing. Similarly, on LinkedIn, it is important to present at least the appearance of activity. By being active, you "look active" (a **trust** indicator), plus you have new ways to reach out to prospects and customers to stay top-of-mind and generate business inquiries.

Posting frequently – posts, articles, and video – as well as being active in LinkedIn groups, in short: a) makes you seem active (and therefore trustworthy), and b) gives you more opportunities to be top of mind among prospects, thereby increasing opportunities for connections and business engagements. Just as at a business networking event, be active and engaged in a serious way. Participation is important!

Remember: LinkedIn is a team sport, and only individuals can post to their own accounts. Getting employees to post and be active is yet another example of why getting all your customer-facing employees "on board" is a key element of LinkedIn success.

LinkedIn Content

You want to distinguish the possible pieces of content you can post to your profile on LinkedIn (we'll cover company Pages in a moment). These are:

> **Text**. As on Facebook, you can literally just log in to LinkedIn and share an idea or thought, such as, "It's Monday! And I am super psyched because Monday means the start of my work week!"

Photos. You can upload a photo with or without some text. Imagine taking a picture of your lead salesperson at your booth at the Consumer Electronics Show.

Videos. LinkedIn has gone "all in" on video and is favoring "native" video uploaded to the platform. You can also post a link and summary to a YouTube or Vimeo video.

Articles. LinkedIn has its own "native" or "internal" blogging platform. Thus, you can write a long-form article and leverage LinkedIn's algorithm to push it out to fellow travelers on the platform.

As on Facebook and other networks, you can (and should) include *#hashtags* in your post. LinkedIn has worked hard to increase the use of hashtags on the network, as it tries to be not just the place to search for jobs but the place for industry updates and continuing education.

Let's review LinkedIn Content one by one.

Texts and Photos

This is the easiest to understand. When you log in to LinkedIn, you'll see a box with "Start a post," and to the right of that, icons for a photo, a video, or a document (which allows you to upload a PDF, for instance.). Just start typing and share a thought. If you want to include an image, just click the image box/camera icon and upload a photo from your phone or desktop. Here's a screenshot:

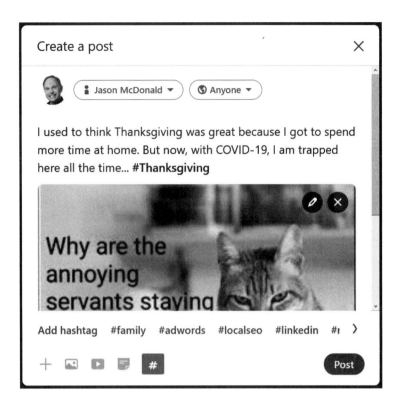

At the top, click on the downward icon under "Anyone," and LinkedIn gives you options such as to share to the public, to only people connected to you, and to public + Twitter (if you attached Twitter to your account). The hashtags then become clickable and discoverable across LinkedIn.

You can also include a **link** to an external resource (such as your blog, your book on Amazon, or a landing page on your website). LinkedIn will automatically shorten the URL for you, which is pretty neat. Once you make a post, you can then click to *Me > Post and Activities*, and you can get data on how many likes, comments, and shares your posts are getting. Here's a screenshot of a post by me with some data:

As you post text, links, videos, photos, memes, infographics, and the like, you can measure their success by scrolling through your timeline. Go to *Me > Profile > Activity > See All Activity* to see this data. This will show you all your recent posts. Then, you can drill into an individual post to see engagement. Here's a screenshot of a tongue-in-cheek post I did on using polls on LinkedIn:

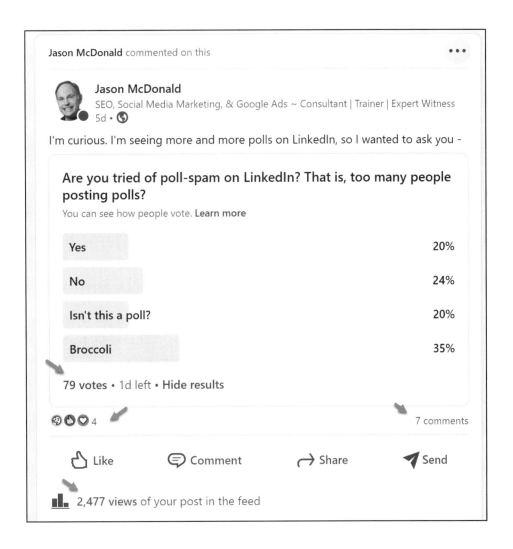

In terms of engagement, this post received 2,477 views, 79 votes, 4 likes, and 7 comments. Pretty good for an easy poll; notice how "Broccoli" came out the winner at 35%.

Thus you can measure your posts (and the posts of your employee team members) to see what type of content is being favored by the LinkedIn algorithm and getting the most engagement. Remember: just as on Facebook, if you share a *post* to your profile and I am a 1st level connection, then that *post* has a good chance of showing in my *news feed*. The news feed on LinkedIn is the first content that greets a person when he or she logs in. You're looking for likes, comments, and shares as metrics that indicate engagement.

Content is king, and queen, and jack on LinkedIn as on all social media. Turn back to your Content Marketing plan, and remember you'll need both other people's content and your own content to share on LinkedIn as *posts* or as *articles* to LinkedIn (more on articles in a moment). But first, here are some ideas of what you can share as *posts* to LinkedIn:

- **Blog Post Summaries**. To the extent that you have an active external blog and are posting items that fit with LinkedIn's professional focus, post headlines, short summaries, and links to your blog.

- **Quotes**. People love quotes, and taking memorable quotes (on business themes) and pasting them on graphics is a win/win.

- **Comments and Engagements on Industry Items**. Identify, comment, and share items that are relevant to your industry and especially to the interests of your target customers. Be that "helpful expert" on LinkedIn that people turn to for what's happening.

- **Infographics and Instructographics**. Factoids, how to articles, top ten lists, seven things you didn't know lists, especially ones that are fun yet useful, are excellent for LinkedIn. **Memes** are also great content.

- **Quizzes, Polls, and Response-provoking posts**. Ask a question, and get an answer or more. Great for encouraging interactivity, especially when the interaction is business-oriented. A great idea is to mention a project you are working on and ask for feedback before, during, or after.

Turn to the content marketing section of the *Marketing Almanac* for a list of tools that will help you find other people's content and create your own. I recommend Hootsuite (**https://www.hootsuite.com/**) to manage all your social postings across platforms. I recommend Feedly (**http://www.feedly.com/**) as a way to organize industry blogs and the content of other people so that you can be a useful sharer of third-party information on LinkedIn.

Articles

One opportunity not to be missed on LinkedIn in terms of posting is articles on LinkedIn. LinkedIn is aggressively trying to grow its role not only for job seekers but for the fully employed. (Check out LinkedIn learning at **https://www.linkedin.com/learning/**, and you can even apply to be an instructor at **http://jmlinks.com/46f**, which is a great way to showcase your talents as a "helpful expert" on LinkedIn.)

Let's return, however, to articles. *Articles* post to LinkedIn's internal blog, and anyone (including you) can easily post an *article*. Be sure to get the LinkedIn lingo: a *post* is when you share something external to LinkedIn, such as a link to a blog post on your company blog, whereas an *article* is when you write (and share) something to LinkedIn's *internal* blogging platform.

To get started, search for articles posted to LinkedIn that are relevant to your social media keywords and themes. LinkedIn, unfortunately, doesn't have a very good way to search for articles. So go to Google and type in:

site:linkedin.com/pulse {keyword}

as for example:

site:linkedin.com/pulse petroleum

You can also use the "Tools" menu on Google at the far right and filter for articles posted in the last year or month. To check out a sample search, visit **http://jmlinks.com/45z**.

In this way, you can find native articles to LinkedIn posted by persons in your industry. For example, here's a screenshot of an article entitled, "From Play Concept to Discovery: New Emerging Oil Plays in the Frontier Basin of Pakistan:"

You can see it got 164 likes and 11 comments. In this way, you can quickly research what articles others are posting natively to LinkedIn and what extent of engagement they are incurring.

You can also click on the author's name and even "follow" him, which is not the same as connecting. You can now "follow" people on LinkedIn in a public way, which is akin to following them on Twitter or on Medium (**https://medium.com/**), which are 100% public platforms. The difference between following and connecting is that in the former, you see their posts in your newsfeed, but they do not see yours; in the latter, both of you see each other's posts.

In this way, you can research what's being published on LinkedIn that's getting engagement in your industry, follow "competitive" people on LinkedIn, and stay competitive yourself.

As you brainstorm topics to write your own *articles* for LinkedIn, here are the steps:

1. **Identify a topic** that will interest your prospects and customers, such as an industry trend or a common "pain point" in your industry or, more generally, in business. Pay attention to trending topics that appear at the far right when you

log in to LinkedIn or search by keyword in your industry. The "trend is your friend," so to speak.

2. **Brainstorm and identify keywords** using tools like Google suggest, Ubersuggest, or Answer the Public. (See **http://jmlinks.com/smmdash** for these tools under the "keywords" section). Pay attention to what's trending on LinkedIn and which authors are getting engagement in your industry and why.

3. **Write a strong article with a great headline**, a catchy first paragraph, and some substantial content that will be useful to readers and position you as a "helpful expert."

4. **Tag your article with relevant tags and use hashtags** – these influence whether your article will show in their news feed and/or relevant searches.

Inside LinkedIn, articles live under the icon "Write an article." Here's a screenshot:

To write an article, just click on "Write an article" and start writing. LinkedIn is very keen to promote articles. The platform is trying to grow beyond job search to be more a site for "lifetime professional learning." Piggyback on this trend, and LinkedIn will promote your articles not only to your own connections but even to people you do not know. For this reason, articles on LinkedIn is a great promotion strategy!

For example, you can see a LinkedIn article by me on "United Breaks Noses: What United's Latest Really, Bad Day Teaches about Social Media Marketing" at **http://jmlinks.com/31h**. If you are the article owner, LinkedIn will also show you nifty metrics on who viewed the article and what types of people they were. Here's a screenshot:

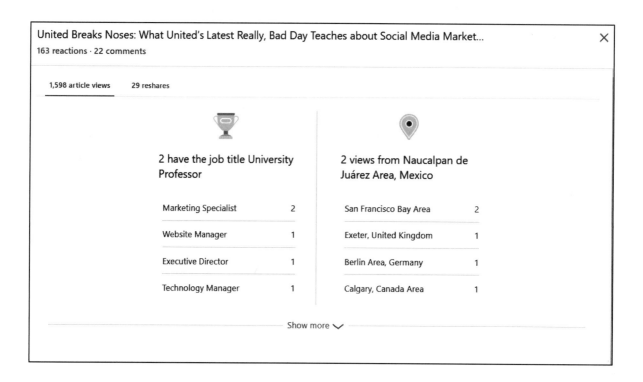

This means that it got 1,598 views, 22 comments, and 29 reshares – proof that if you hit a good trending topic, LinkedIn will promote your articles pretty wide and far.

Articles Reach Beyond Your Connections

LinkedIn articles also allow individuals with whom you are NOT 1st level connections on LinkedIn to "follow you." Even better, when you share your LinkedIn article on other social networks (e.g., Twitter, Facebook, Pinterest) and encourage people to cross over to LinkedIn, LinkedIn monitors this activity. If you get enough momentum, an article can "go viral" and really supercharge your LinkedIn connections.

LinkedIn's own marketing team is keen to promote articles, so if you've written something substantial, be sure to tweet your articles to LinkedIn Marketing at **https://twitter.com/LinkedInMktg**. In summary, mix posts to LinkedIn from your own blog, content from others, and native articles on your LinkedIn timeline.

Video

LinkedIn has gone all-in on video and now allows native video by both profiles and pages. In fact, rumor has it that their algorithm favors "native" video over posts that link to competitors YouTube, Vimeo, or Facebook.

It's not hard to post a video, either on the phone or by uploading it on your computer. The hard part is creating the video. Just as with any content, brainstorm:

- **Your target audience**. What do they want to watch and why?

- **The content itself**. For a video, storyboard, or at least outline what you're going to talk about in your video.

- **The technical aspects**. Fortunately, LinkedIn videos need not be technologically spectacular. It's more important that it be authentic and useful to your audience than slick and Hollywoodesque.

Many videos on LinkedIn are commentary on industry events; a common type is a person at an industry show sharing his or her perspective on "goings-on" at the show. To upload a video, just click on "video" on either the mobile app or desktop and upload. Note that the upload can be very slow, so do not close the browser window before it's uploaded. To view the help file about LinkedIn video, visit **http://jmlinks.com/46b**.

Tip: once you post a video to LinkedIn, find it in your feed and click the three dots top right and find the "share link:"

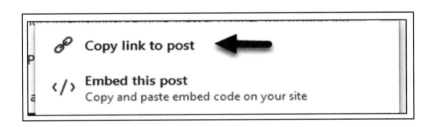

Copy that link and save it somewhere because once your feed ages, it can be very difficult to find your video posts. You can also embed the post on your website or blog as you do with a YouTube video. To see an example, check out this video from leading LinkedIn guru Viveka von Rosen at **http://jmlinks.com/46c**. As far as I know, there is no way to search for "native videos" on LinkedIn, but you can try to search content for "video" plus your keywords as in "video organic" and then browsing to see which video is native.

How frequently should you post?

Now that the LinkedIn news feed is very crowded (and the reality is that only a few people outside of job seekers and outbound marketers check their feed daily), you can safely share posts and/or articles quite frequently, even several times a day. But this differs with your audience, so pay attention to your shares by monitoring thumbs up and comments (*for LinkedIn posts*) and stats (*for articles*). Your goal is to be interesting, informative, useful, and friendly as trust indicators and hopefully get social spread among your LinkedIn connections, especially via articles. Note that you can see who responded to your posts, and this gives you an opportunity to connect with them. Finally, an *article* should be a more thoughtful, in-depth piece of content vs. a *post* to LinkedIn, which can be short and simple, as simple as just your thoughts on something trending in your industry or a short headline and link to an interesting article written by someone else.

Create a LinkedIn Content Marketing Plan

For your next **TO-DO**, download the **LinkedIn Posting Worksheet**. Sit down with your team and work together for a plan, as a company, and a plan, for each key employee. For the worksheet, go to **http://jmlinks.com/2023smm** (then enter the code '**2023smm**' to register your workbook), and click on the link to the "LinkedIn Posting Worksheet." You'll create a systematic plan for posts to LinkedIn, both your own content and the content of others.

As much as it is fun and easy to post, the reality of LinkedIn today is that outside of job seekers, not everybody checks LinkedIn on a daily or even weekly basis. So while frequently posting to LinkedIn is a good idea, recognize that LinkedIn does not have the sheer volume of Facebook in terms of active engagement. Keep that in mind when you measure the ROI of posting to LinkedIn.

> **VIDEO.** Watch a video tutorial on how to share posts and articles on LinkedIn at **http://jmlinks.com/16t**.

» BE ACTIVE ON LINKEDIN: CONNECTIONS, COMMENTS, AND GROUPS

Interactivity is where it's "at" on LinkedIn, so get your team to interact with their connections and followers on LinkedIn. Let's review some of the interactive opportunities on LinkedIn to stay top of mind with customers and prospects.

Connections and Comments

When you log in to LinkedIn, you'll see your news feed. LinkedIn prioritizes content by your connections, so you'll generally see content posted by connections first. This is a good opportunity to scan new content quickly and then like, comment, and share. Note that when you do, LinkedIn will notify the person who created this content. For example, here's a post by Christian Terry about Facebook memes, and he's asking for comments. When I wrote mine, this means that he'll get a notification as well as will people to whom I am connected. My interactivity pays off by helping me to stay top of mind with everyone I'm connected to on LinkedIn:

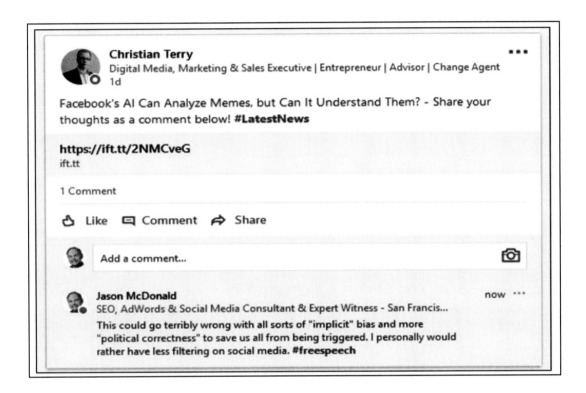

Note as well that when you comment on something, it shows in your "posts and activity," which you can get to by *LinkedIn > Me > Posts & activity*. Another good idea is when you log in to LinkedIn, look at the far right of the screen under "LinkedIn News" Here's a screenshot

:

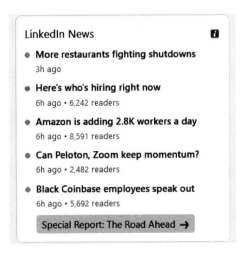

This means, for example, that 2,482 persons are engaging with the article entitled "Can Peloton, Zoom keep momentum?" You can then click on this trending article, see posts on it, and chime in with your own two cents. Using **interactive content** is a great way to schmooze yourself into the hearts and minds of other folks on LinkedIn. Here are your steps:

1. Research content on LinkedIn by looking at hashtags, trending topics, or doing keyword-focused searches for "content" in the top bar.

2. Peruse content on that theme that is of interest to you and your target customers.

3. Like, comment, or share the content of others. Note that when you comment on their content, they get a notification (!).

4. As people react to your comments, reach out to them with connection requests.

Leveraging **interactive content** is a fantastic way to increase your visibility on LinkedIn. As opposed to just viewing your news feed, go up to search, click on the blank search bar, and just click "content" at the bottom without typing anything in. Here's a screenshot:

This gives another view of content related to you that is different than the news feed. You can also enter a keyword such as "marketing" or "proteomics" and quickly scan content that is relevant to your industry. Using the pull-down menus, you can filter by date, by connection level, and by industry. Here's a screenshot for Content > Proteomics:

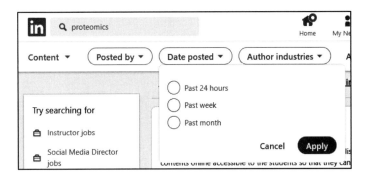

Scroll through it and comment on relevant articles by folks in your industry. For any person, you can hover by their name and see whether they are a 1st, 2nd, or 3rd level contact, as well as view shared connections. Here's a screenshot:

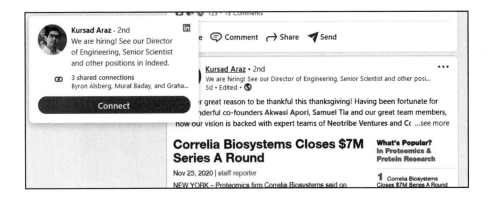

Notice how Kursad is a 2nd level contact, which means I can then comment on his post or article, get his attention, and possibly begin a relationship. I can also see 1st level connections that he and I share in common. Identifying and interacting with relevant contact by 2nd or 3rd level contacts is yet another great way to schmooze and grow your network on LinkedIn.

Search by Keyword for Content

You can also search LinkedIn for content by keyword. Just go back to the search bar and follow these steps:

1. Click on the search bar.

2. Type your keyword into the search bar.

3. Click "see all results" at the bottom.

4. Click "Content" in the gray at the top.

It's a little hard to do, so play around with it. Just be sure you are both entering a keyword and searching ONLY content. Then scroll down the results and find interesting content and people and like, comment, or share their posts or articles. This is a fantastic way to identify relevant content and people quickly and schmooze. Here's a screenshot for a search for "petroleum" content:

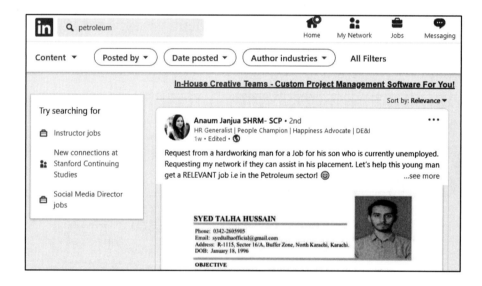

I can either add a comment, or I can reply to the comments of others. Again, each time I comment or reply, LinkedIn will notify the recipient, thus building buzz around me on LinkedIn and giving me opportunities to schmooze with more people. Obviously, do not spam people – be useful and engaging, so focus on content in which you actually have something useful to contribute!

Hashtags on LinkedIn

LinkedIn also features **hashtags**, which are "conversation themes" similar to Twitter. Look for their usage in content that matters to you. You can "follow" a hashtag which will then appear on the far left column when you are logged in. Then click "followed hashtags" to see a list of all the hashtags you are following. It's a little hard to get to, so use **http://jmlinks.com/54y** to get directly to it when logged in to LinkedIn. Then, you can bookmark this link or add it to your Start.me page. Finally, just as with a pro-active search, you can drill into a hashtag such as *#proteomics* or *#petroleum* and quickly find content by others to like, comment, and share, thus building your own visibility quickly and efficiently. For example, here's a screenshot of the hashtag #socialmedia, which has 19,784,951 followers (including me):

I can thus quickly scroll through content posted to this hashtag/theme and interact with others, such as Dr. Kakade, via likes, comments, and shares. This "**interactive content**" strategy is a real time-saver for your LinkedIn outreach.

Groups

With LinkedIn's growing emphasis on "professional learning," it should come as no surprise that LinkedIn has a growing ecosystem of groups on every topic imaginable. Compare LinkedIn groups to the "break out" sessions at your industry trade show: interested parties show up, listen to each other, participate in discussions, and showcase their questions (and answers) on professional topics. Oh, and occasionally, they use groups as yet another opportunity to **schmooze** *(surprise!)*. By participating tactfully in LinkedIn groups, you can grow your prestige (and that of your company). It's a soft sell environment, however. Anyone who is a member of a group that you are a member of is a good prospect to become a LinkedIn 1st level connection.

To find relevant groups, simply search LinkedIn by keyword, click on "See all results," then "More," and then "Groups." Groups can be standard, open, or closed, meaning for some groups, you have to ask to join, and for others, you just join up. By clicking "ask to join," you are requesting the group moderator to approve your membership.

Once you've joined a group, you may see posts from group members in your news feed, or you can click to groups by going to *My Network > Groups*. You can also visit **https://www.linkedin.com/groups/** as LinkedIn strangely makes it hard to find your groups. To learn more about LinkedIn groups, read the official help file at **http://jmlinks.com/31j**.

Group Promotion Strategy

LinkedIn is a serious social media platform, so please don't "spam" groups with self-serving "buy my stuff" messages. Instead, join relevant groups, pay attention to the ongoing discussions, and post informative and useful content. It's a soft sell environment. Let group members realize how smart and useful you are, and then reach out to you directly.

As you research (or join) groups, pay attention to the quality of the discussions. Some groups are fantastic: full of motivated, informed, honest people. Other groups are quite spammy, with everyone talking and few people listening. Just as at a professional trade show, be choosy with your time and efforts. Not all groups are created equally.

Your **TO-DO** for groups is simple:

- **Log on** to your LinkedIn account.

- **Search for relevant groups** by keyword.

- **Identify** interesting and useful **groups**, and join them (or apply to join if it's a closed group).

- **Monitor** and begin to **participate**.

- Diplomatically position yourself (and your company) as a **helpful expert**.

Join the Groups of Your Customers

Here's a pro tip. Don't just join groups that are relevant to your professional interests; join groups that interest your target *customers*. A WordPress web designer, for example, would join groups on WordPress to boost her professional skills but also join (and participate in) groups for small business owners, where she could contribute to the discussion and, in a very "soft sell" way, showcase her skills on WordPress.

Your to-do's here are thus:

1. Identify keywords *relevant to your customers* (i.e., pain points or desires that they have and might be joining LinkedIn groups to explore).

2. Identify LinkedIn groups that your customers are joining.

3. Join those groups yourself.

4. Participate in a useful way in these groups. Don't be spammy!

5. Interact with and connect with potential customers as you participate in these groups as a "helpful expert."

By joining groups *relevant to your customers* and being a "helpful expert" in those customer-facing groups, you can build your brand and leverages LinkedIn far more effectively than by joining groups *of your peers (and competitors)*.

» USE LINKEDIN COMPANY PAGES

Like Facebook, LinkedIn offers company Pages. And like Facebook, you must first have an individual profile to create (or manage) a company page. To view the official LinkedIn information on company pages, visit **http://jmlinks.com/3h**. The steps to start a business Page on LinkedIn are:

1. Sign in to your personal profile.

2. Click on Work at the far right, top, and then "Create a company page" at the bottom or just go to **http://jmlinks.com/3j**.

3. Add your company name and your email address, matching the company website domain.

4. Enter your company name.

5. Enter your designated Admins.

Now that you have created a company Page, it's time to optimize it. Log in, first, to your personal profile. Next, click on Me, and the pull-down arrow. Find your company on the list as indicated by *Company Page*. You can also just search for your company by name and click "Manage Page." Next, when you're on your Company Page, then click on the various "pencil" icons you'll see throughout. These allow you to update your background photo, company description, and specialties. Here's a screenshot:

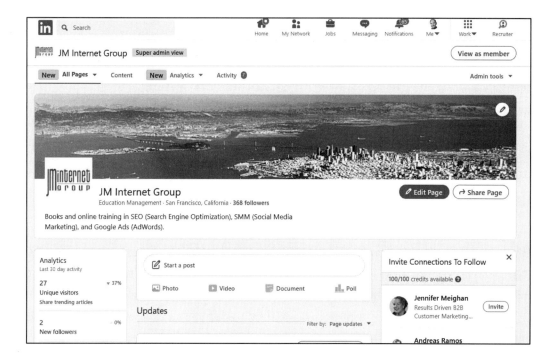

Click on the "pencil" at the far right to edit your Page, including your tabs. There's not much to a LinkedIn Company Page. You can only optimize:

- **Page Info**. Enter or adjust your company name accordingly.

- **Buttons**. Add specific buttons with links.

- **About**. Enter a keyword-heavy yet relevant description of your company. Explain your value proposition: what can you do for LinkedIn members?
    - **Description**. Describe what your company does; focus on what you do for customers.
    - **Other Items**. Enter your website URL, phone, industry, company size, company type, years founded, etc.

- o **Specialties**. Enter keywords that match what your company does.

- o **Hashtags**. Enter hashtags that match your business focus.

- o **Featured Groups**. Enter groups that match what your company does.

- **Designated Admins**. Located under *Admin Tools > Manage*, here, you can add or remove Admins. Any Admin has full `control of the page; so if you terminate an employee, remove them first!

- **Cover Photo**. Similar to the Facebook cover photo, you can change your LinkedIn (cover) image.

- **Company Logo**. Similar to the Facebook profile picture, you can change your LinkedIn Profile picture.

For a fee, you can add a "career" tab to your LinkedIn Company Page as well as a "Life" tab. These are useful really only if your company is using LinkedIn to recruit employees, not for marketing to customers. Learn more at **http://jmlinks.com/53j**.

The reality is that few people "search" LinkedIn to find companies. So the bread-and-butter of your company page is to post interesting items (both your own content and that of other people) to people who follow your page because, externally, they have already decided to follow you. For example, existing customers or people who find your blog interesting might "follow" your company on LinkedIn to stay updated.

For tips from LinkedIn on how to nurture effective company Pages, please visit **http://jmlinks.com/3k**.

Page Posting Strategy

Although most of the action on LinkedIn is at the profile-to-profile level, you can post via your company Page as well. Just as with a profile, the trick is to identify interesting, engaging content (both your own and that of others) to post to the Page. In reality, you can cross-post content on both employee profiles and the company page. For example, if the director of marketing writes an informative piece for LinkedIn articles, you can "cross-post" this to your LinkedIn company feed. Similarly, you can identify interesting industry-related articles on Feedly and share this content at both the profile and Page levels.

To share a *post*, just log in to your Company Page, and click on "Start a post" link. Just as with a personal profile, you can share either just text, text with a photo, video, or link to an external website or native video. Company Pages can now post articles on

LinkedIn, though I would still recommend that key persons (such as your CEO) post your articles since people, and not companies, actually write articles.

Essentially, you are trying to position your company as a "helpful expert" on a relevant topic, by posting:

- **Your own content** such as your company's blog posts, videos either on YouTube or native to LinkedIn, infographics / instructographics, reports, eBooks, industry studies that deal with industry issues in an informative way;

- **Other people's content** similar to the above. Remember to post the content of your own employees!

- **Self-promotional content** like announcements of free Webinars, eBooks, upcoming trade shows, new products, etc.

Note that your **posting rhythm** of *fun, fun, fun, fun, buy my stuff* on Facebook translates on LinkedIn to:

useful, useful, useful, useful, useful, useful, useful, attend our webinar, useful, useful, useful, useful, useful, useful, useful, download our free eBook, useful, useful, useful, useful, useful, useful, visit us at the trade show...

Get Employees to Post Your Content as Well as Your Company Page

And remember, LinkedIn marketing is a **team sport**: if you have a great blog post, video, or infographic, have it posted not only to your company LinkedIn page but have key employees share it as an update on their own LinkedIn profiles as well!

In other words, make 80% or more of your posts useful, and only 20% or less, shameless, self-promotional announcements. If you like, you can "pin" a company update to the top of your company Page. Simply find the update, and click the "three dots" and then "Pin to top."

Here are some examples of effective LinkedIn company pages:

- Thermo Fischer Scientific at **http://jmlinks.com/36k.**

- Intel Corporation at **http://jmlinks.com/36m.**

- Bayer at **http://jmlinks.com/53k**.

- Social Media Examiner **http://jmlinks.com/36p**.

To find companies to emulate, either search LinkedIn directly by keywords or use this Google trick. Go to **https://www.google.com/** and enter:

site:linkedin.com/company {keyword}

site:linkedin.com/company {company name}

as for example:

site:linkedin.com/company "organic food"

You'll find that LinkedIn is fast becoming a better home for more "serious" or even "boring" companies than Facebook; companies whose business value proposition is more *business-to-business* rather than *business-to-consumer* and whose customers engage when they are in their work / professional / business mode. Find and follow competitors and companies you admire on LinkedIn. You'll also find that the organic reach of business Pages on LinkedIn dwarfs that of business Pages on Facebook.

In sum, if your business is *business-to-business* such as professional services like Web design, accounting, business attorneys, computer services, SEO, social media marketing, marketing services... any business-to-business, professional service, then a company Page on LinkedIn can be a very effective marketing tool.

❯ PROMOTING YOUR LINKEDIN PROFILES, POSTS, AND PAGES

Once you and your employees have established their individual profiles, begun to share posts or articles, set up a company Page, and begun to populate it with posts on a regular basis, you've essentially "set up" your social media party on LinkedIn. Now it's time to send out the invitations. In and of itself, nothing on LinkedIn is truly self-promotional.

Remember: social media is a **party**. You must have yummy food and entertainment for people to show up and stick around. So as you promote your LinkedIn **content**, always keep front and center "what's in it for them" – what will they get by connecting with your employees on LinkedIn or following your company LinkedIn page?

Generally speaking, people on LinkedIn are looking for informative, educational, useful, and professional content relevant to their industry and job so that they can stay informed and educated. If on Facebook, the name of the game is *fun*, on LinkedIn, the name of the game is *useful*.

FACEBOOK IS ABOUT FUN; LINKEDIN IS ABOUT USEFUL

Assuming your employee Profile(s) and company Page(s) have lots of useful content, here are some common ways to promote your LinkedIn accounts:

- **Real World to Social.** Don't forget the real world! If you are a serious technology vendor of single board computers, and you're at the industry trade show, be sure that the folks manning the booth recommend to booth visitors that they "connect" with your employees and "follow" your business LinkedIn Page. *Why? Because they'll get insider tips, industry news, free eBooks, and webinars – stuff that will keep them abreast of the industry and better informed at their jobs.*

- **Cross-Promotion**. Link your website to your LinkedIn profiles and Page, your blog posts to your profiles and Page, your Twitter to your profiles and Page, etc. Notice how big brands like Intel (**http://www.intel.com/**) do this: one digital property promotes another digital property.

- **Content**. Don't think of content on LinkedIn as post it and forget about it. Rather think about content as a promotion strategy. Post interesting and engaging content, and then as people respond, respond back to them. Also, work on interactive content: search LinkedIn weekly or even daily for discussions going on about topics that matter to you and your business. Chime in with your two cents. Being interactive with content on LinkedIn is a promotion strategy as much as a content strategy.

- **Hashtags**. LinkedIn is increasingly promoting hashtags, so include relevant #hashtags in your posts. To find them, search the existing posts of others by keyword and look for the "#" symbol, guess at them (e.g., #organic). Once you follow a hashtag, you'll see it on the far left of your feed.

- **Email**. Email your customer list and ask them to "connect" with key employees and/or "follow" your Page. Again, you must have a reason why they'll do so:

what's in it for them? Have a contest, give away something for free, or otherwise motivate them to click from the email to your profiles or Page, and then connect.

- **LinkedIn Internal**. More at the profile level than on the Page level, participation on LinkedIn in an authentic way can grow one's follower base. LinkedIn articles are especially useful for this, as are LinkedIn groups. Internal promotion is not particularly strong on LinkedIn, but it should still be in the mix.

- **Use LinkedIn Plugins**. LinkedIn has numerous plugins that allow you to "embed" your LinkedIn content on your website and thereby nurture cross-promotion. To learn more about plugins, visit **http://jmlinks.com/31k**. In this way, your blog can promote your LinkedIn content, and your LinkedIn content can promote your blog. Similarly, your YouTube videos can promote your LinkedIn Page, and your LinkedIn posts and articles can promote your YouTube Videos and vice-versa.

- **Leverage your Customers**. People who already have connected with you and your company are your best promoters. Remember, it's *social* (!) media, and encouraging your customers to share your content is the name of the game. You want to leverage your connections as much as possible to share your content. On LinkedIn, it's all about being useful! Indeed, a timely article to LinkedIn can be picked up by key influencers, go viral, and exponentially increase your personal and company reach.

GET YOUR CUSTOMERS TO HELP PROMOTE YOUR LINKEDIN CONTENT

» ADVERTISE ON LINKEDIN

One of the best ways to promote your LinkedIn content is through **advertising**. LinkedIn offers highly focused targeting options for its ads. Here are the basic options:

Sponsored Content. On your LinkedIn company page, find a post. At the top of the post, click on the gray "Sponsor Now" button and follow the instructions. This is similar to "boosting" a post on Facebook.

Message Ads. LinkedIn allows you to send "Sponsored InMail," which is a type of email marketing. Yes, it's a bit spammy, but you can essentially use LinkedIn to send out targeted (unsolicited) emails to prospects.

Text Ads. These ads appear at the far right of the LinkedIn screen and in the app and are links to external websites. This is a great way to promote a business webinar, eBook, or some type of lead generation form.

Video Ads. With the migration to video, you can now advertise native video on LinkedIn.

Follower Ads. These are ads used to promote a Company Page and thus grow its follower base.

We'll discuss LinkedIn targeting in a moment, but let's look at these options not from the perspective of the format but rather from the perspective of your advertising objective:

Objective #1: Use LinkedIn to Promote Your Website. Like most social networks, LinkedIn makes it easy for you to set up an ad that goes FROM LinkedIn TO your website. An example might be setting up an ad on LinkedIn to promote a webinar on a new product. You'd set up a demographic target (such as people in the Proteomics industry), set up a "text ad" on LinkedIn, and then pay by click. LinkedIn would show your text-based ad to people who are in the Proteomics industry, and they'd click over to your website and register for your webinar. Ads appear at the top and top right on LinkedIn.

Objective #2: Use LinkedIn to Promote Your Posts and Company Page. Here, you're using LinkedIn advertising to grow the follower base of your Company Page and/or to boost the reach of posts by your Page. You'd set up a demographic target (such as people in the Proteomics industry), boost the post (or choose a Follower ad), and LinkedIn would promote the Post and/or your Page to persons who would see (and hopefully engage with) your content. Note: within a Post, click on the "Sponsor now" link at the top to "boost" a post (that is, advertise it).

Objective #3: Use LinkedIn to Generate Highly Targeted Leads. Here, your objective is a little spammy. LinkedIn will allow you to send "unsolicited InMails" to members via "Message ads." These ads can only be sent in the name of a *person* (not a *Page*), so you'd choose a person such as your CEO or Business Development Manager, and then follow the steps after "Lead Generation" in LinkedIn ads to send a "Message ad." These ads can be personalized to include the name of each person sent, company name, job title, and/or industry, and appear in their InMail InBox. An example would be sending a sponsored InMail from the CEO to invite an individual to attend a real-world event at Proteomics world or perhaps a targeted webinar online.

Message ads, in my experience, are the most effective form of advertising on LinkedIn. They're unique in the social media landscape in that they are essentially like unsolicited email advertising. Here's a screenshot of what it looks like inside LinkedIn when someone clicks on their messages:

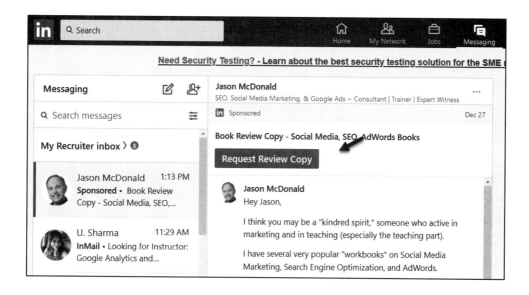

If you look closely, you'll see that it's marked "Sponsored" in the top left. You can turn "on" or "off" the clickable blue box in your ad. I have it turned on and formatted to say "Request review copy," as this "Message ad" is used to promote my books. This third option is thus a little like ads in Gmail, Google's free email platform. Be aware that because this is very much like unsolicited email, it is both highly effective and highly obnoxious. Use "Message ads" with discretion.

Visit LinkedIn's information center at **http://jmlinks.com/31m** to access more detailed official information on LinkedIn's advertising opportunities.

Demographic Targeting

As on Facebook, you can **demographically target people** on LinkedIn based on their interests. Whether you're promoting a Page post, advertising an offlink to your website, or using Message Ads, LinkedIn allows you to demographically target:

By **geography**. Target by country, state, city, or town.

By **followers**. Target only to people who already follow your Company Page or exclude your followers.

By **targeting criteria**. Target people specifically by:

> *Company name*
>
> *Company industry*
>
> *Company size*
>
> *Job title*
>
> *Job function*
>
> *Job seniority*
>
> *etc.*

In this way, you can take a piece of content and laser-target it to LinkedIn users based on who they are down to very specific attributes. The big challenge, however, is that aside from job seekers, many people do not frequently check their LinkedIn news feed. So, whereas Facebook reaches nearly everyone *frequently* (but they're in friends, family, fun mode), LinkedIn tends to reach people outside of job search only *sporadically* (when they're in business learn mode). Therefore, the *reach* of LinkedIn advertising is a bit of a challenge, and the cost per click can be pretty high as well.

Use Your Company Page and Employee Profiles in Tandem

LinkedIn does not currently allow you to directly promote individual profiles or the posts/articles of individuals via advertising. Only *Pages* (not *Profiles*) can advertise. How can you thus use your company, LinkedIn Page, to assist your employee posts and articles? Here's how:

1. Have the employee **post** to his or her **blog**; and/or

   o Have the employee create an **article** for LinkedIn.

   o Find the link to that article by clicking on the top right, three dots.

2. **Pay to advertise** this content via your Company Account by following the steps at LinkedIn Campaign Manager (**http://jmlinks.com/53g**).

In this way, you can use your company Page to grow the following of individual key employees as well as advertise their content for thought-leadership and brand purposes. You can thus use your Company Page to help promote your employee profiles and your employee profiles to help promote your Company Page. It's a team sport.

New for 2023: similar to Facebook, LinkedIn offers a "tracking pixel." Install the pixel on your website, and as with Facebook, you can integrate how you track users on LinkedIn and on your website, even defining custom audiences and sub audiences to better target your LinkedIn advertising. Learn more at **http://jmlinks.com/57j**.

» MEASURING YOUR RESULTS

LinkedIn offers more metrics at the company level than at the personal profile level.

LinkedIn Profiles

First, let's look at the profile level. Log in to LinkedIn. Then, on the far left, find "Who's viewed your profile" and click on it. Here's a screenshot:

This will show you data on who's viewed your profile. Depending on whether you have a free or premium account, you can see who's viewed your profile and then reach out to them with a connection request.

You can also see at the top left your follower count. Click on "Posts and Activities" and then on "Followers." Here's a screenshot:

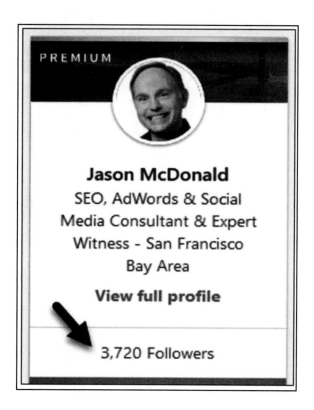

Right underneath that, click on "your followers," and you can see who's following you. You can then follow them back. To see your connections, go to *LinkedIn > Me > View Profile > Connections*. Here's a screenshot:

LinkedIn Posts

You can also see data at the post level. For example, here's a screenshot of a post with data:

You can see that this post had 132 views, 8 likes, and 1 comment, for example. You can also toggle between articles and posts at the top; just remember that an article is a post to LinkedIn's internal blog system. As with posts, you can see views, likes, comments, and shares.

If you post an article to LinkedIn, stats on its performance will also be visible. Go to *LinkedIn > Me > Posts and Activity > Articles* to see this data. There isn't yet a video tab, so you have to scroll through "All activity" to find any native videos you uploaded. For any piece of content, you can see likes, comments, and shares. Your objective is to figure out what your audience likes and give them more of it.

LinkedIn Pages

LinkedIn Page data is more robust. If you are logged in as the company, simply click on the "Analytics" tab, and LinkedIn provides lots of graphical data about your Page and its reach. Click on "Notifications," and you can see likes, comments, shares, and mentions in more detail.

In summary, LinkedIn lets you see how people interact with your Page and updates as well as those made by individual profiles.

»» CHECKLIST: LINKEDIN ACTION ITEMS

Test your knowledge of LinkedIn! Take the *LinkedIn marketing quiz* at **http://jmlinks.com/qzli**. Next, here are your LinkedIn **Action Items**:

❑ **Research** whether your customers (and competitors) are on LinkedIn. What are they doing? What interests them? Why?

    ❑ Identify a few **customer profiles** that match your *buyer personas* and determine how active they are.

    ❑ Identify **companies** to "reverse engineer" who are doing a good job on LinkedIn. Remember to look at the company employees' **profiles** as well as the company Page.

❑ **Optimize the LinkedIn Profiles** of key employees vs. target keywords; be sure that each Profile clearly explains the "value proposition" to a target customer.

❑ Strategize how to **grow the 1st level connections** of key employees, including recommendations and endorsements.

❑ Brainstorm **content ideas** that give you something enticing to "offer" to 1st and 2nd level connections (e.g., free eBooks, webinars, interesting articles to LinkedIn, wine and cheese events at industry trade shows, etc.).

> ❑ Begin sharing useful posts to LinkedIn aimed at your target customers.

> ❑ Begin occasionally posting useful articles to LinkedIn aimed at your target customers.

> ❑ If possible, consider doing "native video" on LinkedIn.

❑ Identify, join, and participate in **customer groups** on LinkedIn; do not spam!

❑ Set up a **LinkedIn Company Page** and begin posting useful content.

> ❑ Strategize how to grow/promote your Company Page, including **advertising,** to promote your Page content as well as the posts of key employees.

❑ Evaluate whether **LinkedIn advertising** such as boosted content or "Message ads" to targeted prospects might help your LinkedIn efforts for a decent ROI.

❑ **Measure** your **KPIs** on LinkedIn for both Profiles and Pages, such as the growth of your connections and the interactivity of your posts and articles.

Check out the **free tools**! Go to my *Social Media Marketing Dashboard > LinkedIn* for my favorite free tools on LinkedIn. Just visit **http://jmlinks.com/smmdash**.

»» DELIVERABLE: A LINKEDIN MARKETING PLAN

Now that we've come to the end of our chapter on LinkedIn, your **DELIVERABLE** has arrived. For your final **TO-DO**, download the **LinkedIn Marketing Plan Worksheet.** For the worksheet, go to **http://jmlinks.com/2023smm** (then enter the code '2023smm' to register your workbook), and click on the link to the "LinkedIn Marketing Plan Worksheet." You'll brainstorm your strategy for LinkedIn at both the employee (profile) and company (Page) level.

6
TWITTER

Do you Tweet? Should you? Twitter is among the most misunderstood of all social media platforms. On the one hand, it dominates the news and pop culture, giving Twitter a brand presence second only to Facebook and Instagram. *Katy Perry tweets. The Pope tweets. CBS News tweets.* And so the logic goes, *you better tweet, too.* On the other hand, Twitter is so full of noise, news, and craziness that it isn't necessarily a good marketing venue for many businesses. In fact, many businesses tweet, and no one is really listening, so Twitter becomes a complete zero in terms of return on investment.

Twitter can be an **effective marketing channel** for your business, or Twitter can be a **huge waste of time**. Which is it? Should you use Twitter, and if so, how? The answer, of course, is "it depends." It depends on whether your customers are on Twitter and whether you can systematically implement a Twitter marketing strategy. And with the recent acquisition of Twitter by Elon Musk, one can only wonder at the business and political implications faced by Twitter in this New World Order. It's in turmoil.

In this Chapter, you'll learn how Twitter works, how to figure out if Twitter is a good opportunity for your business, how to set up your Twitter account, and – most importantly – how to tweet effectively. Throughout, I will point you to free tools and resources for more information, as well as worksheets to guide you step-by-step. Even if you are already tweeting, you'll learn how to use Twitter for marketing as opposed to just pecking endlessly at 280 characters.

Let's get started!

TO-DO LIST:

» Explore How Twitter Works

» Inventory Likes and Dislikes on Twitter

» Create Twitter-friendly Content

» Tweet to Journalists, Bloggers, and Influencers

» Brainstorm and Execute a Tweeting Strategy

» Promote Your Twitter Account and Tweets

» Advertise on Twitter

» Measure your Results

»» Checklist: Twitter Action Items

»» Deliverable: A Twitter Marketing Plan

» EXPLORE HOW TWITTER WORKS

One easy way to understand Twitter is to think of it as a **microblogging** platform. Blogs are all about having inspiration for a blog post, composing a strong headline, and writing detailed paragraphs about the topic. Twitter is very similar, just a lot shorter - 280 characters, to be exact.

Let's compare writing a blog post and composing a tweet.

When you write a blog post, you a) conceptualize a **topic** (*one of interest to your target audience*), b) write a **headline** and the **blog post** itself, c) append an **image** or perhaps embed a **video** as an optional feature, and d) **promote** the post. Similarly, within the constraints of a 280-character tweet, you a) conceptualize a **topic** of interest to your (potential) followers, b) write a **headline/tweet** (they're basically one-and-the-same on Twitter), c) append an **image** or **video** as an optional element, and d) **promote** your tweet.

TWITTER IS MICROBLOGGING

One difference between Twitter and blogging is that a tweet often points *outward* to an in-depth blog post, a video, an infographic, or an image. A tweet can be just a "headline" pointing out the "rest of the story;" think of Twitter as a "headline" service pointing to your blog, offer on your e-commerce website, YouTube videos, etc. But, tweets can be self-standing as well. And tweets can be conversational as when one person responds to others, and whole groups of people tweet into a conversation.

As for content, tweets can be:

- **Just text.** Start typing a thought, idea, reaction, news announcement, or whatever up to 280 characters.

- **A photo or image.** You can upload a photo on your computer or via your phone and the Twitter app.

- **A video**. Twitter, like all the platforms, has gone gaga for video. Upload a short video of less than 2 minutes and 20 seconds. You can also "go live" with live video on Twitter.

Check out the official tutorial on how to use Twitter at **http://jmlinks.com/46h**.

Twitter is Like Facebook (and Instagram, LinkedIn, and Pinterest...)

Structurally speaking, Twitter also shares many similarities with other social media. Like Facebook, LinkedIn, Pinterest, and other social media, your Twitter account (a.k.a., "Page") can be "followed" ("liked") by others who are alerted in their news feeds when you tweet new items. In addition, tweets can be discovered through *#hashtags*, plus people can *retweet* (share) your tweets, respond to them, or favorite them, thereby drawing the attention of their followers to you.

In fact, as Twitter becomes more visual and Instagram becomes more textual, these two are on a "collision course," and the world may not be big enough for both of them!

The names may have changed, but the basic structure of Twitter works pretty much like that of other social media platforms:

- Individuals have *accounts* on Twitter ("Profiles" on Facebook).
    - Companies also have *accounts* on Twitter ("Pages" on Facebook).

- If an individual *follows* your account on Twitter ("likes" your Page on Facebook), then when your company tweets it will show up in the *news feed* of that individual (technically their Twitter *timeline*).

- Individuals can
    - *like* a tweet – "like" a post on Facebook;
    - *respond* to a tweet – "comment" on Facebook; and/or
    - *re-tweet* a tweet to their followers (reshare posts on Facebook).

- They can also create *lists* and *moments*, which are compendia of tweets.

The structure of Twitter is thus quite similar to that of Facebook; the big differences are that Twitter is shorter, faster, and noisier than Facebook. In addition, Twitter is dramatically more **conversational** than any other platform. Especially about politics, pop culture, and trending topics, folks go on Twitter to *converse* – many would say *argue* – about trending topics. Twitter is a rough-and-tumble 24 hour street **conversation**. Thus, for your content marketing strategy, you should focus not just on "your own content" but on "interactive" content – **conversations** you can have with prospects, customers, superfans, and "influencers" such as bloggers, journalists, or other superstars in your industry.

TWITTER IS A CONVERSATION!

What's Unique about Twitter?

Twitter is the most open of all social media. Anyone can set up a Twitter account in literally minutes and start tweeting – there's no required authentication. And anyone can listen in. There's no required friending or connecting as on Facebook or LinkedIn. Indeed, even people who do not follow you can easily find and read your tweets. They can even contact you without your pre-approval. Let me repeat these important Twitter facts:

Anyone can instantly set up a Twitter account and start tweeting: no authentication required;

Anyone can listen in to anyone on Twitter: no friending required; and

Anyone can converse with **anyone** via Twitter: it's completely open.

TWITTER IS OPEN

So anyone can talk on Twitter, a fact that, in combination with its focus on news and pop culture, may explain why Twitter is the most "no holds barred" of all the social media. Because it is so open, however, Twitter also offers unique marketing opportunities oriented on precisely this openness; you can tweet to journalists, the President (or not), the followers of your competitors, anyone and everyone – and everyone can listen in and discover new and engaging content. Twitter's openness gives it reach unrivaled by networks like Facebook or LinkedIn.

Lots of folks are tweeting and talking on Twitter (including bots, which are automated robots pretending to be people), but is *anyone really listening?* That's a different question, and the answer varies a great deal based on your industry, your status, and your skill at building an audience on Twitter. As with all social media, your first to-do is to investigate whether your target audience is on Twitter and, if so, how you can reach them as a marketer.

Twitter is Noisy, Really Noisy

Because of its openness and because of its focus on short, newsy content, Twitter is a blizzard of information with lots and lots of noise obfuscating the interesting stuff. Whereas Facebook is all about friends, family, and fun, "as if" you are at a company picnic or family reunion, Twitter is "as if" you were listening to all talk radio stations and all cable TV stations at the same time.

To get started, search for competitors and brands to emulate. On the desktop and on the app, just click on the "magnifying glass" and start a search. For instance, type in "organic" and then click over to people. Here's a screenshot:

In this way, you can find companies or brands on Twitter that focus on "organic." Then click into a company such as *@OrganicConsumer* and click the "follow" button to "follow" them.

Here's a power tip. Use Twitter's free tool, TweetDeck (**https://tweetdeck.twitter.com/**), enter a term to search, such as "organic food," and then click on the expansion icon at the top right. This opens up advanced search in TweetDeck, which allows you to filter by time, account, the prominence of the accounts, and even engagement. Here's a screenshot:

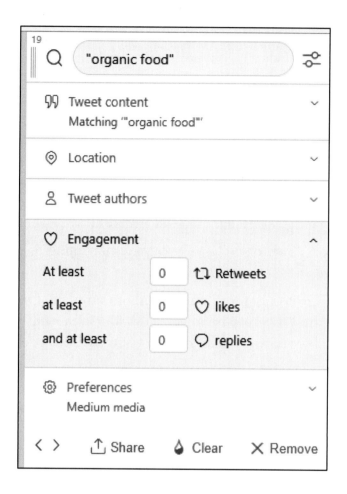

You can also browse Twitter for trends. On the app, click on the magnifying glass and then click "trending," "news," "sports," "fun," or "entertainment." The Twitter algorithm will give you the most popular, trending content by genre. On the desktop, click on the *#Explore* icon on the left, and then you'll see "For You," "News," "Sports," etc. Here's a screenshot:

Rather than paying attention to massive pop culture or news trends, I recommend you drill down by search. Look for persons to follow, companies or brands to emulate, influencers, superfans, and others who are focused on your industry. The trick is to drill down into the niches in your industry and realize that if all you see are the rather silly or outrageous headlines on Twitter, you're missing its opportunities. "Riches are in the niches" on Twitter, very much so.

Twitter's Culture

Twitter's culture is fast-paced and used primarily to share news (about everything) and/or to share gossip (about pop culture and politics). It's also rather rude and even full of cyberbullying. Inappropriate, mean-spirited comments are rife on Twitter. Twitter is where pop culture is discussed, Twitter is where politics is argued over, Twitter is the 24/7 news cycle on steroids, Twitter is full of crazy, fun, over-the-top, crude, and inappropriate hashtags and conversations. Twitter is ground zero for political correctness. Twitter is ground zero for AntiFa and the Alt Right. Twitter is home to insanity, but Twitter is also powerful because of its incredible reach into every nook and cranny of the culture.

Twitter is a complete, insane mess. Twitter makes you believe we are living in the end times. Twitter has been responsible for revolutions, and cat videos gone viral.

I love Twitter!

I hate Twitter!

In fact, Twitter is even home to *Twitter mobs*, which are crowds that attack people who are "beyond the pale," with "pale" being the other side of whatever the frenzied mob doesn't seem to like. See **http://jmlinks.com/46j**.

Is Twitter for You? Tuning In and Tuning Out

With all these pros and cons, the question becomes whether or not Twitter is for you, whether or not your customers are on Twitter, and – if so, whether you can use it to market to them. If, for example, your business lives in an industry that thrives on news, Twitter may be great for you. If, for example, your business is connected to politics, news, or pop culture, Twitter may be essential to your marketing efforts. If you are a nonprofit that advocates into the public square, Twitter is definitely a must. If you are a politician, you absolutely have to be on Twitter. If your business is about coupons, special deals, and foodie events, Twitter may be an amazing marketing opportunity. If you attend industry trade shows or want to reach specific journalists hungry for story ideas, Twitter can be your secret marketing weapon.

Throughout, keep your eye on how to *tune in* to the appropriate conversations on Twitter and *tune out* the blizzard of useless Twitter noise. Like talk radio or the 365 channels on cable TV, it's all about *tuning in* to an audience to succeed at Twitter marketing.

> *Tune in to Twitter conversations that matter to your business, and tune out of Twitter conversations that don't.*

While Twitter is not for the faint-hearted, with some skill and knowledge, you can "tune in" to relevant content and conversations for your brand and "tune out" of the over-the-top insanity that gives Twitter a bad name.

Sign up for Twitter

If you haven't already signed up for Twitter, simply go to **http://jmlinks.com/1h**. For complete information on setting up your business, go to **http://jmlinks.com/1i**.

The basics of setting up a business Twitter account are as follows:

- **Your Account / Your Username / Twitter Handle**. A username such as **@jmgrp** becomes your Twitter handle or URL (**https://twitter.com/jmgrp**) and shows up in your tweets. Choose a short username that reflects your brand identity. **Shorter names are better** because, although they no longer count in the character count, tweets are limited to 280 characters, and long usernames look somewhat stupid. As with most social media, you need an email address to sign up, or you can use a mobile phone number; unlike Facebook pages, you can only have one email address/password / user – or you can use third-party apps like Hootsuite (**http://www.hootsuite.com/**) or Tweetdeck (**https://tweetdeck.twitter.com/**) to let multiple people access your account.

- **Profile Photo**. This is essentially the same as a profile photo on Facebook. The recommended image size is 400x400 pixels. It shows on your Tweets when viewed in a follower's news feed.

- **Bio**. You have 160 characters to explain your company brand, products, and/or services. Be sure to include an http:// URL link to your company website. You can insert *#hashtags* and *@mentions* in your bio, and these are now clickable. Branded hashtags have thus come to Twitter bios just as on Instagram.

- **Header Image**. Similar to the Facebook cover photo, you get 1500x500 pixels to run as a banner across your account page.

- **Pinned Tweet**. You can "pin" a tweet to the top of your Twitter account so that it shows first when users click up to your Twitter page. For example, compose a tweet that promotes your email newsletter, and then "pin" this to the top of your Twitter account.

Here's a screenshot of how to "pin" a Tweet:

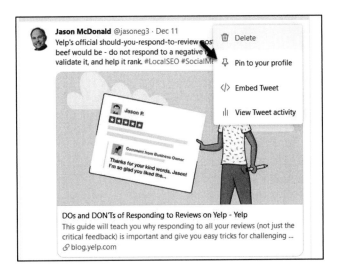

Essentially, find the tweet you want to pin, click on the downward arrow, and then click on "pin to your profile page."

To access any of the other settings and features, go to your page on Twitter (as for example, **http://twitter.com/jmgrp**), be sure you are logged in, click on the small profile picture at the top right, click "profile," and finally, click on the "edit profile" button in the far right of the screen. If you're logged in, you can also just go to **http://jmlinks.com/31v** or **https://twitter.com/settings/account** when logged in.

Not much can be customized, but in this day of Internet hacking and piracy, I recommend that you turn on **login verification**, which will require a mobile phone code for any new login.

Following and Followers

Now that you've set up your account, you can "follow" people or brands on Twitter by finding their Twitter accounts and clicking on the "follow" link. Similarly, people can follow you on Twitter by doing the same. No approval is necessary – just find people or accounts that interest you and click "follow." Twitter is like YouTube or Instagram (and not Facebook or LinkedIn) in that there is no real distinction between a "brand" and a "person" on Twitter. Everyone just has an account or handle, so it's @jasoneg3 (for me as a person) and @jmgrp (for the JM Internet Group as a brand), and they function the same.

As you are logged in to your account (either personal or business, it doesn't matter), start searching for and following persons and brands that interest you. Just remember that outsiders can see whom you follow, so if you're going to follow competitors, I'd follow them with your personal account, not your business account.

For example, to follow the outdoor retailer REI, you'd search for REI on Twitter to find their account or visit **https://twitter.com/REI** and click the blue "Follow" button. Here's a screenshot:

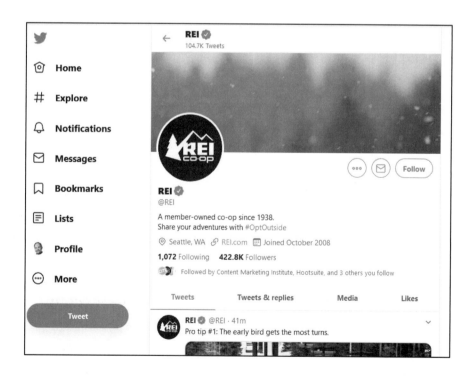

Note as well how after you click "follow," Twitter suggests other similar accounts such as @Patagonia. You can see that REI has 422.8K followers and is following 1,072 accounts. At the very top, you can see that they have made 104.7K tweets. The blue check indicates it is a Twitter-verified account (something necessary for big brands or famous people to preclude fraud).

The more followers an account has, the more powerful it is. The more people follow it, and the fewer people it follows, the more powerful it is. If you see an account that has about the same number of followers as it is following, then many of its relationships are "follow for follow," which is indicative of weakness.

Just as in High School, the most powerful people are followed by "everyone," while they tend only to follow other high-profile people. Here's a screenshot of Oprah's account on Twitter, showing she is followed by 42.7 million people yet follows only 309:

The same goes for anyone on Twitter. The more followers they have, the more important they are. The fewer people they follow, the more important they are. Pay attention as well to the content areas that they play in. Oprah is an expert on pop culture, for example, not on auto repair. REI is an expert on outdoor activities, not cooking, and so on and so forth. Look for "powerful" influencers or superfans in your industry as measured by what they tweet about and how many followers follow them. *#HighSchoolNeverEnded.*

Following Content Marketing on Twitter

In terms of content, Twitter works the same as Facebook or LinkedIn. When people follow you on Twitter, they see your tweets in their news feed (Twitter *timeline*) subject to the clutter of the rapidly-moving Twitter news feed and a secret algorithm in Twitter that attempts to prioritize interactive Tweets (e.g., similar to the Facebook *algorithm*).

Similarly, you can share the tweets of others (called *retweeting* or *RT*) to your own followers, and others can share your tweets to their followers. It's *social* media, after all.

As you're researching Twitter, look for a) accounts of competitors and/or b) accounts of people or brands to emulate. Here's a pro tip. You can create a "list" on Twitter by clicking on the "lists" tab to the left. Then name it by topic, such as "organic" for people in the organic industry, "outdoors" for companies like REI or Bass Pro Shops, or perhaps "competitors" for people that you compete against. You can make your list public or private. Then when you're logged into Twitter, you can click into your list to filter out all the noise and filter in just the accounts you've put into your list. To see an example, check out my list of movers and shakers in the SEO industry at **http://jmlinks.com/53m**. Here's a screenshot:

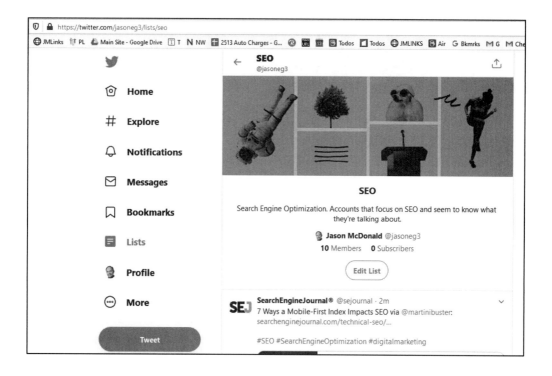

Understand a Tweet

Tweets are the heart and soul of Twitter and correspond to *posts* on Facebook. A tweet is limited to 280 characters. If you use an app like Hootsuite, that app will also give you a character count. Or you can use a service like **http://www.lettercount.com/** and pre-count your characters. As you compose a tweet, you can also string together more than one tweet in a thread. Here's a screenshot:

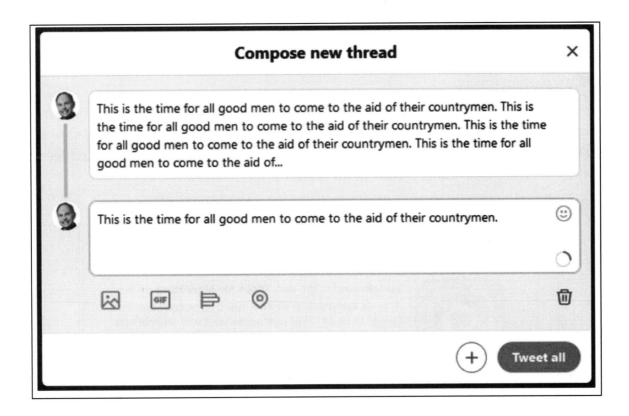

Think of a tweet as a news headline or a very short microblog post with just a little supporting information. If you tweet a link to a blog post or other Web page, use a URL shortener like **http://bitly.com/**, **http://tinyurl.com/**, or the "short link" feature in WordPress, so as not to waste characters. Twitter has a built-in shortener as well. You can create a self-standing tweet, or you can tweet "outlinks" to blog posts, videos, or images. You can tweet either on the phone, on your computer, or through a third-party app like Hootsuite.

Most tweets these days combine elements. They have text with a link to an external blog or video and then a photo or video underneath. Here's an example:

This tweet by *@terrywhalin* has a short "headline" plus a "mention" plus an outward bit.ly link plus an image.

Notice that if your tweet references an external URL and that URL has a featured image, Twitter will display the image from the website. For example, here's a screenshot of a tweet by me to a blog post I wrote about technical tips for Instagram marketing with the image and headline being pulled from my blog:

Thus, if you don't manually add an image to Twitter, it will pull the image from the blog post or website. As a marketer, this speaks to having coherent titles and featured images on any and all website content.

You can also post a "native" video to Twitter, and then the video itself becomes the image:

And on any tweet, you can see at the bottom replies (comments), retweets (shares), and likes. For instance, on the tweet above, you can see it had 5 comments, 21 retweets, and 29 likes.

The goal is obviously to get your fans to reply, retweet, and like your company's tweets!

If you click on a tweet (just click somewhere in the middle of the text), you can view the conversation going on around that tweet. For example, if you click on the tweet above, you'll be shown the comments and conversation around that tweet. Here's a screenshot:

Note that you're not in control of the conversation! Twitter is open, meaning fans, friends, haters, hecklers, and just plain crazies can chime in on any tweet.

Remember: it's *social* media, so be aware that anyone, anywhere, can tweet right back at you – in agreement, in disagreement, good, bad, ugly, or just plain crazy. More than any other social media, Twitter conversations can be rather rough and rather rude (*that's the downside*). More than any other platform, with the possible exceptions of YouTube, TikTok, and Instagram, however, Twitter allows people to discover new content that is not "in" their circle of friends (*that's the upside*).

And each reply can garner more replies, retweets, and likes. Twitter is the 24/7 social conversation going on around everything.

Understand Hashtags

A **hashtag** (#) in a tweet indicates a keyword or theme and is clickable in a tweet. Think of a hashtag as a keyword/subject / theme about which people are talking: *sports, the Oakland A's, global warming, the 2020 presidential campaign, the Academy Awards*. Hashtags should be short and can NOT include spaces. Anyone can create one, and the success, or failure, of a hashtag, is a function of whether many or just a few people use them. And, yes, because Twitter is totally open, there is no control: anyone can use them for any purpose, and a hashtag can overlap two discussions.

Nota Bene: *Anyone can create a hashtag! Anyone can chime in on a hashtag! No one controls a hashtag!*

How a hashtag is used, however, is a function of the crowd: the crowd decides what the hashtag really means.

To find existing hashtags, use **https://ritetag.com/** or simply search Twitter using the # hashtag in front of a topic such as *#organicfood* or *#free*. Note that hashtags can NOT include spaces. So it's *#organicfood*, not *#organic food*. Or just search Twitter by keyword and look for the # hashtag symbol. For example, here's a screenshot of a tweet with hashtags *#natural*, *#organic*, *#mommyandme*, and *#gifts*:

You can click on any one of these hashtags to discover more tweets and thus more hashtags. Hashtags, after all, are "conversations" around a topic and are clickable in a tweet to discover more tweets on that topic. To see the "conversation" on Twitter on *#organic*, visit **http://jmlinks.com/31p**. I recommend that you research, identify, and maintain a running list of *hashtags* that are important to your company.

#HASHTAGS DESIGNATE CONVERSATIONS ON TWITTER

In the tweet above, the hashtags *#organic* and *#natural* are "themes" around which people converse on Twitter. By including hashtags in your Tweets, you can be found by non-followers who are interested in and following that topic on Twitter. For example, if you are a seller of organic baby food and have a new flavor out, you might tweet with hashtags as follows:

Hey followers! Our super baby plum recipe is out. **#babyfood #organic #natural #food**. *http://bit.ly/1234*

These hashtags become clickable in a tweet, and for people who are interested in that topic, your tweet becomes part of an enormous conversation around that theme. So, finding popular, relevant hashtags and tweeting on them is a good promotion strategy on Twitter. Remember, however, that you have to stand out and get attention amidst all the noise!

VIDEO. Watch a video tutorial on how to use #hashtags on Twitter and Instagram for marketing purposes at **http://jmlinks.com/16u**.

Understand the @ Sign or Handle

The @ sign designates a Twitter account, often called a "handle" on Twitter. When included in a tweet, it does two things:

- It becomes **clickable**. Anyone who sees this tweet can click on the @handle and go up to that account to view the account and possibly follow that person on Twitter; and

- It **shows up in the news feed of that person** and **sends an email alert** to him or her that they have been mentioned. This is called a "mention." A *mention* means essentially that: someone has mentioned you (your Twitter account) in a Tweet. Nowadays, people also use the word "tag" to mean including the *@account* in a tweet or a post to Instagram, though technically, "tag" is more photo-centric.

Here's a screenshot:

Raw Halo (@*RawHaloUK*) has tweeted to its followers an announcement about a competition and, inside that, has included @*SoilAssociation*. Anyone seeing this tweet can click "up" to @*SoilAssociation*'s account, and @*SoilAssociation* would have received a "mention" notification in their account news feed.

In fact, anyone can tweet to anyone. Just search for the account, and then on the far left, click on the "Tweet" to button. For example, if I want to tweet to @*Peetscoffee*, the Bay Area's best coffee chain, I visit their account and then look for the "Tweet" button on the left:

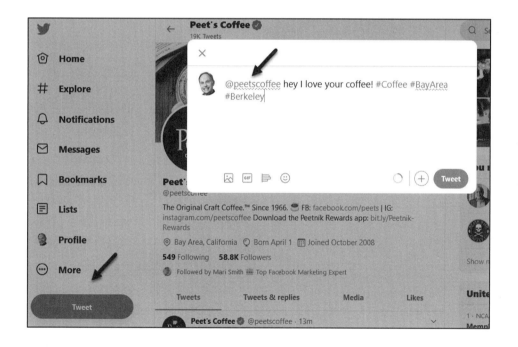

When I click on the "Tweet" link, Twitter then pre-populates my tweet, as indicated above. It begins with @*peetscoffee,* which is both a "mention" and a way to tweet "to" a person or account. Now here's the deal. Twitter is totally open; you can find anyone on it and tweet to anyone (except the very weird minority that has made their accounts private). When you include their handle as in @*peetscoffee* in your tweet, this "mention"

triggers an alert to them in their feed. This means that you can tweet to anyone on Twitter regardless of whether you follow them or they follow you. It's completely open.

USING THE @ SIGN,
YOU CAN TWEET TO ANYONE

Unlike Facebook or LinkedIn – you do not need "pre-approval" to converse with someone via Twitter. Again, when your Tweet contains the @*handle* of someone else, that generates an alert in their news feed and often via email. **Via Twitter, you can tweet to anyone!** (*More on this in a moment*).

> **VIDEO.** Watch a video tutorial on how to use the "@" sign or "handle" on Twitter for marketing purposes at **http://jmlinks.com/16y**.

Understand Mentions and Retweets

We've already explained a **mention**. When someone includes your @*handle* in their Tweet, that's called a *mention*: clickable by anyone following them to go "up" to your account and learn about you or your business.

A **retweet** is a special type of mention designated by "*RT*" on Twitter. In it, person *A* retweets the tweet of person *B*. Meaning, he takes your tweet and tweets it out to his followers. Imagine if Ellen DeGeneres recapped your joke on her TV show, or imagine if one of your vendor partners tweeted out your product or service announcement to their followers. To retweet a tweet, find a tweet that interests you and click on the two arrows at the bottom. You can then add your own message to the RT:

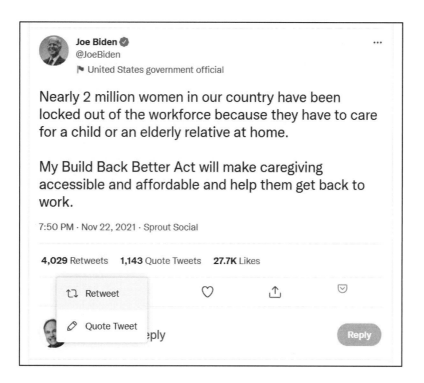

"Retweet" just instantly pushes it out via your account. "Quote tweet" means you want to add some commentary:

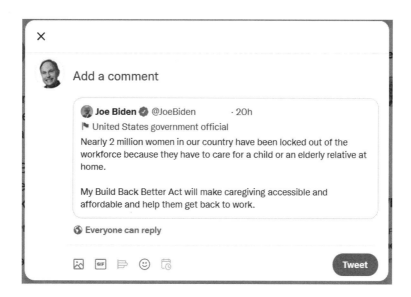

You can **retweet** tweets that interest you, and more importantly, your own followers can retweet your tweets to their followers, thus expanding your reach. Getting retweets should be a prime objective of your Twitter marketing. A mention or "retweet" of your tweets would spur followers of followers to learn about you and might result in a massive increase in your follower count. Retweets also show as "mentions" in the account of the person or brand that initially composed the tweet.

You can also, of course, **comment** on the tweets of others; they get notified that you've commented on their tweet, and this also tends to show in the newsfeed of people who follow you. Interactivity is essential for content marketing on Twitter, so follow, like, comment, and retweet the accounts of people in your industry, whether they be competitors, industry luminaries, or even customers.

Here's a screenshot of a retweet, designated in Twitter lingo by *RT*:

Robots-and-AIs @Robots_and_AIs · Sep 13
RT @Yale : Yale initiative that marries data science & neuroscience receives \\$8.5 million @NSF grant to "improve artificial intelligence and machine learning by drawing on lessons of the prodigious learning ability of the human br... bit.ly /2CPHVRX

@Robots_and_Ais is retweeting *@Yale* (Yale University), which tweeted about a data science and neuroscience grant, which includes a "mention" of *@NSF* (the National Science Foundation). In this way, the followers of *@Robots_and_Ais* learn about the tweet by *@Yale*. This is how information can spread from one account to another on Twitter.

You don't have to be a Hollywood star to do this: identify essential people in your industry and converse with them via the @sign (handles). Your followers can see this conversation, and their followers can see it too (if the person responds to you) – thereby cross-pollinating your accounts. (See technical details below).

Tweet (Privately) To Someone

Here are some esoterica about mentions or retweets. When you tweet directly to someone (by including their account (@ sign) <u>at the very beginning</u> of your tweet), that tweet is visible to **only** those folks who follow **both** accounts. If you put a dot "." before the @ sign, your tweet shows up in the news feed (officially called your "timeline" on Twitter, but not to be confused with the "timeline" of Facebook) of all of your followers, even if they do not follow the mentioned account. For example, if I tweet:

@katyperry love your music, give me free concert tickets!

(This tweet shows to ONLY those people who follow @jasoneg3 AND @katyperry) and it shows in Katy Perry's own timeline (if she actually checks it)).

vs.

.@katyperry loved your concert, give me free concert tickets!

(This tweet shows to ALL people who follow @jasoneg3, AND it shows in Katy Perry's own timeline (if she actually checks it)).

And, if Katy responded, then she and I would be having a public conversation viewable to her fans and to my fans. In other words, if I can provoke a person "more important" than me to engage in a public Twitter conversation, I have the opportunity to get her followers to follow me. (Unfortunately, Katy never responded).

Note: there has been some controversy about how all this works; I've tested it again and again and, despite what Twitter officially says and despite what the cognoscenti of the blogosphere say, the "old rules" seem to still apply. If you want your tweet to show in your feed to everyone, start it with a "dot." If you want it to be more private, start it with the @ sign. In both cases, realize that nothing is really private on Twitter. You can also DM (Direct Message) a person on Twitter, which is a step more private. However, **never** fall into the trap of thinking anything on the Internet is truly private. For both yourself and your brand, think of all your social media content (and emails, for that matter) as something that might ultimately come out to haunt you later. Be on your best behavior.

To read more about the "dot" in front of the "@" sign in more detail, visit **http://jmlinks.com/2k**. For the official Twitter guide to Twitter for Business, visit **https://business.twitter.com/,** and for the official Twitter help files, visit **https://support.twitter.com/**.

» INVENTORY OF LIKES & DISLIKES ON TWITTER

Now that you understand the basics of how Twitter works, it's time to research whether your customers are on Twitter and identify competitors in your industry who are on Twitter and/or successful businesses on Twitter to make an inventory of your likes and dislikes.

Find Accounts on Twitter

Stay signed into your Twitter account. There are several ways to find accounts to follow on Twitter:

- **Visit their Websites**. Most big brands will have a prominent link to Twitter, right on their Website. For example, go to **http://www.rei.com/** or **http://www.wholefoods.com/**, find the Twitter link, click on it, and hit follow. Go to your competitors' websites and do the same.

- **Search on Twitter**. While logged in to your account, go to the top right of the screen and in the "Search Twitter" box, enter the names of competitors, businesses you like, or keywords. To find stuff on Twitter about organic food, just type in "organic food" into the search box. Then, when you find an account you like, just click "follow," and you will now see its tweets in your news feed.

- **Advanced Search on Twitter**. You can find Twitter Advanced Search by first doing a search, then clicking on "Search filters" on the left, and then "Advanced Search" at the bottom. Or, just visit **http://jmlinks.com/46k**. You can also use TweetDeck (**https://tweetdeck.twitter.com/**), which has an even more sophisticated search interface.

Use Google to Find Twitter Accounts

Outside of Twitter, go to Google and type in *site:twitter.com* and your keywords. For example, on Google, type in *site:twitter.com "organic food"* and the trusty search engine will identify Twitter accounts with that keyword. Google is often a better way to find Twitter *accounts*, whereas Twitter search is a better way to browse individual *tweets*. Remember: there is no space between site: and twitter – it's *site:twitter.com* not *site: twitter.com*. An example would be on Google, *site:twitter.com "organic food"* to find tweets that contained "organic food" in them.

Once you follow companies, you can browse their Twitter pages easily by clicking on the "following" link at the top left of the page while you are logged in to your Twitter account. In this way, you can see who they follow. Here's a screenshot –

So if you click on "following," you can see the accounts and persons I follow. If you click on "follower," you can see who follows me. Now, think like a marketer. You can identify competitors, click on folks following them (a.k.a., their customers) and follow them, or even tweet to them. There are no secrets really on Twitter, including the customer lists of your competitors.

For example, I can be an up-and-coming organic grocer in Austin, Texas, and I can research and identify accounts on Twitter that are competitors to me, such as Farmhouse delivery (@*texasfarmhouse*). Then I can click on their followers and reach out to them. Here's a screenshot of the followers of @*texasfarmhouse*:

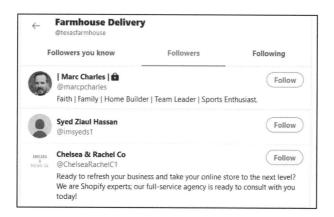

I can not only identify but also follow and tweet to their followers or customers. I can also review their tweets to see which ones have the most interaction, participate in those conversations, and even follow or tweet directly to those people who make comments. Indeed, I can even create Twitter ads that specifically target the followers of my competitors.

You can also easily find influencers on Twitter. Here's how:

- Use Google and other tools like LinkedIn or Buzzsumo.com to identify Twitter accounts of key influencers, competitors, journalists, etc.

- Search Twitter for "journalist" or "blogger" and your target keywords. Do the same on TweetDeck.

- Tweet "to" these key influencers with a free offer like your latest eBook or a free product sample.

- Look at who they follow (and tweet to those people).

- Look at who follows them (and tweet to those people).

Even if you aren't using Twitter to connect with your customers directly, you can use this "tweet to anyone" strategy in combination with Google and/or LinkedIn to literally communicate with anyone via Twitter! This feature of "Tweet to anyone" is unique to Twitter and is, in my opinion, the coolest feature for marketers.

Returning to company set up issues, your **TO-DO** here is to identify companies on Twitter, both in and outside of your industry, so that you can inventory what you like and dislike. Here are some inventory questions:

- **Username**. Usernames should be short yet convey the brand. Do you like/dislike the usernames of brands that you see?

- **Profile Picture**. As is true in all social media, the profile picture shows when viewed on someone else's timeline. Do you like/dislike the profile pictures of various companies on Twitter? Why or why not?

- **Header Photo**. Similar to the Facebook cover photo, this wide banner dominates the account visuals. How are competitors and other businesses using the header photo on Twitter?

- **Pinned Tweets**. Are any brands using the pinned tweet feature? If so, how?

- **Account Bio**. How are brands using their bio to market via Twitter? Do you see any opportunities or pitfalls here?

- **Following and Followers**. Whom are they following, and who follows them? What does this tell you about their effectiveness on Twitter? Are there opportunities to steal their followers? Why and how?

- **Lists**. Have they created lists? Are they on the lists of others? What does this tell you about bookmarking vis-à-vis this company and/or its themes?

Posting or Tweeting Strategy

You'll quickly realize that Twitter offers little customization and that most of the action on Twitter has to do with *posting strategy* or *tweeting strategy*. What are businesses tweeting, and why? What is their *tweeting rhythm*? Similar to all social media, the idea is to spur interactivity, get replies, retweets, and likes, and drive traffic to desired actions such as website visits or visits to your eCommerce store.

Pay attention to companies in your industry as well as hashtags (see below) in your industry, all the while asking the question: are our customers on Twitter? If so, what are they tweeting about? What are they interacting with, and why?

Let's review some accounts on Twitter and reverse-engineer their posting strategies. Do the same for businesses that you like and/or competitors in your industry.

Twitter Marketing: Common Uses

Here are common uses for Twitter and example accounts:

- **Celebrities**. Examples are Katy Perry (**https://twitter.com/katyperry**) , Justin Bieber (**https://twitter.com/justinbieber**), Ellen Degeneres (**https://twitter.com/TheEllenShow**).
  - o **Marketing Goals**: stay top of mind, get social shares, use Twitter to cross-promote their concerts and TV shows, **posting rhythm** of *fun, fun, fun, fun, buy my concert tickets,* etc.
- **Politicians**. Examples are Hillary Clinton (**https://twitter.com/hillaryclinton**), Bill de Blasio (**https://twitter.com/billdeblasio**).
  - o **Marketing Goals**: stay top of mind, get social shares, use Twitter to motivate followers to take political action. **Posting rhythm** of newsworthy, newsworthy, newsworthy, take political action or donate...
- **Political Causes and Non-Profits.** Examples are Greenpeace (**https://twitter.com/greenpeace**), Red Cross

(**https://twitter.com/redcross**), Catholic Charities (**https://twitter.com/ccharitiesusa**).

- o **Marketing Goals:** stay top of mind, get social shares, use Twitter followers to take political action or make donations. Posting rhythm is similar to politicians.

- **Brands.** Examples are REI (**https://twitter.com/rei**), Gucci (**https://twitter.com/gucci**), Martha Stewart Living (**https://twitter.com/marthaliving**).

  - o **Marketing Goals:** stay top of mind, get social shares, use Twitter followers to connect to buy actions, also use Twitter as an "insider" or "best customer" channel for secret coupons, inside deals and information. **Posting rhythm** is fun, fun, fun, fun, buy my stuff.

- **Restaurants and Food Trucks.** Examples are Kogi BBQ (**https://twitter.com/kogibbq**), Ricky's Fish Tacos (**https://twitter.com/rickysfishtacos**), Newark Natural Foods (**https://twitter.com/newarkfoods**).

  - o **Marketing Goals.** stay top of mind, get social shares, use Twitter to drive real-world traffic to a store or restaurant, usually looking for insider information or special deals/coupons.

For most for-profit businesses, common marketing goals for Twitter are:

- **Stay top of mind / one touch to many.** To the extent that your users are on Twitter (usually to follow up-to-the-minute news), you can use Twitter to continually remind users about your company, product, and/or service.

- **Insider / loyalty programs**. If you are a brand with a core group of loyal customers (e.g., REI's loyal group of outdoor fanatics or Gucci's loyal group of fashion addicts), you can use Twitter to stay in touch with this elite group and reward them with insider information, tips, special deals, and even coupons.

- **Coupons / bargains**. If you use coupons or discounts, especially in retail, customers commonly scan Twitter for coupons and special deals.

- **Foodies / coupons / bargains / what's cookin'.** Especially in the food truck industry, but in any big downtown area with a lunch scene, foodies look to Twitter to identify special deals, coupons, and what's cookin'.

- **Discussions on Timely Topics.** By using #hashtags (e.g., *#AIDS, #globalwarming, #obamacare*), you can participate in an ongoing global discussion and thereby market your products. A special case of this is trade shows, which often use a hashtag (*#CES* for Consumer Electronics Show, for example) to allow participants to converse via Twitter.

- **Branded Conversations.** People who "love" a brand often discuss it in detail on Twitter, especially via a branded hashtag. An example would be *#Gucci* for the fashion brand or *#REI* for the outdoor brand. You can either listen in on competitor brand conversations and/or create your own.

- **News Alerts.** To the extent that you generate and/or participate in news, Twitter is the go-to service for breaking news (especially vis hashtags and trending searches).

- **Political Action.** For non-profits and political groups, Twitter is the go-to place to organize politically and discuss politics. If you or your organization is into politics, you gotta be on Twitter!

- **Twitter Chats.** You can have a public chat on Twitter, usually using a custom hashtag. In this way, you can engage and interact with your super fans. See SproutSocial's guide to Twitter chats at **http://jmlinks.com/31q**.

IDENTIFY COMPANIES THAT DO TWITTER WELL AND REVERSE ENGINEER THEM

For your next **TO-DO**, download the **Twitter Research Worksheet**. For the worksheet, go to **http://jmlinks.com/2023smm** (then enter the code '**2023smm**' to register your workbook), and click on the link to the "Twitter Research Worksheet." You'll answer questions as to whether your potential customers are on Twitter, identify brands to follow, and inventory what you like and dislike about their Twitter setup and marketing strategy.

» CREATE TWITTER-FRIENDLY CONTENT

Content is king on Twitter, just as it is on all social media. We've already covered the basics, but let's review them:

- Each tweet is limited to **280 characters**, though you can string tweets together.

- **Hashtags**, designated by the # symbol as in *#organic* or *#organicfood* designate conversational themes and are clickable in tweets.

- The **"@" sign** designates a handle and is clickable in a tweet; even when you are not following or followed by a person, using their handle (as for example *@jasoneg3*) is a "mention" and generates an alert to that person.

- **Followers** can view, like, comment on, and share or retweet content on Twitter.

No one is in control of anything on Twitter, and the pace is very fast. In terms of content, you can:

- Tweet just **text**.

- Tweet **text** with **@ signs and #hashtags** to reach out to persons and/or conversational themes.

- Tweet text and **images / photos**.

- Tweet **links** to external websites like blogs.

- Tweet **short-form video** that is "native" on Twitter.

In terms of actual content, you want to tweet things that are of interest to your customers. If you're a brand, you want to tweet news announcements, new products or services, links to new blog posts or YouTube videos, etc. You also want to tweet and comment on industry news.

TWEET INTERESTING STUFF #DUH #DONTBEBORING

Take a look at a big brand account like REI (*@REI*) and "reverse engineer" their content strategy. You'll see: a) tweets about the outdoors, b) tweets with links to their blogs and YouTube videos, c) contests or challenges, d) special deals or coupons as well as "insider" alerts on new products, e) new product alerts, and f) surveys. Compare that with an author or public figure such as the author *@StephenKing*, who tweets out a lot of social commentaries as well as interesting stuff relating to his novels. (*Whether his political or social commentary helps or hurts his brand is a question for his marketing team*). Or take a look at *@kogibbq*, the Korean / Mexican fusion barbeque chain in Los Angeles. They tweet 80% the location of their trucks in LA, and 20% is fun photos, what's cooking, and some interaction with their fans.

Each account is filling a content marketing pipeline with tweets that are relevant to its brand and alternate on a continuum between commentary on industry events or news up to in-your-face, "buy my stuff" content. As with all social media content, it should be 80% or more, *fun fun fun fun fun fun fun fun* and 20% or less *buy my stuff buy my stuff buy my stuff*.

Twitter Content is What You Make of It

Twitter content, in short, is what you make of it. It's the kind of content that is engaging to your fans and can be as simple as a coupon code, as complex as a link to a blog post on climate change, or as silly as your response to *#mondaymadness*.

Do not miss the importance of **interactive** content on Twitter. Twitter is conversational. For example, here's a screenshot of some of the conversation around just one of REI's tweets on the national parks:

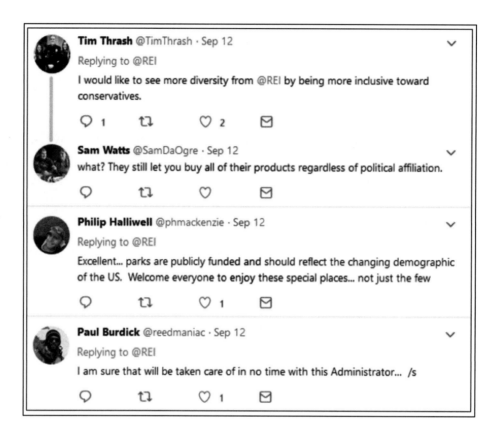

REI does a great job with content, but where is the brand participation here? What is the brand's reaction? Sometimes it's as if the brand, public persona, or other person is conspicuous by their absence in interactive content on Twitter. That's a mistake.

Interacting with your fans and others is a key content opportunity on Twitter. So join in the conversation as a brand!

Your to-dos with respect to Twitter content are to identify:

- **hashtags** or topics that you want your brand's message to be part of the conversation;

- **text, images, photo**s, and even **videos** that you can post natively to Twitter on these themes;

- **external links** to your blog or website with summaries posted to Twitter;

- **interactive conversations** between your brand and customers that are relevant and positive for your brand; and,

- an awareness of and readiness for **pushback** from customers and hecklers, as no one is in control of Twitter.

Always look at the problem from the perspective of your target customers. Why will they want to follow you on Twitter? What will they get out of your content? What's in it for them? Is it as simple as a coupon or special deal? Is it participation in an insider or superfan event? Is it a sense of belonging to a "cool club?" Is it a conversation with you and others on Twitter about the news of the day?

The *why* is as important as the *what* when it comes to a Twitter content marketing plan.

Think Before You Tweet

On a cautionary note, make your team aware that Twitter (and the Internet) is like an elephant. *It never forgets.* Because Twitter is so immediate, people often shoot off their mouths or their tweets without thinking worse than they do on any other social media platform. As the Russians say:

"A word is not a bird; once it flies out, you can't get it back."

If you don't have something nice to say (even on Twitter), it's probably better not to say it at all. Stay positive, and stay classy. If you're a big brand, have a policy that more than one person needs to look at and approve each and every tweet before it goes out. It's easy to click and tweet, and it's very, very hard to call back a tweet you wish you hadn't sent in the first place.

Just ask the TV star Roseanne (@*therealroseanne*), whose racist tweet ended up getting her TV show canceled in May 2018 after a firestorm of social media outrage (See: **http://jmlinks.com/46m**). One has to wonder where her sanity was and where her marketing team was *before* she tweeted. If you have a hot-blooded CEO or executive, ask yourself this question *before* an inappropriate tweet causes a social media train wreck for your brand. It's a truism that day-in and day-out celebrities and brands have to "apologize" for their latest stupid tweet. Pro tip: **think before you tweet!**

❯ TWEET TO JOURNALISTS, BLOGGERS, AND INFLUENCERS

One of the uniquely valuable uses of Twitter is a "deep dive" into using this ability to tweet to anyone. Using Twitter's openness, you can identify journalists, bloggers, or other influencers in your industry and tweet to them. They don't have to pre-approve or "like" you. Twitter is 110% open.

In fact, because Twitter is where news breaks first, it is probably the favorite social media channel of journalists. Thus, since journalists and bloggers actively monitor Twitter for news, they are "hungry" for you to "pitch" them story ideas.

Journalists and bloggers love Twitter, so tweet your news directly @ them.

Let's say, for example, that I want to send a free review copy of my *Social Media Marketing Workbook* to journalists and bloggers who write on small business. First, I'd go to Twitter and identify journalists and bloggers through Twitter and Google searches (*site:twitter.com*) for keywords like *small business journalist*, or *small business blogger*. Then, I'd go to each Twitter account, click on the "Tweet to" icon located just below their profile picture, and copy/paste the following message:

> *Hey! I see you write on #smallbusiness. Are you interested in a free review copy of my Social Media Marketing Workbook 2022?*

Here's a screenshot of my tweet to journalist Kai Ryssdal (@kairyssdal) for the 2022 edition of my SEO Workbook:

A response from Mr. Ryssdal would show in my "notifications" tab. Remember that when you start a tweet with the @sign at the very beginning of a Tweet, your tweet is generally *not* broadcast to your own followers (though it is still public and discoverable). If, instead, you put a period "." in front of the @handle, then it is visible.

In this way, you can use Twitter to send "unsolicited tweets" to journalists and bloggers without annoying your own followers. It's not unlike the way you use LinkedIn to reach out to 1st and 2nd level contacts.

Using LinkedIn and Twitter in Combination

Indeed, you can even use LinkedIn in combination with Twitter. First, search LinkedIn by keywords, click on *People*, and then browse any level (1st, 2nd, or 3rd), click into a person in the search results, and then click on *See contact info* to find their Twitter account (if they inputted it to LinkedIn). Here's a screenshot of Kai Ryssdal on LinkedIn (with whom I am NOT connected), showing that you can use LinkedIn to "find him," click on contact info to find his Twitter account, and then use Twitter to tweet to him.

In this way, you can combine the power of LinkedIn's social rolodex to identify journalists, bloggers, and influencers, and the openness of Twitter to reach out to them via "unsolicited" tweets. Here are the steps:

1. Research journalists, bloggers, and other influencers in your industry via Twitter and LinkedIn.

2. Have a "carrot" ready such as a free eBook, webinar, wine-and-cheese event at an industry trade show, etc.

3. Tweet to them a solicitation essentially saying, "*@journalist* Hey I see that you are a journalist / blogger / influencer interested in {*keyword*} and I have this {*carrot*}. Are you interested?"

As is always true on social media, however, don't be spammy. Have a legitimate and interesting reason why you are reaching out to them and be respectful. If they do not show interest, move on to the next target.

» BRAINSTORM AND EXECUTE A TWEETING STRATEGY

Optimizing your account on Twitter is pretty straightforward. As indicated above, a good way to do this is to compare / contrast pages that you like and use your inventory list to identify to-dos. Next, the real work begins. *What will you tweet? Who will care?* Let's reverse engineer some companies and their **tweeting strategies**:

> **Kogi BBQ (https://twitter.com/kogibbq).** Their tweeting strategy is 90% about the location of the taco truck, with a few tweets about "what's cooking" or "insider specials," and the occasional back-and-forth with a hard-core Kogi fan about the joys of Korean BBQ. That's it.
>
> **REI (https://twitter.com/rei).** Their tweets are largely off-loads to blog posts, YouTube videos, and Instagram photos about the fun of outdoor activities, some participatory contests for hard-core REI fans, headline links to in-depth blog posts on outdoor fun, and about 10% shameless "buy our stuff isn't this a cool product" tweets. Like many retailers, REI uses Twitter as a place to communicate deals, insider information, and special offers to its most devoted customers.
>
> **Woot (https://twitter.com/woot).** Their tweets are 100% about discounts and bargains, as Woot (owned now by Amazon) is all about discounts and special deals. It's the home shopping network gone Twitter.
>
> **Greenpeace (https://twitter.com/greenpeace).** This non-profit tweets photos that inspire about wildlife and nature, links to blog posts about environmental issues, and political calls to action.
>
> **Cato Institute (https://twitter.com/catoinstitute).** This political action organization tweets about politics from a conservative perspective, with offlinks to its blog and videos plus the occasional call to action.

Throughout, your job is to reverse engineer competitors or companies you admire in terms of their tweeting strategy. What are they tweeting (blog posts, pictures, infographics, videos), and why are they tweeting it (to stay top of mind, sell stuff, get viewers on YouTube). Who is following them, and why? What's in it for the followers? How does all this tweeting activity ultimately lead to some sort of sale or business action? Summing up, Twitter is used most commonly to:

- stay top of mind, pestering and reminding customers to "look at me, look at me!";

- communicate with influencers, superfans, and fans, i.e., people who are passionate (or potentially passionate) about your brand;

- leverage *#hashtags* to reach a wider audience and participate in society-wide discussions; and/or

- reach out to journalists, bloggers, and other influencers.

For your next **TO-DO**, download the **Twitter Tweeting Strategy Worksheet**. For the worksheet, go to **http://jmlinks.com/2023smm** (then enter the code '**2023smm**' to register your workbook), and click on the link to the "Twitter Tweeting Strategy Worksheet." You'll answer questions to help you understand what other companies are doing on Twitter and begin to outline your own tweeting strategy.

Content is King

As you work on a tweeting strategy, you'll quickly realize you need a lot of content! Remember to create a **content marketing system** of:

- **Your own content**. Twitter is all about off-loads to blog posts, infographics, images, photos, videos, Memes, and other types of your own content. Twitter and blogging go together like peas and carrots, while Twitter and video go together like scotch and soda.

- **Other people's content**. Relevant content in your industry. By curating out the garbage and identifying the cool, fun, interesting stuff, you can use other people's content to help your tweets stay top of mind.

- **UGC Content.** Use hashtags like *#contest* or *#challenge*, or create a branded hashtag (if enough of your customer base is on Twitter). Motivate your superfans and followers to share their own content around your branded themes.

- **Interactive content**. Twitter is perhaps the most **interactive** social media platform. ""Like" the tweets of others. "Comment" on the tweets of others. "Retweet" them to your followers with comments. *@mention* people constantly. "Tweet to" famous people, superfans, and influencers, even if you don't know them. By interacting with the content of others, you can open the door to "real" relationships.

To identify relevant content from other people, I recommend setting up a Feedly account (**http://www.feedly.com/**) and using tools like Buzzsumo (**http://www.buzzsumo.com**), and Google Alerts (**https://www.google.com/alerts**). You can also create Twitter lists by topic and thus pre-organize whom you follow into easy-to-access and content-specific lists. Use a tool like TweetDeck to take this to the next level. Organize your content into topic groups, and then as you find the content useful to your target audience, "tweet out" that content. Also, monitor key *#hashtags* in your industry and chime in with relevant tweets (and retweets) on topics that are trending.

Use a tool like Hootsuite to schedule your tweets in advance. Or, inside of TweetDeck (now owned by Twitter), you can use its built-in scheduler.

As for your own content, Twitter is best used by staying on topic and sharing original, useful content such as in-depth blog posts, free eBooks or webinars, infographics and instructographics, videos on YouTube. Twitter is a headline service pointing to the "rest of the story" on your blog, video, or infographic.

» PROMOTE YOUR TWITTER ACCOUNT AND TWEETS

Once you've set up your Twitter account and begun to populate it with tweets on a regular basis, you've essentially "set up" your party on Twitter. Now it's time to send out the invitations.

In and of itself, a Twitter Page will not be self-promoting! You've got to promote it!

Assuming your Twitter account shares lots of yummy, useful, fun, provocative content that when seen by a user will entice him or her to "follow" you on Twitter, here are some common ways to promote your Twitter account and Tweets:

- **Real World to Social.** Don't forget the real world! If you are a museum store, for example, be sure that the cashiers recommend to people that they "follow" you on Twitter? *Why? Because they'll get insider tips, fun do-it-yourself posts, announcements on upcoming museum and museum store events, etc.* Get your staff to promote Twitter in that important face-to-face interaction. If you're a barbeque truck in Los Angeles, post signs to "follow us on Twitter" on the trucks, and have staff cajole customers to "follow you." *Why follow you on Twitter? To learn where the taco truck is, to get special deals, and to learn what's cooking.* Use the real world to promote your

Twitter account, and be ready to explain "why" they should follow you on Twitter. What's in it for them?

- **Cross-Promotion.** Link your website to your Twitter Page, your blog posts to your Twitter Page, your YouTube to your Twitter Page, etc. Notice how big brands like REI do this: one digital property promotes another digital property.

- **Email.** Email your customer list and ask them to follow you on Twitter. Again, you must explain what's in it for them.

- **Twitter Internal.** Interact with other accounts via the @ sign, share their content, comment on timely topics using #hashtags, and reach out to complementary pages to work with you on co-promotion. (See below).

- **Use Twitter Plugins.** Twitter has numerous plugins that allow you to "embed" your Twitter Page on your website, and thereby nurture cross-promotion. To learn more about plugins, visit **https://publish.twitter.com/**. Among the better ones –

  o **The Tweet Button.** Make it easy for people to tweet your content (e.g., blog posts).

  o **The Follow Button.** Make it easy for Web visitors to follow you on Twitter.

- **Leverage your Fans.** People who like your Twitter Page are your best promoters. Do everything you can to get them to retweet you to their own followers. Remember, it's *social* (!) media, and encouraging your customers to share your content is the name of the game. You want to leverage your fans as much as possible to share your content.

DON'T FORGET THE REAL WORLD AS A TWITTER PROMOTION STRATEGY

Three Special Ways to Promote via Twitter.

Twitter has three very special ways to promote yourself or your company that are much stronger than on other social media.

Use #Hashtags to Promote Your Company

The first is the **hashtag**. Because Twitter is all about news, the use of hashtags on trending or controversial topics is bigger on Twitter than on any other social media. Identify trending or important hashtags and include them in your tweets. Use **https://ritetag.com/** to identify hashtags in your industry, and don't forget about major trade shows, which often have (and promote) their own hashtags. Then include these hashtags in your tweets, and make sure that your tweets are not only on topic but also offlink to something useful, provocative or important. In that way, they'll discover you via a hashtag and then follow you permanently.

> **VIDEO.** Watch a video tutorial on how to use the "#" sign or "hashtag" on Twitter for marketing purposes at **http://jmlinks.com/16u**.

Industry Trade Shows and Hashtags

Here's a hashtag use you do not want to miss: industry trade shows. Nearly every industry has THE trade show or a few KEY trade shows. Nowadays, these will have hashtags, such as *#CES2022* for the 2022 Consumer Electronics Show. Obviously, this show occurs every year, and the 2023 hashtag *(#CES2023)* is rather easy to guess in advance. My prediction? There will be a 2024 hashtag as well, and so on and so forth.

Thus, **pre-identify** the hashtags of your own industry trade show(s) as well as subordinate, session, or topic hashtags, and start tweeting on those themes before, during, and shortly after the show. Attendees know to look for the show hashtags to find out what's cool, exciting, and worth visiting.

Episodic Usage of Twitter for Marketing

For many businesses, simply knowing the hashtag of "the" industry conference and tweeting during the yearly, or twice yearly, trade conference in and of itself will justify using Twitter for marketing:

> *Hey, #CES2024 attendees! Come by our booth at 2:30 pm for a free laser wand give-away.*

Identify the Twitter account of the industry trade show(s), and they'll easily show you the relevant hashtags. Make sure you have a robust Twitter account set up before the big show, and then during the show, start tweeting on show-related hashtags. For many businesses, this "trade show" use of Twitter is the most important marketing use of Twitter.

Here's something *devious*. Identify the hashtags for all your industry shows, including the ones you do *not* attend in the "real world," and insert them into your tweets during show time. In this way, you can tweet "to" attendees of a show without actually being there!

@Someonefamous

The second promotion strategy is what I call **@someonefamous**. The idea here is to reach out and "have a conversation" with someone more famous (with more followers) than you. Think of it like Dr. Phil making it on the Oprah Winfrey show: her audience saw this new "doctor," and some of her fans became his fans. The trick is to find business partners, complementary companies, or other people/companies on Twitter who are influencers and who have more and/or different fan bases than you.

A useful tool to use is Buzzsumo (**http://www.buzzsumo.com/**). Search for your keywords and identify influencers tweeting about those topics. Identifying them is the easy part. The hard part is getting them to engage in a Twitter conversation with you. You have to convince them to have a conversation with you on Twitter, and then once you're talking to their fans... convince their fans to follow you, too. You can also use TweetDeck's advanced search to filter for engagement and accounts which have a sufficient number of followers.

> **VIDEO.** Watch a video tutorial on how to use the "@" sign or "handle" on Twitter for marketing purposes at **http://jmlinks.com/16y**.

Pitch Journalists via Twitter

We've discussed this already, but you want to think of journalists and bloggers on Twitter as a promotion strategy:

@journalists. Identify journalists on Twitter, find their handles, and tweet "to" the journalists, pitching them on story ideas. Journalists love Twitter because it's where stories break first. They listen to their Twitter feeds as businesses, organizations, and individuals "pitch" them on story ideas via Twitter.

Indeed, you can even advertise to select lists of journalists by using username targeting on Twitter. One simple trick is to just search Twitter for the word "journalist" plus a keyword like "organic" and then click on "people." Here's a screenshot:

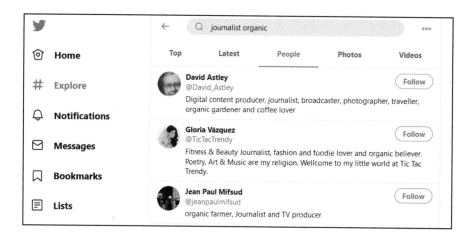

In this way, you can quickly build a targeted list of journalists who cover the organic industry. Follow them, tweet to them, and pitch them on your content. Isn't Twitter amazing?

Get Retweeted

The third Twitter promotion strategy is the **retweet**. By posting items that are funny, scandalous, interesting, shocking, outrageous, or otherwise highly contagious, you get people to retweet your tweets, thereby (again) allowing their followers to see you, and hopefully, begin to follow you as well. To research what is retweeted in your industry, simply do a Twitter search with the letters "RT" in front of your keywords. For an example, visit **http://jmlinks.com/21** to see a search on Twitter of retweets of *#organic* as in "RT organic" searched via Twitter search.

Here's a sample RT:

» ADVERTISE ON TWITTER

Besides these organic promotion methods, there's paid advertising on Twitter. You can promote your tweets as well as create custom advertising campaigns to promote your account and/or clicks to your website. To begin advertising, log in to your account and click on your profile at the left. Then click on *More > Professional Tools > Twitter Ads*. Here's a screenshot:

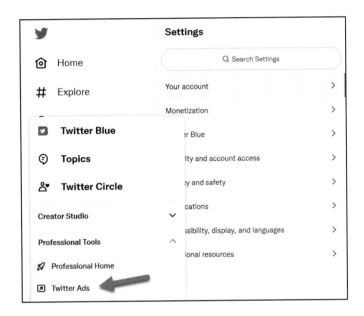

This gets you to the dashboard. You can then set up *Campaigns > Ad Groups > Ads* and target them to audiences. Click to *Tools > Audiences* to see Twitter's targeting options. As you create a Campaign, you'll be prompted either to promote your account or an individual tweet. You can then choose demographic targeting. Here's a screenshot showing people who show interest in "organic:"

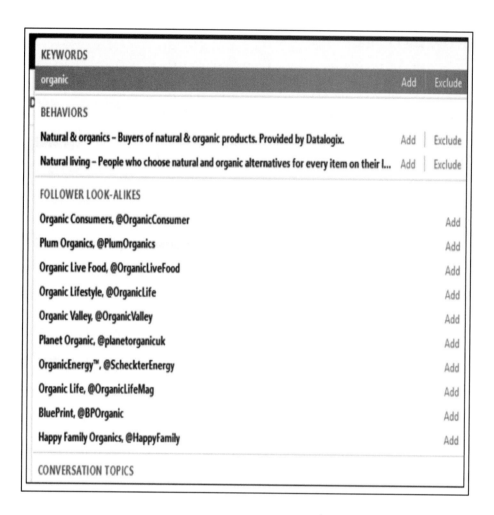

Note that you can target the followers of any account, meaning you can target people who follow your competitor, or people who follow an industry trade show, etc.

To learn more about advertising on Twitter, visit **http://jmlinks.com/31t** or **https://ads.twitter.com/**. Because journalists and bloggers often follow Twitter intensely for breaking news, one of the smartest strategies is to make an "influencer list" on influencers on Twitter and then advertise your tweets directly to those high-impact Twitterers. To learn more about username and follower targeting on Twitter, visit **http://jmlinks.com/1k**.

Twitter Blue: New for 2023?

Twitter's new owner, Elon Musk, seems to be focused on monetizing Twitter beyond ads. One of his innovations, as of this writing, is "Twitter Blue." The idea is to allow people to purchase a verified Twitter account for around $8 / month, remove many ads, have their posts be prioritized by the algorithm, and be a "higher class" of Twitter users. It bombed so badly at deployment that they paused it, so stay tuned as to whether they will refine it and reopen it. Here's a screenshot of "Twitter Blue" options:

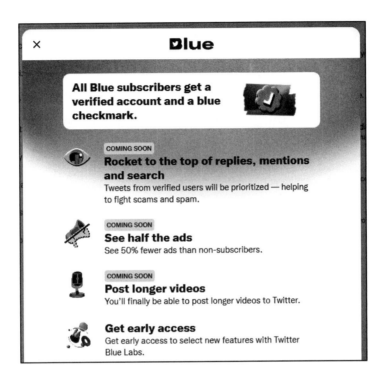

To set up Twitter Blue, you have to use the mobile app version. On the desktop, click *More > Twitter Blue*. Another feature is paid-subscription "Twitter newsletters," which are also under *More > Creator Studio > Newsletters*. This is a competitor to Substack (**https://substack.com/**). Stay tuned as Mr. Musk is clearly trying to monetize Twitter and get it to actually "make money" rather than just "make controversy."

» MEASURE YOUR RESULTS

Measuring the success or failure of your Twitter marketing can be a challenge. Let's look at it from the "bottom up" in terms of items a marketer might want to know or measure vis-a-vis Twitter:

- **Sales or Sales Leads**. Have tweets or Twitter marketing resulted in actual sales leaders (completed feedback forms for a free offer, consultation, eBook, download, etc.) and/or eCommerce sales?

- **Branding / Awareness**. Has Twitter increased our brand awareness and/or improved our brand image?

- **Top of Mind / One Touch to Many**. Has Twitter helped us to stay "top of mind" by reminding potential customers of our company, products, and/or services?

- **Tweet Interactivity**. Have people read our tweets? Have they interacted with our tweets by favoriting them and/or retweeted our tweets?

- **Twitter Account**. Is our follower count increasing, and if so, by how much and how fast? Where are our followers physically located, and what are their demographic characteristics?

The last of these is the easiest to measure: simply record your Twitter follower count each month, and keep a record of it month-to-month. I generally do this on my *Keyword Worksheet*, where I also track inbound links to my website and my review count on review media such as Google, Facebook, and Yelp.

Analytics Inside of Twitter

Inside of Twitter, click on *More > Creator Studio > Analytics*. Here's a screenshot:

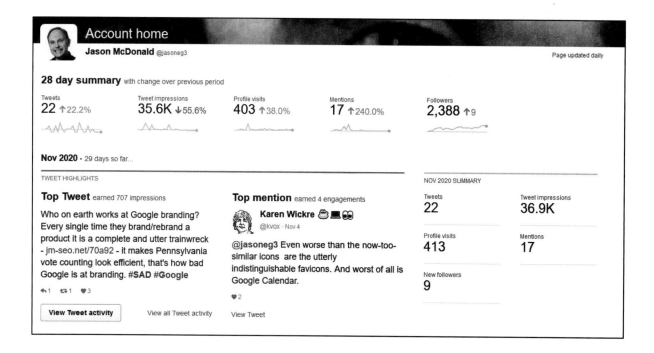

There you can see which tweets gained the most impressions, as well as engagements by Tweet such as clicks, follows, and retweets. Twitter will also tell you whether links you are sharing are getting clicked on and so on and so forth. Twitter also has a feature called **Twitter cards** that bridges your website to/from Twitter activity If you enable Twitter cards on your Website, you get attribution for your Web content plus more data on that inside of Twitter. Learn more at **http://jmlinks.com/31u**.

In sum, inside of Twitter, you can see how people interact with your Twitter account and tweets. Inside of Google Analytics, you can see where they land on your website and what they do after they arrive.

»» CHECKLIST: TWITTER ACTION ITEMS

Test your knowledge of Twitter! Take the *Twitter marketing quiz* at **http://jmlinks.com/qztw**. Next, here are your Twitter **Action Items**:

❑ **Research** whether your customers (and competitors) are on Twitter. What are they doing? What interests them? Why?

> ❑ Identify a few **customer profiles** that match your *buyer personas* and determine how active they are.

> ❑ Identify **competitors** and **companies** to "emulate" or "reverse engineer" who are doing a good job on Twitter.

❑ Set up a **Twitter account** (learn the basics like #hashtags, @mentions, and retweets) and begin posting useful content following the 280 character limit and Twitter lingo.

> ❑ Brainstorm a **Twitter content marketing strategy** of your own content, the content of others, UGC content, and interactive content on industry trends and topics. You need a lot of content to succeed at Twitter!

> ❑ Strategize how to **promote** your Twitter account and tweets, including **advertising** to promote content and grow your followers.

❑ Identify, join, and participate in **relevant #hashtags** on Twitter used by your target customers; do not spam!

❑ Identify **key influencers** (e.g., journalists or bloggers) and note their @*handles*. Where appropriate, tweet to these key influencers when you have highly interesting content or free offers such as eBooks, key news, new product samples, etc.

❑ **Measure** your **KPIs** on Twitter such as the follower growth, likes, comments and retweets of your tweets as well as traffic from Twitter to your website or eCommerce site.

Check out the **free tools**! Go to my *Social Media Marketing Dashboard > Twitter* for my favorite free tools on Twitter. Just visit **http://jmlinks.com/smmdash**.

»» DELIVERABLE: A TWITTER MARKETING PLAN

Now that we've come to the end of our chapter on Twitter, your **DELIVERABLE** has arrived. For the worksheet, go to **http://jmlinks.com/2023smm** (then enter the code **'2023smm'** to register your workbook), and click on the link to the "Twitter Marketing Plan." By filling out this plan, you and your team will establish a vision of what you want to achieve via Twitter.

7
INSTAGRAM

Instagram boasts five hundred million *daily* users with literally *millions upon millions* of photos and videos shared each day to the platform. In the minds of many social media experts, Instagram is more important than its parent, Facebook. It's certainly perceived by younger people as much cooler than "Grandpa Facebook" or crazy "Meta." (Many do not even know that their beloved Instagram is a subsidiary). And now, with "stories" and "reels," Instagram is clearly the true source of innovation. But you don't care about the business strategies at Facebook / Instagram. You care about you. You care about your business. You care about your customers. The question is: "Is Instagram for you?"

In this Chapter, we'll start with the basics of how to use Instagram, proceed to how to research and identify brands to emulate, and turn to tips, tricks, and techniques to leverage Instagram's free and paid opportunities. Along the way, we'll look behind the scenes to "reverse engineer" companies that do Instagram well. By Chapter's end, you'll have a good idea as to whether Instagram is just a waste of time for you (*because either your customers aren't on it in a meaningful way, or because you can't connect your brand to the fun, family, photos, and fake of Instagram, or both*), or whether Instagram is a social media network that will help you not only photograph, but bring home, the marketing bacon.

Let's get started!

TO-DO LIST:

» Explore Concepts and Brands on Instagram

» Reverse Engineer Instagram Strategies

» Set up Your Business Page on Instagram

» Learn Technical Tips to Using Instagram

» Master Instagram Shopping

» Video: Instagram Stories, Videos, and Reels

» Inventory Likes and Dislikes on Instagram

» Brainstorm and Plan an Instagram Marketing Strategy

» Promote Your Instagram Account and Posts

» Work with Instagram Influencers

» Measure Your Instagram KPIs

»» Checklist: Instagram Action Items

»» Deliverable: an Instagram Marketing Plan

» EXPLORE CONCEPTS AND BRANDS ON INSTAGRAM

Instagram is phone-first. 99.9% of your users will use Instagram on the phone or tablet, and I doubt that many people even know you can access Instagram on the desktop (although you can). For personal use, it's best to use Instagram on your phone, and as a marketer, I recommend that you do so as well so that you experience Instagram how it's meant to be experienced, i.e., how most of your users will experience your content on the platform.

It's probably easier for purposes of marketing research, however, to use Instagram on the desktop. Once you have installed it on your phone with a username and password, just visit **https://www.instagram.com/** and log in to your account. You (and your team) can now browse, research, and "reverse engineer" competitors and other brands from your big-screen desktop. For purposes of easy explanation, I recommend you start out by visiting and following a youth-oriented consumer brand such as Chipotle (**https://www.instagram.com/chipotle/**) or Wendy's (**https://www.instagram.com/wendys/**). Both are Instagram superstars. Let's walk through their Instagram accounts step-by-step. Our goal? To get the hang of looking behind the scenes at what Chipotle, Wendy's, and other consumer-facing brands are up to on Instagram.

Despite how "fun" Chipotle and Wendy's make Instagram seem, remember that social media marketing is not just about throwing a fantastic party. It's about throwing **a party with a purpose**, namely to grow your brand and, ultimately, to sell more stuff (or more burritos and burgers).

The Elements of an Instagram Profile

Starting on Chipotle's and Wendy's business profile on Instagram, let's review the basic elements:

> **Profile Picture.** This is the big smiling red icon that represents the brand. Notice how Wendy's is a smile and not a frown because it is all about friends, family, fun, photos, and fake. Everyone is having a good time on Instagram, and if they're not, they're supposed to fake it!

The Timeline. It may not be officially called a "timeline," but as on a Facebook business Page, any user can click "up" to the account and see the "timeline," a series of posts by the brand (or a friend) to his or her account. These are represented by square boxes. Note in the top right corner of any Instagram post that there is often a video camera icon (indicating a video post), or if the icon is missing, it's just a photo. Unlike other networks, Instagram requires photo or video content; you can't post text only.

Status Stats. Across the top, you can see whether you are "following" an account, as well as the number of posts, of followers, and of those being followed. As of December 2022, Chipotle had 375 posts, 1.1 million+ followers, and is following 207; Wendy's had 218 posts, 1 million+ followers, and is following 203. Just as on Twitter, this is public knowledge; anyone can see who follows whom, and even follow the followers of a competitor and interact with them to gain their attention.

The Bio. Any profile on Instagram, whether that of a person or of a brand, has a bio and the bio is allowed one (*and only one*) **clickable website link**. This is the place to explain your business value proposition (your answer to the question, why follow you on Instagram?) and use the clickable link to get customers from Instagram and to your website, e-commerce store, or another place to take an action such as buy your stuff.

Story Highlights. Just below the bio, "Story Highlights" may appear. Check out another savvy consumer brand, RusticCuff (**https://www.instagram.com/rusticcuff/**), as they tend to use highlights as does REI (**https://www.instagram.com/rei/**). These are selections from their Stories, often, though not always, in video format.

Shopping. Shopping is big on Instagram, really big. (We'll discuss it in a special subsection below). You can only see shopping on the app, so choose a big brand like REI (@*rei*) or Bass Pro Shops (@*bassproshops*) and you'll see "View shop" on the app. Click in and you can browse products and buy them.

Video. Click on the right-facing arrow, and you'll see the brand's videos and/or reels. New for 2023: all videos posted to Instagram are considered "reels." Check out how Chipotle is using it at **https://www.instagram.com/chipotle/reels/**. Reels are discoverable both in the feeds of people who follow a brand and in the feeds of people who do not follow the brand but share interests in the same content.

Person Icon. Click here and you can see how a brand has been "tagged" by others.

Branded Hashtags

Encouraging UGC is a top priority on a consumer platform like Instagram. Thus brands often create and promote "branded hashtags" so users can share content around the brand. For example, Bass Pro Shops (@*bassproshops*) promotes *#bassproshops* and encourages users to "tag your outdoor photos" with it.

Here's a screenshot:

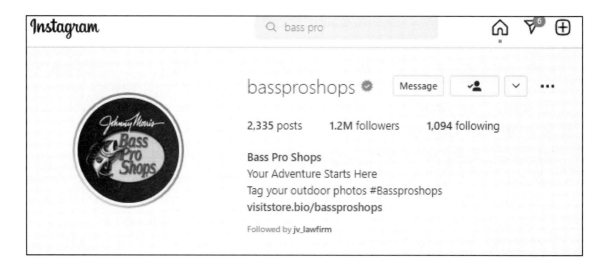

That "branded hashtag" encourages Bass Pro Shops fans to post content around outdoor hunting, fishing, and other activities and feature Bass Pro Merchandise. It has over 300,000 posts. Here's a screenshot:

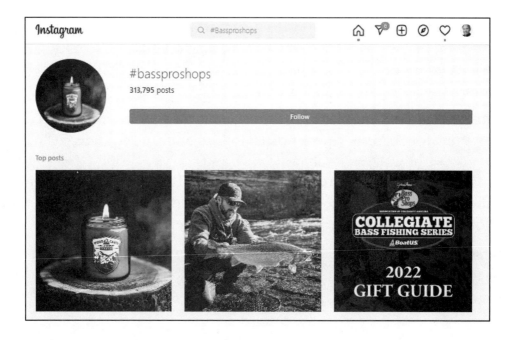

Many big brands have "branded" hashtags, even if they do not feature them in their bios. You can usually guess if there is a branded hashtag by simply searching by the brand name on Instagram. For example, try typing in *#Chipotle* and you'll see something like the following pop up via Instagram autocomplete:

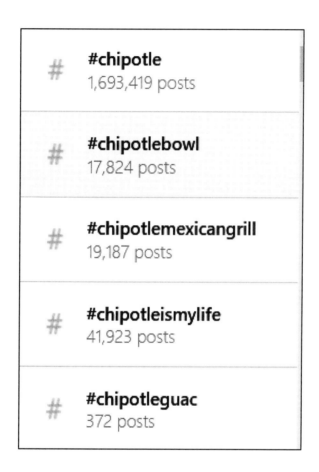

This means that there are 1.6 million posts around Chipotle on Instagram. Massive user engagement means massive free publicity for the brand. But this didn't just happen. Chipotle nurtures its **branded hashtag** with publicity, shoutouts to key fans, contests, and challenges. Your to-do here is to figure out if you have (or can nurture) enough superfans to make a branded hashtag worthwhile for your own company.

Inventory Competitors and Companies-to-Emulate

As with all social networks, look at competitors and big brands through the prism not only of a user but of a social media marketer. What do you like? What do you dislike? What features are enabled, such as the clickable contact links, branded hashtags, or the new shop feature? Take this knowledge back to your own Instagram account, and enable what you like, and disable or ignore what you don't.

1. Identify **competitors** and **companies-to-emulate** on Instagram.

2. Inventory their **structural features** such as profile picture, shop, story highlights, reels, bio, tabs, etc.

3. Drill into key features such as "**reels**" or "**shop**" and investigate whether these might work for your own company.

4. Look for **user-generated content** around the brand, especially via branded hashtags.

Once you know a question such as "How do I set up shop tags on Instagram?," you can literally "Google it" to find an answer, visit YouTube for helpful videos, or visit the Instagram help files at **https://help.instagram.com/**. Instagram also has a more advertising-focused resource for businesses at **https://business.instagram.com/**.

The Elements of an Instagram Post

While superfans will visit and follow the profiles of key brands, most of the action on Instagram is on the feed itself. Thus, beyond the account setup issues, you want to research the "posting strategy" of competitors and companies to emulate. Let's dig into the posting strategy of these three brands – Chipotle, Wendy's, and Rustic Cuff.

The simplest is a post that has a caption plus an image. Here's a screenshot from Rustic Cuff promoting a holiday bracelet:

Make a note of the key elements, such as:

- **A beautiful photograph**. Instagram is all about photography, so your photos or videos need to be done well.

- **A relevant caption**. Instagram allows you to write a short summary. Here the brand is asking its followers to "Take a stroll down candy cane lane."

- **Hashtags**. Instagram is very friendly to hashtags. Just as we saw on Twitter, hashtags are conversational themes on Instagram. Thus *#TisTheSeason* is a more general hashtag, and *#RusticCuff* is the branded hashtag.

Note as well that Instagram is very open. You can not only see the "likes" and "comments" to this post. You can also click into any person who engaged with this and see their account. You can even follow them. If you hover with your mouse over them, Instagram will pop up some info on that account. Here's a screenshot:

You can thus see Sandi Patty as a follower of Rustic Cuff. As on Twitter, you can click over to her account. You can even message or follow her via the platform. Instagram, like Twitter but unlike Facebook or LinkedIn, is extremely open. Just don't be creepy.

Brands can also post video content. Here's a video posted by Chipotle to its account of two "superfans" who attempted to launch a burrito into space:

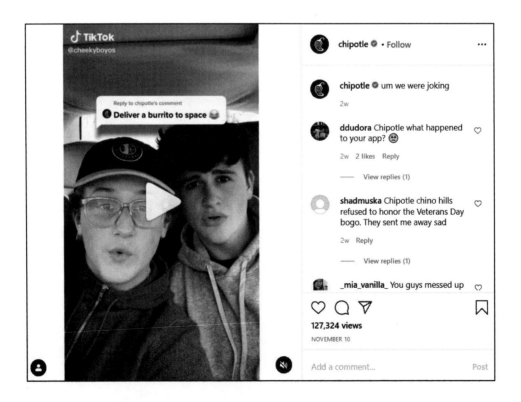

Note that this had 127,324 views! You can watch it at **http://jmlinks.com/54z**. It's really funny, and it's a fantastic example of User Generated Content that has gone "viral."

You can post about anything on Instagram, but the posts by brands that do the best fit the culture of friends, family, fun, and photos. Keep it simple. Keep it fun. And keep it photogenic to succeed on Instagram.

For instance, here's a post by Wendy's just before Halloween:

In terms of content marketing, note how it is piggybacking on a very popular holiday, and it mimics the kind of content that users create and share. The brand is fun, friendly, and (to some extent) fake – just like "real people" on Instagram.

Link in Bio

One of the peculiarities of Instagram is that it does not allow link-sharing in posts. Unlike on Twitter, you can't post a link that goes from Instagram outbound to a website. This is only possible in ads. Thus for organic content, brands usually refer to "link in bio" and direct users to their bio. As we shall see, some brands use services like

Curalate or Link.Tree to work around this limitation. Here's a screenshot of REI, which uses the like2b.uy service:

You can check this out at **https://like2b.uy/rei** and notice how it mimics their actual Instagram account:

And here's a screenshot of that second post in red with the "link in bio" reference:

Instagram Sharing

Another quirky feature on Instagram is the inability for one-to-many sharing. On other platforms, such as Twitter or TikTok, a user can easily reshare ("retweet") a post to his or her followers. Thus *one* user can share to *many* followers, and *one* user of that original sharer can reshare to *many* of his followers, and so on and so forth. This allows content to get shared and reshared quickly and helps content to "go viral."

In contrast, Instagram only allows users to "send" content to their followers. This lack of one-to-many sharing, in my view, is a major flaw in the platform. It prevents users from magnifying content. Be that as it may, no one listens to me at Instagram. Just be aware of the limitations on links and sharing. If your marketing objective is to "go viral," Instagram is not the right venue. In addition, many business users want to curate content; that is, identify and share the best content from their followers or others. To do this, you have to go through a very convoluted process using third-party apps. To learn more, check out "How to Repost on Instagram: 4 Ways to Reshare Content From Other Users" from Hubspot at **http://jmlinks.com/55b**. For these reasons, I would not focus on curated content on Instagram. I would only focus on my own content, UGC content, and interactive content (as you can comment and like on the content of others, including your own fans).

Searching Instagram

As you get started, an easy way to find posts and brands on Instagram is to use the desktop version for market research. This gives you a big screen, and you and your team can work together to research what's relevant to your brand on Instagram.

Just enter keywords like "organic" or "weddings" into Instagram search, and you can browse posts and thus find persons and brands to follow. If you enter "wedding," for example, it will show you possible accounts to follow in the pull-down. Here's a screenshot:

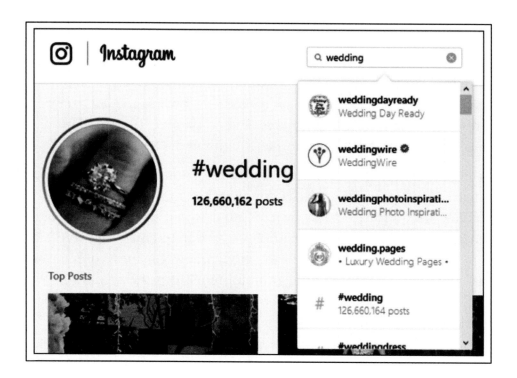

If you put the "#" sign in front, it becomes a hashtag, which is more about finding posts than accounts, as in *#weddings*. Try typing in some of your keywords with the # (hashtag) symbol; just remember that hashtags are always made with no spaces, so it's *#valentinesday* not *#valentines day* or *#valentines #day*. As you find posts, click on them, and you can see the poster's account at the top; you can click up to check them out or just click "Follow" to follow that account. Here's a screenshot:

You can also use Google to search Instagram. Just go to Google and type in *site:instagram.com {keyword}* (no space between site: and instagram.com), as for example, *site:instagram.com organic* or **http://jmlinks.com/45f**. Using these techniques, identify brands that are either competitors to you, in or near your industry, or just doing a great job on Instagram as marketers. Look for ideas in terms of how they set up their account and – most importantly – how and what they are posting to Instagram. Which posts are getting the most likes and comments? Which features such as "stories" or "shopping" are enabled, and why?

Instagram Stories and Reels

Instagram has a feature called *Instagram stories*, which is now averaging 500 million daily users. These are short narrative video clips that tell your story on a day-to-day basis. If someone you are following has a story, their Profile Picture will glow on the phone with a pinkish/red circle around it. Simply click on their icon, and then you can watch a short video of that person's (or brand's) Instagram story. To learn more about Instagram Stories, read the help file at **http://jmlinks.com/27n**.

You can easily see the marketing opportunity for a business to post a fun, provocative "insider" story to Instagram so that your customers, fans, and superfans can get insider information and fun insights about your business. Imagine a pizza restaurant posting an Instagram story of "how we make our incredible pepperoni pizza," or a fashion designer sharing his daily shaving and man-beauty routine. "Insider stories" are what brand stories are ultimately about on Instagram. Check out your competitors and companies-to-emulate and see what they post to their stories; reverse engineer the marketing message nestled inside a good "story." To view a story by a competitor, find their account, verify that their profile picture is encircled in red, and click on it. If they have a story, it will play the video or start the slideshow.

Here's a screenshot of a story from Rustic Cuff:

Rustic Cuff does a great job with stories. Notice how their stories are "behind the scenes" content and that this content is optimized for their "superfans."

Here's a problem as you "reverse engineer" competitors and companies-to-emulate, however. Stories are "temporary." They disappear after twenty-four hours. If a brand or person you follow has a story, you can see it ONLY on the mobile version of Instagram. Here are where and how stories appear:

1. **On your home screen, stories appear across the top in circles.** Click on a circle to view the "story" for a brand or person that your follow. Note: this is the big marketing opportunity for organic reach via stories: get customers to "follow you," create as many stories as you can (especially engaging ones!), and then these stories will appear at the top as your customers log in to Instagram. *#freeadvertising.*

2. **On the timeline of the brand or person.** Search for a brand such as "Chipotle" or "Koolaid." Then tap on their "Profile picture" on the top left to view their story. If they have one, it will pop up. If they don't, nothing will happen. Stories can also appear permanently in "story highlights," which are little circles beneath the profile picture. REI (@REI, **https://www.instagram.com/rei**) has done a very good job using story highlights.

3. **Search by keyword.** Search for a term by tapping on the "magnifying glass" icon. Then tap on the circle around each brand profile picture (NOT the brand name) to browse stories.

Reels: Instagram's Answer to TikTok

"**Reels**" is Instagram's rip-off of TikTok. Users and brands can upload quirky, musically-oriented videos to the platform. Check out Chipotle at **https://www.instagram.com/chipotle/reels/**. Similarly, if you know the account handle, you can quickly see any reels that they have posted. Just substitute the handle for "chipotle" in that URL as in **https://www.instagram.com/burgerking/reels/**. You can also just click into an account and click on the "Reels" icon, both on the desktop and on the phone.

Reels is a very big deal for Instagram. New for 2023, ALL new videos are reels. Essentially, therefore, video on Instagram is reels, and reels are video. IGTV has been discontinued.

Suffice it to say that you can repurpose TikToks as Reels on Instagram and that Reels now show in the "feed" on Instagram. The race is on between Reels and TikTok, and only time will tell which will win!

The other key element about Reels is **discovery**. Whereas posts predominantly appear in the feeds of people who follow your brand, Reels can appear in anyone's feed. Thus, dog people might see your "dog" reel, cat people might see your "cat" reel, and iguana people might see your "iguana" reels, *even if they have not "followed" you on Instagram*. Reels are a big opportunity to get your brand in front of new prospects and customers based on shared interests between your brand and its customers. REI masters this aspect of reels, producing all sorts of fun, informative, "how to" content that extends its brand via **https://www.instagram.com/rei/reels/**.

More Exemplary Instagram Business Accounts

Here are some more brands that do Instagram well. Pay attention to their account setup, including branded hashtags, use of the "shop" feature, stories, story highlights, Reels, etc., and then to what they're posting not just in terms of photos but in terms of captions and hashtags as well as the user engagement.

MadeWell at **https://www.instagram.com/madewell**. Here's the mother ship (for females) of the casual brand. Another excellent example of over-the-top chic materialism on Instagram. "Shop till you drop."

MadeWellMens at **https://www.instagram.com/madewellmens**. This casual-chic brand does an excellent job at connecting Instagram to its shopping feature. Pay special attention to how it "tags" product posts to its Instagram shopping tab.

mDesign at **https://www.instagram.com/mdesign**. Notice how this brand has the fully enabled "Buy on Instagram" feature so users can seamlessly purchase directly via the app. Click on the "shopping bag" icon and then a product. You'll notice that it says "add to bag" rather than "visit website."

Foundr Magazine at **https://www.instagram.com/foundr/**. This magazine uses Instagram as a quote-of-the-day, inspirational message and focuses on entrepreneurs.

Bass Pro Shops at **https://www.instagram.com/bassproshops/**. This outdoor retailer shares content around fishing and outdoor sports and does a great job with contests.

The Pioneer Woman at **https://www.instagram.com/thepioneerwoman/**. Another account that's native to my home state of Oklahoma, the Pioneer Woman shares recipes and cooking tips for those who "love butter" and love to cook. Notice how she uses the "Story Highlights" feature to showcase recipes. Yum!

Museum of Sex at **https://www.instagram.com/museumofsex/**. This New York-based museum pushes the envelope of what's allowable on Instagram and promotes itself as a "must-see" destination in New York City. Instagram is very much part of "pop culture," and "sexy" and "Instagram" are a natural. Try the hashtags *#sexy* or *#muscles*, and note that any brand that can leverage our fascination with the body, hedonism, looking good, and being sexy is a great fit for Instagram.

Banksy at **https://www.instagram.com/banksy/.** Banksy is an "underground" artist who uses social media and social sharing to build one of the weirdest brands on the Internet. Check out his movie, "Exit Through the Gift Shop" at **http://jmlinks.com/45g** for a through-the-looking-glass look at art and brand-building.

Topshop at **https://www.instagram.com/topshop/.** This account is all about women's fashion and trends, with lots of social engagement on Instagram. Check out *#topshopstyle* for its brand hashtag and watch how it engages users to share themselves wearing Topshop styles.

Aeromexico at **https://www.instagram.com/aeromexico/.** The Mexican airline, as we shall discuss in a moment, does a pretty good job of leveraging adjacent fun themes of places to go and see in Mexico, as opposed to just the "boring" aspects of air travel.

Outdoor Voices at **https://www.instagram.com/outdoorvoices**. Yet another brand that is lucky enough to have Instagram shopping fully enabled.

The point is to find competitors, similar companies, and companies to emulate. Then "lurk" behind the scenes and "reverse engineer" what they're doing at a technical level with features like branded hashtags, shop tags, Instagram stories, Reels, i.e., what they're doing at a content level in terms of what they're posting as images, videos, and text captions, and what's getting engagement from their fans (and why).

The Instagram Game: Followers, Likes, and Engagement

As on other social media networks, the game on Instagram is to get people to follow your company, and once they follow you, get them to like, comment, and share ("send") your posts to their friends, family, and contacts.

Engagement is the key to content marketing on Instagram, so you need to brainstorm fun, provocative photo, or video content that engages your users.

LIKE ALL SOCIAL MEDIA, INSTAGRAM CRAVES ENGAGEMENT

Instagram, like Facebook or Twitter, follows the structure of timeline and news feed. What a friend posts to her timeline shows up in my newsfeed. If she posts a photo of herself and her boyfriend having fun at Disneyland, then that photo will show up in my newsfeed, where I can "like," "comment," or "share" it to my own friends. In this way, Instagram is very much *Twitter with pictures*.

Users have profiles and post pictures / videos to their timelines. They can also post Instagram stories, which are collections of photos and videos, sort of a "day in the life" of a friend or brand you follow.

The videos / pictures / stories posted by User A appear in User B's newsfeed if they're connected to each other. Instagram, like Facebook, also monitors interaction in a quasi-Edgerank fashion, ranking which posts are prominent on the newsfeed as measured by previous interaction among the parties. The more interactive you and an account are, the more likely it is that your followers will see your posts prominently in the newsfeed.

Businesses can have brand Pages on Instagram, and when an individual follows a brand (similar to liking the brand's Facebook Page), posts by that brand will appear in the newsfeed of followers if the posts are "engaging" enough as judged by the Instagram algorithm.

Businesses can enable Instagram shopping and, if they're big enough, "buy on Instagram." These new features enable brands to integrate social media with shopping directly. Learn more at **http://jmlinks.com/53n**.

Users can like, comment, or share posts by others to their own followers. Note one weird technical glitch here on Instagram: unlike on Twitter or Facebook, one person can only share with one other person. Instagram does not have a "one to many" share feature, which limits the ability of posts to "go viral" on Instagram.

Reels. Reels works in a different way. On the one hand, if you post a reel to your Instagram account it has the opportunity to appear in the feeds of people who follow you. But it also can be driven by the "recommendation engine" to appear in people who do NOT follow you, yet have a similar interest. Thus a "dog" video can show not only to your followers but also to folks who are interested in "dogs but *do not follow you*. In this way, Reels can help you reach new followers, new prospects, and new customers. Savvy marketers are very excited about reels for this reason.

Business Accounts and Personal Profiles

While there's not a clear distinction between business and personal profiles in terms of the basics, it's best to choose a Business Account for your business. (Note: just to confuse us, it's called a Business *Page* on Facebook and a Business *Account* on Instagram).

A Business Account allows for advertising and also provides reporting. To set up an Instagram account for a business from scratch, however, you must first have a Facebook Page for your business. (To learn how to set up a Facebook Page for your business, visit **http://jmlinks.com/29a**). So, first set up a Business Page on Facebook, and then open up the Instagram App to set up a new Instagram Business Account.

Note: to set up a business profile on Instagram, you'll have to do this first on your phone by "signing up" as an individual. You can read the official step-by-step guide to setting up a business account on Instagram at **http://jmlinks.com/57k**.

Converting a Personal to a Business Account

You can also convert an existing Personal Profile to a Business Account if you mistakenly set up your business as a Personal Profile. (And you can convert back again). However, because a Professional Account on Instagram must be connected to a Business Page on Facebook, be sure that you have first set up a Business Page on Facebook or are ready to do so. Then follow these steps:

1. On your phone, open the Instagram app, go to your profile, and tap "edit profile."

2. Tap Switch to Professional Account.

3. On the Set Up your Professional Profile page, review your business contact information and press done.

4. Connect to your Facebook Page. This is optional but highly recommended. The Facebook Ads platform is difficult to use, and your best option to connect Instagram to Facebook is during this conversion.

A Business Account is recommended as it allows contact buttons such as "email" or "message" near the top of your profile, depending on the contact information you provided. You also get better metrics for a Business Account. To read the help file, visit **http://jmlinks.com/27k**.

Managing Multiple Accounts

Once you have both a personal Instagram and a business Instagram, you can manage both via one app on your phone. Go to the gear icon and then scroll down to the very bottom and find "Add Accounts." You can manage up to five accounts on Instagram via one phone and one app install. Once you have more than one account on your phone, you can switch between accounts. To read the help file on how to set this up, visit **http://jmlinks.com/27m**.

» REVERSE ENGINEER INSTAGRAM STRATEGIES

We'll return to some of the technical features of Instagram in a moment, but let's look at what's happening on Instagram first. Like any social media network, you want to figure out what people are doing on Instagram and what brands are trying to do as marketers. Like any good party planner, you want to figure out if your target customers are on Instagram, and what they're engaged in, and then turn a skeptical eye towards what other companies and brands are doing to "reverse engineer" their marketing strategies.

First up, ponder for a moment what you, your friends, and your family are doing on Instagram, leaving aside companies and brands for the moment. If I take a look at myself as well as my friends and family on Instagram, it's pretty clear that 99% of what people are doing on the network is paying attention to friends and family as they have fun in their daily lives, and taking photos (and videos), along with posting these to their Instagram Stories or Reels. At its core, Instagram is really just a multiperson scrapbook sharing photos and videos largely of the "fun stuff" in one's life.

But there are two big currents on Instagram. One is friends and family that share photos of their lives (admittedly exaggerating the positive and downplaying the negative). The other is consumer brands like Target, REI, and Gucci as well as consumer personalities like the Kardashians and other influencers who are "all in" when it comes to consumerism, materialism, and hedonism.

Is Instagram fake? Absta-INSTA-lutely. Like Facebook, Instagram is more "life as it should be" than "life as it really is." Instagram tends to be very **show-offy** as people post photos of themselves, their families, their friends, and their super cool, amazing, perfect life to "show off" how great their life is (vs. your sad, pathetic, boring life and dysfunctional family). Big brands and celebrities are even more so. The Kardashians, for example, are (probably) an example of this sort of Insta-fantasy. Check out Kim at **https://www.instagram.com/kimkardashian/**, or Khloe at **https://www.instagram.com/khloekardashian/**. I love the Kardashians, don't get me wrong. I just don't particularly believe that what they project about their lives is "reality." There is also a lot of **"virtue signaling"** on Instagram – people live lifestyles, promote causes, support or detract from issues, etc., in such a way as to "signal" that they live a virtuous life (vs. you other shmucks out there, who don't care about global warming, puppies, motherhood, our troops or other fill-in-the-blank virtuous causes plus you have bad skin, don't vacation in interesting parts, and do not partake of fine wines or fine dinners).

Like most social media, Instagram isn't really about reality. It's about projection and perception. You might disagree with it on a cultural level; you might even think it means we are living in a very shallow consumer culture devoid of meaning. But it is what it is. The marketing point here is that smart brands leverage customer **narcissism** and the **desire to show off**; they encourage customers to "showcase" that they are "living their best life" by using the company's products or services.

INSTAGRAM ENCOURAGES BRANDS AND USERS TO "SHOW OFF"

Turning to the other current, we find visual consumerism. A lot of Instagram content is fashion photos. It's as if the old-style glossy magazines of the supermarket went online and took over a platform. Choose your favorite fashion brand, whether it's Gucci (**https://www.instagram.com/gucci/**) or Gap (**https://www.instagram.com/gap/**), Old Navy (**https://www.instagram.com/oldnavy/**) or OshKosh B'gosh (**https://www.instagram.com/oshkoshkids/**), and you'll find brands and consumers using Instagram as a visual shopping platform. See it. Like it. And now, buy it, via Instagram shopping. If you are a B2C brand and you're visual, this makes Instagram a "must do" social platform. The strategy here is simply for brands to visually showcase good-looking clothing, products, and services.

Search by Location

Let's look at some other techniques to browse Instagram and look for marketing opportunities. One good way to see what "real people" are doing on Instagram is to search by location.

Simply go to Instagram and type in a city, such as Pittsburgh, Tulsa, or Houston. To browse Instagram posts on Tulsa, for example, visit **http://jmlinks.com/27p**. Then drill down into a post, and you can snoop into what that person was posting and how their family, friends, and acquaintances reacted. For example, here's an adorable Dad and daughter post that's been tagged with *#Tulsa*:

You can then click "up" to the person who posted it, in this case, @*biggestrayray,* and see what he's posting to his account. (Note how, like Twitter, Instagram is very open – many people have little idea just how public what they do on Instagram is).

You can also find location-based posts by neighborhood or landmarks, which is excellent for a local business in a neighborhood. For example, check out *#downtowntulsa* (Downtown Tulsa, Oklahoma), *#brooksidetulsaok* (Tulsa's Brookside neighborhood), or even *#tulsafarmersmarket* for things around Tulsa's best farmers' market. Search for neighborhoods and landmarks in your city or town, and discover through Instagram what people post that's location-specific. Find brands you like (or compete with) and drill into the accounts of people that are interacting with brands. **Geotags** are a special feature – when you're on the app, click into "add location." These inserts a geotag vs. a hashtag. Geotags help posts appear on the "explore" page of users who are nearby.

If you're a local business, the takeaways here are a) use both local *#hashtags* and *geotags* when you post to Instagram, and b) consider advertising on Instagram, which can also be geo-targeted. Instagram, while mammoth, also has a very local side to it.

Research the Fans of Your Competitors

You can find a competitor and then literally drill into their fans. The easiest way to do this is on the desktop, though you can do it on the phone app, too. Here's how:

1. Find the Instagram account of a competitor or company you want to research. We'll use Peet's Coffee (**https://www.instagram.com/peetscoffee/**), which is the Bay Area's best coffee chain.

2. Click on followers at the top. This then pops up a list of everyone who follows them. You can literally click "follow" in blue to follow that account or **click on** the account name and check them out.

Here's a screenshot of how easy it is to "see" the "followers" of Peet's Coffee:

You can easily research who is following a competitor. You can even follow them. Just don't be creepy about this. Realize that when you follow someone on Instagram, they often follow you back or at least check you out. It's all very public. Plus, there is a limit of 300 accounts to follow each day; 7,000 lifetime limit. So if you rapidly follow accounts, you'll get blocked. But as a research tool, this is a great way to investigate who's following a competitor and how fervently. "Follow for follow" is also a promotional tool; within reason, people whom you follow with your brand account will tend to follow you back (or at least check you out). So consider "following" key people who "follow" your competitors.

You can also drill into a competitor's post (vs. their entire account), and see which posts are the most popular as measured by likes and comments. Simply find a competitor, click into one of their more popular posts, and then click over to those people who liked it or commented on it. Here's a screenshot from Peet's Coffee:

If you click on *@missberberry*, you can see her account. If you click on the 547 likes, you can see all the people who liked this post and click over to their accounts, too. Here's a screenshot:

I would not recommend that you follow each and every person who likes a competitor's account or posts. But in terms of research, it gives you a window into your competitor's Instagram strategy, what they post, what gets engagement, and even the types of people who are engaging with their posts. As you browse accounts, you can see how many followers they have and thus get a crude measurement of their clout on the network. Use the public nature of Instagram in your marketing research by finding companies similar to yours, investigating their posting/content strategy, and even drilling into their fans.

Business Strategies on Instagram.

With some basics under our belt, let's revisit what brands are doing on Instagram. Remember – unlike a person – a brand isn't on Instagram "for fun." Rather, whether it's the camping gear retailer, REI, the Mexican airline, Wendy's, Chipotle, Aeromexico, or Rustic Cuff, brands have an ultimate **goal** for Instagram: **to sell more stuff**. I think you could argue that this is also true for public personas like the Kardashians, who are more brands than real people if you think about it.

If you work backward from the "ultimate goal" of selling more stuff, you can see that many brands are on Instagram to build "brand equity," that warm and fuzzy feeling that tells you when it's time to book a trip to Mexico, you want to fly Aeromexico airlines, when it's time to go camping, you want to shop for a tent via REI, and when it's time to buy a gift for mom or your girlfriend, a trendy bracelet from Rustic Cuff is a good gift to buy online. And when you look to people to emulate as lifestyle leaders, you look to the Kardashians (Or not, depending on your values).

Instagram is about image and the projection of one's "public persona." It's about knowing who your target audience is and who it is not. It's about doing a communicative, visual dance with them via photos and videos.

Consumer Brands on Instagram

By far, the biggest and most active business accounts on Instagram could be categorized as consumer brands. Take a brand like REI (@REI), for example. (You can browse it on your desktop at **http://jmlinks.com/32u**). REI posts photos of cool people doing cool things outdoors, with its clothing, gear, and accessories taking a backseat to just people having a great time enjoying nature. It's pretty easy to see that REI's Instagram marketing strategy is to share fun photos of its customers wearing or using REI gear and to encourage "user-generated content" from customers by having contests and using hashtags like *#optoutside* (**http://jmlinks.com/27q**). As you scroll through REI's account, you can hover to see the number of "likes" and "comments," as indicated by the heart icon and the comment icon, respectively. Because REI does a great job with its photos, videos, and strategy and because outdoor fun is a photogenic fit to Instagram, it's easy to see that Instagram is a huge and successful part of REI's Internet marketing efforts.

REVERSE ENGINEER THE BIG BRANDS ON INSTAGRAM

Or take a brand like Whole Foods (@*wholefoods* at **http://jmlinks.com/32v**), another big retailer, but this time of food. Whole Foods shares fun, colorful photos of healthy, organic foods (which, incidentally, you can buy at its many stores…), as well as uses hashtags like *#Foods4Thought* and *#WholeFoodFaves*. Even more interesting, notice that Whole Foods uses the Instagram shopping service Like2b.uy at **http://like2b.uy (http://jmlinks.com/32w)**) to integrate its Instagram posts with its blog and website. Here's a screenshot:

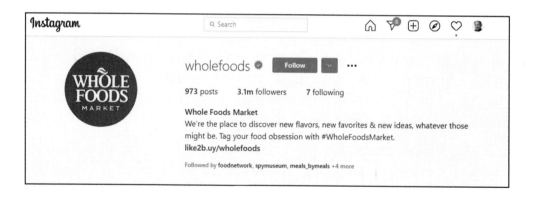

If you click on the Like2b.uy link, you'll see photos that "match up" to Whole Food's Instagram posts, and you can go from there to the Whole Foods website, blog, eCommerce site, etc.

Like2b.uy (**http://jmlinks.com/55f**) is a workaround against the fact that Instagram allows one, and only one, clickable URL in an account in the bio. Another vendor that allows a way around this functionality is Olapic's Tap-shop platform at **http://jmlinks.com/32z**. Still another one is Linktree at **https://linktr.ee/**. The Instagram shop feature (**http://jmlinks.com/45h**) is yet a third option. Rustic Cuff has this feature enabled, so check that out. Major brands such as **@glamglow** (**https://www.instagram.com/glamglow/**) can also have "native" shopping via

Instagram. Refer to my companion, *Marketing Almanac,* for a complete index to the best Instagram resources, including eCommerce plugins and services.

What you'll see on Instagram is brands leveraging photogenic product shots as well as photogenic shots *by and of* happy customers using their products and services. The genuinely great marketers on Instagram, like REI, have figured out how to mobilize their customer evangelists to post, like, comment, and share product photos for them. UGC content is king on the platform; interactive content is queen.

Tap into the Narcissism of Your Customers

There's a certain self-serving narcissism in our modern, ego-centric culture in which you post your "amazing" trip to Machu Pichu (2.1 million posts as of December 2022 at **http://jmlinks.com/27r**), your "incredible" trip to Disney World (16.5 million posts at **http://jmlinks.com/27s**), or your "meaningful" Destination Wedding (14 million posts at **http://jmlinks.com/27t**). The point is that if it's "fun" and it's "photogenic," and especially if people want to "show off" to their friends and family about how much "fun" they're having… it's a perfect fit for Instagram marketing! As a brand, if you can tap into our very human desire to "show off" to our friends how cool, fun, brilliant, smart, incredible, holier-than-thou, moralistic, compassionate, perfect, rich, with it, living-the-life, and any other narcissistic impulse that we share as humans… well, that's the way to market successfully on Instagram. Brand hashtags on Instagram such as *#optoutside*, *#doingthings*, or *#rusticcuff* are examples of how brands leverage consumer narcissism as a marketing strategy on Instagram.

Note also that geographies like Tulsa, Oklahoma, (**http://jmlinks.com/33a**), Niles, California, (**http://jmlinks.com/33b**), or Havana, Cuba, (**http://jmlinks.com/33c**) also have geotags or technically what are called "location tags." You can even create a location, such as your business address, and then promote it to customers for location-tagging. See **http://jmlinks.com/33d**.

INSTAGRAM TAPS INTO OUR HUMAN DESIRE TO "SHOW OFF"

Airbnb (**http://jmlinks.com/32x**), for example, is a brand that truly does Instagram well and taps into this "show off" component of the human ego. Who doesn't want to share photos of their fun Airbnb vacation for a little surreptitious gloating vis-à-vis their friends back home, stuck in cubicle hell at work? REI also fits this mold as people "show off" their incredible communions with nature using REI products.

For a small business, an example of this affinity would be a wedding planner, wedding photographer, or pretty much anything in the wedding industry. Just search Instagram for the hashtag *#wedding*, and you'll find over 240 million posts sharing the fun, faith, and love that is that glorious day (*plus products and services to buy at a convenient wedding superstore near you; act now supplies are limited*). Brainstorm how and why your customers might want to "show off" that they are using your products in a photographic / video way, and you're on the way to real Instagram marketing success.

Non-fun Brands that Connect to Something Fun

If your brand isn't fun, don't despair. You can connect to something *adjacent* that is truly fun. Take air travel. Let's face it; air travel isn't exactly fun these days. Unlike camping or staying in a fabulous Airbnb location, air travel in and of itself is anything but fun. And it's not very photogenic. What would people take photos of besides the planes? I mean, should you have your customers photograph the crowded and dirty seats, the overhead bins, or those crazy, blue, and loud toilets? And now with Covid-19, mask requirements and bossy flight attendants. Hell has come to earth, and it's called air travel.

An airline, therefore, has to "look out the window" to find things that truly are fun (such as travel), and connect these adjacent *fun* things to the *non-fun* experience that is air travel.

Check out United Airlines at *@united* on Instagram (**http://jmlinks.com/33e**), or for an airline that does tend to be a bit more fun, I recommend Aeromexico at **http://jmlinks.com/33f**. The point is if your brand is serious or not-fun, brainstorm ways that you can attach it to more fun types of activities, especially ones that are photogenic. This strategy is at the heart of all the airlines on Instagram. But it goes for B2B or more serious consumer brands as well. Consider Sunrun Solar at **http://jmlinks.com/45j**. That brand posts photos of solar panels, as well as outdoor nature-type photos that highlight the synergy between clean energy and a healthy outdoor environment. Here's a screenshot:

Solar panels in and of themselves are neither fun nor photogenic, so the trick would be to identify photos that ARE fun and photogenic but somehow connect to solar power. Check out the hashtags *#solar* or *#solarpanels*, for instance, for ideas.

Really Unfun Products or Services: What to do?

Next, take a look at the big insurers like Geico (**http://jmlinks.com/33h**), Allstate (**http://jmlinks.com/33j**), or Progressive (**http://jmlinks.com/33k**). Insurance is not only "not fun," it's one of the most expensive, mistrusted, and obnoxious experiences of a consumer's life. (*The policies can be next to impossible to understand, and as my Dad says, the insurers are great at taking your premiums but not so great at paying out when something happens. Regardless of my views on insurance, as an Instagram user, I'm not exactly going to share a photo of me on Instagram going over my life insurance policy!*).

Insurance is boring, unphotogenic, mistrusted, and not exactly something the average consumer would spontaneously share on Instagram. So, what is to be done?

Like the airlines, the insurance companies attempt to attach themselves to something fun and photogenic. Their job is much more difficult because while Aeromexico takes you to Cabo San Lucas or Puerta Vallarta, which are fun and photogenic, you probably won't exactly take a picture of your house burning down and caption it, "Wow! I'm glad I have Allstate." I also doubt I'm going to take a photo of myself in my coffin and say, "Wow! I'm glad I have USAA life insurance!" (Though perhaps my wife will take a selfie with me, *#itsfinallyover*).

Accordingly, the insurance companies are worth looking at on Instagram as examples of "out of the box" marketing thinking. An example would be Progressive's hashtag

#parentamorphosis, which attempts to make fun of the transformation from a hip twenty-something into a boring thirty-something with two kids in tow.

Here's a screenshot:

This post garnered 128 likes, which is far from tremendous, but it shows the strategy attempt by one of the country's biggest brands to attach the non-photogenic, non-fun themes of insurance to the fun, photogenic themes of Instagram.

Gurus and Visual Instruction

If you, or your small business, can explain things to people, and if those things can be explained in such a way as to be visually appealing, then an Instagram guru strategy might work. Consider the fitness industry, for example, which posts photos and short videos to Instagram to teach users how to get fit (and occasionally promotes products and services to buy). Check out Certified Fitness, for example, at **http://jmlinks.com/33m** with 8,840 followers and 3,318 posts as they build a brand that promotes fitness. Or for a bigger brand, check out 24 Hour Fitness at **http://jmlinks.com/33n**. Or check out the 43 million posts to the hashtag *#fishing* and 16 million to #*hunting*. These are visual sports or activities that blend a "Gee! Look at the huge fish I caught" narcissism of the users with the visual "how-tos" of vendors and a good dose of selling and brand identity.

Even outside of the purely visual, brands that explain things can find a niche on Instagram. Sue B. Zimmerman is one of the goddesses of Instagram, and she shares tips, tricks, and pretty much the visual story of her life at **http://jmlinks.com/33p**. Dog guru Zak George uses Instagram to share photos of dogs and dog-training tips at **http://jmlinks.com/55c**, as does the much more successful (at least on Instagram), Cesar Millan (**http://jmlinks.com/33r**). All of these "guru strategies" blend insider tips, tricks, and secrets with a personalized view into the life and viewpoints of the guru, him or herself.

Which Strategy Fits You Best?

The strategic point of all these examples on Instagram is to get you to look deep into your marketing soul and ponder whether:

> You're a **fun brand** in a **fun, photogenic industry** such as travel or jewelry, so Instagram is a natural and easy fit for your online marketing. (Example: @*Airbnb,* @*Disney*, @rusticcuff).

> Or

> You're a **non-fun brand** adjacent to a **fun, photogenic** industry such as airlines, so Instagram fits only if you attach your "non-fun" brand (air travel) to the photogenic outcome, *travel*. (Example: @*aeromexico,* @*united*).

> Or

> You're a **non-fun brand** in a **non-fun, non-photogenic industry** such as insurance, so Instagram only works if you attach your non-fun brand to something fun (hence the attempts by @*Progressive* and @*Geico* to make insurance fun or post things that have little to do with insurance but are visually fun, and then (somehow) connect this back to their brand).

This is even true for nonprofits, which should also identify if they are *fun* or *not fun, photogenic,* or *non-photogenic* for the purposes of their strategy. Your **TO-DO** here is to determine where you fit:

Fun and photogenic: use direct photos of the product or service, and encourage user engagement around the direct use of the product or service (*e.g., Disneyland encouraging users to share photos of themselves having fun at Disneyland*).

Not fun but adjacent to something fun and photogenic. Use photos of the "result" of the product or service in something that is fun and photogenic (*e.g., encouraging persons who tan in tanning booths to share photos of their sexy, tanned bodies at the beach; check out #tanning on Instagram. Another example is how airlines* (not fun) *use travel* (fun) *to promote themselves on Instagram (@SouthWestAir)*).

Not-fun and non-photogenic: attach your Instagram marketing to an adjacent or even unrelated theme. An example would be *@Progressive* on Instagram, sharing photos of their employees enjoying summer at Progressive Field Ballpark in Cleveland. *Baseball is fun, the ballpark is fun, and so… insurance is fun…*

Sentimentality and Aw Shucks on Instagram

Another common strategy is to use quotes and emotion-inspiring photos to attach your brand to something that people will "agree with" because it has a strong emotional component. One of my favorite examples of this is *@Islamic_Teachings* (**http://jmlinks.com/33w**), which shares meaningful quotes about Islam.

So something serious, *religion*, is connected to something beautiful, *a bird*, with a quotation that provides *food for thought*. It's also something we probably all agree on: we should be kind to each other. *Aw shucks*. This post received 18,994 likes. Foundr magazine uses this type of quote strategy as well at **http://jmlinks.com/33x**. So we have "Fear is the disease. Hustle is the antidote" with 9,045 likes in just 22 hours and hundreds of comments:

We'll return to researching and "reverse engineering" brands on Instagram in a moment, but let's dive back into tips and tricks to manage your Instagram efforts better.

» SET UP YOUR BUSINESS PAGE (AND LEARN ITS ADVANTAGES)

You want to use Instagram as a business, not as an individual. So when you set up your Instagram account, be sure to set it up as a business. To do so, follow the steps at **http://jmlinks.com/45r**. If you've mistakenly set yourself up as a personal profile, follow the link to "Convert Existing Account" to convert it.

A business account on Instagram comes with many advantages:

1. **Contact Info**. Business profiles have easy-to-find contact information, which allows users to contact you with questions. If you have an e-commerce store, you can also apply for the new "shop" feature to enable links to the new Instagram shopping experience.

2. **Instagram Insights**. Business accounts get data on user activity, while personal accounts do not.

3. **Advertising**. Business accounts can advertise, which is very useful to grow your followers and engagement. Personal accounts can't advertise.

4. **Post from Desktop Apps**. For business users, Instagram is more accessible via the desktop, including desktop software programs like Hootsuite. This makes it easier to manage.

5. **Connection to Facebook**. Because Instagram is owned by Facebook, Instagram Business accounts are connected to Business Facebook accounts, again making management easier.

6. **Instagram Stories with Links**. Businesses that have more than 10,000 followers can have links in their Stories and Story Highlights via the "swipe up" feature, giving you more opportunities to drive traffic from Instagram to your e-commerce store.

7. **Shopping**. Instagram is clearly moving in the direction of being e-commerce and shopping friendly. Businesses can set up a "shop" on Instagram, tag products in photos, and otherwise enable a seamless shopping experience between their Instagram account and their e-commerce store.

The main downsides are fears that having a business profile will make your business look "salesy" to users and that the organic reach of business profiles will suffer, just as Facebook clobbered the organic reach of business Pages on Facebook. It's likely that at some point, Instagram will REQUIRE businesses to convert, so this risk is there regardless of what you do. You can also try a two-pronged strategy – having a personal profile for the CEO or company spokesperson and a business profile. The former can be more "behind the scenes" and "personal," and the latter more "organizational" and "formal." As always, know your brand and experiment with what will work best for you and your business.

Advertising on Instagram is managed via the Facebook platform. You can set up demographic targets using all the techniques on Facebook (see Chapter 3 on Facebook to learn more about Facebook demographic targeting, which also applies to Instagram). Once you have a Business account on Instagram, you can advertise your posts to:

- People who follow your Business Page on Instagram and/or Facebook.

- People you choose through demographic targeting (such as women, aged 18-24, living in Tulsa, who are interested in weddings, etc.). Facebook and Instagram know a lot about their users, and so leveraging this data to target your Instagram posts is really incredible.

- People you choose through the Facebook Pixel, that is, people who have hit your website. In this way, you can target likely customers who have "hit" your website when they are on Instagram.

Instagram advertising is a great way to gain more exposure for your posts and grow your followers. Learn more at **http://jmlinks.com/45v**.

» LEARN TECHNICAL TIPS TO USING INSTAGRAM

We'll assume that you've set up a business profile on Instagram and done the basics of adding a profile picture, filling out your bio, including a link to your website or eCommerce store. It's a best practice, especially for larger, more consumer-focused brands, to create a company-centric hashtag so that your fans have a virtual way to "tag" their posts about your product or service. Airbnb does this, for example, simply with the hashtag *#Airbnb*, and Southwest Airlines does it with *#SWApic* to encourage its customers to tag photos about their Southwest trips.

Learn a Little Photography

Before we dive into technical tips on Instagram, let's take a moment and talk about **photography**. Instagram is all about photos and videos, so it's very worth your while to become a better photographer. You can Google "how to take better iPhone photos," for example, or go to YouTube and look for tutorials on photography. To read a nice, short article on how to take better Instagram photos, visit **http://jmlinks.com/45u**. But spend some time simply learning how to identify photo-friendly subjects and how to optimize your photos on your camera. The subject and quality of your photos matter a lot.

Indeed, with the rise of Stories, and Reels, Instagram is pushing "vertical video" in a bid to undo nearly a century of horizontal video dominating film. Check out Instagram's tips for vertical video at **http://jmlinks.com/45k** as well as success stories at **http://jmlinks.com/45m**.

Use Instagram Hacks and Techniques

Now, let's dive into some of the technical tips to being a better Instagram user:

Use Hashtags. As has already been discussed, hashtags are big on Instagram. In fact, hashtags are more important on Instagram than on Twitter, and a post can often have five, seven, or even ten hashtags at the end of it. Use a tool like RiteTag (**https://ritetag.com/**) or Hashtags.org (**http://jmlinks.com/27w**) to identify customer-friendly hashtags for your account bio and posts. Also, just search Instagram for your keywords to identify hashtags that have a lot of volume.

Tag People. As on Facebook, you can "tag" people and thereby notify them that they were included on your feed. So, for example, if customer Jane Doe follows your Pizza Parlor, then you can take a picture of her and her friends on her birthday and tag all of them in the Instagram app. In that way, they all get notified that they were "tagged" and are encouraged to share the post with their own friends via Instagram.

Tag Products. If you have enabled shopping, you can take a photo and "tag" products into it. Then when users click or tap on the photo, they can see clickable links from the post to the individual products.

Shopping / eCommerce. Instagram does not allow clickable URLs in posts. Therefore, third-party services have emerged, such as Olapic Tapshop (**http://jmlinks.com/32z**) or Curalate's Like2Buy (**http://jmlinks.com/32w**) that can cross-connect your account to photos that match up with your posts. If you have an active business account, you can also apply for the "shop" feature on Instagram at **http://jmlinks.com/45n**. You can even "tag" a product that will create a link to your e-commerce store.

Link in Bio / Link in Profile. This phrase is commonly used in a post on Instagram to remind people, "Hey! If you want to buy this or check it out on my blog, the clickable link is in my profile," or "Link in my bio" is another way people reference this idea. Use a service like Link Tree (**http://jmlinks.com/45w**) to have a handy index of referenced links.

Add Locations. This is a unique feature of Instagram. When you upload a photo, you can "tag" it to a location such as San Diego or Miami. This improves your chances of showing up in the *Instagram Explore* feature (See: **http://jmlinks.com/27z**), which is where people can go to explore what's up with their friends, connections, and other algorithmically generated accounts and posts. Think of Instagram as an online magazine, and this helps you get into their flippable newsfeed, so to speak.

Multiple Image Posts. Instagram now allows more than one photo per post. Some people hate this feature, but others like it. The easiest way to use it is to access your camera roll and click on "select multiple" to select multiple photos.

Boomerang. This is a quick video plugin for Instagram. Simply find it in the Apple Store or on Google Play by searching for *Instagram Boomerang*. This fun app allows you to shoot a quick, looping video and upload it to your Instagram account. You can download Boomerang on both Google Play and the Apple App Store.

Contests and Challenges. Contests and challenges are huge on Instagram. Have a contest, asking your fans to do something (and enter to win something). Or create a silly "challenge" that challenges them to do something just for bragging rights. Check out the hashtags #challenge and #contest to view what other brands are doing.

Instagram Live. As on Facebook and YouTube, you can "go live" on Instagram. Brainstorm fun, live events for your customers, and "go live" on Instagram. Learn more at **http://jmlinks.com/45p**.

Manage Multiple Accounts. Once you've set up your own personal Instagram account and that of your company, how can you manage both of them? Within Instagram, go to settings (gear icon on the iPhone), and then scroll to the bottom to "add account." You can also use a third-party desktop app like Hootsuite or Buffer to manage multiple business accounts, including posting from the desktop and scheduling your posts.

Instagram Help. Yes, Virginia, there is help on Instagram! Simply visit **http://jmlinks.com/33y**. You can search by keyword for help on a variety of topics. Instagram for business focuses more on advertising issues but can be found at **http://jmlinks.com/33z**. They also have a very good Instagram business blog at **http://jmlinks.com/45q**.

Check out my continually updated post, "Instagram Technical Tips," at **http://jmlinks.com/55d,** which I use in my Stanford Continuing Studies class on social media marketing. The technical tips just keep coming!

Know the Question, and Find the Answer

Remember that *once you know the question, you can find the answer*. One of the best ways to do this is to simply "Google" your question. Just go to Google and type in something like, "How to schedule Instagram posts," or "How to manage multiple accounts on Instagram," and you can usually find a quick blog post or YouTube video that will answer your query. "Once you know the question," I always say to my Stanford students, "You can find the answer." So spend some time reverse-engineering what users and competitors are doing on Instagram, and then formulate a question for Google along the lines of "how do they do such-and-such." A good tip here is to use the Tools menu on the far right of Google and select "Past Year" so as to get recent, up-to-date answers. Here's a screenshot:

» MASTER INSTAGRAM SHOPPING

Let's talk about shopping. Who doesn't love to shop? Instagram is highly visual, highly show offy, and ideal for B2C consumer brands that want to encourage shopping!

A Simple Strategy

The simplest strategy is to proactively link your content to your products or services. Your content can encourage excitement and then subtly (or not so subtly) explain that it's "for sale." Here are the three ways that you can enable a shopping experience for your customers via Instagram:

1. **Mention Shopping Opportunities**. A small company or brand might simply mention that customers can "DM" (direct message) them to inquire about purchasing a product or service in a post. Some companies create unique,

branded hashtags so users can post and inquire via hashtags. By having a business account, you can also enable the "contact" buttons such as email or messaging. As you post, remind customers that what you're posting is "for sale," and they can DM you for more info or click the "email" button, etc.

2. **Use a Link Service**. You can mention "link in bio" often in your posts, thus directing users to your website or, to be more specific, to a link service like Curalate Like2Buy or LinkTree that can match your posts on a one-to-one basis to items in your e-commerce store.

3. **Enable Instagram Shopping and Tag Products**. If you have an e-commerce store on your website, you can activate the Instagram shopping feature. This is the most direct way to enable e-commerce via Instagram. Note that, if enabled, this allows you to "tag a product" via Instagram. Here's a screenshot of a tagged product post by *@outdoorvoices*:

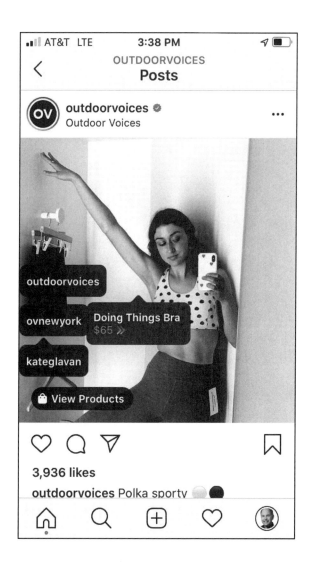

Users can click on "View products" to shop, or click directly on the "Doing Things Bra" and purchase it for $65. Learn more about tagging products at **http://jmlinks.com/53p**.

Enable Instagram Shopping

Returning to the Rustic Cuff Instagram account, notice the "shop" button. (Note: you will see this button only on the mobile version, not the desktop. It's the little "view shop" icon). This new "Instagram Shop" feature is a direct connection to an e-commerce store. Learn more at **http://jmlinks.com/45e**. Here's a screenshot of what you see after you click the "shop" icon on Rustic Cuff's Instagram page:

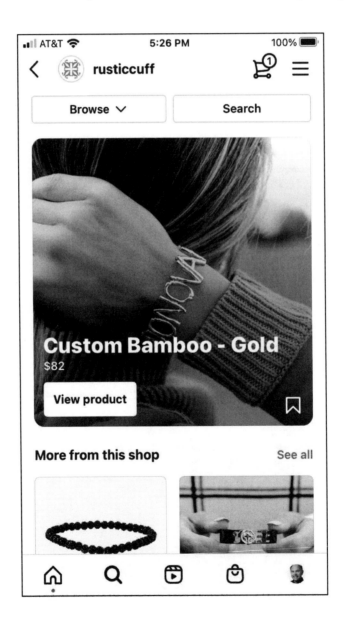

This allows a user to toggle between Rustic Cuff posts that she likes and the e-commerce store and thus purchase them via a direct link from Instagram. Instagram has become a kind of glossy photo magazine for the fashion set; it's an awesome platform for consumer clothing, jewelry, make-up, and accessory brands. Shopping just takes it to the next level.

Within the rubric of shopping on Instagram, let's pause for a moment and investigate the options. You'll need to use the Instagram app on your phone (not the desktop) to see the shopping options as follows:

Non-native Shopping

Examples: @rusticcuff (**https://www.instagram.com/rusticcuff**/) and @target (**https://www.instagram.com/target/**).

Click into the account, then into their shop, click on a product, and you end up on their website to "consummate" the purchase.

Native Shopping

Examples: @inpursuitoftea (**https://www.instagram.com/inpursuitoftea**) and @stickyroosterbrand (**https://www.instagram.com/stickyroosterbrand**).

Click on the account, then into their shop, click on a product, and you remain inside of the Instagram app, where you "consummate" the purchase.

Tagged Products

Examples: @target (**https://www.instagram.com/target/** and @stickyroosterbrand (**https://www.instagram.com/stickyroosterbrand**).

Click into the account, look for posts with the "shopping bag" icon in the top right (or click into product posts), click again on the post and you should see little text pop ups, click on these and you are taking to their store (either native or non-native).

Identify a few brands that have shops and play around with how they integrate their main Instagram feed with shops and products to purchase, including "tagging" products in their posts.

Native Shopping on Instagram: Opportunities

Another way to investigate shopping is to look at it from within the app. By becoming a "native" shop on Instagram, you gain unique promotion opportunities. Read the official help file at **http://jmlinks.com/59a** on how to participate with your products. Inside the app, click on the "shop" icon at the bottom. You'll see "categories," "drops," and "live." Here's a screenshot:

Let's review these opportunities:

> **Categories**. When you participate in Instagram "native" shopping, your products have the opportunity to appear by category. Consumers then browse by category, discovering your products and your brand.
>
> **Drops**. "Drops" are a new type of marketing on Instagram. A "drop" is a product that is usually available in a limited quantity and becomes available only on a specific day, when it "drops." Drops create scarcity for brands, often selling out very quickly. Many young consumers avidly monitor brand drops, buy the products, and in some cases even scalp and resell them. Scarcity and uniqueness drive buzz among the consumer cognoscenti, so try a few "drops" around your brand. Learn more about "drops" at the announcement at **http://jmlinks.com/58z.**
>
> **Live**. You can go "live" with products. Here, you, your staff, and/or customers can have a real event and broadcast this product showcase "live" to Instagram.

It then appears on the "live" tab, and a clickable link to your (tagged) products, as well as in the "story" icon to any follower who is online at the same time.

Instagram, in sum, is "all in" when it comes to shopping. Brainstorm how to build your brand's persona so that customers go from posts and reels to shopping, shop directly to your brand shop, or discover you on the "shop" tab itself including "live."

» INVENTORY LIKES AND DISLIKES ON INSTAGRAM

Now that you have the basics of Instagram down as a user, and you've taken a look at some of the big brands like REI, Airbnb, or Aeromexico that are doing Instagram well, it's time to do your own inventory as a company. Your goal is to identify companies that are doing Instagram well and "reverse engineer" what you like or dislike about their Instagram marketing strategy. Remember: you don't only want to find and follow companies in your industry or niche because many of them may not be that savvy.

In fact, I recommend that you distinguish among and identify three distinct company types. That is, you need to:

1. Find companies *in your niche or industry,* such as competitors.

2. Find companies *in similar niches or industries* (e.g., B2B companies if your B2B, B2G companies if your B2G, etc.)

3. Find some *big brands* that you and your team agree you like.

To start your research, download the "Instagram Research Worksheet." For the worksheet, go to **http://jmlinks.com/2023smm** (then enter the code '**2023smm**' to register your workbook), and click on the link to the "Instagram Research Worksheet." Along the way, pay special attention to the "people" on Instagram and whether (and how) they are interacting with the brands you identify above.

Finding Companies on Instagram

To identify companies on Instagram, start with your keywords and social media themes. Let's take a few hypothetical examples, such as a plumber, a wedding photographer, and a B2B company that sells business insurance. So we'd have keywords such as:

Plumber. *Plumbing, plumber, home improvement, DIY, toilet repair.*

Wedding Photographer: *weddings, marriage, photography, bridal.*

Business insurance. *Insurance, business insurance, small business, risk management.*

Here are the methods to search Instagram by keyword, looking for accounts to follow and reverse engineer:

Method #1: Instagram Search. Go to Instagram, either on the desktop or on your phone. Type your keywords into the search box. Then look at the posts that come back, and click up to the account holders, or look at the comments and likes, and click over to those people who are interacting with the posts. Make a list of those accounts that fit your target.

Method #2: Google Search. Use Google. Go to Google.com, and enter *site:Instagram.com* plus your keywords, as in *site:Instagram.com "business insurance"* (There's no space between *site:* and *Instagram.com*, and use quotation marks around keyword phrases). To see an example, visit **http://jmlinks.com/28c**. Next, scroll down the list, and Google will identify accounts on Instagram that have those keywords.

Method #3: Use a Geotag. Type in a city name such as *Tulsa* (**http://jmlinks.com/28g**) into the Instagram search box. This is a good way to see the posts across a wide range of industries and topics so that you don't get "boxed in" to seeing just posts in your industry.

Method #4: Instagram Explore. Instagram Explore works best if you first configure your personal Instagram account for a few weeks, and be sure to follow competitors and others in your industry. Then, open up your Instagram App, and click the "Magnifying Glass" icon on the bottom. Instagram will suggest photos and accounts to you, based on your interests and behavior. By following competitors and paying attention to things "as if" you were a customer, you can get Instagram to find interesting companies to "reverse engineer." Across the top, you can also swipe by category for suggestions. Here's a screenshot:

So if you clicked on "Style," you'd see posts on that topic and can then click up to follow a person or brand that might be relevant for your marketing research. You can also access *Instagram Explore* on the desktop or at **https://www.instagram.com/explore/**.

Method #5. Explore Account Suggestions. You can also find one brand you like and then click on the downward arrow to the right of "message" in the app to see "similar" companies. It's easy to miss, so here's a screenshot:

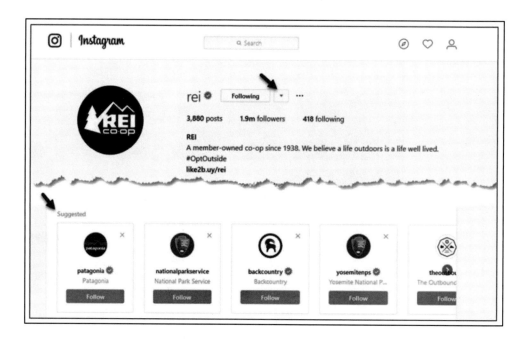

In this way, you can find one brand such as REI and then find similar or competitive brands to follow, such as in this case Patagonia, the National Park Service, and Back Country.

Inventory Companies That You Find

For example, if you search Instagram for *toilet repair* (**http://jmlinks.com/28a**), you'll find posts by people and a few companies on the topic. I found this post, for example:

Bayside Plumbing Instagram post:

bayside.plumbing · Follow

bayside.plumbing Is that flush button just not working like it used to? Is water constantly trickling into the toilet bowl? 🚽

While some problems may seem simple, trying to fix your toilet by yourself can potentially make the problem worse - and you could end up spending lots of money on litres of wasted water!

So when it comes to toilet trouble, it's best to hang up your DIY hat 🎩 and pick up the phone to give the experts a call ☎️

#baysideplumbing #emergencyplumbing #sydneyplumber #sydneyplumbing #toiletrepair #bathroomremodel #bathroomrenovation #bathroomideas #bathroomstyle #plumbersworld #plumbersydney #plumbingservices #plumbingandheating #plumbingrepair #plumbingwork

6w

rambuilt_constructions Love that tool!

6w 1 like Reply

28 likes

OCTOBER 6

Add a comment...

Toilet repair on Instagram, who knew?

As you identify posts and accounts, take some notes as you and your team discuss what you like and what you don't like about:

Profile Picture. Do you like it? Does it convey the brand image?

Bio. What does the bio say? Does it have a link?

Other Technical Features. Is shopping enabled? Is it native to Instagram or does it move to the vendor website? Is a branded hashtag in use? Why or why not? Can you message the account owner? Go through the technical features one-by-one and "reverse engineer" how they are being used.

Followers. How many people follow the account? What type of engagement are you seeing?

Content Strategy. What types of content are being created and why? What is the ratio of "fun" posts to "buy our stuff posts?"

UGC is key on Instagram. Can your company identify and create a unique branded hashtag for your own customers? Would they care enough to post photos tagged in that way? What about having a contest or challenge for the best photos posted to your hashtag? Don't stare at the blank page: inventory and reverse engineer what other companies are doing on Instagram.

Posting Strategy

Next, note the interactivity of individual posts. Which ones stand out as something you – as a user – would take note of on Instagram and even like, comment, or share? Which ones have the most interactivity? Why? Notice, for example, this post (**http://jmlinks.com/28e**) which is a plumber pushup video, with 183 likes, and 21 comments:

Think deeply about each post. Notice, for example, that this isn't a plumber doing plumbing (*boring*), but it's a kind of sexy guy showing off how strong he is by doing push-ups (*fun*). And then (spoiler alert), as you watch it, you realize it's a spoof. It's very similar to posts that "real people" make on Instagram; it's personal, it's funny, and it's photogenic. And notice that it's actually a repost from somewhere else. So this post indicates that @*theTacticalPlumber* is being playful and having fun with Instagram, not just posting boring plumbing stuff.

And yet, it does relate to plumbing, and it does build the company's brand. So what types of posts might you make that would be fun, playful, and photogenic and yet connect to your brand? Don't be boring!

As you look at Instagram accounts that pique your interest, try to "reverse engineer" each company's **posting strategy**. Looking at their posts, are they merely informative, fun, photogenic, or something else? How do they connect to the brand image that the vendor is seeking to project? How frequently are items posted? Look at likes, comments, and shares. Is their posting strategy engaging their users, and why or why not?

A Different Vendor

Let's do this again with another search and vendor. My search on Google for *site:Instagram.com* *"business insurance"* led me to *@WeddingInsuranceGroup* (**http://jmlinks.com/28f**). This is a British company that offers insurance for vendors in the wedding industry. They have 377 posts, 667 followers, and are following 1,193. Note that they are an insurer (*boring!*), but they are adjacent to a very Instagram-friendly business, weddings (*fun!*).

Their bio says:

> *The specialist independent insurance broker for wedding and event businesses. We cover niche professions. Visit our site for a quote.*

Scroll down through their posts and attempt to "reverse engineer" what they've posted and why. You'll see a lot of posts with quotations speaking to the fear that the photography or catering equipment might get stolen, something might go terribly wrong, and hence the need for business insurance. But also take a look at how they use hashtags such as *#WeddingWednesday,* which reaches out not to just their B2B customers but people actually planning weddings who might be interested in insuring the big event (what if the groom gets cold feet?). Notice the use of single images, carousel images, and even videos. Here's a post that is a collaboration with a vendor they insure, Luxury Classic Jaguars:

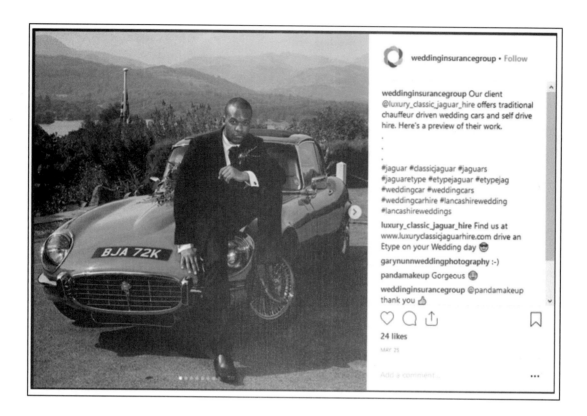

In terms of posting, they have fun images, they use hashtags and emojis, they use "shout-outs" to their partners, and they encourage cross-posting. This is clearly a B2B business that is using Instagram to be visible on a venue that their own customers (Wedding photographers and the like) clearly see as essential. The wedding insurance itself isn't fun, but the way that they connect to the adjacent industry is.

Wrapping Up Your Research

For your **TO-DO**, download and complete the **Instagram Research Worksheet**. For the worksheet, go to **http://jmlinks.com/2023smm** (then enter the code '**2023smm**' to register your workbook), and click on the link to the "Instagram Research Worksheet."

Pay the most attention to **posting strategy**. After all, setting up an Instagram account isn't very difficult. It's what types of photos or videos get posted, how successful they are at generating interactivity, and how all this buzz connects to some business objective that matters. I recommend that you create an editorial calendar for all your social media posts; for Instagram, this would mean planning out what types of photos or videos you are going to shoot, when, where, and how. Like any good party, there should be a lot of systematic planning towards the food and entertainment that needs to be produced on a regular basis! It just looks easy, but that's an illusion.

» Video: Instagram Stories, Videos, and Reels

Instagram, like all the major platforms, is strongly encouraging the move to video. It's a Brave New World of vertical video, clearly hoping to leapfrog YouTube as a major video platform. You can upload videos directly from your phone, or you can pre-edit them in vertical format and upload via your PC. Learn more at **http://jmlinks.com/45s**.

Instagram Stories, in contrast, are short pictures or videos you upload to your "story" as a brand. Stories are essentially a "day in the life" of an individual or brand, told in photo and video format. "Stories" is a direct competitor to **Snapchat** (**https://www.snapchat.com/**). Snapchat, of course, invented many of the aspects "stolen" by Instagram, such as stories or filters, and so far, it looks like Instagram is going to win out. And don't forget you can just upload videos directly to Instagram as a post from your phone.

Instagram is very video-friendly, and the company clearly sees video as its future, so stay tuned. Reels is Instagram's copycat of TikTok. Users can upload short, funny videos, as can brands.

It's Instagram and Reels, not Instagram or Reels

Nonetheless, I'd caution against *either/or* thinking and recommend you do *both/and* thinking. The lion's share of your work will be on Instagram posts of pictures and videos directly to your feed, but you should investigate Stories and Reels.

Reels is the newest; you can learn more about it at **http://jmlinks.com/55e**. Reels is a direct copy of TikTok videos, and focuses less on your social media connections and more on trending content. As on TikTok, Reels tend to be short, fun, and snappy. Many reels use "trending sounds" that become a sort of audio hashtag. Within reels, click on any video and on the lower right for "trending sounds." Trends are the key to reels as the algorithm pays massive attention to which videos a user watches, likes, and comments on. Thus people who love cat videos, see more cat reels. People who love dog videos, see more dog videos, and so on and so forth. Reels works, as does TikTok, on a "recommendation engine" algorithm and not so much on a traditional social network.

» BRAINSTORM AND PLAN AN INSTAGRAM MARKETING STRATEGY

Returning to Instagram, it's time to brainstorm, plan, and execute an Instagram marketing strategy for your company. I'll assume you've researched your customer base and decided they're on Instagram, plus looked at competitors, similar companies, and just brands that "get it," to get a sense of what you like and what you don't like about brand marketing on Instagram. You've completed the *Instagram Research Worksheet*. Now download the *Instagram Posting* and *Instagram Marketing Plan Worksheets*. (For the worksheet, go to **http://jmlinks.com/2023smm** (then enter the code '**2023smm**' to register your workbook)).

Instagram Set Up

The *Instagram Research Worksheet* gives you your basics. Identify a profile picture. Write a bio that includes a link to your website. Decide if you want to enable a clickable email link. And decide if you want to use an Instagram-related link service such as Like2b.uy (**http://jmlinks.com/32w**)   or   Olapic's   Tapshop   platform   at **http://jmlinks.com/32z**. Enable at least one Instagram account for your business, but you'll probably need to manage multiple accounts on your phone. If more than one person is uploading photos and videos, then have multiple people enable it on their phones. Consider using a third-party app like Hootsuite to manage and schedule your posts.

Instagram Posting Strategy

What and how should you post? First and foremost, figure out if you are a *fun* company in a *fun/photogenic* industry, where people will want to share photos of themselves directly using your product or service, or you're a *fun or not fun* company in a *fun or not fun* industry, where you'll have to strategize something adjacent to your industry. Are you an Airbnb that's directly fun? Or are you more like an airline like Aeromexico, where the experience itself isn't that fun, but there's something adjacent (travel) that is fun? Or are you like Allstate Insurance, where your business isn't fun, your industry isn't fun, and it's not really adjacent to anything that's fun, either? So check off:

❑ We're a *fun company in a fun industry*, so we'll post (and get our fans to post) fun photos of them actually using our product or service.

❑ We're a *not fun company adjacent to something fun*, so we'll post (and get our fans to post) fun photos of them using something adjacent to our industry.

❏ We're a *not fun company in a not fun industry*, so we'll really have to think out of the box to use Instagram!

Your **posting strategy** will reflect the reality of how fun and photogenic your products or services truly are.

ARE YOU A FUN COMPANY, OR A NOT FUN COMPANY?

Next, identify who's going to take what photos/videos, when, where, why, and how. Create an editorial calendar to pre-identify Instagram opportunities such as industry holidays or events (think Cinco de Mayo if you're an avocado company, or Christmas if you're an Irish gift store). Other opportunities might be when customers use your product or service in a photogenic way; think "Kodak Moments" like they used to have in Disneyland. A museum store might have a contest among its customers to share a fun photo of mom or grandma with the kids, buying fun stuff in the store. What are your "Instagram moments" for your business? Think ahead for when there are the best opportunities for Instagram buzz, and write those down in your posting strategy worksheet.

Finally, start posting! Instagram – like all social media – requires that you post a lot of content on a regular basis, and you won't know what works until you start doing it. So get started!

The steps are:

1. **Create Engaging Content.** You must create content that engages your customers, sparks their curiosity, and empowers their imagination.

2. **Promote Your Instagram Content.** Content by itself is insufficient. You need to promote your content to customers through every trick of the trade: real-world to social, cross social as in from Twitter to Instagram, Instagram organic as through the use of hashtags, and even advertising.

3. **Have a Clear Call To Action (CTA).** A strong brand encourages customers to take action. That can be an obvious CTA such as a shopping post with tagged items or a more subtle CTA such as "link in bio," but regardless, you as the marketer need to encourage customers to take the final step: buying your products or services either off or on Instagram.

» Promote Your Instagram Account and Posts

The best Instagram account in the world isn't worth a hill of beans if no one sees your posts. Like all "parties" on Social Media, you have to promote your Instagram "party" for it to be successful. First, populate your Instagram account with fun photos, even if you have zero or just a few followers. There has to be something there that people want to engage with before you start promoting.

Once you're up and running, here are ideas on how to promote your Instagram account and posts:

Real World to Social. For most businesses, this is by far the most important tactic and the cheapest. Simply ask your customers to follow you on Instagram at the point of real contact. A museum gift shop, for example, can install placards at check out that say, "Follow us on Instagram," or even better, a small tablet displaying the store's Instagram account in real-time that people can see and click on as they wait in line. Have the clerks ask people if they're on Instagram and ask them to follow the shop. "Why follow us?" you ask. Because we share fun photos, have contests and even communicate special deals and discounts!

Shout outs and Collabs. Identify complementary vendors in your niche, and reach out to them for collaborative Instagram marketing. If you're a wedding photographer, reach out to the wedding florist, the wedding venue, the cake maker, the priest, rabbi, or another officiant at the wedding… ask them to "collab" with you and/or give you a "shout out," and reciprocate.

You Gotta Promote Your Instagram to Be Successful

Hashtags. Instagram is very hashtag-friendly. Be sure to use **geotags** (your location) in your posts, and identify and use relevant hashtags. People use Instagram like a magazine to discover content that they care about, so deploy hashtags that feed that interest and make sure that the content they will discover is "sticky" so that they follow your account. (Use RiteTag (**https://ritetag.com/**)) to find trending hashtags on Twitter and Instagram that are relevant to your brand, and include them in your posts. In addition, identify one or more "branded" hashtags unique to your company to encourage social sharing around your brand. REI does this, for example, with *#optoutside* across all its social media channels.

Website / Other Social Media. Be sure that your website links to your Instagram, easily, and cross-promote from your other social accounts (e.g., Twitter) to your Instagram. Don't forget to use your customer email list and email newsletters to promote and advertise your Instagram. Use one social media to promote another.

Interact with Others. Follow other accounts, and like, share, and comment on posts made by those accounts. Identify your competitors, and look at who follows them. Follow those people and like, share, and comment on their Instagram accounts. **Warning**: Be aware that if you follow/interact with too many accounts too quickly, you can get banned from Instagram! (See **http://jmlinks.com/28r** for more information). So don't be spammy! More tips on being interactive with your fans –

> **Follow Relevant People.** "Follow for follow" still works on Instagram, so identify and follow industry leaders, the followers of your competitors, etc. This means that if you follow them, they will likely follow you back. Warning: do not overdo this, as there is a cap of about 300 follows per day and a lifetime cap of 7000. Don't spam!
>
> **@Mention People.** Mention or "tag" key influencers, your own users and other people in general in your comments and captions. By "shout outs" to others, you'll get their attention. **Tag** people as well.
>
> **Like and Comment on the Posts of Others.** Look at your users, and the friends of your users, and like their posts. Ditto for comments. Comment on what others are doing on Instagram.
>
> **Reshare Your Users' Posts.** Selectively share / or repost some of your users' posts (with their permission). Sharing isn't as easy on Instagram as on Facebook, but you should still do it. For example, you can reach out by email to someone who posts a photo, have them email it to you, post it to your account, and include their @handle in your caption.
>
> **Engage with Your Own Users**. Instagram isn't just about broadcasting to your customers. It's also about interacting with and engaging with them. Pay attention to who follows you already, and interact with their comments to your account. Follow them back. Spend at least an hour a day interacting with your customer. Identify and cultivate superfans that might be willing to promote your business. Ask your fans for comments. Post a picture of a draft product or service, and ask users for their

opinions. Post a survey question and ask users to chime in in the comments field. Post a photo and ask for a caption; have a caption contest, and give the winner a gift card. Be provocative!

Advertise on Instagram. Yes, Instagram has advertising! And yes, you can use it to promote your Instagram business account, as well as offlink to your website or e-commerce store. Since Instagram is owned by Facebook, you manage an Instagram ad through your Facebook account. You need a Facebook Page for your business and need to connect that Page to your Instagram account to be able to advertise. You can read the official help file at **http://jmlinks.com/28w**.

Instagram Contests and Challenges

Among the most important Instagram promotion strategies are **contests** and **challenges**. One easy way to do this is to establish a hashtag for your brand and then ask users to post a photo on that hashtag as part of the contest or giveaway. You select a winner based on the posts. For example, check out *#jorgstyle,* which was a contest based on user photos (**http://jmlinks.com/28s**). Here's a screenshot of the singer Pitbull, who's using the hashtags *#contest, #Pitbull,* and *#Mr305* to promote his brand. Yes, you can go to Las Vegas and see him live – just post a picture of you and your Mom. What's more special than a picture of you and your mom honoring Pitbull? (*A selfie of you and your mom at the Pitbull concert in Las Vegas shared to Instagram, of course*).

A quick way to browse contests and look for contest ideas on Instagram is to use the Google *search site:Instagram.com #contests* at **http://jmlinks.com/28t**. Of course, there are vendors such as Gleam.io that will help you manage Instagram contests (**http://jmlinks.com/28u**). Just Google "Instagram Contests" or "Instagram Challenges," and you can easily find helpful vendors or apps. Read the official Instagram restrictions at **http://jmlinks.com/28v**.

» WORK WITH INSTAGRAM INFLUENCERS

Instagram is probably the most important social media network these days for so-called **influencers**, though influencers are big on YouTube and TikTok, too. What's an influencer?

> *An influencer is a person who has a relevant and substantial social media following and is willing to promote your product or service, usually for a fee.*

Here's where it gets tricky. You want to distinguish among:

Fans and Superfans. These are people who truly use and like your product or service and are active on Instagram, and might promote you "for free" because they basically really love you.

Paid Promotions / Contests / Challenges. This is using giveaways, contests, challenges, or other tactics to encourage your fans and superfans to promote you. You either pay them, or they get some type of free stuff in exchange for spreading your message.

Influencers. This term has come to mean people who have a very substantial following on Instagram and who will promote your product or service for a fee. Make sure that they are relevant to your brand; it's not just about quantity; after all, it's about quality and relevance.

It is also possible that people who have a significant following might be willing to collaborate with you and your brand in exchange not for money but just for free stuff or even because they just truly love your brand, products, and/or services. A hotel chain, for example, might comp a guest to stay at the hotel and in exchange, expect photos, videos, and shout-outs about the brand. Or a restaurant might give discounts to people in the restaurant for similar behavior. So you'll have some "influencers" who might promote you for free because they just really love you, some who want free stuff, and still others who want money.

FTC regulations require persons who are getting free stuff and/or being paid to acknowledge a paid relationship in their posts, but this regulation seems to be widely ignored. Instagram also requires the influencer ("paid") posts to be identified with the tag "Paid partnership with" your company. See Instagram's requirements at **http://jmlinks.com/45t** and check out posts fulfilling this requirement at **http://jmlinks.com/46g**.

To find influencers, look at your branded hashtags and look for fans and superfans who are already engaged. Follow them back and look at how many followers they have. Reach out to them with offers of free stuff and/or money to promote your brand.

Search Instagram by keyword and look for accounts that are relevant. You can also use services like Buzzsumo to find out what type of content is being shared (and by whom), Hashtagify.me (which tracks Instagram in its paid version), and paid services like Pixlee (**https://www.pixlee.com**). Just Google "influencer marketing Instagram" and you can easily find companies and services that broker the relationship between influencers and brands on the platform.

» MEASURE YOUR INSTAGRAM KPIs

Although Instagram does not easily allow links to your website, Instagram marketing can still be measured. Define the KPIs (Key Performance Indicators) that will indicate that your Instagram marketing efforts are either building your brand awareness and/or directly selling more stuff.

Establish some KPIs (Key Performance Indicators), such as:

- **Followers**. Measure your follower count each month. It should go up.

- **Engagement**. Measure, for each post, is it getting likes, comments, and shares. Which posts get the most engagement? Why or why not?

- **Action**. You're not in this for your health. Is Instagram –

  - **Building your brand**? Increasing your brand awareness in a positive way? If so, why? If not, why not, and what can you do to fix it?

  - **Leading to sales** actions such as completed feedback/inquiry forms or purchases at an eCommerce website? For some brands (e.g., Airbnb, Rusticcuff), Instagram CAN lead to real sales, but for others, this isn't a realistic objective.

Your Instagram strategy – working *backward* – should go from a sale/sales lead to better brand awareness, to a fun, photogenic post by you or a fan, to a strong account on Instagram. To devise your strategy, don't start at a conceptual level with the photo or post; rather, start with what you want, such as either better brand awareness or an actual sale (or both), and work backward.

Don't forget to think about user-generated content (UGC). How can you use contests, hashtags, or other prompts to motivate your customer fans to engage with you on Instagram and even create and upload fun content around your brand? Interact with your users and others on Instagram by liking, commenting on, and sharing their posts. Tag people in your photos and videos. Follow individuals, as the "follow for follow" vibe is still very strong on Instagram. Measure whether these outreach efforts are getting resonance or not, and why.

Finally, on an ongoing, monthly basis, measure your Instagram performance vis-a-vis your KPIs and record them as you should be doing for other social media networks like Facebook, LinkedIn, or Twitter. Is your fan base growing? Is your engagement growing? Are you seeing improvements in your brand equity? And are you getting any actual sales performance from your social media efforts? How can you improve?

Measure your Instagram strategy as the Big Picture of why your company is on Instagram in the first place and your posting strategy as the tactical manifestation of this. Everything needs to work together towards a common goal of bolstering your brand on Instagram and ultimately helping you to sell more stuff.

»» CHECKLIST: INSTAGRAM ACTION ITEMS

Test your knowledge of Instagram! Take the *Instagram marketing quiz* at **http://jmlinks.com/qzin**. Next, here are your Instagram **Action Items**:

❑ **Research** -

> ❑ Whether **your customers** are on Instagram. If so, what or who are they interacting with? What **content** engages them, and why? What type of interactive and/or UGC content do you see?

> ❑ Whether **your competitors** are on Instagram. If so, what is their Instagram posting strategy, and does it seem to be working as measured by followers and interaction? Why or why not?

> ❑ Whether **there are similar companies to emulate**. Are there companies (not your competitors) that are doing a good job on Instagram? If so, who are they, and what are they doing?

> ❑ Whether there are relevant **#hashtags** on Instagram or **#geotags** that connect potential customers to themes that make sense for your business.

❑ **Set up** a business profile on Instagram, including –

> ❑ **Profile Picture**

> ❑ **Bio Description with link.** Describe your company's value proposition in a fun way, and use a service like Like2Buy if desired.

> ❑ **Contact Info.** Make sure that your contact information is included in your Business account. If possible, sign up for the shop feature.

> ❑ **Posts.** Begin posting photos and/or videos of your business that fit to the Instagram culture of friends, family, fun, photos, and fake.

> ❑ **Instagram Stories and/or Reels**. If possible, create a daily Instagram story about your brand. Save stories as "highlights" so that they show under your profile. Once you have 10,000 followers, you can embed links as well.

❑ **Instagram Shopping.** If applicable, set up the Shop feature for your e-commerce store. If you're a major brand, consider setting up an Instagram "native" shop.

❑ **Brainstorm** a **content marketing strategy** for Instagram. Are you a "fun company" in a "fun industry," a "not fun company" adjacent to a "fun industry," or a "not fun company" that's not near "anything fun?" Then brainstorm –

> ❑ **Photos** to take of your business, products, and/or services that "fit" with Instagram.

> ❑ **Videos, Stories,** and **Reels** that "fit" your brand narrative.

> ❑ **UGC** or "User Generated Content." How can you get your fans/customers to not only interact with the content you produce but produce content themselves that helps build your brand? Would contests or challenges work for you?

> ❑ **Interactive Content.** Be interactive on Instagram. Follow your fans back, and follow new people to get their attention. Like and comment on what your fans are saying. Make your brand interactive.

❑ **Promote** your Instagram business profile through strategies like *#hashtags*, follow for follow, cross-connections to other digital properties like your website, Twitter, Facebook, etc., and even consider contests or **advertising** on Instagram.

❑ **Measure** your Instagram results such as increase in followers, increases in post interactivity, traffic to your website and/or eCommerce store.

Check out the **free tools**! Go to my *Social Media Marketing Dashboard > Instagram* for my favorite free tools on Instagram. Just visit **http://jmlinks.com/smmdash**.

»» DELIVERABLE: AN INSTAGRAM MARKETING PLAN

Your **DELIVERABLE** has arrived. For the worksheet, go to **http://jmlinks.com/2023smm** (then enter the code '**2023smm**' to register your workbook), and click on the link to the "Instagram Marketing Plan." By filling out this plan, you and your team will establish a vision of what you want to achieve via Instagram marketing, including your KPIs (Key Performance Indicators). Be sure to complete the Instagram research and posting worksheets as well.

8
YOUTUBE

YouTube, in particular, and video, in general, provide a two-for-one punch to your social media marketing. First, video can be the **actual content**, the "stuff" that's being posted and consumed on Twitter, Facebook, LinkedIn, etc. People love, watch, and share video as one of the most popular types of content across social media. Nowadays, however, video doesn't just live on YouTube. It lives on Facebook, Instagram, LinkedIn, TikTok, and even Twitter. Second, as a **social media platform** in its own right, YouTube works much like Facebook or Twitter. People "like" (*thumbs up* in YouTube lingo), "comment on," and "share" your videos. They "subscribe" to your channel and get notifications when you release a new video.

In this Chapter, you'll learn the basics of what makes a good video for any platform. As for YouTube, you'll see similarities to Facebook: setting up a channel ("Page") on YouTube, uploading a video ("post") to YouTube, and the fact that people subscribe to your channel ("like" your "Page"). You'll also learn that video brings three very different marketing mechanisms in its role as content. Video can be used as a **supportive medium**, it can be deployed via **SEO** (Search Engine Optimization) to show at the top of Google and/or YouTube searches, and it can be tweaked for **social sharing** across platforms. And, with the rise of "YouTube Shorts," YouTube has gone full stop into the "**recommendation engine**" pioneered by TikTok. YouTube lets you reach not just folks who "subscribe" to your channel but folks who are searching and watching content on themes that matter to your brand.

Let's get started!

To-do List:

» Get What's So Great about Video

» Explore How YouTube Works

» Inventory Companies on YouTube

» Understand the Four Promotional Uses of Video

» Tell Stories through Video

» Set up Your Channel and Upload Videos

» Advertise on YouTube

» Explore Video on Facebook, Instagram, LinkedIn, and TikTok

» Measure your Results

»» Checklist: YouTube Action Items

»» Deliverable: A YouTube Marketing Plan

» GET WHAT'S SO GREAT ABOUT VIDEO

Video is the fastest-growing form of content on the Internet, and video is the most viral type of content. People love video! But why? In his prescient 1964 book *Understanding Media*, Marshall McLuhan argued that "the medium is the message." *Understanding Media* is a complex, nuanced book, but suffice it to say that McLuhan was one of the first to realize that people would respond to video in an emotional way. Were McLuhan alive today, the social scientist would not be surprised at the popularity of "cat videos" on the Internet, the fact that trends like the "Harlem Shake" or "Ice Bucket Challenge" are able to "go viral" by leveraging both the power of video and the power of influencers, nor the power of video to create political controversy over events at the US border, the relationship between police and minority communities, the 2024 election, or other powerful political images that seemingly sweep across the culture day in and day out. More recently, authors like Richard Brodie and Susan Blackmore have argued that the Internet accelerates the spread of "memes" or "idea viruses" and that video plays a key role in how ideas spread across the culture.

For marketers and business owners, video brings together two key features that exist almost nowhere else in social media:

1. the ability to **leverage emotions** to persuade potential customers to like your brand and buy your stuff; and

2. an increased likelihood of **social sharing** by one user to others.

Video, by its very nature is also an ideal medium for "showing" rather than "telling," so it plays well in the "how to" space as, for example, in popular videos like "how to tie a tie," or "how to get a puppy to stop biting," with 102 million views and 2.7 million views on YouTube, respectively. And, in an era in which (unfortunately) the general population is declining in education and intelligence, video is "easy" to understand vs. reading, which is "hard."

People prefer emotion to reason, showing to telling, and viewing to reading. Video hits all three of these trends. New for 2023, another trend is the movement towards "recommendation engines" in the algorithm. TikTok, in particular, but also YouTube, Instagram, Twitter, Facebook, and other video-heavy platforms increasingly *recommend* videos to users, even if those users do not "follow" the video creator. Cat people get more suggestions of cat videos, dog people more dog videos, and so on and so forth. Trends, in particular, can be more important for the success of your video content than the actual subscribers to your channel on YouTube or followers of your account on TikTok. Indeed, the launch of "YouTube Shorts," which is a copycat of TikTok, speaks to how YouTube wants to evolve from being a social media platform into a recommendation engine, or perhaps a hybrid of the best of both.

Leaving aside the general decline of Western civilization, video is an incredible tool in your marketing toolbox. Imagine videos about your brand, product, or service that touch on emotions, spur social sharing, explain how to use your product (and its benefits), and are so easy to consume as content that the user need merely sit back, relax, and absorb your marketing message. What's not to like about video?

VIDEO IS EASY TO CONSUME AND HARD TO PRODUCE

Production, that's what not to like. Producing video, as compared with still photos or text posts, is difficult. It requires knowledge of visual storytelling as well as production techniques such as scripts, camera, sound, and editing. Even a short YouTube video can be difficult to produce and can be intimidating. With some effort and some tools, however, it's increasingly easy to create videos. So don't be intimidated! Rather, embrace and enjoy the video revolution in marketing.

» EXPLORE HOW YOUTUBE WORKS

Video and YouTube are among the most dramatic, most viral components of the Internet. Who doesn't know the "Harlem Shake" (**http://jmlinks.com/1m**) or the "Ice Bucket Challenge" (**http://jmlinks.com/1n**)? Who hasn't watched "Will it blend?" (**http://jmlinks.com/1o**) or "Dear 16 Year Old Me" (**http://jmlinks.com/1p**)? (Check out the hashtag #challenge on YouTube at **https://www.youtube.com/hashtag/challenge** to see the latest crazes). And who hasn't fallen into the trap of assuming all YouTube is, are silly cat videos, Beyoncé and

Jay-Z videos, and inappropriate High School humor? It is, but YouTube is much, much more than that as a marketing opportunity (and as a social phenomenon).

As we shall see, there are four basic ways that videos can help you with social media marketing:

1. **Video as a supporting medium**: acting as the "content" that you "share" via other social media, including your website. (This is true on your website, on YouTube, on Facebook, and even on LinkedIn or Twitter).

2. **Video as a discovery mechanism via SEO** (Search Engine Optimization), helping you promote your company, products, or services via YouTube and Google search.

3. **Video as a share / viral promotion tactic**, because people love and share provocative videos, not just on YouTube but via on all social media networks like Facebook, Twitter, LinkedIn, or Pinterest.

4. **Video as a Subscription Service:** you become a de facto "TV channel" and people "subscribe" to your channel because they want to learn about a topic, watch you pointificate in serious or humorous ways about trends, or just laugh / engage with you "as if" you / your channel were a TV show. In this model, you make money with "product placements," "internal ads," and "monetization" via YouTube's ad platform.

We should also mention **#5** – video as an *advertising* medium. YouTube presents unique advertising opportunities, and "video ads" are now common on Facebook, Twitter, and LinkedIn. And **#6** – video across platforms from YouTube to Facebook, Instagram, and now TikTok and beyond.

We'll dive into the details in a moment. But first, log on to YouTube and get your bearings. (For the official YouTube starter guide, go to **http://jmlinks.com/1q**). If you're familiar with Facebook and Twitter, you'll see many similarities right out of the gate:

- Individuals (or brands) have an "account" or "**channel**" on YouTube, set up by registering with an email address and using their Google account to manage their account.

- Individuals (or brands) can **upload videos** to their "channel," and when uploading, give each video a TITLE, a DESCRIPTION, and KEYWORD TAGS as well as designate a VIDEO THUMBNAIL.

- Individuals **"subscribe"** to the channels of other individuals (or brands) on YouTube, and when someone you subscribe to uploads a new video, you get a notification in your YouTube news feed as well as via email that a new video has been posted. A unique feature on YouTube is the "bell," located to the right of the "subscribe" button; subscribed users can click it to increase the likelihood of notifications.

- Individuals can **thumbs up / thumbs down videos** (akin to "like" on Facebook of a post), comment, and share the videos via other social media as well as create playlists of videos on YouTube.

- Companies can create **brand channels** on YouTube. They can also post alerts and announcements visible to their fans including via hashtags to chime in on timely topics important to the YouTube community.

- **New for 2023** – videos can now exist in two formats, the older "traditional" horizontal format or the newer **"shorts"** vertical format, optimized for the phone. The latter is a complete rip-off of TikTok, and like Reels on Instagram, attempts to capitalize on short, funny videos that "go viral" via the "recommendation engine" of the algorithm. Learn more about shorts at **http://jmlinks.com/57m**.

Like Twitter or Instagram, YouTube is easy and open: anyone can quickly create a channel. Like Twitter or Instagram, YouTube does not really distinguish between the Channel or Account of an individual vs. that of a company. And like Twitter or Instagram, YouTube really does not authenticate users. It's super easy to set up a Channel and post videos as either an individual or a company.

For assistance on how to set up a company YouTube channel, visit **http://jmlinks.com/1r**. Your first to-do is thus to either set up a YouTube account as an individual or as a brand, and then start searching for, watching, and interacting with videos. What videos pique your interest? What videos seem relevant to your target customers? Which brands or individuals that are relevant to your company are already on YouTube, and what type of video content are they producing that's getting transaction?

» Inventory Companies on YouTube

After you've signed up for YouTube, your mission is to identify competitors on YouTube as well as brands to emulate in order to make an inventory of your likes and dislikes when it comes to YouTube as a channel for marketing. I'll focus largely on how to use YouTube as a brand, but let's distinguish between these three types of YouTubers:

1. **Pure Users**. These are ordinary people who don't post videos but rather just watch video content. They are "content consumers" and not "content producers." These are your target audiences as a marketer. Like Twitter, YouTube reaches pretty much everyone on the planet. "Riches are in the niches," so don't be discouraged by the high-profile pop culture elements on YouTube. There are many fantastic niche users and niche usages!

2. **Amateur Content Creators**. These are people who create and upload videos about their lives, likes, habits, or other things but whose goal isn't to make money or go viral. They are merely using YouTube like they'd use Facebook, TikTok, or Instagram to upload and share content about their lives. Note that an individual can be both a user on YouTube and a creator of content, just as they can be on Twitter or Facebook.

3. **Professional Content Creators or Influencers**. These are individuals who really function as brands. An example would be PewDiePie, with over 111 million subscribers on YouTube (**http://jmlinks.com/44d**). PewDiePie's real name is Felix Arvid Ulf Kjellberg, and this Swedish national was named by Time magazine as one of 2016's most influential people. This type of content creator generally makes money off of Google ads placed on YouTube and/or brand endorsements. Think of this type as akin to "Oprah" on YouTube, where a single individual IS the brand and money is made by product tie-ins and advertising. Patreon (**https://www.patreon.com/**), YouTube subscriptions, and selling "swag" are new ways for YouTube creators to make money off of their videos. You can even find "influencers" eager to accept money in exchange for their "honest" promotion of your product or service.

4. **Brands**. These are companies on YouTube as opposed to individuals who are uploading content and have a marketing agenda of either a) supporting their other social media channels with video content, b) ranking on Google and/or YouTube search and/or c) getting shares by users or even going viral with their brand message.

As you get started with YouTube, start to contemplate whether your business is best served by a brand Channel or by an individual Channel (such as the company CEO or lead celebrity), or perhaps both. Perhaps working with influencers would be higher ROI, or perhaps merely using YouTube as an advertising venue would be best. Regardless, as marketers, realize that you are producing video for the marketing purpose of building your brand and/or selling more stuff, either directly or indirectly. You're not producing video for video's sake any more than you might be producing art for art's sake. We're talking video as *marketing*, not video as *art*.

How to Browse YouTube for Videos and Channels

To get started, you need to explore what individuals or brands are out there that represent competitors, companies to emulate, or just uses of YouTube that you can see might advance your marketing agenda. How do you find Channels and videos?

One obvious way to make your shortlist of companies to follow is to simply visit their websites and look for a link from their website to their YouTube channel. A big brand like REI, Target, or Geico, for example, will usually have the YouTube icon somewhere on their website, often in top right or on the bottom footer. Simply be signed in to your personal YouTube account, click on their link to YouTube, and then once you land on their channel, click the red "subscribe" button. Click the "bell" if you want to ensure notifications. Here's a screenshot:

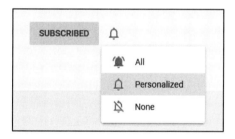

A second way to find companies to subscribe to is to **browse YouTube**. When you are logged in to your YouTube account, simply click on "Browse channels" located on the left-hand side of the screen or in the middle of the screen. This is a bit confusing because once you are an active YouTube user, YouTube hides some of these links, so here are some direct links to click when you are logged in to your YouTube account:

Browse Channels at **http://jmlinks.com/44f.**

YouTube Live at **http://jmlinks.com/44g** as well as at **https://www.youtube.com/@live**.

YouTube Trending at **http://jmlinks.com/44h**.

YouTube Shorts at **https://www.youtube.com/shorts**.

Channels are especially interesting. On each category, you can click on the category name (e.g., *Film and Entertainment*), and drill down to channels in that category. Identify channels that interest you and hit the "subscribe" button. As you subscribe to channels, they will begin to appear on your home screen on the left column under "Subscriptions."

To unsubscribe, just click on "Manage subscriptions" and/or go to the channel and hit the now-gray "Subscribed" button. Notice as well that after you subscribe, when a Channel posts a new video, it will show in your "news feed" under recommended or under the Channel itself. In this way, YouTube is like Facebook or Twitter in that once someone establishes a social media connection, the news feed of the one pushes content when the timeline of the other has something new. As a marketer, you want to drive folks to subscribe to your channel and to hit the "bell" so that they receive your notifications.

How to Search YouTube

Most of the action on YouTube really occurs at the level of the video, and not the channel, however. By this, I mean that most of the high video counts, sharing, and even videos discovered via search occur via individual videos and not channels. You need to be a good searcher to understand YouTube!

> **VIDEO.** Watch a video tutorial on how to search YouTube at **http://jmlinks.com/17a**.

To search YouTube directly, simply type keywords that matter to your company into the search bar at the top of the screen. For example, type *organic food* to find YouTube videos on *organic food*. Here's a screenshot:

Like the Google search engine, YouTube will return a list of the most relevant videos. Simply click on a video to watch it, and then click "up" to the channel to learn more about the channel that produced it. Or you can just hit the red "Subscribe" button directly to subscribe to the channel. Here's a screenshot:

You can also thumb up / thumb down a video, comment on it (using your Google account), and share it. If you click on the share icon below a video, YouTube gives you all the social icons plus a link to "Embed," which provides the HTML code you need to embed a video on your own website or blog.

SEARCH YOUTUBE BY KEYWORDS TO FIND RELEVANT VIDEOS AND CHANNELS

Going back to search, type "organic food" into the search bar. Next, on the top left, click on *Filter*, which opens up a set of parameters by which you can narrow your search. Here's a screenshot:

⇄ FILTER				
UPLOAD DATE	**TYPE**	**DURATION**	**FEATURES**	**SORT BY**
Last hour	Video	Short (< 4 minutes)	Live	**Relevance**
Today	Channel	Long (> 20 minutes)	4K	Upload date
This week	Playlist		HD	View count
This month	Movie		Subtitles/CC	Rating
This year	Show		Creative Commons	
			360°	
			VR180	
			3D	
			HDR	
			Location	
			Purchased	

Click *Upload date > This year*, which will turn on *filter* #1 (videos of the last year), then re-click *Filter*, and then click *Sort by > View Count*, which will turn on *filter* #2 (most popular). In this way, you can find the most popular videos by view count vs. a time period (one year). You can also do this by week or month.

You can also use Filter to search for Channels by keyword. Enter your keyword such as "organic food," and then under Type select "Channel." This is a quick and easy way to find the most popular channels by keyword. Note that as on the Google search engine, a search for "Organic Food" (with quotes) is different than a search for *Organic Food* (without quotes). Play around with your keywords and social media themes to identify the most popular Channels in your niche.

Next, click around at the various videos, and identify what sorts of topics you find people producing and watching in your industry. Pay attention to the thumbs up / thumbs down count and comments per video. Like a good party planner, you are looking to identify the types of entertainment that attract and engage your guests.

With respect to an individual video, pay attention to the total views, thumbs up / thumbs down, and comments. Here's a screenshot of data for the video, "Is Organic Food Worse for You?" at **http://jmlinks.com/53t**:

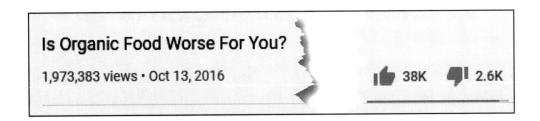

This means that this video had 2.0 million views and 38,000 thumbs-up. (Note that YouTube no longer publicly reveals "thumbs down.") If you scroll down to comments, you can see the **comments** count (3,869 as of December 2022), and you read through them. You can also see the date a video was published. In this way, you can see how "popular" a video is on YouTube and how "interactive" it is vis-à-vis the user base.

Two good tools to get more data are *TubeBuddy* (**http://jmlinks.com/53r**) and *vidIQ* (**http://jmlinks.com/53s**). Each has a free and a premium version. Here's a screenshot of data from vidIQ for this video:

The plugin will also give you data for the channel as a whole, plus "hidden" tags added to the video and the rank, if applicable, for those keywords. Here's a screenshot:

In this way, as you start your YouTube research, you can find channels and videos of competitors and companies-to-emulate and then drill into specific videos to see data about user engagement and the hidden optimization added to the video by the creator. Then, on your own videos, you can use this feature to see how well an individual video is performing.

Search Google for Videos

Another way to find interesting videos by keywords is to search Google. First, type your keywords into Google and then click the *more* > *videos* button. Here's a screenshot:

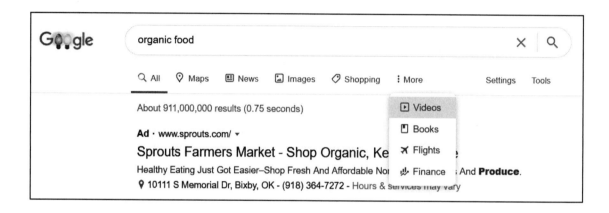

You can also use the button "Tools" on the far right to filter these results by videos of the last year or by source (e.g., CNN.com or YouTube.com), but unlike on YouTube itself, you can't filter by view count.

By browsing, searching YouTube directly, or searching Google for videos, your objective is to identify channels and videos that have high view counts as well as high thumbs up / thumbs down, and comments. What do people like? Why do they interact with it? How can this knowledge be applied to videos relevant to your company? Your goals or questions are:

- Are your potential **customers** on YouTube, and if so, what types of videos are they watching? Which relevant videos have the highest view counts? What keywords or themes seem to be the most popular? Why?

- Are **individuals** ("content creators") and/or **companies** similar to yours on YouTube, and if so, what kinds of videos are they producing? Look out for competitors and companies-to-emulate.

- What types of videos are gaining the most **interactions** as measured by thumbs up / thumbs down, comments, shares, and subscriptions to the channel?

For your first **TO-DO**, download the **YouTube Research Worksheet**. For the worksheet, go to **http://jmlinks.com/2023smm** (then enter the code '**2023smm**' to register your workbook), and click on the link to the "YouTube Research Worksheet." You'll answer questions as to whether your potential customers are on YouTube, identify brands to follow, and inventory what you like and dislike about their YouTube channels and individual videos.

» UNDERSTAND THE FOUR PROMOTIONAL USES OF VIDEO

While YouTube has channels, subscriptions, and social spread just as other social media, the lion's share of activity comes **directly** from the videos themselves. Thus, it is very important to understand the four promotional uses of video.

#1 Use of YouTube: Supportive Use of Video

If a picture is worth a thousand words, a video is worth ten thousand. If you are selling a complex product or service, creating and hosting explanatory videos can really help your sales process. Let's face it. Today's busy consumer doesn't really want to read a lot of text! They like videos because videos convey a lot of information quickly and easily, and videos convey emotional content.

Let's assume, for example, that you are a personal injury attorney in San Francisco. People are going to search for you via Google with keyword searches like "Personal Injury Attorneys SF," or "Auto Accident Attorney Bay Area." Then, they're going to land on your website, see a lot of intimidating text, and want to learn more about you as an attorney. Are you smart? Are you nice? Are you someone that they can trust?

In the old, pre-video days, they'd have to call you on the phone and come in for a quick interview. Then, they'd get in the car with their spouse and have a little chat: *did you like her? Did she seem smart? Could we trust her with our case?* It would be all about "emotional intelligence" and "gut feeling."

Video allows you to post a quick introduction to you and/or your firm on your website and start that process of "emotional intelligence" in just a few clicks of the mouse. In a very non-threatening way, videos give you the opportunity to pitch to a potential customer.

Here are some examples of this "supportive" use of video from the personal injury lawyer community. These videos are not meant to "go viral," but rather to "support" the content of a website:

Farar & Lewis (https://www.fararlawgroup.com/). Notice the introductory video in the center of the homepage at **http://jmlinks.com/53u.**

Walkup Law (http://www.walkuplawoffice.com/). Again, notice the video in the center of the homepage. Note that this one is not hosted on YouTube but rather on their own website.

The hosting location, however, is not important. What's important is that in a complex industry such as legal services, these companies are using video to "support" the content of their website and provide potential customers and "easy" way to acquire some "emotional intelligence" about the law firm.

> *A **supportive** video explains what your company offers, using a friendly, visual video format to communicate emotional trust.*

Another area that uses videos in a supportive way is the technology industry. Take a look at the Analog Devices channel (**http://jmlinks.com/13b**). Watch a sample video from their participation at the *Embedded World Trade Show* at **http://jmlinks.com/1t.** Essentially, they are taking a video recorder to the trade show and recording the "dog and pony show" that each product marketing engineer gives to a prospect who walks up to the trade show booth. The dance goes like this:

> *Hi, what does Analog Devices have new and exciting for engineers that you're exhibiting here at the Embedded World Tradeshow?*
>
> *Oh, hi there, my name is John Doe, Product Marketing Manager at Analog Devices of the super widget. Let me walk you through what we're exhibiting.*
>
> *Thank you. (Mentally: oh that's interesting, that fits what I need, he seems like a nice guy, and they seem like a great company... I'll follow up on doing business together after the show).*

By posting these videos to YouTube, Analog Devices creates linkable, shareable **content** that it can post to its Facebook, Twitter, LinkedIn, and even website pages. It can also email these videos out to prospective clients who inquire but were unable to attend the industry trade show. They are using video to ***support*** their marketing efforts, and none of these videos are designed to "go viral" like a cat video or Beyoncé's latest over-the-top music video. That's not their purpose.

Analog Devices' use of YouTube is all about **support**: using YouTube to reach highly qualified target customers, not to create massive view counts.

> **Tip**. Look for videos in your industry with high share counts, thumbs up, comments, and shares as indicated on YouTube itself at the video level. Even if your goal is only to use video to support your website, you want to research what type of content engages your customers and produce accordingly.

If you sell something complex, something that people use "emotional intelligence" to evaluate, video allows you the opportunity to share that information quickly and easily.

Showing Rather than Telling

If you have "how to" content that is best explained visually, videos can be fantastic for your social media marketing. Any type of content that is better explained by "showing" than by "writing" is an excellent candidate for video. You can also, of course, use video for "after the sale" events such as explanations to commonly asked technical support questions.

The **supportive** use of video, with free hosting of those videos on YouTube and a universal player, is an opportunity not to be missed!

#2 Use of YouTube: Search Discovery or SEO Use of Video

YouTube is the number two search engine behind Google and far ahead of Bing. One of the heaviest uses of YouTube is for "how to" searches. YouTube tries to suggest videos to viewers that they are "likely" to watch.

> **VIDEO.** Watch an official YouTube explanation of how its algorithm works at **http://jmlinks.com/59b**.

As for your own videos and customers, you need to start with keywords. Simply go to YouTube and start typing "how to" and you'll see a list of common YouTube searches.

Here's a screenshot:

```
how to

how to tie a tie
how to get the mammoth skin in fortnite
how to draw
how to make slime
how to wrap a gift
how to basic
how to connect ps4 controller to iphone
how to crip walk
how to train your dragon homecoming
how to get woolly mammoth fortnite
                                        Report search predictions
```

You can also type other words more relevant to your company like "How to grow" or "How to put on," etc. to see more specific "how to" searches relevant to your industry. If your company has any type of "how to" content, especially "how to" content that is best explained in a visual way, you can SEO-optimize YouTube videos to show up for search.

Let's say, for example, that you sell pet food. People who have new puppies are often curious about how to potty train their new puppy. So they'll Google or search via YouTube "How to potty train a puppy." Presto! You now have an idea for an informative video, and in that video, you can embed mentions and links to your website for more information and products to buy. Or let's say that you sell makeup. People are dying to know the best way to put on mascara. So they search "How to put on Mascara." Here's a screenshot of common "how to" searches with makeup:

```
how to put on

how to put on fake eyelashes
how to put on eyeliner
how to put on makeup for beginners
how to put on makeup
how to put on eyeshadow
how to put on a tampon
how to put on a tie
how to put on lipstick
how to put on a wig
how to put on mascara
```

So your first step is to do some keyword research. What types of searches are people making on YouTube that are relevant to your product or service? Use "YouTube autocomplete" by simply typing keywords into YouTube and paying attention to what people enter (this is driven, largely, by keyword search volume). Use a tool like Ubersuggest or Answer the Public, which pull "suggestions" from Google for keyword discovery. If you have a Google Ads account, use Google's Keyword Planner tool to identify high volume, high-value keyword searches on Google (which generally also translate to YouTube). Check out my Dashboard at **http://jmlinks.com/smmdash** > *keywords* for more free tools to research keywords.

A video channel that is 100% built around "how to" searches is *Zak George's Dog Training rEvolution* at 3.6 million subscribers at **http://jmlinks.com/13c**. Notice how each of his videos is optimized for searches that puppy and dog owners do to learn "how to" train their dogs. Here's Zak's video in the #1 spot for "how to potty train a puppy":

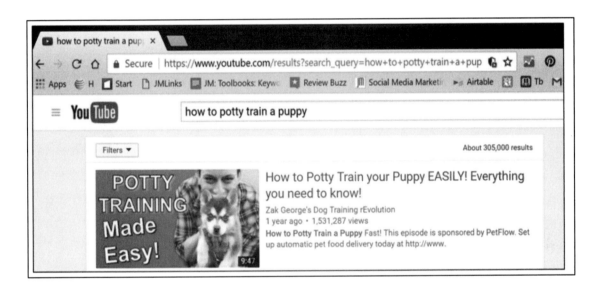

In a similar way, if your company, service, or product touches on something that customers are eager to learn "how to" do, then create videos on these topics and optimize them for relevant keywords. Zak's Channel is a good example of an SEO-focused YouTube marketing strategy.

Branded Keywords: Your Competitor Names

As for keywords, also pay attention to very specific branded searches. If a competitor has a hard-to-use product, and you know that people search YouTube for that product, you can include that product name in your video headline to snag viewers who are searching for the product. Identify adjacent, branded search terms and snag that traffic to your own videos. For example, YouTube searches such as "Netgear router set up" or "How to use a Black and Decker drill" are ripe for this type of adjacent keyword optimization.

Optimize Your Video via SEO for YouTube

Once you've identified keywords that people search on Google and/or YouTube, looking for video content, it's time to optimize your video using the tactics of Search Engine Optimization or SEO. Here's what to do:

1. **Create Your Video**. Obviously, you have to create a short, informative video that explains "how to" do what people are looking to understand. It should be primarily informative but still showcase your product or service.

2. **Optimize the Video Title**. Write a keyword-heavy video title.

3. **Optimize the Video Description**. Write a keyword-heavy video description and include a link in *http://* format to your website for more information.

4. **Optimize the Video Transcript**. YouTube pays attention to what you "say" in the video via voice recognition software, so be sure to "say" the keywords when you are presenting. For example, "In this video, I am going to explain how to tie a tie." If possible, upload subtitles or closed captions to the video.

5. **Optimize the Video Tags**. When you upload the video, be sure to use no more than five keyword-relevant tags.

Tip. It's a best practice to have your keyword-heavy content ready to go upon upload, as the first indexing by YouTube is the strongest. Don't upload first in a temporary version, and come back later to optimize.

Here's a screenshot of Zak's "How to Potty Train Your Puppy" video:

Notice how the video title and video description both contain the exact phrase "How to Potty Train * Puppy." It's obvious that the video regurgitates to YouTube the target keyword phrase.

Learn "How To" Optimize a YouTube Video for SEO

Take a look at the following "how to" searches, and browse the top-ranked videos to confirm how they optimize their video titles and descriptions:

- How to Put on Eyeliner at **http://jmlinks.com/1w**

- How to stop a puppy from chewing on a leash at **http://jmlinks.com/1x**

- Living wills and advanced directives at **http://jmlinks.com/1y**.

It's easy to optimize the video headline, description, and tags (not visible to the user). That's your first step.

Next, you need to think about **engagement**. In rewarding videos with top search positions, YouTube pays a lot of attention to how many views a video has and how engaging a video is, similar to the way that Facebook rewards posts that have high engagement. Indeed, the trend is towards "recommendation engine" in the algorithm and away from subscriptions. Videos that get clicks, watch time, thumbs up / thumbs down, comments, and shares get more eyeballs in the algorithm. Videos that are boring get less. The premium is thus on "shock value" first, engagement second, and subscriptions a distant third.

Now, not every video is meant to "go viral." But nonetheless, think like your target customer. You want users to "interact" with your video: thumbs up / thumbs down, comment, share, and embed. How do you get high video counts and high engagement?

- **Ask.** In your video, ask users to "subscribe to your channel," or "thumbs up" if you like the video, or "enter questions in the comments below." You can drive interactivity simply by asking for it.

- **Cards and End Screens.** "Cards" (see **http://jmlinks.com/31z**) are clickable popups in a video that can lead to actions such as links to your website. "End screens" (see **http://jmlinks.com/31y**) allow you to recommend other videos, playlists, and a call to subscribe to your channel at the end of a video.

Here's a screenshot of the "i" information link that pops up in the top right of a video:

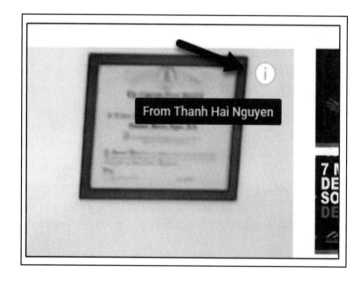

That little "i" pops out a few seconds into the video, and if the user clicks, he sees a little ad. He can then click on this and go to the website. Video "cards" are thus ways to tease your users with "more information."

To see it in action, watch my video on the "Mozon Local SEO Conference" at **http://jmlinks.com/32a** and click on the "i" on the top right of the screen. If you pay attention while watching the video, you'll see that when the YouTube card first appears, it "pops out" a little a message.

You can create clickable links to other videos as well as to the subscribe feature, and you can create messages to users that ask for interactivity. For the official YouTube help article on creating a custom subscribe button for your videos, visit **http://jmlinks.com/32b**. You can watch a video tutorial on cards and ends screens at **http://jmlinks.com/53v**.

SEO & Recommendation Engines: They Work Together

Optimization of your videos for SEO helps with the newer, "recommendation engine," aspects of the YouTube algorithm. There are two interrelated discovery paths:

1. A user goes to YouTube and **searches** by keyword as in "dog training" or "how to get my puppy to stop biting."
2. A user is **watching** YouTube videos on "dog training" and "puppy biting." The algorithm "snoops" on his behavior (which videos he watches, for how long, what does he watch next) and then matches his "behavior" to the "content" of your videos, which show as the next video to watch, or in the suggestion column.

"SEO" means ranking your video in **search**. The "recommendation engine" means getting your video **suggested**. Both require attention to keyword themes, video titles, descriptions, and transcripts.

But that's not usually enough. For success at both, the YouTube algorithm pays attention to video likes, comments, and shares as well as "watch time." Indeed, it's increasingly clear that YouTube rewards videos that have long "watch times," meaning people actually stick around and watch all or most of the video. So as you create video content, pay attention to the watch time data (available in *YouTube Studio* via your YouTube Channel). YouTube wants "sticky" content – content that people want to watch, continue to watch, thumbs up, write comments, and share. Quality, as measured by user **engagement**, is thus job #1 for success on YouTube. All of this goes for YouTube "shorts" as well, though they are discovered by users largely through watch and not search.

Promote Your Videos Externally

Because YouTube rewards videos with high view counts and engagement, promoting your video is a key part of success on the SEO path. Have an external **promotion strategy** ready for every video as soon as you upload it. Since YouTube pays attention to the **view count** (*higher is better*) as well as interactivity, use your other social networks to promote your video. Post your video on Facebook, Twitter, LinkedIn, etc., email your video link out to your email link. Even consider advertising the video upon launch on YouTube (**http://jmlinks.com/13d**), to drive the view count up as well as the interactions. "Embeds" of your video (when your video is embedded or linked to from an external website) and links to your video from external websites are also important signals to help drive a video to the top of search. The more views of your video, the more embeds of your video across the Web, the more links to your video, the higher it will rank in relevant YouTube and Google searches.

CREATE A VIRTUOUS CIRCLE: THE MORE A VIDEO IS VIEWED, THE MORE IT SHOWS IN SEARCH AND IS RECOMMENDED TO OTHERS

Once on the top of YouTube search, a **virtuous circle** can kick in: the more a video shows at the top of YouTube search, the more people watch it, the more they watch it, the higher the view count and interactivity, which drives it higher on search and recommendations, and so on and so forth.

#3 Use of YouTube: Sharing and Viral Videos

Videos are one of the most shared content across social media. We've all seen compelling videos and shared them across Facebook, Twitter, or LinkedIn. Videos are highly shareable! Why? Largely because video can convey **emotional content** in a much easier way than can text or images. And emotion drives sharing: funny, shocking, provocative, outrageous – any of the big human emotions are the ultimate driver of sharing across social media.

VIDEOS GET SHARED BECAUSE OF EMOTIONAL CONTENT

If you have a product or service that people do not heavily search for, then you can attempt to leverage the share path via YouTube. How? First and foremost, identify a logical **emotion** to drive the shares. *Utility* is one emotion, in the sense that people will share a video that is useful with friends or family. For example, a video on "how to make your Facebook completely private" (**http://jmlinks.com/1z**) has over nine million views. So creating something so useful that people share it with friends and family is one way to leverage YouTube sharing to promote your product.

But utility is the weakest of human emotions. **Fear, anger, outrage, humor** – all of these emotions are much, much stronger than mere utility!

For most businesses, the best emotion to tap is **humor** because humor can encourage sharing without having negative side effects on your brand image. A famous example of YouTube sharing is Blendtec Blenders (**http://www.blendtec.com/**). Their YouTube channel, entitled "Will it blend" (**http://jmlinks.com/36v**) is all about taking crazy items and blending them in their powerful blenders: being humorous and yet showcasing their product. One of my favorite viral videos produced by Blendtec concerns Justin Bieber, with over 3.7 million views. Watch it at **http://jmlinks.com/2a**.

If you can connect your product to something insanely funny, then you can use humor as the "fuel" to drive social sharing of your product or service. Just remember it has to be insanely funny. Fun examples are "Girls don't poop" (**http://jmlinks.com/2b**), This Unicorn Changed the Way I Poop (**http://jmlinks.com/44k**), or "The man your man could smell like" (**http://jmlinks.com/2c**). For the latter, I recommend you read the Wikipedia discussion at **http://jmlinks.com/2d**, where you'll learn that "behind the scenes" an immense amount of work and promotion went on to make the video "go viral."

Going Viral

To "go viral," a video must be so highly shared that one person shares it with two, and the two share it with four, and so on and so forth. For a video to go viral, it must have a strong emotional pull, and to get started, it must usually have aggressive external promotion, including advertising.

> *It takes a match to ignite a forest fire, after all.*

Humor is one emotion that can start viral sharing. Another is **sentimentality**. Especially for non-profits, videos that tug on the emotions can be used to encourage social sharing. Examples of this strategy are "Dear 16 Year Old Me" (**http://jmlinks.com/1p**), "Dear Future Mom" (**http://jmlinks.com/2e**), and indeed the majority of the "Dove" YouTube Channel (**https://www.youtube.com/@doveunitedstates**). These videos feature real people, sharing authentic emotional stories about a social cause or problem. People share them to "support" the cause. Another powerful example of using social sharing for a "cause" is the "It Gets Better Project" (**https://www.youtube.com/user/itgetsbetterproject**). Regardless of your political persuasion, there's a lot to be learned from the use of "viral" topics and "social sharing" as a strategy for promotion, whether for a product or a cause.

> **VIDEO.** Watch a video tutorial on how the YouTube algorithm is changing what goes viral, how, and why at **http://jmlinks.com/57n**.

Finally, I want to draw your attention to Mike Tompkins (**http://jmlinks.com/13e**) as an example of a marketer who leverages viral sharing via YouTube. Tompkins produces "covers" of pop songs on YouTube, such as his first video on Miley Cyrus's "Party in the USA" (**http://jmlinks.com/2f**). The strategy is to "piggyback" on popular YouTube searches for "branded content" (e.g., "Party in the USA" or "Party in the USA cover") and then "hijack" users to his own wonderful videos. Then, users "subscribe" to his channel, and he has a promotional vehicle combining YouTube search and viral sharing because his videos are strong and innovative enough to be shareable in their own right.

> *It's not search OR share on YouTube: it's search AND share.*

Indeed a video such as Tompkins' "Starships" (**http://jmlinks.com/2g**) is leveraging search, share, and the use of influencers (the cast of Pitch Perfect) to promote it and get it to "go viral"). Similarly, the "It gets better project" (**http://jmlinks.com/36t**) is leveraging influencers, sentimentality, user-generated content, and a "cause" that many people agree with to get its videos to "go viral" and spread its message.

Dove Real Beauty Sketches

Let's return to one of my favorite viral videos, "Dove Real Beauty Sketches" This is an excellent example of a viral video that has an ulterior marketing motive. *Dove* (the soap and beauty products manufacturer) commissioned a video about stereotypes and cleverly entitled it "Dove Real Beauty Sketches" (**http://jmlinks.com/59d**). (Note the insertion of their brand name in the video title – clever marketing, no?) Please take a moment and watch this incredibly powerful and thought-provoking video; as a consumer. I guarantee it will make you think deeply about the societal messages we embed into young girls. As a father of two young women, it certainly made me think.

But then, "reverse engineer" this video as a marketer. If *Dove* had created a video about soaps, shampoos, or makeup removers, it wouldn't have exactly been an award-winning, viral video. Pretty boring and not exactly a topic people would share. So clearly, *Dove* brainstormed a message that blended into its corporate brand, touched on women's issues, and had the potential to go viral by being emotional and counterintuitive. The brand message (*buy Dove products*) takes a back seat to the socially conscious message about our prejudices concerning what it means to be beautiful as a young woman in today's social media society.

> In an effective **viral video** for a corporate brand, the brand message isn't in the *foreground*. It's in the *background*.

As a marketer, the task is to "reverse engineer" these efforts at sharing and virality and determine if there is a path to viral marketing that *fits your company*. Again, for most for-profit companies, the best emotion is humor, while for many non-profits, sentimentality and causes that people actively support are good mechanisms to spur social sharing. If you can identify a potential concept for a viral video for your company, product, or service, I recommend you watch this YouTube video on "Why Storyboard?" at **http://jmlinks.com/53w**. Before you invest blood, sweat, tears, and budget in an attempt to "go viral," first storyboard your video and test market it.

Here's one final thought. Don't be intimidated by "viral videos." You and your company might not be able to make an over-the-top viral video with view counts in the hundreds of thousands. However, think about the reasons why a user might share your video. Is it funny? Is it humorous? Does it touch on a sentimental emotion? Even if your video doesn't "go viral," you can engineer emotional touchpoints and calls to action to encourage a viewer to share it with friends and family, thus expanding your reach. It's not ultimately *supportive vs. SEO vs. viral* in terms of video production; it can be *both / and*.

#4 Use of YouTube: Subscription

Back when I was a kid in a galaxy far, far away, we had three TV channels. We didn't even have a remote. Then, we got cable TV and suddenly, we had, like, fifty channels. There was a *cooking* channel, there was a *fishing* channel, there was a channel about *country drives* around Oklahoma, and there was even a *porn* channel (which my brother and I continually tried to access by pressing various button combinations on the clunky cable TV remote). You get the picture: there was a channel for nearly everything, and broadcasters started micro-broadcasting. Fisherpeople needed a channel about fishing; cooks needed a channel about cooking, and hormonal teenage boys needed a channel about…. you know, where to go for long drives in Oklahoma.

The fourth use of YouTube is this "subscription" model. You (meaning you, as a person, or you, as your company or brand, produce a channel with informative content. It could be "how to" content such as "how to" fish. Or it could be political content, as in commentary on our crazy political system. Or it might just be "deep dives" into murder and mystery. Your path to success is to define an audience and produce content that that audience wants so much that they will "subscribe" to your YouTube channel and eagerly await your next video.

As for how to make money, your paths to revenue are: subscription fees (often via Patreon), ads via YouTube monetization, embedded ads within your videos (including those for your own products or services), and spin-offs such as paid training or "premium" features to "paid" subscribers.

Here are some examples:

Khan Academy (https://www.youtube.com/c/khanacademy) – a channel focused on teaching kids math and science.

Murder, Mystery, and Makeup (https://www.youtube.com/c/BaileySarian) – a channel that provides "deep dives" into true crime while also showcasing makeup skills.

Economics Explained (https://www.youtube.com/c/EconomicsExplained) – a channel explaining current and historical events from the perspective of economics.

Zach George's Dog Training Revolution (https://www.youtube.com/c/zakgeorge) – a channel on how to train your puppy or dog also soliciting you for Patreon support **(https://www.patreon.com/zakgeorge)** and best-in-class dog and puppy products.

Thus, in the "subscription" model, you build content that people want, and you make money by selling "premium" content or placing ads within your content. More recently, this is also a kind of "influencer" business strategy, in which a channel creator with thousands or millions of followers sells ads on his channel that are "product placements" within that content without necessarily telling his viewers that this is a "paid sponsorship." Is it legal? Probably not (ask the FTC or your lawyers). Is it widespread? Increasingly so.

Which of the Four YouTube Strategies Will Work for You?

To summarize, identify which of the following strategies on YouTube are most relevant for your company:

Supportive. Create and upload videos that support your website and other social media. This is largely using YouTube as a hosting platform as opposed to a promotional system.

Search / SEO / Recommendation. To the extent that people search for keywords near your product or service, you can optimize your videos for discovery by search and recommendation. Then, remember to sell something after they discover your videos!

Share / Viral. To the extent that your videos have emotional content, you can encourage discovery by social sharing and even virality. This viral promotion then builds your brand.

Subscription. To the extent that you are a skilled content creator, you can create content that drives YouTube subscriptions and then sell premium content and/or affiliated products or services.

Remember that in all cases, you usually need to use external promotion tactics such as sharing your videos on Facebook, Twitter, and LinkedIn, reaching out to influencers who will help promote your videos, and even advertising on YouTube to extend the reach of your videos.

≫ TELL STORIES THROUGH VIDEO

Humans love stories. From our prehistoric roots around campfires to today's multimedia digital environment, we've been wired to respond to narrative. Who said what to whom? What happened next? Why are you telling me this? And, above all, where's the emotional thrill in what you're telling me? In the beginning, was the Word (John 1:1), and we're all wired to respond to it.

Video, whether on YouTube, Facebook, Instagram, or elsewhere, is an ideal **storytelling** medium. Look back at some of the videos I've mentioned above. Notice how they follow the elements of story from hook to rising action to climax to falling action. Indeed, whatever video you are working on should follow the elements of story as described by many, including "Ron Popeil," the so-called father of the infomercial.

It slices, it dices, but wait, there's more.

Popeil and others have identified these elements to an engaging story of any type:

1. **The hook.** Capture their attention with an ear- and eye-grabbing first scene. Shakespeare started many of his plays with an explosion, a few witches, or a fight scene in order to capture the audience's attention, and so should you.

2. **The problem.** Here, especially when you're selling something, you need a statement of the problem. It can be simple as, "Your puppy won't stop biting the leash," or as complicated as "The multitudinous ways in which girls can put on eyeliner." But there needs to be a problem or challenge that the viewer wants to solve or at least learn about.

3. **The solution.** Here's where you (and your product or service) come in. You have the solution to the problem, and you ask the viewer to allow you to explain how.

4. **The Soft CTA.** You, implicitly or perhaps even explicitly, begin to explain to the user your call to action. It can obviously be for them to "buy your stuff," but in some way or another, you start to lay the groundwork for them to "want" what "you have."

5. **Credibility.** Why are you an expert? What's so great about your product or service? A problem calls for a solution, but why is your solution so great, and why should the viewer believe you?

6. **The Hard CTA.** Here's the hard call to action, so tell the viewer to "act now" while "supplies last" or perhaps offer a coupon or discount code that expires in 24 hours. You want to motivate them to "pick up that phone" or "click that button!"

7. **The Gush.** This concept comes from Derral Eves (**https://derraleves.com/**), a prominent YouTuber and teacher of everything YouTube. Eves uses "The Gush" to signify that final, often humorous, kickback that comes after the hard

call to action. The camera returns, and we see something funny or intriguing to make us laugh and help us retain the message.

Go back and re-watch the Squatty Potty infomercial on YouTube, "This Unicorn Changed the Way I Poop," at **http://jmlinks.com/44k**. As you watch it, notice how it goes through the seven phases above. Notice as well how it uses outrageous humor and funny, sort of disgusting graphics to hold your attention and motivate you to share this video with your friends and family, if only for the reason that it's funny. It's a great example of an infomercial on YouTube, and with 40 million views, 138K thumbs up, and hundreds of comments, this video has leveraged YouTube's algorithm to help make the Squatty Potty a household word.

This video and all successful videos on YouTube tell a story.

Storytelling isn't easy, but it isn't exactly rocket science, either. Storyboarding is a step-by-step methodology to help you plan and organize the production of your videos. Check out an excellent video on how to storyboard by YouTubers Mary Doodles and Whitney Lee Milam at **http://jmlinks.com/44n**. While you're there, check out the cornucopia of videos about how to do YouTube successfully at the official *YouTube Creators' Channel* at **http://jmlinks.com/44p**. Then, take your own product or service, and brainstorm a "story" around it, perhaps in a straightforward infomercial format or perhaps in some type of question-and-answer format that will appeal to your target customers. Remember: social media is a party and not a prison, so a good story has to be compelling and engaging, or they'll simply stop watching. Search YouTube by keywords that matter to you and "reverse engineer" the stories inherent in the successful videos that fit your niche and delight your target audience.

Live Video is a Story, Too

Even if you're going to do live video on YouTube, you want to think in terms of a story. Imagine you were going to give a live theater or stand-up performance for comedy. You might be very spontaneous, but you'll still have an idea of your hook, the script you'd want to follow, and even the call-to-action you might want from your audience. Even live video is a form of storytelling. You can "go live" either on the YouTube app for your phone or via the desktop – just click the camera icon at the top right and then "Go Live." Here's a screenshot:

If you click "create post," you can now post messages to YouTube that will show to your followers when they log in to YouTube. In this way, YouTube is trying to become a bit more like Facebook or LinkedIn. You can upload a video, create a poll, or upload an image. Learn more about "community posts" at **http://jmlinks.com/53z**. Learn more about how to go live on YouTube at **http://jmlinks.com/55g**.

Write Your (Draft) Story and Get Technical

So your to-do here is to create a draft story. Then, your next to-do is the technical aspects of shooting the video. You'll need a script, actors, a set, and an outline of the scenes. The technical aspects of video production are outside the scope of this book, but just realize that a few Google searches can help you with everything from how to write a short script or storyboard to the best video cameras, microphones, and other technical things you'll need. You can also look for local videographers to come to your place of business and help you shoot one or more videos. Just be aware that, in my experience, those who excel at the art of telling stories (a.k.a., writers) are not necessarily the same people who excel at the technical skills of shooting or editing video (a.k.a., photographers). They possess two different skill sets. Finally, you'll need to either edit your video yourself using software such as Windows Movie Maker, Apple iMovie, or more sophisticated software products like Camtasia. YouTube even has its own built-in editor accessible after you upload your video at **https://studio.youtube.com**.

The end result should be a short, emotion-packed, engaging video that focuses on your solution to the desire or problem your customers have. It may have the goal of supporting your website or other social media channels, of showing up high on YouTube or Google searches, or "going viral" or at least "getting shared." But regardless of which of the three YouTube goals your video is focusing on, it must tell a good story.

Finally, once you upload your video, you'll want to optimize the Video Title, description, and link to more information, plus both cards and end screens, which I'll explain in a moment.

» SET UP YOUR CHANNEL AND UPLOAD VIDEOS

After you've made an inventory of YouTube channels and videos that interest you from a marketing perspective, you're ready to set up your own YouTube channel. Assuming you haven't done this already, the best way to do this is from your Google or Gmail account. Here are the steps:

1. **Login to your Google account** (either via Gmail or an email address for which you have created a Google account).

2. **Go to YouTube** by typing **https://www.youtube.com/** in the browser address bar, or using the Google pull-down menu to go to YouTube.

3. Go to your Channel List at **http://jmlinks.com/31w**.

4. Click on "Create a new channel."

(For the official YouTube help article on how to create a channel, visit **http://jmlinks.com/12z**). At that point, you will be "inside" your new YouTube channel. (If you already have a channel, simply log in to YouTube.) Make sure to keep the email address and password in a safe and secure place, as you need this each time to log in to your Channel.

On the top right of the screen, click on your profile picture and then **YouTube Studio**. Here's a screenshot:

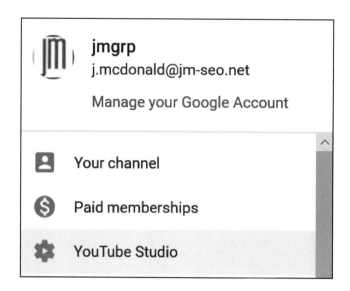

That gets you into *YouTube Studio*. First, set up your community settings. This controls who can comment on your videos. Go to *Settings > Community*, where you can manage the ability of users to post comments on your video. Under "blocked words," for example, you can forbid the use of certain words, as well as ban users who have not behaved well from interacting with your channel. You can also use YouTube filters to control comments and block possibly spammy content from auto-posting (where you then approve or disapprove it).

Click up to "Advanced Settings." Here you can clarify whether you make videos for kids or not. This is important as a kids-oriented channel has many more restrictions than a non-kids channel. Under "Branding," you can add a video watermark, such as your logo to all videos. Under "Feature eligibility," you can use phone verification so that you can upload videos longer than 15 minutes plus get access to custom thumbnails and live streaming capability.

Next, click back to "Your Channel" and then "Customize Channel" in blue. On the left menu, you can set features such as the following.

Videos. This gets you into a list of all the videos you have uploaded to your Channel. You can drill into each video and perform further edits or modifications video by video.

Playlists. Here, you can create a "group" or "playlist" of videos on a topic.

Analytics. Analytics gives you information on your channel and your videos as to how they are discovered, whether users stay engaged, etc.

Comments. Here, you can see comments from users across all your videos and respond to them.

Monetization. This allows you to make money off of YouTube advertising. Unless your view counts run into the millions, I do not recommend turning on monetization.

Audio Library. YouTube gives you a cornucopia of royalty-free music for your videos as well as sound effects.

To change your *profile picture*, go back to the initial view of YouTube Studio, and click the "Your Channel" icon in the top right. It can be a little hard to toggle between the YouTube Studio settings and the "View Channel" settings, so sometimes, just log all the way out and start over at YouTube.com. Or, you can often see the settings on the far right column under your brand icon.

Once you've made it to Your Channel, click on your picture on the top left, hover over it, and click on your Channel cover or icon to change your Channel background image or icon. You can also upload *channel art*, which is similar to Facebook cover photos, by clicking on the large photo in the middle. Fill out your Channel "*About > Description*" section with keyword-heavy but short content explaining what your Channel is about and why folks should subscribe to it. Here, you can also create backlinks to your website and other social media sites. If things are not clickable, find the "Customize Channel" link and then click back into this or that element.

One of the more important things to do is to create a "Channel Trailer." Create a video that explains what your Channel offers and – most importantly – why a user should subscribe. Click on "Customize Channel" and then "Home." You should see two bullet points marked "channel trailer" and "featured trailer," the former being for people who have not subscribed to your channel and the latter being for people who have. Click on each one and select the appropriate video. Learn more from the official help file at **http://jmlinks.com/31x**.

Remember that there are two distinct areas to set up: *Your Channel look and feel* and *YouTube Studio*. If you can't find what you want on one of them, look into the other. There's no rhyme or reason as to how YouTube has organized any of this. One trick I use is to open three tabs in my browser, so I can have all three elements viewable as I "hunt for Red October" to find a feature I want to change. Help is available at the top right under the "Question Mark" or at **https://support.google.com/youtube**.

Monetization

One of the big questions in setting up a YouTube Channel is whether or not to allow monetization. Monetization merely means that YouTube will be able to place ads on your videos. For most businesses, I strongly advise against allowing advertising or monetization on your channel, as your goal once you have a customer viewing your videos is for them to buy your product or service, not to go off and buy someone else's. Why be paid *pennies* by YouTube for ad clicks when you can make *dollars* by selling customers on your own product or service? Note, however, that since mid-2021, YouTube has placed ads on nearly every channel, whether monetized or not. Go figure.

Furthermore, unless your view count is in the millions, you'll earn next to nothing via YouTube monetization. (The only practical reason to monetize a video is if you absolutely insist on using copyright-protected music; for that sort of music to be allowed, you must allow advertising on your video via monetization).

Channel Optimization for SEO

YouTube is the No. 2 search engine, ahead of Bing (but behind its parent, Google). As I have already explained, you should optimize each and every video for YouTube SEO by having a keyword-heavy video title, description, and tags. You should do the same with your channel. Place keywords in your channel keywords field. To enter your channel keywords, click on *YouTube Studio > Settings > Channel* keywords. Here's a screenshot:

On the Advanced tab, you can also link your YouTube account to your Google Ads account, as well as to your Google Analytics account for metrics purposes. Don't forget to associate your YouTube account with your website as well. To do this, fill in your website *http://* address in the "Associated website" field and follow the verification instructions. You can learn more about how to link your website to your YouTube channel at **http://jmlinks.com/59e**. At the end of this process, you should have fully set up your Channel.

Upload Videos

To upload a video, click back to you're your channel dashboard, then select the "upload video" icon in blue. Select a video to upload and start uploading.

Input a:

- **Video Title**: Write a keyword-heavy but catchy video title. Note: if you include a hashtag at the end of the video title, as in #socialmedia or #organic it will show up first on the video title in public display.

- **Description**. Write a keyword-heavy but catchy video description. Include an *http://www.yourcompany.com* link to your website. Be sure to use the http:// prefix, as that makes it "clickable" to your website.

- **Tags**. Identify no more than five relevant keyword tags for your video.

- **Public**: set the video to *public* (anyone can see), *unlisted* (only people with the link can view), or *private* (restricted access).

- **Custom thumbnail**. Upload a custom video thumbnail, which will appear in YouTube search. Or, YouTube will automatically create three options for you.

Custom thumbnails are worthy of attention. Your video thumbnail will show in YouTube search and alongside other videos or at the end of a video. They are your "teaser" or "hook" to get a user to click through and begin watching the video. They need to function like ads. The best thumbnails include photos of people (you, your CEO, or someone key to the company come to mind) plus some very big and bold text. Try a search on YouTube for your keywords and evaluate which videos have a lot of views and interaction, and look at their thumbnails. Learn more about custom thumbnails from *YouTube Creator Academy* at **http://jmlinks.com/44q**. I strongly recommend that you create custom thumbnails for each and every video.

» ENABLE CLICKABLE LINKS IN YOUR VIDEO

Be sure to include a clickable link in your video description, preferably right after the first sentence, and in the format of **http://www.yourwebsite.com/**. It MUST be in the *http://* format to be clickable! You can then reference the link for "more information" in your short video ad, such as telling the viewer, "Click on the link in the video description to learn more!"

Here's a screenshot from the famous Dollar Shave Club video's description, showing the clickable link from the video description to their website:

That link - **http://dlrshv.es/b3FELr** - gets the user to the Dollar Shave website with just one easy click, so you gotta have one in your video!

Create Cards and End Screens in Your Video

"Cards" and "End Screens" on YouTube are yet another way to drive traffic from your video to your website. Cards are clickable links in the video itself. "End screens" occur at the end of a video and are also clickable links. In order to create YouTube cards or end screens that link to your website, however, you must link your YouTube account to your website, and you must join the YouTube Partners Program. (See **http://jmlinks.com/49u**). This requires more than 1,000 subscribers, so it will not be available if you have a brand-new account.

To add a "card" to your video, first, click on a video via YouTube Studio. Next:

- Click on the "pencil" icon for the video.
- Scroll down on the right and find "cards." Click the "pencil icon."
- Fill out the link, card title, call to action, and teaser text.
- Position the "card" by scrolling back and forth in the video timeline. This controls where and for how long the "card" will appear.

Finally, save your work and then test out the video on a new screen to verify that your "card" works and it is where you want it in the video.

"Cards" are Clickable Links in a Video

VIDEO. You can read the official Google help file on YouTube cards at **http://jmlinks.com/27h**.

Cards appear in the top right of a YouTube video and "pop out" when they appear. Users can click on them to learn more and then click from the card to your website. Here's a screenshot showing the card in the top right corner:

Just remember as you set up videos and/or video ads on YouTube to be on the lookout for where it will allow you to put clickable links: in the video description, in cards, in call-to-action overlays, and in the new call-to-action extension. All options are not always available, so just be aware that you may or may not see them. To learn more about cards and end screens, visit **http://jmlinks.com/53y** for the official YouTube explanation.

For your second **TO-DO**, download the **YouTube Setup Worksheet**. For the worksheet, go to **http://jmlinks.com/2023smm** (then enter the code '**2023smm**' to register your workbook), and click on the link to the "YouTube Setup Worksheet." You'll answer and outline the basic setup issues for your YouTube channel.

» ADVERTISE ON YOUTUBE

YouTube offers robust advertising options. You can use advertising to expand the reach of your YouTube videos, especially for persons in "search mode" on YouTube by keyword or those who are easy to target demographically, such as persons who love to fish, people who want to try out cosmetics, or perhaps religious people who want to watch Christian videos. You can use YouTube advertising to boost your video view count and engagement, and in that way, YouTube advertising can work to support your organic YouTube efforts. (See **http://jmlinks.com/32f** for the official guide to YouTube advertising).

To create a video campaign, you'll need a Google Ads account, preferably linked to your YouTube account. Although you can place text and graphic ads on YouTube, we'll assume you have a video you want to promote through advertising. With that video in hand, here are your steps.

If you already have a *Campaign > Ad Group* on YouTube, you can skip this section. If not, to create a video campaign, log in to Google Ads, and click the blue circle. Select "Create a campaign without a goal's guidance" and then *Video* as the campaign type. Select "custom video campaign." Follow the steps to define:

Campaign Name. Give it an easy-to-remember name, such as *Cat Boarding: YouTube*. I recommend you put YouTube at the end so you can see in an instant that this is a YouTube Campaign and not a Search or Display Campaign. Note there are two formats on YouTube that are commonly used, and I recommend you create separate campaigns for each format.

Bid Strategy. This will default to "Maximum CPV," which is maximum cost-per-view, as you pay by view on YouTube (more on this in a moment).

Budget and Dates. Enter your campaign budget and any date constraints.

Networks. Here, choose **YouTube Search Results** (i.e., users are pro-actively searching), **YouTube videos** (i.e., the YouTube algorithm is placing your videos "near" or "at the end" of videos users or watching), and/or **Video Partners** (*not recommended*, as these are non-YouTube websites).

Locations. Select your geo-location, such as the entire United States, or just a city or region, as in "San Jose, California." You will need a decent-sized population for the video to run, so I do not recommend something as tight as a zip code, although you can do that.

Follow the instructions on any other settings, which are self-explanatory. For example, you can target conversions, devices, a frequency cap (the maximum number of times a user is shown a video), ad schedule, etc. And then name your Ad Group. Give it a name that is self-evident, as in "*JM Cat Boarding: YouTube.*"

Next, be careful with the targeting. The first time you set up an ad, Google Ads forces you to go through every step, but do not choose multiple targeting methods (!). These are demographics, audiences, keywords, topics, and placements. **Do not mix and match targeting methods in a single ad group!** I would recommend for your first group that you choose relevant keywords such as, in my example, "cats" or "cat boarding."

YouTube has different types of ads. Here are the most important ones:

Skippable In-stream Ads occur in what YouTube calls the **Video Action** ad format, meaning you pay, if and only if, a person clicks thru on your ad, watches more than 30 seconds, or half of the video ad (whichever is lesser). This is the most common format.

Non-skippable Instream Ads. These are video ads that generally appear before a video. The user is forced to watch up to five seconds, and then he or she can click on the ad or click "skip." If you are going to use this type, name your Campaign something like *JM Cat Boarding: YouTube – Instream.*

In-feed Video Ads. These appear "in the feed,", especially on the app or mobile phone. This is a good way to get your videos "next to" those of competitors.

Bumper Ads. These are short, six-second, non-skippable ads, before, in the middle of, and after a video. These are usually used by major brands for "branding" and "awareness" rather than results.

Other Formats. YouTube also offers other formats such as Outstream Ads (on partner sites), Non-skippable in-stream ads (ads that the user cannot skip), and Bumper ads (short six-second ads that are non-skippable), but these are generally used only by very large advertisers who want to use YouTube like television for branding purposes.

Learn more about ad formats at **http://jmlinks.com/59f**.

Next, create your video ad. Enter the exact URL of the video you want to promote here. Select a format such as *In-stream ad* or *bumper ad* ("browse mode") or *video discovery* ("search mode") ad as explained above. Select a thumbnail, and write a headline and description. If you are using the "Skippable in-stream ad," then enter a URL such as your website landing page. For a "video discovery ad," no URL is inputted. Add a "call to action" and select or upload an image. These appear at the far right of the video and allow users to learn more.

Again, similarly to regular Google Ads, Google stupidly makes you go through every step, even if you are not ready. Once a *Campaign > Ad Group* is created, however, you can then insert new Ad Groups and Ads much more easily, adjust targeting, etc. Just go through the steps to create your first *Campaign > Ad Group > Ad,* and then it will be much easier to manage. What's stupid about this is you only have to do this the very first time, and then from then on, it's much easier to manage.

At the end of this process, you should have your first *Campaign > Ad Group > Ad*. Pause it so that it doesn't start running until you are completely ready.

Location Targeting in YouTube

Importantly, you can geotarget on YouTube. For example, Jason's Cat Boarding Emporium could target people watching "cat videos" who also live in San Francisco. Or a pet store could target people watching videos on dog and puppy training who live in Oakland, Berkeley, or El Cerrito, California.

LOCATION TARGETING WORKS ON YOUTUBE

Geotargeting makes it easy to get your ads right to people near your local business and is one of the most exciting features of YouTube advertising. Accordingly, select your Geotarget (e.g., United States, or drill down to a specific city or state). You do this by being at the Campaign level and selecting *Locations* on the left. For example, since I am only interested in people who live in San Francisco and have cats, I could target cat videos on YouTube, but by setting the geotarget to San Francisco, only people who are physically in San Francisco would see my ads. This is a fantastic feature of YouTube advertising as you can have your cake and eat it too – meaning target very broad video types (e.g., "cat videos") but to very narrow locations (e.g., "San Francisco").

Mobile Bid Adjustment

You can also control your mobile bid adjustment on YouTube if you do/do not want to run on phones and/or tablets. Once you've created a Campaign, click on *Devices* on the left and configure your device targeting by setting bid adjustments up or down. An example here might be a probate attorney who would figure that the most serious people would be watching her videos on their computers, so she would set a bid adjustment of negative 100% for mobile. If you think there is a strong pattern between mobile vs. desktop vs. tablet, this is yet another useful YouTube targeting refinement.

Target Your Ad: Video Targeting

Now that you've inputted your ad to YouTube, it's time to dive into targeting options. Targeting "lives" at the Ad Group level, just as in regular Google Ads. Click into your Ad Group on YouTube, and you'll see targeting options on the left. As with the Display Network, it's a best practice not to mix and match targeting options (though you can in some situations). Let's review targeting options.

> **Keywords.** Here, similar to the Display Network, enter **keywords** that you think someone might be searching on YouTube and/or that might describe similar or adjacent videos. **This is the most common and most powerful way to target your videos.** In our *Cat Boarding* example, we'd enter keywords like *cats, cat boarding, cat care, kittens*, etc. Google has taken away a lot of YouTube targeting features, so I wouldn't worry about plus signs, quote marks, etc., just enter keywords and remember that, as on the Display Network, the targeting is pretty loose on YouTube. Note that Google uses how they search not only on YouTube but on Google for keyword-based targeting.
>
> **Audiences.** Here you will see *Search | Browse* at the top. Click into *Browse*, and you should see:
>
>> **Who They Are.** This is demographic targeting based on attributes such as Parental Status, Marital Status, Education, and Homeownership.
>>
>> **What their interests and habits are.** These are "affinities," such as whether they're into Banking & Finance, Beauty & Wellness, Food & Dining, etc.
>>
>> **What they are actively researching or planning.** This refers to "in-market audiences," such as people who are "in the market" to buy a house or a car. If relevant to you, this is one of the best targeting options.

How they have interacted with your business. This leverages your remarketing audiences via Google Analytics. So, for example, you can "tag" people who visit your website and then show them your video ad as they browse YouTube videos. You can also expand to "retargeting" using Google AI to expand to people "similar" to those who have already hit your website. Learn more about remarketing (now called "data segments") on Google / YouTube at **http://jmlinks.com/57p**.

Your Combined Audiences. This is a new feature that allows you to use "And" statements to combine any of the above features.

Your Custom Audiences. This allows you to use remarketing, that is to "reshow" your ads to people who have already visited your website.

Demographics. You can see and target the age, gender, parental status, and household income of the people who have viewed your YouTube advertising.

Placements. This is unique on YouTube. You can find videos or channels that allow advertising and then copy/paste their URLs here. However, if a channel or video is not "monetized" (meaning that the owner does not allow YouTube to place ads), this is all in vain. Double-check to see if you see ads on any relevant placements. Google doesn't enable clickable links here, so open up a new browser window and search YouTube by Channel or Video name to find out if it allows advertising. If you see ads, it does. If you don't, it doesn't.

Learn more about targeting options at **http://jmlinks.com/59g**.

Evaluate Your YouTube Advertising Performance

Once your ads are up and running on YouTube, evaluating the performance is similar to the rest of the Display Network. Click into an Ad Group. Then, along the left column, click:

Keywords to browse the keywords the triggered your video ads. As elsewhere on Google Ads, you can create "negative keywords" to block your ad.

Audiences to learn characteristics about the audiences reached.

Demographics to see age information (if available).

Placements and then *See where your ads appeared* to see which videos/channels ran your ad. As on the Display Network, you can block your ad from placements.

You can also go into Google Analytics to view clicks coming from YouTube to evaluate what happens "after the click." To do this, create a Segment by clicking on the *Segments* tab in Google Analytics, and then *Custom*, and source as *YouTube.com*.

And within your YouTube Channel, you can click on *Creator Studio > Analytics* to browse information about your videos.

Returning back to your YouTube Channel (not Google Ads, and not Google Analytics), you can go to *YouTube Studio > Analytics* and then drill down into an individual video to see key performance indicators such as watch time, view duration, views, geographies, genders, traffic sources, and playback locations. In summary, there is really a wealth of information in Google Ads, Analytics, and YouTube about what happens with your videos!

» EXPLORE FACEBOOK, LINKEDIN, INSTAGRAM, AND TIKTOK VIDEO

Video is more than YouTube, of course. A video can live on your website, for example. Or, you can place so-called "native" videos on Facebook, Instagram, LinkedIn, and TikTok, not to mention short videos on Twitter. As you work on your video marketing strategy, therefore, don't miss opportunities on the other platforms.

I will now review each platform but before I do that, let's talk about some commonalities – across platforms.

1. Video is the fastest-growing content type across all social media platforms.

2. Each platform (Facebook, Instagram / IGTV, Twitter, YouTube / Google, TikTok) tends to favor "native" video, that is, video hosted on its platform.

3. All platforms, including YouTube, have video as a "share" path, wherein consumers share videos with each other, but YouTube alone dominates the "search" path as when a consumer is pro-actively searching for a video explaining "how to tie a tie."

4. Videos that get shared across all platforms tend to have emotional, shocking, counterintuitive, etc., content. The more emotional, the more counterintuitive, the more shocking a video is, the better it does.

5. All platforms reward videos that spur engagement as measured by views, comments, shares, and "watch time."

The three big differences between YouTube and the offer platforms are thus a) that only YouTube has videos that really respond to user proactive search queries, b) only

YouTube has an easy-to-use repository format so you can have a Channel as a place to permanently store your videos, and c) only YouTube offers an easy "embed" code so that you can embed your videos on your website. Some of these features exist on Facebook, Instagram, or LinkedIn (such as embed code), but they are so hard to manage that you're better off using YouTube for those purposes.

Facebook Video

Facebook is keen to become the #2 player in video, but the way that video works on Facebook leverages only the "supportive" and "share/viral" use of video. Don't think of Facebook video as an *alternative* to YouTube but rather as a *complement*.

Conceptually, there are two marketing paths to video success on Facebook:

> **Supportive**. Upload your video directly to Facebook as a "native" video. This use of video on Facebook "supports" your marketing message by providing content for you to post and share on Facebook. Facebook favors "native video" in its algorithm vs. non-native videos hosted on YouTube, so if reach on Facebook is your goal, native is the way to go.

> **Share/viral**. A video on Facebook can be shared or even go viral. As with YouTube, it's emotional videos that get a lot of shares or go viral on Facebook. Again, because Facebook favors its own videos, you will get better organic traction with a native video. In addition, you can advertise the video via Facebook advertising. Facebook live video also has a heavier reach as promoted by the Facebook algorithm. (Learn more about Facebook live at **http://jmlinks.com/36w** and YouTube live at **http://jmlinks.com/36x**).

Facebook, unlike YouTube, isn't a very good storage repository for video, nor does it have the SEO / discovery use of video. (You can have a video tab on your Facebook Page, but there is no cross-Channel discovery on Facebook, and the organic reach of videos is pretty poor). Accordingly, you might think of launching your video simultaneously on Facebook AND YouTube but then in the long term, nurturing only the YouTube version as an "evergreen" video.

To upload a video to Facebook, you first need to have a business Page. You obviously also need a video to upload, generally in the MP4 format. Once you have set up a business Page and have a video you want to upload to Facebook, then simply go to that Page either on the desktop or on the mobile phone and look for the "upload video" icon. Here's a screenshot from the desktop:

For example, check out the Antiques Roadshow videos on Facebook at **http://jmlinks.com/44v**. Notice how they've enabled the "video" tab on their Facebook Page.

Facebook also has a rather new feature called "Facebook Watch" at **https://www.facebook.com/watch**. As on YouTube, users can follow a Facebook Page to be alerted when new videos are uploaded. This is an attempt at direct competition with YouTube. A business Page on Facebook can thus host videos on Facebook, which show up on its video tab, and on the "watch" page. The problem is that the organic reach of Facebook is poor compared to organic reach and discovery on YouTube, and few users even know about Facebook watch, so it is not much of a destination website in the way that YouTube clearly is.

Facebook is also encouraging "creators," that is, individuals who post videos that are heavily shared or even go viral, to move to Facebook (or "Meta") via its new "Creator" page type. You can learn more about the Meta creator program at **http://jmlinks.com/44w**.

All in all, the main opportunities on Facebook for video are really the "supportive" or "share / viral" use of video. To succeed on Facebook, you need to budget some advertising dollars to promote your videos, or they won't be seen by many people.

Instagram Video

Instagram, of course, is owned by Facebook. So it's not surprising that many of the opportunities are the same. Instagram favors native videos in its algorithm as well, and

Instagram has gone "all in" on reels to such an extent that all videos posted to Instagram are now "reels." "Reels," of course, are the newest thing – you might consider having the same video on TikTok, Reels on Instagram, and Shorts on YouTube, as all three have the same vibe.

As on Facebook, the main reach is either people who already follow you on Instagram or videos that "go viral" due to lots of social sharing. It isn't yet much of a competitor to YouTube for long-term video hosting or discovery. Note as well that on both Instagram and Facebook, brands can have "stories," which are daily video summaries of events and highlights. Learn more about Facebook stories at **http://jmlinks.com/44z** and Instagram stories at **http://jmlinks.com/45a**.

LinkedIn Video

LinkedIn is the latest social platform to embrace video. Obviously, the personality of LinkedIn is more serious, professional, B2B type marketing, so the videos that will do well on LinkedIn are going to fit its unique culture. The structure and setup is very similar to Facebook, so LinkedIn isn't much of a stable repository for video but rather a network for distributing video to your existing users. Video will show in their news feeds and if a video is controversial, emotional, or counterintuitive enough, the video has the chance to "go viral" and get shared by people on LinkedIn.

LinkedIn seems to favor "native video" over YouTube-based video, so – again – you're better off uploading video directly to the platform.

Once you have a video in MP4 format, simply log in to your LinkedIn personal profile or your LinkedIn company page. Simply click on the "video" link and upload your video. Here's a screenshot:

To learn more about native videos on LinkedIn, visit **http://jmlinks.com/45b**.

TikTok Video

Like YouTube, TikTok (**https://www.tiktok.com/**) is 100% video content. Since we cover it in the next Chapter, suffice it to say it's a really big deal. I would not shortchange TikTok by thinking it's "just for teens" or "it's just silly videos." In fact, if you're going to invest in vertical video for Instagram, then you already have the digital asset you need for TikTok. Don't ignore it; it's going to be big(ger) than it already is.

» MEASURE YOUR RESULTS

Owned by Google, YouTube provides very good metrics on both your channel and your videos. From inside your YouTube account, click on *YouTube Studio > Analytics*. Next, you can drill down to any video and investigate:

> **Views.** Total views and views over time.
>
> **Estimated Minutes Watched.** Total minutes watched.
>
> **Engagement.** Variables such as likes, dislikes, comments, shares, videos in playlists, and subscribers generated by the video.
>
> **Demographics.** Your top countries and gender distribution.
>
> **Traffic Sources.** How people found your video. Click on "top traffic sources" to view the actual search keywords, "external" to view referrer websites, "suggested videos" to view related videos that generated traffic. If you click "YouTube Search," it will show you which keywords users inputted to find your video. If you click "Suggested videos," you can see which videos preceded yours, and thus your video became a "suggested video" to that one.

YouTube is very keen on watch time, so click on "Average View Duration," and YouTube will show you your video and the user spikes or drop-offs as you watch the video. This is a very useful way to learn what's working and what's not in terms of user engagement.

Google Analytics

For many of us, we want to drive traffic from YouTube to our website, even to our e-commerce store, or to download a free eBook or software package to get a sales lead. Sign up for Google Analytics (**https://analytics.google.com/**) and install the required tracking code. Inside your Google Analytics account, on the left column, drill down by clicking on *Acquisition > Social > Overview*. Then on the right-hand side of the screen, you'll see the word "Social." Click on that, and then find YouTube on the list, and YouTube to your Website, giving you insights into what types of video people find attractive.

You can also create a custom Segment to look at only YouTube traffic and its behavior. For information on how to create custom Segments in Google Analytics, go to **http://jmlinks.com/1f**. For the Google help files on Segments, go to **http://jmlinks.com/1g**.

In sum, on YouTube, you can see how people interact with your channel and videos. Inside of Google Analytics, you can see where they land on your website and what they do after they arrive.

»» CHECKLIST: YOUTUBE ACTION ITEMS

Test your knowledge of YouTube! Take the *YouTube marketing quiz* at **http://jmlinks.com/qzyt**. Next, here are your YouTube **Action Items**:

❑ **Research** whether your customers (and competitors) are on YouTube. Start with keyword searches on YouTube. What videos seem to be engaging? Which videos generate the most interaction, including shares? Why?

　　❑ **Brainstorm** for your company/industry, especially which type(s) of videos make the most sense: ❑ supportive ❑ search/discovery ❑ viral / sharing or ❑ subscription.

❑ Set up your **company channel.** If you see opportunities on YouTube, set up your company channel, including a profile picture, cover photo, the "about" section, and at least one video explaining what you do and who should care.

　　❑ If you have more than one video, consider a "**Channel trailer**" that answers the question of why they should subscribe to your channel.

❑ **Promote** your **video**(s) through SEO (Search), cross-promotion on your other social channels, the real world, and even **advertising** on YouTube.

❑ **Measure** your **results** in ways such as video views, thumbs up / down, comments as well as the growth of your Channel subscribers. Use YouTube cards or call-to-action overlays to send traffic from YouTube to your website and measure conversions such as sales that originate from YouTube.

❑ Finally, consider **Facebook, Instagram, TikTok**, and **LinkedIn** as alternatives for video. Don't think in either/or terms. Take your video content and "repurpose" it across platforms in both horizontal and vertical formats.

Check out the **free tools**! Go to my *Social Media Marketing Dashboard > YouTube* for my favorite free tools on YouTube. Just visit **http://jmlinks.com/smmdash**.

»» DELIVERABLE: A YOUTUBE MARKETING PLAN

Now that we've come to the end of our chapter on YouTube, your **DELIVERABLE** has arrived. For the worksheet, go to **http://jmlinks.com/2023smm** (then enter the code '**2023smm**' to register your workbook), and click on the link to the "YouTube Marketing Plan." By filling out this plan, you and your team will establish a vision of what you want to achieve via YouTube.

9
TIKTOK

In my opinion, TikTok has been the most innovative social media platform since the creation of Facebook. First, TikTok "cracked the code" of allowing regular users to **easily create videos** via their phones. Creating a video for TikTok is easy, fun, and fast. Second, TikTok perfected the concept of a "**recommendation engine**." Yes, people want to see what's going on with friends, family, and brands that they "follow." (That's what Facebook is for). But arguably, many more people just want to "be entertained." They want quick "snackable content" that is funny, provocative, and entertaining. TikTok gives cat lovers more cat videos, dog lovers more dog videos, and Cardi B (*@iamcardib*) fans more Cardi B content.

To get started, just download the app, follow the prompts, and spend some time "liking" videos that interest you and "swiping through" videos that do not interest you. Before you can say "Chinese Communist Party" (since TikTok is a Chinese company), TikTok will be serving up an endless series of highly addictive videos. Soon you'll join the nearly one billion monthly users on the platform who not only consume videos but are enticed to "join in the fun" by creating quirky content themselves.

Many people dismiss TikTok as silly videos for teenage girls. That's short-sighted. It's much more than that, and it's growing fast – very fast. In fact, TikTok was the most downloaded app of 2022. Ignore it at your peril.

Let's get started!

TO-DO LIST:

» Explore How TikTok Works

» Search TikTok and Identify Accounts to Follow

» Inventory Companies on TikTok

» Explore Content Opportunities

» Master Technical Features

» Measure Your Results

»» Checklist: TikTok Action Items

»» Deliverable: A TikTok Marketing Plan

» EXPLORE HOW TIKTOK WORKS

TikTok is like other social platforms, especially **Instagram**, in that users and brands have accounts, and then other users or brands can "follow" them at the account level as well as like, comment, and share videos. TikTok is similar to **YouTube** in that it is video-centric. Much of the logic of content marketing for video applies to the platform. But TikTok is unique, especially in the wealth of **User Generated Content** on the app, the conversational back-and-forth of much of its content, and in how the algorithm feeds addictive content to users. As TikTok combines the best of Instagram with the best of YouTube, it's useful to compare/contrast TikTok with Instagram and YouTube to orient yourself to marketing on the platform.

First, download the app from either the Apple App Store or Google Play. Like Instagram, TikTok is 100% on the phone. Like Instagram, you can have either a user or a "professional" (business) account. Set up a business account as you get better analytics. Like Instagram, you can access TikTok on the desktop at **https://www.tiktok.com/** after you first create an account on your phone. But like Instagram, no real users use the desktop. It's phone-centric.

Here are other features that TikTok shares with Instagram:

TikTok is a True Social Media Platform. Unlike Snapchat, which is really more of a messaging platform, TikTok is a truly social platform. Users find and follow each other, and if User A posts something to his TikTok account, then User B has the opportunity to see it in his feed (and vice-versa).

TikTok is Open. Like Instagram, pretty much anyone can follow anyone. That's the point. It's not about "secret friends" and "you must like me before you can talk to me," as on Snapchat or Facebook. It's more like *see and be seen*, like Twitter or Instagram. TikTok is a profoundly public and open 24/7 crazy party video party.

TikTok is Video-Centric. Like Instagram or YouTube, TikTok is visually centric. But unlike Instagram, TikTok takes this to the next level. No still photos are allowed. It's all about video. In this, therefore, it is more like YouTube.

TikTok Is One Link Only. Like Instagram, TikTok's goal is to keep users on the platform, so you cannot share any link other than the one, and only one, "link in bio."

TikTok's Culture is Show Offy. Even more so than Instagram. TikTok is where users go to "get famous" and measure their self-worth by the follows, likes, comments, and shares that they get on their accounts. If TikTok isn't about living your best life, it is definitely about "showing off" your best life (even if it's fake). TikTok is full of FOMO (fear of missing out), as users jump on trends and attempt to break out to high video counts. It's not just the content *consumption* that goes viral on TikTok. It's the content *creation* – and that is truly unique.

But TikTok isn't precisely like Instagram. Here are two significant differences. First and foremost, TikTok is more a "**recommendation engine**" than a "social network." Whereas Instagram still has one foot in the "social media" idea of following friends, family, and brands (yet is clearly moving towards being a recommendation engine), TikTok is nearly 99% about recommendations. Yes, you can "follow" and "like" content, but what shows in your "for you" feed is generated more by the recommendation engine than by follow / follower patterns. This is a key point:

Secondarily, whereas Instagram is increasingly cluttered, TikTok is about video, only. It's laser-focused on being the "fun" video platform, where creators post videos, and users "lean back" and are passively "entertained." TikTok is doing so well with young users that Zuckerberg and his team have even mentioned it by name as a major competitive threat.

TIKTOK IS A RECOMMENDATION ENGINE

In simple terms, the content on TikTok is extremely focused on engagement. TikTok is meant to "addict" users by showing them more and more content that they find engaging. Every time a user "likes," "comments on," or just "watches" a video, the algorithm is lurking in the background snooping and cataloging user behavior. You can learn more by reading TikTok's official explanation of how the "for you" page works at **http://jmlinks.com/59h**. Note that this is different than the "discover" page, which can be accessed by clicking on the "discover" magnifying glass on the app.

Here's the bottom line. If you are a dog person and like, comment, or just watch a lot of dog-related videos, you will see more of them. If you are a cat person, ditto. If you are a Democrat, ditto. If you are a Republican, ditto. If you like dance videos, ditto. If you like conspiracy theories, ditto. Users quickly go down a rabbit hole of **addictive content.**

On the other hand, the recommendation engine spices up content with new and weird stuff unrelated to interests – trending videos, trending sounds, hashtags, etc. – so that the feed doesn't get boring. It's the perfect balance of "oldies but goodies" when it comes to user interests plus "new and trending" content. It's perfectly designed to engage users, with many teens spending two to three hours per day and the average time on the app at fifty-two minutes. Whether this is good for society is a separate question, but as marketers, we must realize that TikTok – more than any other platform – puts engaging, dare I say, "viral" **content** – front and center as our marketing goal.

Secondly, TikTok is **conversational** in a way that Instagram is not. And not just among users who know each other but across users who do not know each other. While users can simply create an account and post "stories" about their lives, most users are engaging with trending songs or sounds, trending controversies or ideas, or building themselves up as superfans and influencers. There are even **duets** between videos and the ability to embed comments in a video and comment to the comment in a video. A good way to think about TikTok is that it is a truly "**social conversation**" conducted in video form. TikTok also connects strangers to strangers, making it a lot like Twitter in its openness and conversational vibe. But so far, it's not negative and snarky like Twitter: it's fun and friendly.

If Instagram is "here is my life, check me out," TikTok is "you said this-or that?," "well, I respond this-or-that," "you did X," "here is me imitating you doing X," and so on and so forth. It's like a dance contest that mutated into a humor, conversation, trending topic contest. TikTok is a video conversation as much as it is a social platform. TikTok, in essence, is the world's first **social video** platform.

Third, TikTok is **AI-centric**. Many users don't even check who they are following or do much more than "like" or "swipe" videos. The artificial intelligence (AI) algorithm figures out what they like, and shows them more of that, regardless of whether they actually are following that user or not. Sure, follows and followers still exist, but most of TikTok is led by its AI. For this reason, "riding the trend" is as essential, if not even more essential, to success on TikTok than increasing your follower count.

TikTok is AI-Centric

What about YouTube? TikTok, like YouTube, focuses exclusively on video content. It has the four basic uses of video:

> **Supportive**. You could conceivably use TikTok videos to "support" your brand as when a cooking channel puts out short TikToks about how to make a quick recipe or a quick cooking tip. Or, how a celebrity brand might show insights into their daily life as they do on Instagram or Facebook Stories. Since TikTok is very much about "pop culture," users can follow brands they like, such as the TV Show Stranger Things (**https://www.tiktok.com/@strangerthingsoficcial**), and yes, they spelled "official wrong" because a user stole the "official" spelling.

And yes, hundreds of thousands of fans follow the hashtag #strangerthings at **https://www.tiktok.com/tag/strangerthings**.

SEO. TikTok is not easy to search, but users can follow hashtags and content themes. This is not yet a big use of the platform, but, as on YouTube, the "how to" category is growing. The largest category of search is by keyword or hashtag. Many reports indicate that "Gen Z" is turning not to Google or YouTube, but to TikTok as their information discovery tool.

Viral / Sharing. Here, unlike Instagram or even YouTube, TikTok is a huge platform for viral and sharing content. Users piggyback on trending sounds, songs, hashtags, ideas, controversies, etc., and then both the videos themselves and the "theme" go viral. In fact, the "discover" tab on the app is literally about trending hashtags, and the app has built-in share capability not just to other users on the app but to other platforms like Instagram. TikTok is cleverly using other social platforms like Facebook, Twitter, and Instagram to build its audience and pull users off of those platforms.

Subscriptions. Again, like YouTube, individuals, creators, and brands try to build out "addictive" content so that users a) subscribe to their TikTok accounts and/or b) see and re-see their content via the "recommendation engine," which realizes that you "like" to see videos by so-and-so. Not surprisingly, TikTok has a vibrant "influencer" marketplace where brands can purchase endorsements at **https://creatormarketplace.tiktok.com/**.

Although videos on TikTok are shot in "vertical format" and are generally short (< 1 minute, though users can now upload long-form content), the principles of good storytelling apply as on YouTube. **Emotions** (especially humor, controversy, trending topics, and outrage) drive viral shares, plus stuff that is just plain funny. Humor is the #1 emotion on the platform, followed by controversy/outrage and a general sense of "surprise" or "this is counterintuitive." Each video needs to have a very strong and fast "hook" in the first few seconds, tell a quick story with a rising action, climax, and falling action, and then prompt users to "like," "comment," or "share" the video to feed the algorithm.

In summary, TikTok is very much like Instagram, Twitter, or YouTube in that users have "accounts" and users can follow each other. It is very much like them in that content is king. It is very much like them in that emotional video gets the highest engagement, and emotion needs to be the centerpiece of your content strategy. It differs strongly in the very high level of User Generated Content, in the "conversational" tone of video back-and-forth on the platform, and in the extreme dominance of the algorithm over relationships in what people discover.

The best way to understand TikTok is to start using it and identify creators and brands to follow. It is to this task that we now turn.

❯ SEARCH TIKTOK AND IDENTIFY CREATORS AND BRANDS TO FOLLOW

As on YouTube, TikTok has the following sorts of users:

> **Average Users.** These are people who just view videos and consume content without producing any of their own. Or, they produce videos but mainly for friends and family and none of this content "goes viral" or becomes "massively popular."

> **Creators.** These are people-as-brands, that is, people who are using the platform for personal branding. Often they are actors, musicians, or comedians. Many of my favorite content creators are comedians as for example - **https://www.tiktok.com/@tuckercomedy** or **https://www.tiktok.com/@jessejosephgeneau**. But others such as Rachel Ray (**https://www.tiktok.com/@rachaelrayofficial**) or Shaun T (**https://www.tiktok.com/@shaunt**) use the platform for "how to" content such as cooking or getting in shape.

> **Brands.** These are brands such as Chipotle (**https://www.tiktok.com/@chipotle**) or Wendys (**https://www.tiktok.com/@wendys**) that have fully embraced the platform and are cleverly using it to reach their target demographic (young people). Not surprisingly, most of the best brands on TikTok are consumer- and youth-oriented brands.

As on Instagram and YouTube, you can easily see who follows whom on TikTok. Just visit an account on the app and click "following." (Note: some of the features do not work on the desktop, only the mobile app version). Just go to an account and click on "followers."

Here's a screenshot of who is following Wendy's:

You can also click into any follower account and see how many people they are following vs. how many people they follow, a good metric for their brand strength just as on Instagram or Twitter. Here's a screenshot of Wendy's:

Wendy's thus follows only 238 accounts, is followed by 1.2 million, and has received 9.8 million likes on its videos. Note that as on Instagram, only one link is allowed. Wendy's has its main URL in its bio. Similar to Instagram, you have a profile picture, short text bio, and link. That's about it in terms of account optimization. Wendy's has a "blue check," which is also a status symbol indicating that this is a verified account.

Finding Competitors and Brands-to-emulate

On TikTok as on all social platforms, you want to identify people and brands that are doing a good job so you can "reverse engineer" their content marketing strategies. It's not hard to search TikTok. Simply use the **search feature** on the app and input the name of a brand (or competitor). Then follow them on your own account (not your business account), and you can stealthily see what they are up to on TikTok. Alternatively, you can search by keyword. Once you enter a keyword or brand name, you then get a response screen with "Top," "Users," "Videos," "Sounds," and "Hashtags" across the top. To find the brand, generally, tap on "Users."

IDENTIFY AND FOLLOW "COMPANIES-TO-EMULATE" ON TIKTOK

Once you build out a list of **competitors** and **companies-to-emulate** on TikTok and start following them, remember that TikTok is algorithm-centric. You will not always see the content of accounts you follow on your primary feed. Instead, as a "market researcher," you need to tap into your profile and then tap on "following" to find brands you are following.

Here's a screenshot:

By clicking on "following," I can browse creators and brands I follow and see what they are up to vs. depending on the algorithm, which will strongly prefer content that I have heavily engaged with.

Search by Keywords

You also want to search by keywords or themes to discover creators, brands, trending topics, or hashtags. Simply open the app, tap on the "discover" magnifying glass at the bottom, and type in a keyword or theme into the search bar. Here's a screenshot of the keyword "organic" on TikTok:

Again, you can tap across the top for "Top," "Users," etc. to drill into categories. Find brands, creators, hashtags, etc., that are relevant and follow them into your account. **Hashtags** are heavily used on TikTok, and you can "follow" a hashtag. Simply click on it and click "Add to favorites." The same goes for "Sounds" and "Effects." As you find them, simply tap into them, and add them to your favorites.

Favoriting a video is a little non-obvious. Find a video you like, then press into the video. Here's one of my favorite marketing videos, "Sending a Burrito to Space," which appears on the @Chipotle account. After I press and hold on it, I can click "Favorite" (bookmark icon / lower right) to bookmark it to my favorites. Here's a screenshot:

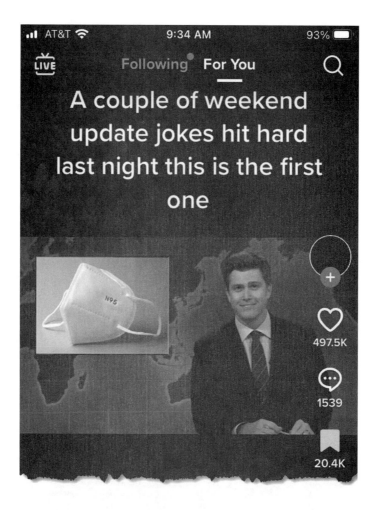

Once added to "Favorites," I can return to this video to rewatch it (and "reverse engineer" the marketing magic in it) by clicking into my profile and then the "bookmark" icon in the middle. I can also click on "liked" to see videos that I "liked." You can also download the video to your phone. And, if you are working as a team, you can copy the URL on the desktop and email that to your team. For example, the URL of a famous video by Chipotle called "Sending a Burrito to Space" at **https://www.tiktok.com/@chipotle/video/6888800963797323013**.

In this way, you can be a very sophisticated market researcher and keep an eye on and eye out for content creators and content that you may want to imitate. Don't try to "reinvent the wheel" on TikTok; rather, pay attention to what others are doing and what is getting engagement.

"REVERSE ENGINEER" WHAT'S WORKING FOR BRANDS ON TIKTOK

Because TikTok is also available on the desktop, you can log in to your account on the desktop and manage many of the features there as well. As the desktop version does not include a search feature, you can use the **site:tiktok.com {keyword}** format on Google to search by competitor or brand name, keyword, or even hashtag, thus using Google to search TikTok for content. For example, to see the search for "burritos" on TikTok, go to **http://jmlinks.com/55q**. You can substitute your own keyword and use Google as a quick way to search TikTok on the desktop.

At the end of this exercise, you should have identified brands, content creators, hashtags, videos, and even sounds that are relevant to your own company or project. I recommend following these in your (private) personal account vs. your (public) business account, as they will be visible to the outside world. The objective here is not only to orient yourself to what's going on on TikTok but to research whether your competitors, companies-to-emulate, and customers are on the platform and, if so, what types of content are engaging them.

» INVENTORY COMPANIES ON TIKTOK

As a marketer, your objective is to "reverse engineer" what other companies are doing and figure out if you can do something similar. Because the platform is so new, you may find that zero competitors in your industry are using it or using it effectively. Even some big brands are absent from the platform at the time of this writing! That's good news because the playing field is wide open. That said, I recommend you go into some key brands and "reverse engineer" what they are doing both at a structural level and at a content level.

Let's look at a few brands, starting with @Chipotle (**https://www.tiktok.com/@chipotle/**). At a structural level, take a look at their brand page. You'll immediately notice there isn't a lot that one can do at the account level. You simply see a brand icon for the profile picture, a text summary of "Less Tok, More Guac," and the single, solitary link allowed by TikTok. Here's a screenshot:

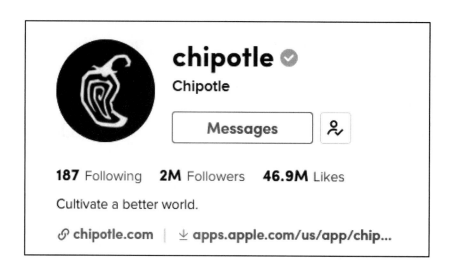

You can see "following," "followers," total "likes," a "bio," a link to their website, and (for apps), a link to their app download page. The "messages" icon allows users to "message" the brand via the TikTok app.

That's about it. The real engine of TikTok is content – content produced by the brand, including content "nurtured" by the brand via hashtags, contests, challenges, and "piggybacking" on trending content. Go to the search feature and type in the brand name, i.e., "Chipotle," and look for related content. This is an easy way to see User Generated Content. Here's a screenshot:

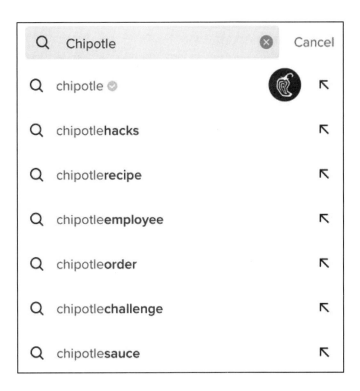

You can then tap into these terms and see related content. Often content such as "chipotlechallenge" or "chipotlehacks" has been "nurtured" by the brand. Don't assume that this all "went viral" all on its own. Chipotle is a smart brand, and it fostered a user-friendly environment on the platform, and so can you.

Next, within a brand channel, you can see the view count of videos. You can thus see which videos have the highest view counts, i.e., are the most popular. For example, here's a video that is co-branded between Chipotle and Bill Nye the Science Guy at 303.9K views:

Along the right column, you can see it had 71.1 thousand likes, 933 comments, and 706 shares. You can watch it at **http://jmlinks.com/55r**. As you work through a brand, pay a lot of attention to the videos on their channel and categorize them. Chipotle has a lot of videos that are a) influencers or famous people, b) challenges or contests, c) silly user-generated content, such as users who are pleading with Chipotle to give them free burritos for life.

Here are some other brands that are doing a fantastic job on TikTok. Click or tap over to each and check them out with an eye to the "party with a purpose" aspect of their TikTok marketing strategy.

Zach King (**https://www.tiktok.com/@zachking**) – note that some of his videos cross into influencer marketing, in which he "endorses" a brand. For example, watch his video supporting GrubHub.

Block Masonry (**https://www.tiktok.com/@blockmasonery**) – who thought masonry would be video-centric? Block Masonry makes the boring, fun.

Crocs (**https://www.tiktok.com/@crocs**) – the shoe type that will just never die.

Jimmy Fallon (**https://www.tiktok.com/@jimmyfallon**) – where does the comedian end and the brand begin? Fallon is a smart example of a content creator that "gets" what's so amazing about TikTok.

Tuyen (**https://www.tiktok.com/@lifewithtuyen**) – here is a "recipe" or "foodie" brand, building out and cooking super yummy food and showing you how to cook. Notice the clever link in bio (**https://www.lifewithtuyen.com/links**), which is a branded way to deal with the single link problem.

Wendys (**https://www.tiktok.com/@wendys**) – another consumer brand that, like Chipotle, is excelling on TikTok as they do on Twitter. Don't miss their video piggybacking on the Fleetwood Mac song *Dreams* at **http://jmlinks.com/55s**.

Sugar Hero (**https://www.tiktok.com/@sugar.hero/**) – a consumer-facing (personal) candy brand that is crushing it (pardon the pun). Notice the "how we make it" theme to many of the videos.

Sticky Lollies (**https://www.tiktok.com/@stickyaustralia**) – another consumer-facing candy brand that is sticky. Similar to Sugar Hero, but in this case a true brand and also heavy on the "how we make it" theme. Note the use of Link.Tree at **https://linktr.ee/stickylollies** as we have seen on Instagram.

Throughout, pay attention to how much of the content strategy is "fun" and "humor" just like real consumers vs. an aggressive "buy our stuff" tone. The "buy our stuff" message takes a back seat to the "we are cool just like you teens" message. Your objective here is to look at the total package of brand content on TikTok with an eye to how you might structure not only your account (which is easy) but your content strategy (which is where the real fun begins). Think fun, think funny, think customer-centric, think user-generated, think viral, think sharing, think visual, think video, think story, think piggybacking on trends – think, in short, like a teenage consumer to make TikTok work for you.

Content, especially User Generated Content, is the name of the game on TikTok. The way to think this through is to blend an understanding of the technical features or opportunities with how brands leverage users to subtly promote their brand message. Let's work through some examples.

Quirky, fun posts. This is the bread-and-butter of TikTok. Here, users and brands simply create their own content that is so quirky, so funny that it will be found by the algorithm and users will engage with it enough to be promoted.

How To's. This is another type of brand content. Brands such as Rachel Ray and Shaun T (food and fitness) create a lot of this type of content. If your brand is a "helpful expert," then this is a big opportunity for supportive content on the platform, but it will not likely go viral.

Challenges. Brands promote challenges that usually require users to do something silly or fun that involves the brand. In some cases, users can win prizes. Try entering a brand name plus "challenge" via Google as in *site:tiktok.com Chipotle Challenge* (**http://jmlinks.com/55t**). There may even be a hashtag such as *#chipotlelidflip* with 325 million views at **http://jmlinks.com/55u**. This type of content is probably the easiest to nurture and encourage in terms of user-generated content and sharing.

Contests. Contests can be as simple as "enter to win" or as complicated as requiring users to go through various steps. Again, simply search TikTok for "contests" to browse current contests and mine them for ideas. Or follow the hashtag *#contests* on the app at **https://www.tiktok.com/tag/contest**. Notice that there are two types of contests:

1. **Contests by Brands**. These are more "formal" contests where money and prizes can be won.

2. **User-generated Contests**. These are really more like "challenges" in that users create, follow, and engage with contests to do this or that. In this way, the difference between a "contest" and a "challenge" can be a bit blurry.

Influencer Outreach. As we see on Instagram and YouTube, influencers are 'for sale' on TikTok. So much so that TikTok has an official "influencer creator marketplace" at **http://jmlinks.com/55v** where talent and endorsements are literally for sale. If you look back at the Chipotle account, for example, you'll see quite a few cross-promotions with influencers; whether money was exchanged or not is not exactly obvious. Sorry FTC regulators – you are way behind the app!

The types of content listed above all have their counterparts on other social media platforms. The uniqueness is in the short-form, vertical video format, and the quirky, funny tone that is common to TikTok. TikTok is not the place for horizontal videos nor for "serious" videos such as "Dear Future Mom" or "#*Always* Like a Girl," as we saw on YouTube. Brands keep it short, funny, and viral. For an official video on how to create engaging content on TikTok, check out **http://jmlinks.com/56y**.

Rapid Fire Content Ideas

Content is king on TikTok! You've gotta create content around your brand that grabs the attention of users, holds it, and spurs engagement as measured by likes, comments, shares, and watch time.

Here are some "rapid-fire" content ideas:

Hook. The first few video seconds are critical. You must "hook" the viewer with a puzzle, a claim, an out-of-body experience, an over-the-top "hook," either visually or audible. **What's your hook?**

Trending Sounds. Trending sounds are as big, if not bigger, than trending hashtags. Follow the trending sounds and hop on, or – if you're a big brand – create your own sound and encourage it to "go viral." Remember that you can "see" the sound in any video on the lower right corner. Click on it and see all videos that use that sound.

> **Trending Music.** Music is critical to many successful TikToks, so look for trending songs, especially but not only top 40 hits, and embed this in your video.

> **Silly Statements.** Another common trending sound is the latest guffaw by Joe Biden, a silly statement by Nancy Pelosi, or a celebrity quote. Piggyback on the humor in these "quotes" as "TikTok sounds."

Contests and Challenges. Both are big; the difference being a contest means money is paid, and a challenge is just "bragging rights." Research the hashtags *#contest* and *#challenge* to see what's going viral and might work for your brand.

Hacks. Hacks and hidden features are yet another content trend. Lots of content is a hidden "cooking" hack or a funny "wedding" hack, etc. Look up the hashtag *#hacks* for ideas.

Behind-the-scenes. As on Instagram Reels or Facebook stories, bigger brands get to show us what goes on "behind the scenes," as in how a Gucci purse might be made, how chocolate is gelled, etc. **What's your "behind the scenes" story?**

Outrage. While not as political as Twitter, *#outrage* does have its place on TikTok. This is especially useful if you are a political or nonprofit brand.

Humor. TikTok remains the funniest platform out there. It has more than its share of "stand-up comedy" type of posts, and many content creators are exclusively humorous. Have fun with your brand and leverage humor for your own content as well as the UGC content of your customers.

"Man bites Dog." This is news. "Dog bites man" is not. What's "**counterintuitive**" about your brand story? What will make people stop in their TikTok tracks and want to see more? Think trainwreck, explosion, or other "I can't believe you did that" type of content.

Trending Hashtags. Hashtags are big, as we have discussed, and they trend. Find and follow key hashtags and jump on them. Make your own branded hashtag. Make your own contest or challenge hashtag.

Infomercial. Many brands create content around their brands that are shameless infomercials. *It slices. It dices. And you can buy it via link in bio.* Think of fun, humorous, over-the-top ways to sell your brand while simultaneously entertaining users.

Ads that Look Organic. TikTok doesn't seem to care about FTC regulations or other brand restrictions. It's hard to see "what's an ad" vs. "what's organic." Jump on that trend with your own ad that "looks like" organic content.

Superfans and Influencers. Collaborate with your most famous "fans" or reach out to "influencers." Cross-pollinate by making fun videos with "influential" people in your niche. Who are the influencers in your industry? Which ones are on TikTok?

Have fun. TikTok is the funnest platform in social media today. Don't be boring with your content. Embrace the zeitgeist of TikTok and be fun, be funny, be outrageous, be over-the-top, be a contest, be a challenge, be crazy, be dancing. But most of all, engage and motivate your customers with "great" content.

❯ MASTER TECHNICAL FEATURES

TikTok has some technical features such as likes, comments, tagging, and hashtags that are similar to other platforms, and we have already noted that — like Instagram — it has a one link only policy. Here are some unique technical features that are also marketing opportunities.

Trending Sounds and Songs

First and foremost, TikTok has trending **sounds** and **songs**. TikTok has a strong music orientation, and thus a sound clip can "go viral." Brands can then piggyback on that sound by creating a funny video that utilizes it. For example, Fleetwood Mac's 1977 hit "Dreams," had a renewed life on TikTok as a viral hit. TikTok users were mesmerized by a young skateboarder chugging Ocean Spray juice along to the tune. Once that went viral, brands such as Wendy's capitalized on it as for example, at **http://jmlinks.com/55s**. Here's a screenshot of Wendy's piggyback to that trend:

On the app, you can tap on the bottom right spinning icon, which is the sound, to see more videos that use this "trending" sound. Here's a screenshot:

That will bring you to a page full of other videos that also share this sound. **Sounds, on TikTok, are thus like "hashtags."** Content can be created and shared around a sound.

Another way to find trending sounds is to look on your "explore" tab, which is the magnifying glass on the app. Scroll down until you see "trending sound" as a designation. Here's a screenshot:

In this way, you can find trending sounds, create video content that employs this sound, and "piggyback" on that trend. You can also often see hashtags that have an interrelated sound and create content that is both a hashtag and a trending sound. You can also search by keyword and then click over to sounds to see related sounds. Inside a trending sound, swipe up to browse videos that use the sound. Trending sounds are one way that the Tiktok algorithm favors content.

Duets

Duets are another fun technical feature on TikTok. Here, one user talks back to another user using the duet feature. Think of it like a video conversation or "split-screen" as on a traditional TV news show. Many duets are tagged using the *#duet* hashtag (**http://jmlinks.com/55w**). Here's a screenshot showing 1702.1 billion views of the hashtag:

The feature is so popular that TikTok has an official video on how to make a duet at **http://jmlinks.com/55x**. Check it out and check out some of the better duets. Then look for trending duet content and chime in as a brand.

Another way to use TikTok is to create your own **branded sounds** and/or your own branded contests or challenges around duets. Chipotle has done this through its "original sound" channel at **http://jmlinks.com/55y**. Thus the brand strategy is to literally create an "original sound" and then promote content around that sound. Other fun things that brands do are respond to comments and embed those comments in their videos with responses, something similar to a duet. I would go so far as to say

"Piggybacking" is a legitimate content strategy on TikTok. So ask yourself – what might you and your brand "piggyback on?"

Other Technical Features

TikTok has a few other technical features that are worth noting. First, there's tagging as on other platforms. By tagging an account that is "more important" than you are, you can encourage a social interaction. Second, there are text overlays. Adding text overlays to a video (such as captions) can help increase interaction as people like to both "see" and "hear" content at the same time. Third, there are comments. You can comment on a video in text, but also you can do a "video reply," thus creating a video type of interaction. You can learn more about this at **http://jmlinks.com/56w**. As on other platforms, you can also "go live" on TikTok. You can plan an event, allow fans to book a notification, and when you "go live," TikTok will push out notifications to users. You can learn more about best practices for "going live" on TikTok at **http://jmlinks.com/56x.**

» MEASURE YOUR RESULTS

Professional or business accounts on TikTok have more bells and whistles than just simple user accounts. As you might expect, you can track video views, followers, and profile views. You can see views by geography, etc. Most importantly, you can see which videos are trending. Of course, when you just start out, you are not going to see a lot of trending activity. You can also drill into an individual video and see the engagement aspects of it. In sum, TikTok Analytics is very similar to YouTube analytics.

Since TikTok also allows URL sharing and shares, you can track clicks from TikTok to your website or eCommerce store. However, 99% of TikTok is about engagement and branding, so don't expect it to be easy to monetize. It's more about the feel than it is about the spending, so to speak. More about making your brand cool and talked about than getting sales directly. But if you are a consumer-facing brand, you gotta consider TikTok!

»» CHECKLIST: TIKTOK ACTION ITEMS

Test your knowledge of TikTok. Take the TikTok quiz at **http://jmlinks.com/qztt.** Here are your TikTok **Action Items:**

❑ **Research** whether your customers (and competitors) are on TikTok. What are they doing? Why? Be sure to distinguish among individual accounts, creators, competitors, and companies-to-emulate. Be sure to understand how to follow accounts, find them (and their content), plus "train" the algorithm to give you what you like.

❑ **Set up** a **business account** on TikTok as well as a personal account. Do your market research in your personal account as you can follow competitors there without being obvious. Remember that everything is public, so make sure your brand account is 100% your brand identity.

❑ **Brainstorm** a **content strategy** for TikTok. As on YouTube, you have primarily:

> ❑ **Your Own Content**. This is quirky, funny, brand-centric content that you create and post to your account.
>
>> ❑ **Trending Content**. This is content that you create, but that piggybacks on trending *hashtags* or *sounds* on TikTok.
>>
>> ❑ **Rapid Fire.** Go through my list of "rapid-fire" ideas, and identify easy-to-produce content for your own videos, such as #hacks, behind-the-scenes, or duets on trending topics.
>
> ❑ **User Generated Content**. Here, you nurture UGC through contests, challenges, branded hashtags, and even clever sounds or songs that you create and promote as a brand for users. Chipotle and Wendys are masters at this strategy.
>
> ❑ **Interactive Content**. Create "Duets" as well as use user comments (and/or comment on other videos). TikTok is conversational – so join the video conversation.

❑ **Repurpose Content**. TikTok's short, vertical format makes it excellent for cross-posting to Instagram, including Instagram stories. Make your content go further by repurposing it to/from Instagram Reels, TikTok, and YouTube Shorts.

❑ **Promote Your Content**. Encourage content that will be "sharable" or even "go viral," plus use your other platforms to alert your fans about your TikTok account. Use strategies like #*hashtags* and trending sounds. Consider **advertising** if TikTok is a strong "yes" for you and you have the budget.

❑ **Measure** your results on TikTok by likes, comments, and shares. Measure whether your account is growing. The platform is still new, so be patient and realize that it takes only one "hit" to really get visibility.

Check out the **free tools**! Go to my *Social Media Marketing Dashboard > TikTok* for my favorite free tools on TikTok. Just visit **http://jmlinks.com/smmdash**.

»» DELIVERABLE: A TIKTOK MARKETING PLAN

Now that we've come to the end of our chapter on TikTok, your **DELIVERABLE** has arrived. For the worksheet, go to **http://jmlinks.com/2023smm** (then enter the code '**2023smm**' to register your workbook), and click on the link to the "TikTok Marketing Plan." By filling out this plan, you and your team will establish a vision of what you want to achieve via TikTok.

10
PINTEREST

Some social media platforms like Facebook, YouTube, and LinkedIn are broad, reaching many people with diverse interests. Others are narrow, reaching only specific people (demographic groups like *young folks* or *women*, for example) or specific usages (e.g., *finding a plumber*, *commenting on the news*, etc.). Yelp, Tumblr, Instagram, Twitter, and Pinterest fall into this latter category. They are very strong in certain niches but not so strong as truly mass platforms. If your specific customer segment or usage case is active on one of these media, in particular, it can work spectacularly well. If not, then all your hard work bombs out into oblivion.

> Pinterest is such a platform: incredibly strong in **online shopping**, **do-it-yourself** (DIY), and the **female demographic**, and all but absent from nearly everything else.

Shoppers use Pinterest to browse the Internet and "pin" items they might want to buy onto "boards." Do-it-yourselfers use Pinterest to share ideas on how to build this or that, knit this or that, or construct this or that. And women, always a heavy shopping and craftsy demographic, use Pinterest as a "buying/idea platform" and as a great platform for do-it-yourself crafting and recipe-sharing.

Pinterest, in short, is *the* network for consumer retail, *the* network for craftsy do-it-yourself, including recipes, and *the* network for women (or, not to be sexist, the network for anyone who loves to browse and shop).

Let's get started!

TO-DO LIST:
- » Explore How Pinterest Works
- » Search Pinterest and Identify Stuff to Follow
- » Inventory Companies on Pinterest
- » Set up and Optimize Your Account
- » Brainstorm and Execute a Pinning Strategy

» Promote Your Pinterest Account, Boards, and Pins

» Measure Your Results

»» Checklist: Pinterest Action Items

»» Deliverable: A Pinterest Marketing Plan

» EXPLORE HOW PINTEREST WORKS

For a basic introduction to Pinterest, check out the official guide at **http://jmlinks.com/36z**. Next, in terms of marketing opportunities, the best way to understand Pinterest is to grasp the concept of an **idea board**. Imagine a virtual corkboard in the Internet cloud to which you (and others) could "pin" sticky notes, photos, videos, and other content around a theme.

Let's use the example of someone planning out her ideal dorm room for freshman year at college. First, she signs up for Pinterest and creates a profile. Compared with Facebook, Pinterest is very basic. Not a lot of information is displayed in a Pinterest profile, pretty much just a profile picture and a very brief description. Next, she should download and install the Pinterest button (see **http://jmlinks.com/54a**) as well as the Pinterest app (available for both Android and iOS). Once installed, she can now surf the Web (or use the Pinterest app for iPhone or Android) and "pin" interesting items to "boards" that she sets up.

For example, she'd set up a board called "my dream college room" or even more specific boards like "my dream bathroom supplies" or "my dream desk." Let's say she goes to Amazon and finds an amazing desk light. She can "pin" this desk light to her "dream desk" board. People who follow her (or this board) on Pinterest thus see this desk light in their Pinterest news feed, whereupon they can comment on it and (*gasp!*) even buy it for her. And, of course, she would pin not just one desk light but several possible desk lights, several pencil holders, several ink pads, a few art posters for above her desk, and on and on. It's as if she's building a collage of desk possibilities from which she can select the perfect accessories. As she creates idea boards for her dream desk, dream closet, dream door room, and dream bathroom supplies, she can invite her friends, her Mom, or her sorority sisters to collaborate by commenting and pinning to the boards as well.

Another example would be a person like myself that is crazy about dogs. I love dog photos, tips on how to get your dog to behave, dog toys that you buy on Amazon or elsewhere, tips on dog snacks, DIY dog toys, etc. I love dogs! I especially love Labradors! So I can create boards to help myself follow what's out there in the "dog world" and then follow persons who have more time than I do and who share their own passion for dogs, dog toys, dog tips, Labs, black Labs, Lab puppies are the cutest dogs, etc. And if a person likes dogs but also, for example, likes football (which doesn't interest me), I can follow only his "dog toy" board and not his "I love Raider football" board. Pinterest makes it easy for me to share, learn about, follow, comment, love, like and engage with other dog lovers wherever they may be in a visual way and interact with folks who share my passion for dogs but not other passions that I have, or that they have. It's a really awesome system and unique in social media.

Pinterest, in short, is a **visual bookmarking** and **idea board** system, one that can be social as well, and one that makes online shopping as easy as discover, click, and buy. People also use it before purchase in the real world as a social scrapbook to group together products and services they might want to buy at a brick-and-mortar store. And do-it-yourselfers use it to share ideas about how to build this or that, how to cook this or that, etc.

THE ESSENCE OF PINTEREST IS THE IDEA BOARD

The structure of Pinterest in a nutshell, is:

Individual profile: me, Jason as a person, or Wells Fargo as a brand.

A board: collections of items from the Web on topics like my "dream dorm room," "dog toys to possibly buy," "do-it-yourself Christmas decorations," or "recipes for summer parties."

Pins: I can "pin" things I find on the Web such as blog posts, videos, images, or products to buy to my "boards" as a collection of ideas, things to buy. I can also upload items directly.

Search. I can browse Pinterest, search Pinterest, or search the Web for interesting things to "pin" to my boards.

Collaboration: I can invite others to comment on my board or pins, and to pin items to my boards directly. I can also pin things to their boards.

Social: I have a news feed, wherein Pinterest shows me the pins of people, brands, and boards I follow as well as suggestions based on my (revealed) interests. People can also follow my boards and me, and like, comment, and reshare items that I am pinning. Through collaborative boards, we can pin and share ideas together.

To get the hang of Pinterest, create your personal and/or business profile, create some boards, download the "Pin it" button, and start playing with the Pinterest app or using it on the desktop. Using Pinterest is the best way to begin to understand how to market on Pinterest. For example, to view a Pinterest search for "dream college dorm rooms," visit **http://jmlinks.com/2o**. To visit some sample idea boards, visit **http://jmlinks.com/13f**. Here's a screenshot of a search for "dream college room":

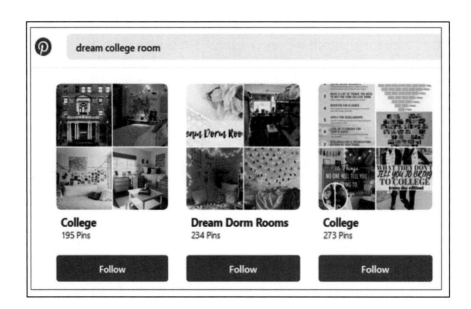

Notice how people use Pinterest as a **visual bookmarking system** of ideas (largely, but not exclusively, of stuff to buy or make), and how others can comment on, and even contribute to these boards in a collaborative fashion.

Let's look at how brands structure their Pinterest accounts. For example, consider the Target strategy on Pinterest. The massive retailer has "drill down" elements, such as:

Account. This is the entire Target account (**https://www.pinterest.com/target**). Users who love everything about Target can follow the *entire* account and thus get notifications in their newsfeed when Target posts *anything*.

Boards. These are listed under "saved" (**https://www.pinterest.com/target/_saved/**). These are "collections" that are category-specific boards of pins created by Target. Users who do not want to follow all of Target can choose instead to follow just specific boards such as Kids Toys (**https://www.pinterest.com/target/kids-toys/**) or Gifts for her (**https://www.pinterest.com/target/gifts-for-her/**). Boards allow for a more specific relationship between users and the themes that they want to follow.

Shop. The new "shop" element (**https://www.pinterest.com/target/_shop/**) is Pinterest's shameless connection of product themes to the instant gratification of being able to shop for something. Just like boards, shops can have sub-themes like "wall décor" but users cannot follow these sub-themes. The "shop' feature enables an easy purchase flow between Pinterest and the brand website.

Pins. These are individual items similar to tweets on Twitter or posts on Instagram. For example, the "All Things Avocado Gift Kit" (**http://jmlinks.com/57q**) lives under the board, "Gifts for Her," under the master Target Account.

Idea Pins. This is Pinterest-speak for video content, similar to "stories" on Instagram or Facebook. Upload a short video, and this gets pushed out to your fans.

Brands like Target thus want to not only get their pins out there into users' newsfeeds but also motivate users to follow the brand as a whole or specific boards.

Boards create a unique marketing opportunity. Expectant mothers might follow the "things for pregnancy" board, fishermen might follow the "outdoor products board," and swimmers might follow the "things for your pool" board, and so on and so forth. As a marketer, you thus must brainstorm not just an *account strategy* but also a *board strategy* on Pinterest. Which content themes will position your brand as a "helpful expert?" Fishermen want to follow a board on fishing tackle, rods, and tools; pregnant women want to follow a board on sleep aids, skin creams, and preparing for baby. Your marketing strategy thus becomes a) identify your own products that match a user need vs. a theme, b) create boards around those themes, and c) remember that you can "pin" not only your own products or services to your board but those of others as well, and you can also pin blog posts, videos, images, etc. A "board" is a collage of items, some of which are "buy my stuff" and some of which are "this is interesting and useful."

Turning to pins specifically, there are two basic marketing opportunities on Pinterest:

> **Direct**. Get your items "pinned" to the boards of others, or have them show up in relevant Pinterest searches. This is a direct buy path: customers "discover" your pins and then buy the product or service referenced by them. (These can also be links to blog posts or videos).

Indirect. Create "idea boards" of your own that are relevant to your product or service. This is more indirect, in the sense that customers find your boards interesting or helpful and then "follow" your boards, thus learning about your products or services that have been "pinned" to your boards as well.

Once you understand the idea of visual bookmarking or "idea boards," then you've "got" Pinterest. Once you grasp the idea of being a "helpful vendor" with "helpful boards" that identify fun, lively things to do, buy or make, and you grasp the idea of encouraging your customers to "pin" your products to their boards, you've "got" the idea of marketing via Pinterest.

For example, when I find a post on Pinterest about a DIY dog toy, I can then pin it to my board of DIY dog toys. Here's an example:

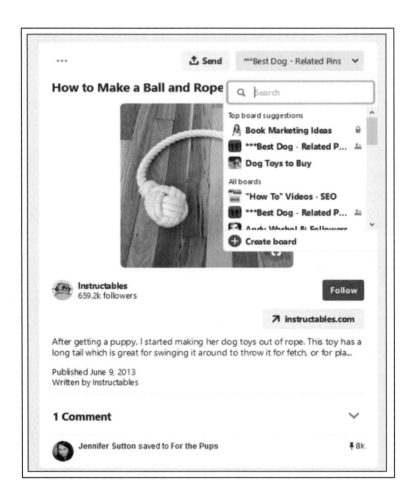

At the top right, you can see Pinterest prompting me to save it to one of my boards, such as my "Best Dog-Related Stuff" board. Then notice at the bottom left, how it indicates Jennifer Sutton saved this Pin as well to her own board titled, "For the pups." I can then click over to her or her board and discover a fellow dog lover to follow on Pinterest. In this interactive way, people browse stuff on Pinterest, save it to their own boards, and discover folks with similar interests.

Using the Pinterest button, you can also surf the Web and pin items you find to your boards. So, for example, I can go to Amazon, find a dog toy that interests me, and pin it to my board. Here's an example of this:

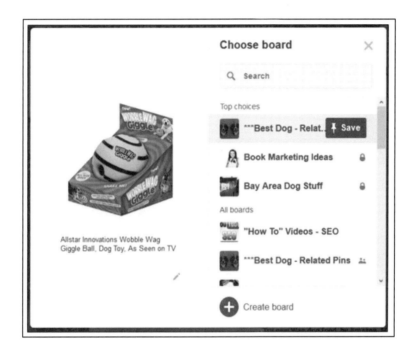

In this way, Pinterest is very "outward-looking." You as a brand should do everything you possibly can to encourage people to pin FROM your website or e-commerce store TO their Pinterest boards. Pinterest offers a free "save from your website" button that enables this feature on your website or e-commerce store easily; learn more at **http://jmlinks.com/46p**. Obviously, you need a visually appealing, highly shoppable type of site (preferably an e-commerce one) for this to work well. Another feature is so-called "rich pins," which transmit data in real-time from your e-commerce store to your pins on Pinterest (such as price, colors, and other options). Learn more at **http://jmlinks.com/46q**.

In this way, Pinterest is unique as a **social bookmarking system**. People find interesting stuff on the Web and pin it to their Pinterest boards. Others connected to them then follow and/or engage with that content, giving Pinterest a unique niche in the interaction between the Web and social media content, in e-commerce, and in visual content such as DIY (do-it-yourself).

Your Pinterest News Feed

As on other social media, people can "follow" other people or brands (or just their boards), and when that person, brand, or board has a new pin, that new pin shows in their news feed. In addition, notifications are generated when someone likes, comments, or repins one of your pins (or boards, or account).

Once you've done some basic research and identified persons/companies, boards, and hashtags to follow, when you log in to Pinterest, you'll see their new pins in your news feed. This is the same structure as on Facebook. If I follow you, and you post a pin, then it shows in my news feed (and vice-versa if you follow me back). You can also click on "Following" on the top left when you log in to see the newest pins from folks you follow. Here's a screenshot:

You can then click on the "+Person" icon top right to access yet another way to find new folks or boards to follow on Pinterest.

Now, flip this around. As a brand, you want to create pins and boards that people **want to follow**. Why? Because you, as the "helpful expert," are identifying and posting intriguing content – content that interests and excites potential customers. That content could be your own content (pins of products, services, videos, blog posts, top ten lists, how to's, DIY's, etc.), or curated content (content by others on these topics). And, yes, you can encourage UGC and interactive content as well, but for now, start with those two types – your own content and curated content.

» Search Pinterest and Identify Stuff to Follow

You can search Pinterest directly by keyword, or by clicking on the categories button, and you can browse Pinterest by categories. Let's review how to do each. As you search Pinterest, you're looking for:

- **Individuals**. These can be power Pinterest folks who are really active on the platform. These are superfans, influencers, and other "brand advocates."

- **Companies or brands to follow**. These might be direct competitors, companies in your industry, or just big brands that seem to be doing a great job at Pinterest like Target (**https://www.pinterest.com/target/**) or Martha Stewart Living (**https://www.pinterest.com/marthastewart/**).

- **Boards**. This is unique to Pinterest. You can either follow ALL of Target's content, or you can drill into a specific board such as Kids Toys (**https://www.pinterest.com/target/kids-toys/**).

- **Hashtags**. Like Twitter and Instagram, Pinterest is very hashtag-friendly. Just start typing keywords into Pinterest search and looking for *#hashtags* as in *#kids* or *#dogtoys*.

Once you find something interesting, just click the red and white "follow" to either follow that company, person, or board. Like Instagram or Twitter, there is no required acceptance at the other end. Pinterest is very open and public and primed for discovery.

If, for example, you were an organic baby food maker, you'd identify keyword themes like *organic, organic food, organic baby food*, etc., and then search Pinterest for companies, people, boards, and hashtags to follow. So search by keyword and start to find pins, people, and boards that you like or that are relevant to your company. When you find an interesting pin, you can then save it to a board you create on the fly or have already created.

For example, I have a board called "Best Dog-Related Pins," and I can save interesting pins to that board. Here's a screenshot:

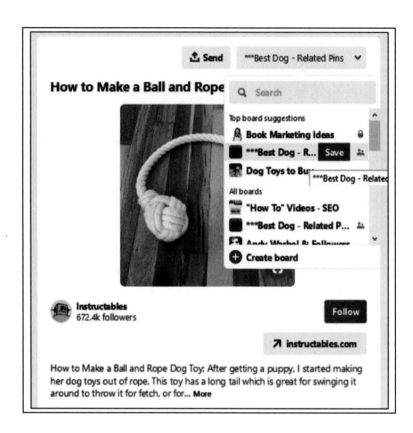

If a pin has a lot of engagement, you can also click down into the comments and find who pinned this pin to which board. For example, Bob Spangler saved this pin to his board "Garden 2":

You can also see that Natural Living Ideas has 55.6 thousand followers and that "Garden 2" has 7,000 followers itself.

In this way, you can search by keyword and find the most popular pins, boards, and people to follow. Pinterest is a search engine, in a sense, as well as a social media platform. With the basics in hand, let's review the available methods to discover pins, people or brands, or boards to follow.

Method #1. Keyword Search. Simply type into Pinterest one of your keyword themes, such as "organic gardening," and then on the left menu, search **all pins** (the universe of all pins on the topic), **product pins** (these are specific products to buy), **people** (this is both real people and brands or companies on Pinterest), and **boards** (these are idea boards on the topic). Here's a screenshot showing the pull-down menu on the left:

Search each category and begin to follow people/brands and/or boards that are relevant to your company. Look for engagement as measured by repins and comments. For example, here's a "quote" pin by Muhammed Ali, "If your dreams don't scare you, they aren't big enough," and here's a screenshot showing the comments and repins:

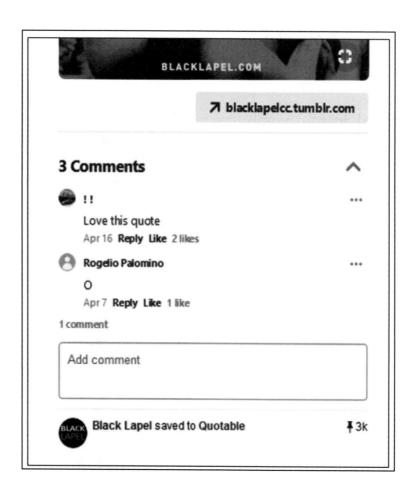

When you simply type a keyword into a Pinterest search, you can also just pay attention to the suggestions that occur just beneath it. Here's a screenshot for "organic:"

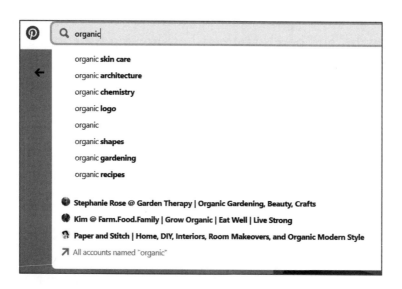

Method #2. Browse Pinterest by Category. Pinterest has sort of hidden this feature, so type this URL into your browser to access it: **https://www.pinterest.com/ideas**. This will then bring up a category index of Pins. Here's a screenshot:

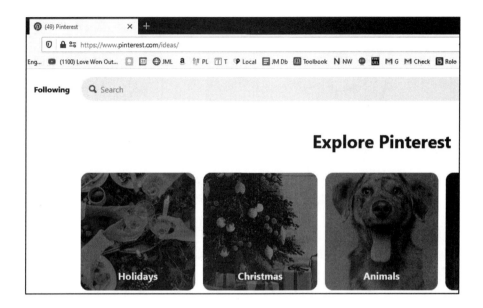

You can then click into a category and see pins as well as subcategories. For "Animals," for example, you get suggestions like "Dogs and puppies" or "Cats and kittens." Click on these, and you will get more suggestions and subcategories.

Method #3. Browse by URL. This is a little geeky, but it's a great way to see which URLs have the most traction on Pinterest as a competitor or a big brand. To do this, you create a very special type of URL, and type the URL of a domain into the search bar. It's not perfect, but it tends to pick up those pins that contain that domain. For example, here's **rei.com** via Pinterest search:

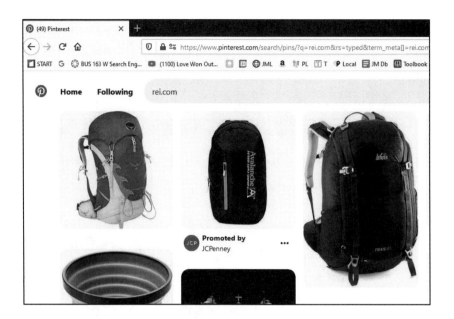

Simply replace *rei.com* in the string above with your own domain, and then copy/paste the complete URL into the address bar of your browser. Do this for your company on a regular basis (bookmark the URL), and you can see what customers and potential customers are pinning from your website; within Pinterest analytics, you can verify ownership of your website and get even more details on your own site.

Method #4. Use Google. Finally, you can go to Google and enter *site:pinterest.com {keyword}* as in *site:pinterest.com "organic food"* or **http://jmlinks.com/46n**. You can use the Tools menu at the top right to select past year, past month, or even past 24 hours to see trending and new topics on Pinterest. You can also do this for a competitor as in *site:pinterest.com rei.com* via Google.

At the end of this process, you should have built up a list of persons or companies, boards, and hashtags to follow on Pinterest. Note that hashtags are only clickable on the phone and then only in the Pin description.

❯ INVENTORY COMPANIES ON PINTEREST

The best way to decide whether Pinterest has any value to your marketing is to **research** other companies on Pinterest and observe how their fans interact with them on the platform. First, you need to understand how to find companies on Pinterest. Second, you should make a list of companies (and boards) to follow on Pinterest (and follow them with your personal profile). Note: it's important to realize that you can and should follow BOTH companies AND boards, as one company (e.g., Whole Foods) can have multiple boards (best soups, ideas for grilling, salad concepts, etc.). Third, you need to know how to determine what customers are doing on Pinterest, and fourth, you must assess whether any of this has potential value for your company's marketing strategy.

VIDEO. Watch a video tutorial on Pinterest marketing basics at **http://jmlinks.com/17c**.

Remember that you're not really or necessarily a true Pinterest user. You're a brand researching what's going on and figuring out if Pinterest is for you, and if so, what content strategy will work the best. You are more interested in how competitors and other companies use Pinterest as a marketing vehicle in *your* industry. To find companies in your industry, look at the pins returned for your searches as listed above, and at the bottom, look for URL's that sound corporate or pins that indicate "promoted pins."

For instance, if you are in the dog toy industry, you might end up at any of these companies' Pinterest pages:

Waggo Pet (https://www.pinterest.com/WaggoPet/) - Lifestyle brand and purveyor of design-driven, happy-centric goodies for home and pet. You'll see that they have a board called "ETC" focused on dogs at **https://www.pinterest.com/WaggoPet/etc/**.

Collar Planet Online (https://www.pinterest.com/collarplanet/) - specializes in unique Martingale Collars, Pet Jewelry, Jeweled and Leather Dog Collars and Leashes. Large assortment of dog costumes, dog clothes, and more!

Swanky Pet (https://www.pinterest.com/swankypet/) - Stylish dog collars and more! All items are made-to-order --- let them know what to make for you!

A quick way to find companies after a search is to hit CTRL+F on your keyboard (COMMAND F on Mac) and type in "promoted." That will highlight the promoted (company) pins. These are pins that are being advertised and consequently will originate from companies as opposed to individuals. When you click on these, you'll go to their websites. But you can then put their name back on Pinterest to find their brand pages. The reality is that brands that are advertising are also putting a lot of effort into organic on Pinterest as well.

IDENTIFY COMPANIES WHO DO PINTEREST MARKETING WELL. REVERSE ENGINEER THEM.

As you research companies via your keywords, look for companies with many followers and whose boards/pins show a great deal of interaction: many pins, likes, repins, and comments. Pinterest, after all, is a *social* medium, and your goal is to identify companies that "get" Pinterest well enough to build large, engaged follower communities.

Not surprisingly, since Pinterest is so successful in consumer retail, many of your large retailers have the most sophisticated marketing efforts on Pinterest. Identify a few consumer retailers you like, follow them on Pinterest, and "reverse engineer" their marketing strategies. Here are some of my favorites:

Target at **https://www.pinterest.com/target/**.

Martha Stewart Living at **https://www.pinterest.com/marthastewart/**

Chobani at **https://www.pinterest.com/chobani/**.

Birchbox at **https://www.pinterest.com/birchbox/**.

Everyday Health at **https://www.pinterest.com/everydayhealth/**.

Free People at **https://www.pinterest.com/freepeople/**.

Intel at **https://www.pinterest.com/intel/**.

Amazon at **https://www.pinterest.com/amazon/**

While we're looking at retailers, let's look at some nifty tricks on Pinterest at the pin level. (Note: this works only on the mobile app version, not the desktop).

First, do a search for your keyword (e.g., "elves"). Next, find a pin that sparks your interest – especially one that is a product photo. Click on the pin. Tap on the pin to reveal a small magnifying glass in the bottom right corner of the image. Drag the corners of the selected area until you have highlighted the entire image or one aspect of it. Pinterest will then search for this image across its database.

Here's a screenshot:

Second, in some cases, the Pinterest algorithm will "tag similar products" in a pin. You'll see a shopping icon in the far right bottom of these posts. Tap on that, and you'll see a listing of the products with clickable links to pins where you can make a purchase. Here's a screenshot of this:

As a brand, you can also tag products in your own Pin. Learn more about tagging products in pins at **http://jmlinks.com/57r**. Since, in many categories, Pinterest will make "similar products" recommendations, I recommend that you tag all your pins with product links.

Third, another method to see what's being shared on Pinterest about a specific domain is to use a tool like Buzzsumo (**http://www.buzzsumo.com/**). Simply type in the domain of interest into Buzzsumo, sort the Pinterest column on the right, and you can see the most popular content on Pinterest for a particular domain. Here's a screenshot using Buzzsumo to research the most shared content from Marthastewart.com:

Don't be afraid to "follow" companies via Pinterest (even your competitors). In fact, I strongly encourage it: by "following" companies you actually "like," you'll experience them marketing to you, and you can then reverse engineer this for your own company. As on other platforms, Pinterest has "stories" (called "idea pins") and shops as well.

For your first **TO-DO**, download the **Pinterest Research Worksheet**. For the worksheet, go to **http://jmlinks.com/2023smm** (then enter the code '**2023smm**' to register your workbook), and click on the link to the "Pinterest Research Worksheet." You'll answer questions as to whether your potential customers are on Pinterest, identify brands to follow, and inventory what you like and dislike about their Pinterest setup and marketing strategy.

» SET UP AND OPTIMIZE YOUR PINTEREST ACCOUNT

Now that you've got the basics of Pinterest down, it's time to set up or optimize your Pinterest page. Remember, people have "profiles," and businesses have "accounts" on Pinterest, often also called "Pages." You'll generally want a business account, or Page, on Pinterest. To set one up for the first time, go to *Pinterest for Business* at **https://business.pinterest.com/**. You can also convert a "profile" to a business "account" if you mistakenly joined as an individual at **https://business.pinterest.com/** and click on the "Join now" text and then "Switch to a business" or go to **http://jmlinks.com/32h**.

Since you are joining as a business, be sure to claim or verify your website. Follow the instructions at **http://jmlinks.com/46r**. This will give you better analytics, the ability to tag products, and mark pins that link to your domain with your profile picture.

Once you've joined, you have only a very basic set up – your profile picture, username (URL), "about you," location, and website. That's it. Once you've filled out this information, you're set up on Pinterest as a business.

Next, set up some boards by clicking on the "Create a Board" on the left of the screen. Here's a screenshot:

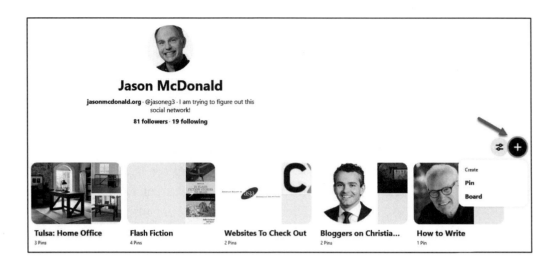

When you create a board, give it a name, a description, a category, a map or location (useful if you are a local business). Be sure to include keywords, as this is critical for discovery in Pinterest search, but don't be spammy. Write in natural English, yet include your keywords. If you're just building out the board, you can also temporarily make it *secret* and then change it to *public* at a later date.

Ask for Collaborators

Pinterest boards can be collaborative, meaning you can have more than one "manager," and you can even invite customers or others to help pin stuff to your boards. If your company has superfans, this is a great way to engage with them. If you want to make a board collaborative, you identify "collaborators" by typing in their names or email addresses. Pinterest will then invite them to start pinning items to your board. The easiest way to start pinning items to your board is to download the "Pinterest button" onto your browser. You can also manually copy URLs over to pin an item. With the concept that a board is an "idea board," start identifying and pinning items from the Web, such as blog posts, images, or photos, and yes, even products from your eCommerce store to your new board.

Board Strategy

Social media is a *party*, not a *prison*, and so it goes with your Pinterest boards. Your boards should attract people to follow them by providing something useful, something visual, something fun. Ask these questions. What is the board "about"? Who will want to "follow" it, Pin stuff from it (or to it), comment, share, and click from the board to your products? Take a board like "Gifts for Dog Lovers" at **http://jmlinks.com/3a** vs. the board "Dog Gifs" at **http://jmlinks.com/3b**. The purpose of the former is to identify fun dog gifts to BUY, while the purpose of the latter is to share funny pictures of dogs and build the brand image of *BarkPost* (**http://barkpost.com/**), a New York-based blog on dogs that also sells dog-related products. Both are legitimate social media marketing users of Pinterest – the former is just a more direct plea to "buy our stuff," whereas the latter is more a "look at this cool stuff" (and by the way, check out all the cool stuff we sell).

> *Hard sell* or *soft sell*: both work on Pinterest.

In sum, it is incredibly important to brainstorm your boards! The questions are:

- **What is this board about?** What ideas does it collect, and how does it function as a useful "idea-generator" on a particular topic?

- **Who will be interested in this board?** What value are you providing as the board-creator and board-curator by having this board? A board on dog toy ideas "saves time" for people who a) love dogs and want toys and/or b) need to buy a gift for a person who loves dogs and wants toys. Your value is curating "in" the cool stuff, and curating "out" the dumb stuff. A board that collects funny pictures of dogs is meant to give viewers a quick and easy way to get a few laughs during their busy day, and a board that collects do-it-yourself ideas for cheap dog toys helps dog lovers save money, and have fun, by building their own dog toys. Who will be interested is a function of what the board is about.

- **What will you pin to this board, and where does that content live?** Is it stuff from your eCommerce store? Stuff on Amazon? Blog posts, or how to articles? Items from your own blog? YouTube video? Content is king, on Pinterest, as on all social media.

For your second **TO-DO**, download the **Pinterest Setup Worksheet**. For the worksheet, go to **http://jmlinks.com/2023smm** (then enter the code '**2023smm**' to register your workbook), and click on the link to the "Pinterest Setup Worksheet." You'll answer and outline the basic setup issues for your Pinterest business account (page) and boards.

❯ BRAINSTORM AND EXECUTE A PINNING STRATEGY

Content is king, queen, and jack. Now that you've set up your Pinterest Page, you need to think about posting (or rather pinning). Turn back to your Content Marketing plan, and remember you'll need both other people's content and your own content to pin:

- **Photographs and Images**. Pinterest is very visual, and you'll need to systematically identify photographs and images that fit with your brand message and ideally encourage likes, comments, and repins (shares).

- **Videos**. With the advent of "idea pins," Pinterest is aggressively promoting video. As on other platforms, you can upload a video to Pinterest, and the algorithm will favor its distribution to your followers.

- **Blog Post and Content Summaries**. To the extent that you have an active blog and are posting items that fit with the common uses of Pinterest, pin your blog posts to Pinterest.

  o Note that the first or "featured" image will become the shareable image. Choose striking, fun images for your pins, even if what you are pinning is just a blog post!

- **Quotes**. People love quotes, and taking memorable quotes and pasting them on graphics is a very popular type of content.

- **How to's and DIY**. Pinterest isn't only about shopping. The "how to" and "DIY" themes are very big on the platform. If you are in an industry such as quilting, for example, posting DIY content that helps your followers can be a big win.

- **Infographics and Instructographics**. Factoids, how to articles, especially ones that are fun, do-it-yourself articles, lists, or collections of tips or products, are excellent for Pinterest. Anything that helps a person organize ideas about products or services to buy or make will work well on Pinterest.

- **Items to Buy**. Yes! You can (and should) pin items to buy on your Pinterest boards. Unlike most other social media users, Pinterest users are "in" the shopping mode in many ways, so tastefully pinning cool items that can be bought is not just expected but encouraged.

Indeed, Pinterest realizes that buying is a logical way to monetize the site, and so they have announced "Shopping on Pinterest" at **http://jmlinks.com/55h**. Another option here is so-called *rich pins*, which are dynamically updated pins from your eCommerce store. Learn about them at **http://jmlinks.com/55m**.

Clearly, Pinterest will help you shamelessly promote, link to, and sell your stuff via Pinterest! In this sense, it is unique among social media in being so unabashedly pro-e-commerce.

» PROMOTE YOUR PINTEREST PAGE, BOARD, AND PINS

Once you've set up your Pinterest business account and begun to populate it with boards and pins on a regular basis, you've essentially "set up" the party. Now it's time to send out the invitations. In and of itself, neither a Pinterest Page nor a Pinterest board will be self-promoting!

MAKE YOUR BOARDS USEFUL, FUN, AND MESMERIZING FOR YOUR USERS

Remember: social media is a **party**. You must have yummy food and entertainment for people to show up and stick around. Thus, as you promote your Pinterest Page, always keep front and center "what's in it for them" – what will they get by "following" your Pinterest page and/or Pinterest boards and checking them out on a regular basis?

Assuming your Page and/or boards have lots of useful, provocative content, here are some common ways to promote your Pinterest account and boards:

- **Real World to Social.** Don't forget the real world! If you are a museum store, for example, be sure that the cashiers recommend to people that they "follow" your Pinterest Page and/or boards? *Why? Because they'll get insider tips, fun do-it-yourself posts, announcements on upcoming museum and museum store events, selected items from your online museum store, etc. Oh, and we'll share collections of do-it-yourself tips as well as gift ideas for that hard-to-buy-for someone in your life.*

- **Cross-Promotion.** Link your website to your Pinterest Page, your blog posts to your Pinterest Page, your Twitter to your Pinterest Page, etc. Notice how big brands like REI do this: one digital property promotes another digital property.

- **Email.** Email your customer list and ask them to "follow" your Page or boards. Be specific: you can drill down to specific **subgroups** and match their interests with **specific boards**. Again, you must have a reason why they'll follow it: what's in it for them? Have a contest, give away something for free, or otherwise motivate them to click from the email to your Page, and then "follow" your page or board.

- **Pinterest Internal**. Interact with other Pages, Pins, and Boards, repin their content, comment on timely topics using *#hashtags*, and reach out to complementary Pages to work with you on co-promotion. Experiment with the Pinterest "ideas" feature, which pushes out short video "stories" to your followers.

- **Pinterest SEO / Search**. People use Pinterest to generate ideas, especially before shopping for something big like a wedding or a dorm room, and therefore search is very big on Pinterest. Research your keywords and name your boards and pins after those keywords, and include keywords in your description. As you get likes, pins, and repins, the Pinterest algorithm will reward your pins with higher placement in Pinterest search results.

- **Be Interactive.** Pinterest is a social media platform, so be social. Like, comment, and follow the boards and pins of others. Comment on the fans of competitors. Interactive content is probably the most undervalued strategy for content and outreach.

- **Leverage your Fans**. People who like your Page are your best promoters. Remember, encouraging your customers to share your content is the name of the game. You want to leverage your fans as much as possible to share your content. Asking key influencers to participate in a board is a great way to both build content and encourage publicity.

ENCOURAGE YOUR FANS TO CONTRIBUTE TO YOUR BOARDS AND SHARE YOUR CONTENT

Here are some specific items worth mentioning:

Group boards. Group boards allow you to collaborate with your employees and customers on Pinterest. Check them out at **http://jmlinks.com/54b**. Brainstorm a collaborative project between you and your customers, and use Pinterest as a means to cooperate online.

Rich Pins and "Product" Pins. These two mechanisms link your eCommerce store to/from Pinterest. They are not promotion mechanisms per se, but they make the buying process as easy as possible. Check out the links at **http://jmlinks.com/55n** (rich pins) and **http://jmlinks.com/55p** (product pins) to learn more about these cross-linking strategies.

Hashtags. Like Twitter and Instagram, Pinterest has hashtags which are ways that people can communicate on a theme. Anything marked with a *#hashtag* is clickable in a pin. Here's a screenshot of a pin with the hashtag *#weddingdresses* highlighted:

And here's what happens if you click on that link: **http://jmlinks.com/13h**. It generates a search on Pinterest for *wedding dress*. So the long and short of it is that by including hashtags in your pins, you become more findable in Pinterest search, whether directly or by the search engine function. Identify relevant hashtags and include them in your best pins.

Pinterest SEO (Search Engine Optimization). Throughout, remember that search is very important on Pinterest. Make sure that you know your keywords and that you weave these keywords into the titles and descriptions of your pins and boards. People use Pinterest as a "search engine" to find interesting products and ideas, similar to how people use Yelp to identify fun restaurants and great plumbers.

Search, and therefore search optimization, should be a major part of your Pinterest promotion strategy.

Advertise. Advertising is increasingly important to success on Pinterest. I've mentioned *rich pins* and *buyable pins*, which are integrations between your online store and Pinterest. "Promoted pins" function much the same way as "promoted posts" on Facebook: you identify a pin to promote, and by advertising, Pinterest pushes these pins to the top of the news feed and search functions on the site. Learn more at **https://ads.pinterest.com/**.

» MEASURE YOUR RESULTS

Once you set up a business account and boards on Pinterest, Pinterest gives you decent metrics on how popular they are. To find them, click on the "analytics" link on the left of the Pinterest web page when you're logged in as a business account. Here's a screenshot:

That will transport you to **https://analytics.pinterest.com/**. You can also confirm your website and Pinterest will show you what people are pinning from your website or blog. (Note: analytics are only available for corporate accounts, not personal profiles).

»» CHECKLIST: PINTEREST ACTION ITEMS

Test your knowledge of Pinterest! Take the *Pinterest marketing quiz* at **http://jmlinks.com/qzpi**. Next, here are your Pinterest **Action Items**:

❏ **Research** whether your customers (and competitors) are on Pinterest. What are they doing? Why? Be sure to distinguish among individual accounts, business accounts, pins, boards, and hashtags. Be sure to understand how to both search and browse Pinterest.

❏ **Set up** a **business account** on Pinterest as well as one or two boards that represent customer interests.

❑ **Brainstorm** a **content strategy** for Pinterest at both the board and pin level. Be systematic and diligent about pinning. Be interactive, including asking your superfans to participate in your boards.

>   ❑ If appropriate, enable **rich pins** and/or **buyable pins** for your eCommerce store.

>   ❑ Tag products or services in your posts.

>   ❑ Experiment with Pinterest "ideas" as the "story" equivalent to Instagram or Facebook.

❑ **Promote your pins** both on Pinterest by strategies like #hashtags and SEO, and off of Pinterest by real-world to Pinterest promotion, cross-promotion, etc. Consider **advertising** if Pinterest is a strong "yes" for you and you have the budget.

❑ **Measure** your results on Pinterest at the pin, board, and account level (are you getting interactivity from real customers?) and whether activity is translating into better brand awareness and even eCommerce sales.

Check out the **free tools**! Go to my *Social Media Marketing Dashboard > Pinterest* for my favorite free tools on Pinterest. Just visit **http://jmlinks.com/smmdash**.

»» DELIVERABLE: A PINTEREST MARKETING PLAN

Now that we've come to the end of our chapter on Pinterest, your **DELIVERABLE** has arrived. For the worksheet, go to **http://jmlinks.com/2023smm** (then enter the code '**2023smm**' to register your workbook), and click on the link to the "Pinterest Marketing Plan." By filling out this plan, you and your team will establish a vision of what you want to achieve via Pinterest.

11
EMAIL MARKETING

Email marketing is the "Rodney Dangerfield" of social media marketing. Dangerfield, of course, was an American stand-up comedian with a rather campy, self-deprecating style. He'd say, "Take my wife," and then pause and say, "No, take my wife – *really*, please take my wife." Another famous Dangerfield quip was that he "Don't get no respect." Of course, he was one of the most successful comedians of his day. Like Dangerfield, email marketing doesn't seem to get "any respect." Yet, like Dangerfield, email marketing is far more effective than its trashy brand image implies.

In this Chapter, we'll explore the basics of email marketing, and we'll connect email marketing both forward and backward to other social media channels. You can drive email signups, for example, from Facebook, and you can use your email list to drive social media events such as video views on YouTube, Facebook, or LinkedIn. And you can use email marketing to drive e-commerce events. What's not to like?

Let's get started!

To-do List:

» Respect the Intimacy of Email

» Master the Steps to Success at Email Marketing

» Use Your List Forward and Backward

»» Checklist: Email Action Items

»» Deliverable: an Email Marketing Plan

» Respect the Intimacy of Email

Customers may follow you on Twitter, like you on Facebook, or watch you on YouTube. It's not a big deal to "follow" someone on social. It's like meeting up for coffee. But getting customers to give you their email address – well, that's another story. And getting them to give their "real" email addresses, not the one used for spam or junk, that's yet one story more. Getting customers to "opt-in" to subscribe to your email alerts is more than just a cheap date. It's intimate. An email sign-up is like a wedding night – they really love you, and they trust you enough to give you access to their email inbox. Those who sign up for your email list are likely to be superfans and micro-influencers, folks who are really "into" you, your brand, or "into" the industry, sector, or topic that you represent.

Think about that for a moment.

The person who is most likely to be willing to give you intimate access to their email inbox is exactly the person who is most likely to be a superfan.

And superfans are key to influencer marketing, social shares, and promotion across the entire social media marketing universe. You'd be crazy not to use email marketing. Crazy.

Email marketing is the best way to communicate with your superfans. Better than Facebook, better than Twitter, better than LinkedIn. I'd even argue it's better than your own company trade show because email marketing is available 24/7, and you can communicate with superfans throughout the year. Email, when done well, combines "interrupt" marketing with "permission" marketing. When done well, email means that people want to get your communication and can't wait to be "interrupted" to hear your latest message.

Email is awesome!

But people hate email marketing. It's perceived as spammy and trashy.

Why? That's easy. Because it's so *valuable* and because it's so *vulnerable*, email is heavily abused by spam and spammers. If you think about it, however, you'll realize that the *outrage* against spam and spammers is just the flip side of the *intimacy* of email. People are outraged about spam because spam is, to be blunt, a kind of digital assault. It's a forced interruption into an intimate space, which is why spam is so nasty and terrible, and spammers are just awful, horrible human beings. Spammers and robocallers should be confined to a special circle of Hell.

Flip this around, and you'll see that if you can honestly gain customer permission and earn customer trust, then having a consensual email relationship can be great for both you and your customers. You need their trust and permission. For a great read on this topic, check out Seth Godin's *Permission Marketing* (**http://jmlinks.com/43a**).

Email is Owned Media

Indeed, email can be considered "owned" media vs. "rented" media. While you build out your Facebook or Instagram following, grow your connections on LinkedIn, or encourage views of your YouTube channel, you are ultimately not in control. Each platform creates its own rules and has its own algorithm. Indeed, years ago, brands built out their Facebook Pages and enjoyed tremendous organic reach for free. But nowadays, Facebook has taken away or at least severely curtailed organic reach on the platform. You don't own your Facebook follower list; you rent it. The same is true across all the other platforms: no matter how great they are, today, there is no guarantee that they won't dramatically change organic reach and the terms of service tomorrow.

EMAIL IS OWNED (BY YOU)

Email, in contrast, is something you own. While you may use a provider like AWeber or Constant Contact, **you own your list**. You configure it, and you send out the email blasts. There is no algorithm to worry about other than the spam-fighting algorithm of all the email providers like Yahoo, Outlook, or Gmail. Because you own your list as opposed to renting it, your email list is arguably a much more valuable digital asset than the number of your Facebook Page followers or views of your YouTube Channel.

Email can even be used *forward* and *backward* with your other social media marketing assets (as I will explain in a moment), making it a prime catalyst to effective digital marketing. Email can be used to encourage reviews on Yelp, Google, or even Amazon.

» MASTER THE STEPS TO SUCCESS AT EMAIL MARKETING

How do you use email successfully? First of all, identify what's in it for your audience. Why would a customer sign up for your email list? What's in it for him? Is it a free eBook? A detailed tutorial? Perhaps insider information, special discounts, or free offers? The "reason for subscribing," the reason why they want to receive and read your email list, is the anchor to your email marketing strategy. Start with something free, something compelling, and something non-threatening.

For example, Jordie van Rijn (**https://www.emailmonday.com/**) is a top-notch email marketer. He offers an incredible free newsletter on email marketing. On the right of every page on his website, there's a big red "get our newsletter" box. Click this, and you see his offer:

Remember "carrot" and "outreach" marketing? Notice here the yummy carrot – new content, professional insights, practical email marketing tricks, etc. Once you click and submit your email (thus giving him your contact information and the privilege of emailing you), you get a fantastic email newsletter.

Your to-dos here are a) identify competitors and companies-to-emulate that offer email newsletters and other types of email offerings, b) sign up for their lists, and c) "reverse engineer" their offers, their content, and the mechanics of their email marketing systems. Pay particular attention to personalization. Many lists ask for your first name, company, etc., and then regurgitate this information to you in the form of a "personalized" email message. Indeed, Mr. van Rijn has a saying for how email marketing should work: "right message, right person, right time."

As is true for all social media, your "posts" to email (that is, the e-blasts that you send out and the content within that email newsletter or other blast) should thus be 80% or more "fun, fun, fun," and 20% or less "buy my stuff." The reason for subscribing needs to always be some type of "carrot," some type of content or offer that's very yummy and ongoing, and then each blast needs to be configured to be a type of "sub carrot" as it were. Yes, you can send out an e-blast that is very much "buy my stuff," but the total email marketing package to subscribers needs to be 80% or more "fun, fun, fun," and only 20% or less "buy my stuff."

Always: make it clear that you won't spam them. Don't frighten them away with "hard sells." Don't abuse the trust relationship.

Technical Issues with Email Marketing

Next, there are the technical issues of email – choosing an email provider like AWeber, MailChimp, or Constant Contact, for example. To be honest, there aren't huge differences between them. All provide very good technical support. And all provide a lot of good technical help as to how to build lists, create sign-up forms, manage email blasts, unsubscribes, etc. I recommend you use a formal email provider as the technical mechanics of getting your email to recipients, even recipients who have pro-actively subscribed to your list are not easy. Outgoing emails face aggressive "spam filters" so much so that even a subscriber who has pro-actively subscribed to your list may not see your email or may even mark it as spam.

Getting email reliably delivered is no easy feat, so use a paid service.

There is the actual sending of the emails. Will it be done on a daily, weekly, or monthly basis? Will it be an email newsletter of one size fits all? Will it be more narrowly customized? Or will it be a **DRIP** campaign? (Drip marketing is the strategy of sending "drips," or pre-written emails automatically via a computer program. Amazon does this all the time – a few days after you make a purchase, you're sent a "please review us" email, for example, and a few days after you browse Amazon, you'll be sent a "you may also like" email. DRIP campaigns can also be set up with eBooks and other free tutorials as the first offer, and then plugs for paid services coming next.) The mechanics have to do with the sign-up, sending, and measurement of email messages and email marketing. You can also segment your list into sublists so that people who like dogs get specific messaging, people who like cats get another set of messages, and people who like iguanas get their own specific content. The more personalized and the more customized you can make your emails, the better.

Promote Your List

Third, there's the issue of promotion. How will potential customers and existing customers find out about your list? What will get them excited about signing up? What are the mechanics of signing up? What are the mechanics of unsubscribing, so that they feel "safe" subscribing to your list in the first place? To grow your list, you want to make sure it's a prominent action on your website, easy to find on your social profiles, and a desired action on many of your posts. If you launch a new, free eBook or webinar, for example, you can use these reasons as a way to drive subscribers. Or, for instance, after a webinar is successfully completed, you can require folks to sign up for your email list to get the recording, and so on and so forth.

» USE YOUR LIST FORWARD AND BACKWARD

Email, like all of social media, is not an end in itself but rather a means to an end, that is a way to build your brand and ultimately sell more stuff. As you work on email marketing, a good way to think about your list is to think forward and backward. As for "forwards," I mean thinking of email along the customer journey or sales funnel as an intermediate step between the coldness of just learning about your brand on Facebook and the hotness of actually making a purchase on your e-commerce store (or becoming an active sales lead via a feedback form).

For example:

1. A customer learns about your brand on Facebook through a post.

2. He signs up to "like" your Facebook Page.

3. Over time, through posts via Facebook, he learns you have an email list with even more interesting content – perhaps content reserved for superfans, perhaps special deals or offers, perhaps inside information on the brand, etc.

4. He signs up for your email list.

5. You then feed him information on your brand, consisting of 80% or more "fun, fun, fun" content and 20% or less "buy my stuff" information.

6. He then ultimately clicks from one of your "buy my stuff" posts to your e-commerce store and makes a purchase.

Facebook is less intimate than email, and email is less intimate than becoming a paid subscriber. You are using email in a "forwards" direction to move customers along the customer journey, or sales funnel from Facebook to email to a sales lead to a sale.

Using Email in a Backward Direction

Email can also be used in a backward direction? How so? Having read this far in the Workbook, you should know that *reviews* matter a lot on Yelp, Google, and Facebook, and that *video views* matter a lot on YouTube, Facebook, Twitter, and LinkedIn. Because email is more intimate than true social media, you can leverage the enthusiasm of your superfans on your email list to grow your social media following and reach. Let's say you've launched a new video on YouTube, you can then:

1. Announce via your email list that you have a beefy, new video on YouTube on topic such-and-such.

2. You can ask your email list fans to watch the video, thumb it up, comment on it, and even share it.

In this way, email can increase the view count and engagement of a video on YouTube, and because the YouTube algorithm pays attention to the velocity of engagement, using email at a strategic moment can help propel a video to the top of YouTube search and shares. The same goes for videos on Facebook, Twitter, and LinkedIn. All platforms reward views, engagement, and velocity – again, meaning that you can use email to prime the pump.

As for reviews, you can offer bonus content for books (as I do) or merely use email to push out requests for reviews on Google, Yelp, Facebook, and other local platforms. Not surprisingly, paid services like GatherUp and Reviewbuzz rely heavily on email (and text messages) to juice reviews. Use the Campaign URL Builder (**http://jmlinks.com/57s**) to set up "utm" codes in your outbound links. These will allow you to track in Google Analytics visits from your email list to your website, thus giving you valuable insights into what happens "after the click."

In summary, email is not an end in itself but rather a means to an end, and email can fit into pretty much any phase of the customer journey, moving forward or backward.

Email is awesome!

»» CHECKLIST: EMAIL ACTION ITEMS

Here are your email **Action Items**:

❑ **Research** -

❑ Whether **your customers** might be interested in signing up for an email newsletter or email notification. Why or why not?

❑ Whether **competitors** and their email marketing efforts. Sign up for their email lists in "stealth mode" and monitor how they use email for marketing.

❑ Whether **there are similar companies to emulate**. Look beyond your own industry, and sign up for the email lists of leading companies that use email well.

❑ **Set up** an email account on one of the big providers, such as Aweber, Constant Contact, or Mailchimp, and begin building your list.

❑ **Identify a "carrot" for your list.** Brainstorm why people will want to sign up for your list and create a "carrot" (the big reason), and then as you create a message, ensure that each message or at least most messages have "carrots."

❏ **Begin sending emails.** Start with content that people will want to get in their email inbox and then brainstorm a –

> ❏ **Forward path** – that is, getting people to subscribe to your list, in the first place, and then using email as an intermediate step between awareness and a desired action such as an e-commerce purchase or a sales inquiry.

> ❏ **Backward path** – that is, using email to support other social media efforts such as reviews on review sites or video views.

❏ **Measure** your email success via subscriber growth, click-throughs, and unsubscribes to your list.

Check out the **free tools**! Go to my *Social Media Marketing Dashboard > Email* for my favorite free tools on email marketing. Just visit **http://jmlinks.com/smmdash**.

»» DELIVERABLE: AN EMAIL MARKETING PLAN

Your **DELIVERABLE** has arrived. For the worksheet, go to **http://jmlinks.com/2023smm** (then enter the code '**2023smm**' to register your workbook), and click on the link to the "Email Marketing Plan." By filling out this plan, you and your team will establish a vision of what you want to achieve via email marketing, including your KPIs (Key Performance Indicators)

12
EPILOGUE

There's always something new! That's what makes social media fun, isn't it? Come on, admit it: you can't wait for the next new thing. (*Just kidding, you probably can wait, but it won't wait for you*). I guarantee there will be a next new thing, and I guarantee that they will hype it in such a way that you just "gotta" be doing it.

As we end our journey through the world of social media marketing, I want to point out some of the newer opportunities (ones that do not yet have substantial traction for small businesses) and give you a conceptual framework to think about and evaluate them.

Finally, I want to motivate you to "just do it" and "never stop learning."

Let's get started!

To-Do List:

» New Kids on the Block

» Just Do It

» Never Stop Learning

»» Deliverable: a Social Media Marketing Plan

» A Final Favor

» New Kids on the Block

There seems to always be a "new" new thing in Social Media. TikTok remains the "new kid" on the block among major social media platforms. It's the darling of teenagers and has revitalized short, quirky videos. TikTok shows, among other things, that there is room in social media for innovation. The big providers like YouTube, Facebook, and Instagram failed to capitalize on the hunger for authentic, silly, and – let's admit it – *narcissistic* videos. Will it succeed? Who knows, but I would argue that the same rules of video that apply to marketing on YouTube will ultimately apply to TikTok. Create great, engaging content that "builds your brand" and ultimately "sells more stuff," but in a soft-sell kind of way.

Another trend is the politicization of social media. TikTok, for example, is banned in India due to concerns about its Chinese ownership, and it's not beyond thinking that it might become banned or restricted in the United States. Twitter is now owned by zillionaire Elon Musk, and amidst that controversy, who is to say what the "future" of Twitter really is? One possible model is a rebirth of Twitter not as a political platform but as an all-in-one social platform similar to WeChat in China.

Snapchat (**https://www.snapchat.com/**) is another one that's hard to place. Snapchat isn't really a social media app; it's a *messaging* app with ads. So far, the main opportunities for brands are in the "stories" feature (organically) and via advertising. It's not clear if Snapchat will survive the competitive onslaught from Instagram, which seems to constantly steal its features. It is clear that Snapchat's model of being more "private" messaging than "social media" is something that Mark Zuckerberg in particular, is keen to imitate, hence Facebook Messenger (**https://www.messenger.com/**). Watch for both Facebook and Instagram to trend towards being closed vs. being open. Twitter, in contrast, seems to be going in the opposite direction.

Yet another one to watch is Medium (**https://medium.com/**), which seems to be the up-and-coming place for long-form content. And still another one – the growth of podcasting as on Stitcher (**https://www.stitcher.com/**). Reddit (**https://www.reddit.com/**) isn't exactly new, but it remains THE place where memes, rumors, conspiracy theories, and just everything that's anything to any super fans seems to get started. Quora (**https://www.quora.com/**) is still one more that's not exactly new but rather niche – it's a place to ask and answer questions. As for niches, there are platforms like GoodReads (**https://www.goodreads.com/**), which is THE place for book lovers and authors to interact, and then there's Meetup (**https://www.meetup.com/**), which helps events "self-organize." There are even sites like "OnlyFans" (**https://onlyfans.com/**) that focus on adult hookups (if you're into that).

"Riches are in the niches," someone once told me, so I advise you to keep an eye out for new social platforms and/or niche social platforms that might be THE place where YOUR customers hang out. Social media is ultimately all about YOU and YOUR CUSTOMERS, not about the latest cool thing for teens, be that Snapchat or TikTok.

The best advice I can give is that for most small to medium businesses, wherever you see opportunities, use them! What is critical for one company may be irrelevant to another, and not just a network (e.g., Snapchat) but a feature (such as "Reels"). It's not one size fits all. And watch out for backlashes as well. I predict oversaturation soon for "influencer marketing" and a backlash against the rather dirty trend of influencers being paid to promote things without really being honest about this fact with their audiences. Privacy is yet another backlash in the works, both from governments (such as CCPA in California or COPPA at the federal level) and from users (who are sick and tired of their data being sold).

Here are my recommendations:

- **Keep your eye out for** new social media platforms that might be relevant to your business, like TikTok, Snapchat, Instagram, or Medium.

- **Sign up for a user account**, and find the business help files or "how to advertise" information. Begin your research.

- **Research** whether your potential customers are "on" this social media and – if so – figure out what they are doing.

- Keep an eye out for **competitors** or **big brands**. **Reverse engineer** what they are doing in terms of marketing, and translate their actions into doable items for your own company.

- **Brainstorm** how you and your company can participate in an authentic way and yet still have a marketing objective. Is it possible to use TikTok, Snapchat, or Instagram Stories to interact with potential customers? How or how not?

- Start slowly, **learn by doing**, and don't be too heavy-handed.

In most cases, you'll see many similarities between the "new" social media like TikTok, Snapchat, or Instagram and the "old" social media like Facebook or Twitter. Snapchat, for example, is beginning to overtake Twitter as a place for real-time or instantaneous communication, as well as a way for brands to offer exclusive information, coupons, or deals to their most avid fans. The fact that a "snap" disappears over time isn't really that different from a tweet. Instagram, in turn, isn't that different from photo-sharing on Facebook (it's really just the photo element of Facebook), plus some similarities to Twitter. Remember Flickr? It was really just Instagram before its time. TikTok? It's just Periscope reimagined. Pinterest? It may be doomed to irrelevancy if it doesn't get beyond shoppers and DIY types.

Indeed, once you see how Snapchat and Instagram are "going after" Twitter, it makes a lot of sense why Twitter has earned the dubious title of the "troubled" social media.

The attempted rebranding of the company as "Meta" and the focus on the "Metaverse" may be the most brilliant business move of the decade, or it could turn out to be the dumbest self-delusion of an overly pampered wunderkind ever recorded. Only time will tell. But beyond TikTok, Snapchat, and Instagram, you may find social media platforms like Tumblr (**https://www.tumblr.com/**) or even ones overseas. (China, in particular, has its own unique set of social media platforms). New ones will no doubt pop up, but the structural realities of social media make them all members of the same genus if not the same species.

Along the way, keep your eye on established social media platforms like Facebook, LinkedIn, Twitter, and YouTube as they are also innovating and adding new features. Facebook's move to native video, for example, has opened up new marketing possibilities for "native" video on the platform. Facebook Live, and YouTube Live are other examples of new opportunities "within" a platform as opposed to on a totally new platform. I am also very excited about LinkedIn as a blogging platform for B2B. Reels? Yes, please. As an information strategy, identify the official blogs for the media most relevant to your company and follow them. I use Feedly (**https://feedly.com/**) as an easy aggregator for official and unofficial blogs that cover social media. Check out the dashboard (**http://jmlinks.com/smmdash**) > *Social Media Conferences and Social Media Publications* for my favorite resources to stay informed.

» JUST DO IT

Voltaire said, "The perfect is the enemy of the good," and today's Nike corporation said, "Just do it!" before it, too, got embroiled in controversy. In both cases, the thought is to "learn by doing," to not be afraid to be bold, and to just "get started."

- Don't be intimidated!

- Do some research, make a plan, and get started!

- Just do it!

Many companies get stuck in "analysis paralysis," always researching and never doing. Don't be one of them! Others get stuck in "doing with no strategy," as in tweeting 24/7 when none of their customers are on Twitter.

Do it! But keep your eyes and ears open to strategy, tactics, and results. If it isn't working, try something else. Don't be afraid to try and fail. (Good advice even for Nike).

Everyone – including myself- is just learning how to "do" social media marketing. Don't be intimidated. There are no real experts. Only fools like me who pretend to know what we're doing.

So just do it, please. *(And email me your ideas, thoughts, suggestions, and questions. I learn more from my students than from anyone else).*

» NEVER STOP LEARNING

If you haven't already, download my *Marketing Alamanac*, and turn to the Chapter on publications and conferences. Read the social media blogs (I'm partial to the *Social Media Examiner* (**http://www.socialmediaexaminer.com/**)). If possible, try to attend the yearly trade show, *Social Media Marketing World*, which is really a fantastic learning opportunity for those who have already mastered "the basics."

Never stop learning!

»» DELIVERABLE: OUTLINE A SOCIAL MEDIA MARKETING PLAN

Now that we've come to the end of the book, go back to the "Party On" chapter. If you haven't already completed it, your **DELIVERABLE** has arrived. For the worksheet, go to **http://jmlinks.com/2023smm** (then enter the code '**2023smm**' to register your workbook), and click on the link to the "Social Media Marketing Plan Big Picture Worksheet." By filling out this plan, you and your team will establish a vision of what to do at the top level, and then by filling out the plans and worksheets for individual media like Twitter, Facebook, or Instagram, you'll know what to do for each individual medium. So get started, and in the immortal words of Garth Algar of the movie Wayne's World, "Party On!"

» A FINAL FAVOR

If you've read this far, well, I'm impressed. I feel like, at this point, I should give you the ultimate secret to social media and life in general. I think it's some combination of "never stop learning," "be humble," and, most of all, "be kind to other people." We're all God's children, and if we could just learn to see that in everyone we meet… well, the Earth would be a lot nicer. But I digress.

I hope you've enjoyed this journey with me, and if the Spirit moves you, I would really appreciate a short, honest review of the *Social Media Marketing Workbook* on Amazon. Simply fire up your browser, go to Amazon.com, and search for the book. (You can also click on **http://jmlinks.com/smm**). Click on "customer reviews" and then on "Write a customer review."

Thanks in advance.

SURVEY OFFER

CLAIM YOUR $5 REBATE! HERE'S HOW -

Visit **http://jmlinks.com/survey**.

1. Take a short, simple survey about the book.

2. Indicate whether you want a $5 rebate or want to make a contribution to our scholarship fund.

WE WILL THEN -

- Rebate you the $5, or thank you profusely for helping a deserving young marketer.

~ $5 REBATE OFFER ~

~ LIMITED TO ONE PER CUSTOMER ~

SUBJECT TO CHANGE WITHOUT NOTICE

GOT QUESTIONS? CALL 800-298-4065

NOTES

NOTES

NOTES

NOTES